Yours faithfully
Frank E. Stevens

THE
BLACK HAWK WAR

Frank E. Stevens

HERITAGE BOOKS
2011

HERITAGE BOOKS
AN IMPRINT OF HERITAGE BOOKS, INC.

Books, CDs, and more—Worldwide

For our listing of thousands of titles see our website
at
www.HeritageBooks.com

A Facsimile Reprint
Published 2011 by
HERITAGE BOOKS, INC.
Publishing Division
100 Railroad Ave. #104
Westminster, Maryland 21157

Entered according to Act of Congress, in the year 1903, by
Frank E. Stevens
in the office of the Librarian of Congress at Washington, D.C.

— Publisher's Notice —
In reprints such as this, it is often not possible to remove blemishes from the original. We feel the contents of this book warrant its reissue despite these blemishes and hope you will agree and read it with pleasure.

International Standard Book Numbers
Paperbound: 978-1-55613-859-1
Clothbound: 978-0-7884-8826-9

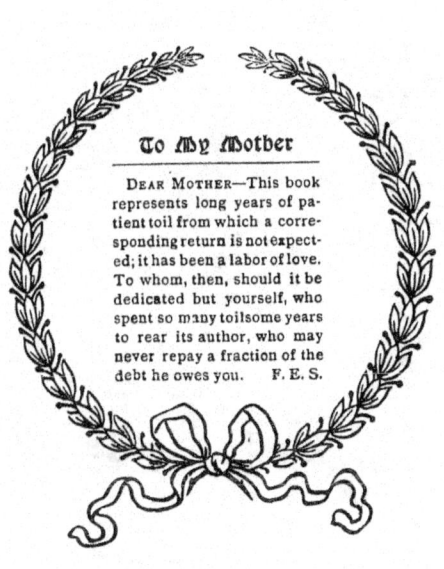

To My Mother

DEAR MOTHER—This book represents long years of patient toil from which a corresponding return is not expected; it has been a labor of love. To whom, then, should it be dedicated but yourself, who spent so many toilsome years to rear its author, who may never repay a fraction of the debt he owes you. F. E. S.

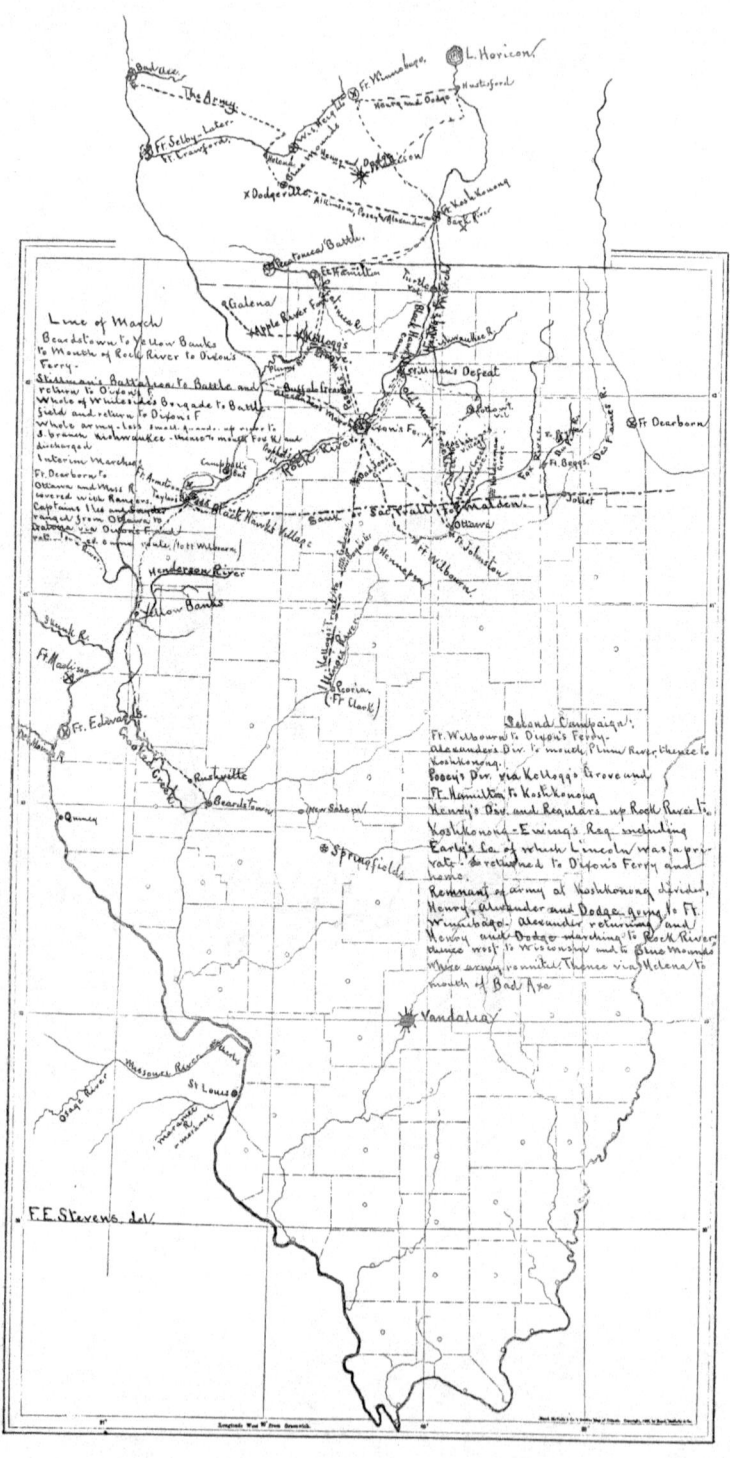

INTRODUCTION

In the autumn of 1871, I began the collection of materials for the book which is just completed; at a time when many original sources existed from which to draw. Since that time, no opportunity wherein I might see and talk with persons who were in the Black Hawk campaigns has been lost, and from those interviews I have been able to gather information, old letters, commissions, muster rolls and papers obtainable by no possible system of correspondence.

I have endeavored to be thorough, and to be thorough has required space. I deplore the necessity which forbids an expression of thanks to each individual by name who has contributed documents, valuable portraits and information from which this work has been constructed. I thank them all as generously as I have borrowed, which has been much. Especially must I thank Mrs. Catherine Buckmaster Curran, of Alton, Illinois, who furnished me with a complete set of papers, without which I could never have finished my work as it should be finished.

Mrs. Colonel William Preston Johnston, of New Orleans, who, at great inconvenience and sacrifice of time, secured a copy of the journal kept by Lieut. Albert Sidney Johnston during his service in those campaigns.

Dr. J. F. Snyder, Virginia, Illinois, President State Historical Society.

Prof. B. F. Shambaugh, Iowa City, Iowa.

Mr. R. G. Thwaites, Madison, Wisconsin.

Charles Aldrich, Des Moines, Iowa.

Miss Caroline M. McIlvaine, Librarian Chicago Historical Society, Chicago.

CONTENTS

	PAGE
CHAPTER I.—Birth, Personal Description and Character of Black Hawk. Not a Chief. Made a Brave. Expeditions against the Osages. Death of Pye-sa. Period of Mourning. Expedition against the Osages. Expedition against the Cherokees. Expedition against the Chippewas, Osages and Kickapoos. The first Appearance of the Americans	17
CHAPTER II.—British Intrigue against the Frontiers. Hatred of the Americans. Treaty of 1804	25
CHAPTER III.—Treaty of 1804 and Black Hawk's Version	31
CHAPTER IV.—Treaty of 1804	34
CHAPTER V.—Erection of Fort Madison. Rumors of Indian Attack. Black Hawk joins Tecumseh. Returns to his Village. Attacks Fort Madison. The Siege	37
CHAPTER VI.—Black Hawk enlists with the British in the War of 1812. Deserts. Foster Son story. Keokuk made Chief	41
CHAPTER VII.—Expedition of Governor Clark to Prairie du Chien. Lieut. Campbell's Battle	46
CHAPTER VIII.—Major Taylor's Battle. Battle of the Sink Hole. Various Murders. British Agents withdrawn from Rock River Country	52
CHAPTER IX.—Treaty of Portage des Sioux, 1815. Treaty of St. Louis, 1816	60
CHAPTER X.—Fort Armstrong built. Black Hawk as a Fault Finder. Annihilation of the Iowas	66
CHAPTER XI.—Treaties of 1822-4-5. Winnebago Outbreak. Attack on the Boats. Arrest and Discharge	71
CHAPTER XII.—The Military Tract. Perils of Frontier Life. Gathering Settlements about Black Hawk's village. Friction. Attempted Compromise. Complaints. Gov. Reynolds calls out Militia. Notifies Clark and Gaines. Correspondence. Gaines at Fort Armstrong	77
CHAPTER XIII.—Council. Militia Organized. March to Black Hawk's Village. Flight. Village Burned. Treaty of 1831	92
CHAPTER XIV.—Unrest. Messengers and War Parties sent out. Attack on the Sioux. They Retaliate. Attack on the Menominees. A Council	100
CHAPTER XV.—Ne-a-pope's Mission. Keokuk's Village. Council. Black Hawk Moves down Iowa River and up the Mississippi to Rock River. Atkinson Moves up to Ft. Armstrong	109
CHAPTER XVI.—Council. Atkinson calls for Troops. Reynolds' Proclamation. Black Hawk Defiant. Gratiot's Journey	112
CHAPTER XVII.—The Militia Moves to Rock River	116

THE BLACK HAWK WAR.

CHAPTER XVIII.—Roster. Movement up Rock River Begun. The Prophet's Village Burned. Forced March to Dixon's Ferry...... 122

CHAPTER XIX.—Dixon's Ferry. Plight of Reynolds' Messengers. Stillman's Defeat..... 129

CHAPTER XX.—Call for Additional Troops. Burial of the Dead. Arrival of Atkinson. Lead Mines Militia. Erection of Forts. Dodge's March to the Four Lakes Country..... 139

CHAPTER XXI.—Atkinson Moves up Rock River. Indian Creek Massacre. Narratives..... 145

CHAPTER XXII.—General Panic. Independent Companies Raised. Atkinson's March Continued. Insubordination. Army Disbanded. Interim Regiment Raised..... 159

CHAPTER XXIII.—Various Illinois Murders, including those of Sample, Payne and the St. Vrain Party..... 165

CHAPTER XXIV.—Atkinson's March to Mouth of Fox River. Dodge's March to Meet Him. Capt. Iles' March..... 172

CHAPTER XXV.—Capt. Snyder's Battle. Murders in the Lead Mines Country. Battle of Pecatonica. Capt. Stephenson's Battle..... 176

CHAPTER XXVI.—Attack on Apple River Fort..... 185

CHAPTER XXVII.—Organization of Forces at Ft. Wilbourn and Disposition of Same. Murder of Phillips. March to Dixon's Ferry..... 188

CHAPTER XXVIII. March to Dixon's Ferry. Dement's Battle..... 197

CHAPTER XXIX.—Murders near Ottawa. Posey's Division Ordered Forward. Alexander's Division Ordered to Plum River. Henry's Division, with Regulars, Moved..... 202

CHAPTER XXX.—Consolidation of the Divisions. Capt. Dunn Shot. Henry, Alexander and Dodge Detached to Move to Ft. Winnebago. Posey sent to Ft. Hamilton. Disintegration of Army. Alexander's Return..... 208

CHAPTER XXXI.—Ft. Winnebago Reached. Stampede. Henry's Treatment of Disobedient Officers. Black Hawk's Trail to Westward Discovered. Forced March. Battle of the Wisconsin. At Blue Mounds..... 213

CHAPTER XXXII.—Pursuit Resumed. Battle of the Bad Axe..... 221

CHAPTER XXXIII.—Throckmorton's Narrative. Atkinson's Report. Black Hawk's Flight. Capture. Delivery to Gen. Street. Council..... 226

CHAPTER XXXIV.—Stambaugh's Expedition..... 234

CHAPTER XXXV.—Examination of the Indians. Black Hawk a Prisoner..... 238

CHAPTER XXXVI.—Scott's Expedition. Treaty..... 242

CHAPTER XXXVII.—Movements of the Michigan Militia..... 243

CHAPTER XXXVIII.—Prison Life. Eastern Trip. Return. Council at Ft. Armstrong. Black Hawk's Apology. Black Hawk Released..... 259

CHAPTER XXXIX.—Second Trip East. A Quiet Life. July Fourth Toast at Ft. Madison. Interview with Iowas. Death. Burial. His Grave Robbed. Bones Recovered. Consumed by Fire. Death of Madam Black Hawk..... 268

APPENDIX: Abraham Lincoln in the Black Hawk War..... 277

APPENDIX: Jefferson Davis in the Black Hawk War..... 290

List of Portraits and Other Illustrations

	PAGE
ABERCROMBIE, LIEUT. J. J. From photograph deposited by Hon. A. J. Turner, of Portage, Wis., in the Wisconsin Historical Collections.	293
ALEXANDER, GEN. M. K. From daguerreotype owned by his daughter, Mrs. J. A. Judson, of Paris, Ill.	192
ANDERSON, LIEUT. ROBERT. From ivory miniature owned by his daughter, Mrs. E. M. C. A. Lawton, Washington, D. C.; by her copyrighted in 1901, and now first published.	293
ARCHER, COL. WILLIAM B. From a steel plate owned by F. J. Bartlett, Marshall, Ill.	225
ARENZ, FRANCIS. From an oil painting owned by his son, Albert W. Arenz, of Jacksonville, Ill.	93
ATKINSON, GEN. HENRY. From oil painting owned by his grandson, Captain B. W. Atkinson, U. S. A. Now first published.	112
BAD AXE BATTLEFIELD. From oil painting owned by Wisconsin Historical Society	224
BAILEY, MAJOR DAVID. From oil painting owned by his son, D. G. Bailey, of Delavan, Ill. Now first published.	133
BAKER, LIEUT. E. D. U. S. Senator, Hero of Ball's Bluff. From rare plate in sketch of his life, by Joseph Wallace, published in 1870.	130
BAKER, MRS. E. B. From photograph by Chiverton, Dixon, Ill. She still lives at Dixon, Ill.	137
BALL, CAPT. JAPHET A. From old photograph owned by John M. Ball, of Chatham, Ill.	130
BARNES, CAPT. ROBERT. From oil painting owned by R. M. Barnes, of Lacon, Ill.	159
BARNEY, CAPT. BENJAMIN. From photograph made in 1870.	119
BARNSBACK, CAPT. JULIUS L. From daguerreotype made in 1845, owned by Mrs. Clara P. Jones, of Edwardsville, Ill.	125
BEACH, MAJOR JOHN. From Fulton's Red Men of Iowa.	37
BEALL, MAJOR ALEXANDER. From photograph made in 1862, owned by William A. Peak, of Exeter, Ill.	123
BEGGS, REV. STEPHEN R. From "Kirkland's Chicago."	167
BENSON, JAMES. Private in Captain McClure's Company. At Stillman's battle. From photograph owned by McLean County Historical Society	136
BLACKBURN, COL. JAMES M. From his only portrait.	225

THE BLACK HAWK WAR.

	PAGE
BLACK HAWK (1 and 2). From American Phrenological Journal for November, 1838. Second number. (3) From portrait by George Catlin. (4) From Patterson's First Edition of Black Hawk's Autobiography. (5) From oil painting owned by Wisconsin Historical Society at Madison by R. M. Sully. (6) From McKenney and Hall's Indians....................	17
BLACK HAWK'S POWDER HORN. Owned by Iowa Historical Society at Iowa City. Photographed by Prof. B. F. Shambaugh.........................	272
BLACK HAWK'S PROMISSORY NOTE. From the original, owned by Mrs. Fannie Anderson, of Louisiana, Mo. Unpaid..................................	272
BLACK HAWK'S TOWER. As it appears to-day...............................	272
BLACKWELL, ROBERT. Paymaster. From daguerreotype owned by Mrs. J. J. Brown, of Vandalia, Ill.	124
BLISS, MAJOR JOHN. From portrait in Minnesota Historical Society's rooms at St. Paul.	97
BOONE, CAPT. LEVI D. From an old photograph owned by C. B. Rhodes, of Hillsboro, Ill.	126
BOONE, COL. NATHAN. Son of Daniel Boone. Only picture. From daguerreotype loaned by his grandson, N. B. Craig, of Hanover, Ill................	293
BOUCHARD, EDWARD D. From a tintype made in 1875, owned by his son, Dr. William L. Bouchard, of Chicago. Only portrait and now first published..	143
BOYD, JAMES M. Second Lieutenant. From photograph owned by Dr. H. B. Tanner, of South Kaukauna, Wis.......................................	235
BRACKEN, LIEUT. CHARLES. From daguerreotype owned by Thomas Bracken, of Mineral Point, Wis.	175
BRADY, GEN. HUGH. From oil painting owned by George N. Brady, of Detroit, Mich. Now first published.	120
BREESE, LIEUT.-COL. SIDNEY. U. S. Senator, Chief Justice, etc. From his first portrait, an oil, owned by his son, Sidney S. Breese, Springfield, Ill., and now first published.	197
BRISTOL, JOHN E. Still alive. From photograph owned by author...........	135
BROWNING, O. H. U. S. Senator, Secretary Interior, etc. From the engraving published with his life.	119
BUCKMASTER, MAJOR NATHANIEL. From his first picture, a daguerreotype, owned by his daughter, Mrs. Catherine Buckmaster Curran, of Alton, Ill., and now first published.	97
BURNS, CAPT. JAMES. From daguerreotype furnished by Hon. George Vernor, of Nashville, Ill.	193
BUTLER, CAPT. PETER. From daguerreotype owned by R. O. Butler, of Monmouth, Ill...	195
CALHOUN, JOHN, of Capt. Goodan's Company. The County Surveyor who furnished Abraham Lincoln with instruments and employment as deputy. He was president of the Lecompton Constitutional Convention. From three-fourths length oil painting owned by Kansas Historical Society, Topeka.	280
CARLIN, GOV. THOMAS. Then Captain. From oil portrait in Executive Mansion at Springfield, Ill...	94
CARPENTER, WILLIAM. Paymaster. From a steel plate....;................	124
CARTWRIGHT, REV. PETER. Private in Captain Reuben Brown's Company. From the plate in his autobiography..	281

THE BLACK HAWK WAR. 7

PAGE

CASEY, ZADOCK. Paymaster. Later Lieut.-Gov. Member of Congress, etc. From oil painting owned by his son, Dr. John R. Casey, of Joliet, Ill...... 179

CASSELL, ADJUTANT HENRY K. From photograph made in 1863, owned by Mrs. Richard Curphy, of Scranton, Iowa.............................. 160

CASS, LEWIS. Secretary of War in 1832. From the engraving made by the U. S. Bureau of Printing and Engraving.............................. 100

CHETLAIN, A. L. From photograph owned by author....................... 142

CHETLAIN, LOUIS. Father of last above. Both in Dodge's Squadron. From old photograph owned by the son... 142

CHRISTY, COL. SAMUEL C. From oil portrait owned by his daughter, Mary F. Scanlan, of St. Louis, Mo... 93

CHOUTEAU, COL. AUGUSTE. From fine plate owned by grandson, J. Gilman Chouteau, of St. Louis... 32

CHOUTEAU, COL. PIERRE. From oil painting owned by Pierre Chouteau, of St. Louis... 32

CLARK, LIEUT. MERIWETHER LEWIS. Of Gen. Atkinson's Staff. From oil painting owned by Mrs. Meriwether Lewis Clark, of Louisville, Ky., made in 1832... 113

CLARK, GOV. WILLIAM. From engraving owned by grandson, John O'Fallon Clark, of St. Louis... 54

COFFEY, CAPT. ACHILLES. From frontispiece of his book, entitled, "History of the Regular Baptist Church," published in 1877....................... 190

COPES, WILLIAM. Private in Capt. Covell's Company. Still alive. Present at dedication of monument at Stillman's battlefield in 1892. From life....... 138

COWEN, LIEUT.-COL. WILLIAM. From old portrait owned by his son, Robert A. Cowen, of Chicago... 159

CRAIG, CAPT. JAMES. From the original, owned by his son, N. B. Craig, of Hanover, Ill... 141

DANLEY, LEVI. Corporal in Captain McClure's Company. At Stillman's battle. From plate owned by McLean Co. Hist. Soc............................ 136

DAVENPORT, GEORGE. An assistant quartermaster of militia. First settler on Rock Island. From oil painting in Supervisors' room at Rock Island..... 113

DAVIS, LIEUT. JEFFERSON. From an ivory miniature owned by Mrs. Davis and copied by her for this work....................................... 290

DEMENT, MAJOR JOHN. From portrait owned by author.................... 179

DICKSON, CAPT. JOSEPH. From daguerreotype owned by his son, Joseph P. Dickson, of Platteville, Wis.. 216

DIMMETT, WILLIAM. Private in Capt. Covell's Company. At Stillman's battle. From photograph owned by McLean Co. Hist. Society................. 136

DIXON, ELISHA. Private in Capt. McClure's Company. At Stillman's battle. From photograph owned by McLean Co. Hist. Society................. 136

DIXON'S FERRY. From oil painting owned by Miss F. Louise Dixon, of Dixon, Ill.. 129

DIXON, JOHN. From photograph owned by author........................... 129

DODGE, A. C. U. S. Senator, Minister to Spain, etc. From photograph owned by his son, W. W. Dodge, of Burlington, Iowa............................ 299

DODGE, COL. HENRY. Governor, U. S. Senator, etc. From portrait owned by his grandson, W. W. Dodge, Burlington, Iowa........................ 141

THE BLACK HAWK WAR.

Dodge, Col. Henry. In uniform as a U. S. Ranger, by George Catlin. From the original, owned by W. W. Dodge, of Burlington, Iowa.............. 141
Duncan, Gen. Joseph. Later Governor of Illinois. From the oil painting in Executive Mansion, in Springfield.................................... 94
Dunlap, Adjutant Samuel. From daguerreotype owned by Mrs. J. M. Wagner, of Newman, Ill.. 192
Dunn, Capt. Charles. Chief Justice, etc. From the oil painting in the rooms of the Supreme Court of Wisconsin, at Madison.................. 191

Eaton, Lieut. Nathaniel J. From daguerreotype made in 1848, owned by his daughter, Mrs. Harriet Eaton Root, of Alton, Ill..................... 113
Eddy, Henry. Quartermaster-General. From daguerreotype owned by his son (recently deceased), John M. Eddy, of Shawneetown, Ill............ 115
Edwards, Lieut.-Col. Abraham. President First Legislative Council Mich. Ter. From portrait owned by Mich. Pioneer and Hist. Soc., Lansing...... 255
Edwards, Cyrus. From a steel plate owned by his daughter, Mrs. George K. Hopkins, of Alton, Ill.. 122
Edwards, Ninian. First Governor of Illinois Territory, U. S. Senator, etc. From portrait in Executive Mansion, at Springfield...................... 54
Elkin, Capt. W. F. From an old picture owned by Lee B. Elkin, of Springfield, Ill. 95
Ewing, Major W. L. D. U. S. Senator, etc. From miniature made in 1835, owned by his daughter, Mrs. Margaret M. Dale, of Kansas City, Mo...... 224

Feaman, Capt. Jacob. From photograph owned by Elias Feaman, of Chester, Ill. 198
Flood, Capt. William G. From old photograph owned by his daughter, Mrs. W. E. Boswell, of Carthage, Ill...................................... 123
Ford, Thomas. Governor, Etc. Private in Whiteside's Battalion in campaign of 1831. From painting in Executive Mansion, Springfield, Ill........... 94
Fort Armstrong. From an original etching by Mrs. Alice C. Walker, of Moline, Ill., and loaned for use in this work................................... 66
Fort Crawford. From the oil painting made by Arthur Brower.............. 121
Fort Dearborn. From picture in rooms of Chicago Historical Society........ 167
Fort Dixon. From oil painting owned by author........................... 161
Fort Madison. From a rare print in the "Annals of Iowa," furnished by Mr. Charles Aldrich, of Des Moines................................... 37
Fort Madison. Ground plan, from drawings in the War Department, at Washington. 37
Fort Snelling. From oil painting in collection of Minn. Historical Society at St. Paul. 77
Fort Winnebago. From painting owned by Hon. A. J. Turner, of Portage, Wis. 308
Fry, Col. Jacob. From an old photograph owned by his son, William M. Fry, of Carrollton, Ill. 95

Gaines, Gen. E. P. From engraving after the portrait by J. W. Jarvis....... 93
Gear, Capt. H. H. From photograph owned by Gen. John C. Smith, Chicago.. 299
Gillespie, Adjutant Joseph. From daguerreotype owned by C. E. Gillespie, of Edwardsville, Ill. 96

GILLHAM, LIEUT.-COL. JAMES. From photograph owned by his son, W. A. Gillham, of Riggston, Ill. 196
GIVENS, CAPT. WILLIAM T. From an old tintype owned by his son, Robert S. Givens, of Waverly, Ill. 126
GRATIOT, LIEUT. CHARLES. Of Capt. Dowling's Company. From daguerreotype owned by his son, Henry R. Gratiot, Gratiot, Wis.................. 142
GRATIOT, COL. HENRY. From oil painting owned by Wisconsin Historical Society, at Madison. Furnished by Hon. Hempstead Washburne, of Chicago, a grandson. 115
GRATIOT, CAPT. J. R. B. From an ivory miniature painted by the Swiss artist, Peter Reinderpacker, owned by daughter of Captain G., Mrs. Ninette Hempstead, of De Soto, Mo.. 141
GRIDLEY, LIEUT. ASAHEL. Of Capt. Covell's Company. At Stillman's battle. From photograph owned by McLean County Historical Society, of Bloomington, Ill.. 135
GRIGNON, AUGUSTIN. From oil painting in Wisconsin Historical Collections.. 235

HAACKE, DAVID. Of Capt. David W. Barnes' Company. Dressed in uniform of captain of militia of the time, to which office he was appointed in 1833.. 132
HAINES, ALFRED. Of Capt. John G. Adams' Company. From daguerreotype owned by his brother, James Haines, of Pekin, Ill........................ 135
HAINES, JONATHAN. Of Capt. Adams' Company. From daguerreotype owned by his brother, James Haines, of Pekin, Ill. At Stillman's battle, with his brother, next above. 135
HALL, OLIVER W. From tintype owned by his daughter, Dr. Lucinda H. Corr, of Carlinville, Ill. 133
HAMILTON, COL. WILLIAM S. From the original, owned by the Wisconsin Historical Society, at Madison 182
HARDIN, COL. JOHN J. From oil painting made of him in 1832, owned by his son, Gen. M. D. Hardin, of Chicago 95
HARNEY, CAPT. W. S. From his first portrait done in oil in 1825, owned by Mrs. John M. Harney, of St. Louis, Mo., and now first published.......... 120
HARRISON, GOV. WILLIAM HENRY. From the oil portrait owned by Betty Harrison Eaton, of North Bend, Ohio.................................... 32
HAWS, CAPT. WILLIAM. From photograph owned by J. W. Thornton, of Magnolia, Ill. 159
HEADEN, WILLIAM. Surgeon. From oil painting owned by Walter Headen, of Shelbyville, Ill. 124
HOGAN, LIEUT. JOHN S. C. Of Capt. Kercheval's Company. Second Postmaster of Chicago. From "Kirkland's Chicago.".......................... 120
HOLLIDAY, CAPT. JOEL. From an old tintype owned by his son, James H. Holliday, of Rileyville.. 190
HORN, REV. REDDICK. From his only picture, owned by H. M. Horn, of Republican City, Neb., and now first published.................................. 137
HORN, SYLVIA HALL. From photograph owned by her granddaughter, Mrs. Samuel Dunavan, of Leland, Ill... 154
HORNEY, SAMUEL. Quartermaster. From portrait secured by John S. Bagby, of Rushville, Ill. 123

THE BLACK HAWK WAR.

                                                                                                PAGE
HUBBARD, LIEUT. GURDON S. Of Capt. Alex. Bailey's Company. From photograph by Mosher. 175
HUSSEY, NATHAN. Brigade Wagonmaster. From beautiful daguerreotype owned by grandson, J. Y. Hussey, of Williamsville, Ill. 195
HUSSEY, WILLIAM S. Fourth Sergeant of Capt. Claywell's Company. From old photograph owned by J. Y. Hussey, of Williamsville, Ill. 198

ILES, CAPT. ELIJAH. In whose company Abraham Lincoln was a private. From photograph made by Anderson, of Springfield. 175
IRWIN, LIEUT. ALEXANDER J. From oil painting in rooms of Wisconsin Historical Society, at Madison. 235

JACKSON, ANDREW. President in 1832. From engraving made from portrait by Earl. 54
JAMES, MAJOR THOMAS. From oil painting owned by his son, Dr. Lewis James, of Racola, Mo. 143
JEFFERSON BARRACKS. From an old print—very rare. 100
JENKINS, CAPT. A. M. From oil painting owned by his daughter-in-law, Mrs. M. E. Jenkins, of Washington, D. C. 196
JONES, COL. GABRIEL. From an old tintype owned by Adelia G. Gordon, of Chester, Ill. 217
JONES, GEORGE W. U. S. Senator, etc. From his first picture, owned by his daughter, Mrs. J. Linn Deuss, of Dubuque, Iowa. 299
JOHNSTON, LIEUT. ALBERT SIDNEY. From an ivory miniature in the family of Mrs. William Preston Johnston, of New Orleans. Published formerly by the "Century Company." 225
JOHNSTON, LIEUT. JOSEPH E. From the steel plate in his "Narrative." 246

KE-O-KUK. From the oil painting—the only one made of him from life—secured by I. G. Baker, of St. Louis. 27

LECLAIRE, ANTOINE. The Interpreter. From oil painting in Court House, at Davenport, Iowa. 27
LEE, WILLIAM H. Of Capt. Samuel Huston's Company. Still alive. Remembers distinctly that Gen. Atkinson swore in the Illinois troops at the mouth of Rock River, including the company of Lincoln. The author is under many obligations to him for valuable information. 281
LETTER OF MAJOR NATHANIEL BUCKMASTER determining what officer swore Capt. Abraham Lincoln into the U. S. service. Owned by Mrs. Catherine Buckmaster Curran, of Alton, Ill. 284
LINCOLN, CAPT. ABRAHAM. From his first picture, a daguerreotype, owned by Hon. Robert T. Lincoln, of Chicago. Copyrighted 1895-6 by S. S. McClure Company. Use permitted here. 277
LINCOLN, CAPT. ABRAHAM. Discharge signed by him. From the collection of Mr. Oldroyd, of Washington. 281
LINCOLN, CAPT. ABRAHAM. Muster roll made by him and in the possession of the author. 279
LOGAN, DR. JOHN B. Father of Gen. John A. Logan. From oil painting owned by J. V. Logan, of Menard, Ill. 196

THE BLACK HAWK WAR. 11

LONG, MAJOR THOMAS. From oil painting owned by his son, T. W. Long, of Taylorville, Ill. 119

LOWE, CAPT. GIDEON. From oil painting owned by his granddaughter, Mrs. E. S. Purdy, of Portage, Wis. 128

MACOMB, GEN. ALEXANDER. Major-General commanding U. S. A. in 1832. From engraving after the painting by T. Sully. 308

MADDING, CAPT. CHAMPION S. From daguerreotype owned by his son, L. B. Madding, of Woodstock, Wis. 194

MAP OF ILLINOIS. Showing marches, forts, etc. Made by author. ....Facing Introduction.

MAP OF ILLINOIS. Showing "Military Tract." Made in 1822, after LeSage's Atlas. 77

MAP OF THE LEAD MINES DISTRICT. Made in 1832. From Tanner's Guide.... 140

MARSAC, CAPT. JOSEPH. From oil painting owned by Michigan Pioneer and Historical Society, Lansing. Capt. Marsac was also interpreter at the making of the Cass Treaty. 255

MASON, CAPT. R. B. From miniature made in 1846, owned by his daughter, Miss Nannie Mason, of Louisville, Ky. 225

MASON, GOV. S. T. From oil portrait which hangs in the State House at Lansing, Mich. 255

MATHEWS, CAPT. CYRUS. From photograph owned by Mrs. James R. Mathews, of Jacksonville, Ill. 160

MAUGHS, CAPT. MILTON M. From a tintype made in 1850, owned by W. B. Langley, of Chicago. Captain Maughs was founder of Mauston, Wis. 139

MAYO, CAPT. JONATHAN. From old photograph furnished by LeRoy Wiley, of Paris, Ill. 193

MAYO, WALTER L. 194

MENARD, CAPT. PETER or PIERRE. From daguerreotype owned by A. H. Menard, of Tremont, Ill. 160

MOFFETT, CAPT. THOMAS. From photograph owned by George M. Brinkerhoff, of Springfield, Ill. 198

MONUMENT AT INDIAN CREEK MASSACRE. From photograph owned by Mrs. Samuel Dunavan, of Leland, Ill. 154

MONUMENT AT KELLOGG'S GROVE. From photograph owned by J. B. Timms... 175

MONUMENT AT STILLMAN'S BATTLEFIELD. From photograph owned by author.. 132

MORRISON, LIEUT. JOHN. Father of Hon. William R. Morrison. From photograph owned by latter. Of Capt. J. S. Briggs' Company. 197

MUNSON, RACHEL HALL. From a photograph made by W. E. Bowman, of Ottawa, in 1865, and now owned by author. 154

MCCLERNAND, JOHN A. Assistant Brigade Quartermaster. From daguerreotype made in 1843, when he was in Congress. Owned by his son, Col. E. J. McClernand, U. S. A. Never before published. 190

MCCONNEL, MAJOR MURRAY. From oil painting owned by his daughter, Mrs. Lilla M. Boothby. 217

MCCULLOUGH, WILLIAM. Of Capt. Covell's Company. At Stillman's battle. From plate owned by McLean County His. Soc., at Bloomington. 138

McKee, William. Private of the company of Capt. Ralls. Same regiment as Capt. Lincoln. ... 138
McMurtry, Capt. William. From an old daguerreotype. ... 195

Naper, Capt. Joseph. From daguerreotype owned by C. A. Naper, of Naperville, Ill. ... 167
Newhall, Dr. Horatio. From photograph owned by Mrs. William C. Barrett, of Galena, Ill. ... 140

Onstott, Capt. John. From daguerreotype owned by J. H. Songer, of Xenia, Ill. ... 191
Order of May 22, to Whiteside. Special No. 11. ... 162
Order of May 25, to cause injury. ... 132
Order to forbid firing of arms. ... 280
Orear, George. From photograph owned by his son, T. B. Orear, of Jacksonville, Ill. ... 123
Orendorf, James K. Private in the company of Capt. Covell. At Stillman's battle. From daguerreotype owned by McLean County Hist. Soc., Bloomington, Ill. ... 138
Ottawa. At the time of the Black Hawk War. From an old sketch owned by W. E. Bowman, of Ottawa, and now first published. ... 130

Parker, Leonard B. Quartermaster. From rare old silhouette owned by his son, George W. Parker, of St. Louis, and now first published. ... 193
Parkinson, Capt. D. M. From oil painting owned by granddaughter, Miss M. L. Parkinson, of Mineral Point, Wis., and now first published. ... 217
Parkinson, Nathaniel T. Of Dodge's Squadron. From tintype owned by Miss M. L. Parkinson, of Mineral Point, Wis. ... 142
Parmenter, Isaac. Adjutant. From daguerreotype furnished by H. T. Goddard, of Mt. Carmel, Ill. ... 194
Pa-she-pa-ho, Chief. From "McKenney and Hall's Indians." ... 27
Patterson, J. B. From photograph owned by his daughter, Miss Tina Patterson, of Peoria, Ill. ... 27
Pecatonica Battlefield. From oil painting owned by Wisconsin Historical Society, Madison ... 182
Pecatonica—Plan of battlefield. From History of Henry Dodge, by William Salter ... 182
Pike, Lieut. Zebulon M. From the engraving by Edwin, in a "History of the War of 1812." ... 32
Pointer, William, of the company of Capt. Seth Pratt. Still alive. He was an old acquaintance of Capt. Lincoln. ... 280
Powell, Capt. Daniel. From an old photograph owned by H. B. Trafton, of Norris City, Ill., a grandson. ... 195
Powell, Lieut. Starkey R., of the company of Capt. William B. Smith. From daguerreotype owned by his daughter, Mrs. Mary Catherine Peffer, of Rochester, N. Y. ... 125
Preuitt, Capt. Solomon—later Lieut. Col. in campaign of 1832. From the "History of Madison County." ... 97
Price, Capt. Daniel. ... 127

THE BLACK HAWK WAR. 13

PRICKETT, COL. DAVID. From oil painting owned by daughter, Miss Christiana G. Prickett, of Springfield, Ill. 122
PUGH, CAPT. ISAAC C. From old photograph owned by Mrs. Mira H. Marks, of Decatur, Ill. 127
RAUM, MAJOR JOHN, From daguerreotype owned by his son, Gen. Green B. Raum, of Chicago 190
REMANN, MAJOR FREDERICK. From photograph owned by Mrs. Fred G. Remann, of Vandalia, Ill. 224
REYNOLDS, GOV. JOHN. From the plate in his "My Own Times." 93
RICE, MATTHEW, of Capt. Solomon Hunter's Company. From photograph owned by his daughter, Mrs. M. E. Smith 198
RICHARDSON, W. A. Ass't Quartermaster Maj. James Odd Battalion. Lieut.-Col. Mexican War, Member of Congress, Gov. of Nebraska, and U. S. Senator to succeed Stephen A. Douglas. From photograph owned by his son, W. A. Richardson, of Quincy, Ill. 127
ROBINSON, ALEXANDER, Chief of the Pottowatomies. From "Kirkland's Chicago." 166
ROBISON, JOHN K., of Capt. Gear's Company. From photograph owned by his daughter, Mrs. Amelia McFarland, of Mendota, Ill. 299
ROMAN, RICHARD, Surgeon. From photograph owned by Richard Roman, of Washington, D. C. 96
ROSS, FIRST SERGEANT LEWIS W., of Capt. John Sain's Company. From photograph owned by his son, P. C. Ross, of Lewiston, Ill. 137
ROSS, CAPT. THOMAS B. From oil painting owned by grandson, Robert W. Ross, of Vandalia, Ill. 192
ROSS, COL. WILLIAM. From picture owned by Hon. A. C. Matthews, of Pittsfield, Ill. 119
ROUNDTREE, CAPT. HIRAM. From photograph owned by his daughter, Mrs. Etta Roundtree Stubblefield, of Hillsboro, Ill. 143
ROUNDTREE, CAPT. JOHN H. From photograph owned by Miss Lilly M. Roundtree, of Platteville, Wis. 143
RUTLEDGE, THOMAS O., of Capt. Covell's Company. At Stillman's battle. From old photograph owned by McLean Co. Hist. Soc., Bloomington, Ill. 137

SANDFORD, CAPT. ISAAC. From oil painting owned by O. S. Sandford, Tuscola, Ill. 191
SCALES, CAPT. S. H. From photograph owned by Samuel Scales, of Shullsburg, Wis. 140
SCOTT, MAJ. GEN. WINFIELD. From his autobiography. Made of him about the time of the Black Hawk War 246
SCOTT, MAJ.-GEN. WINFIELD. Headquarters at Ft. Armstrong 246
SEMPLE, JAMES. Later U. S. Senator, etc. From "History of Edwards County." 96
SHA-BO-NA, or SHAB-BO-NA. Spelled both ways in this work, as both are used by the best authorities. One "b" should, however, be considered preferable. From an old tintype owned by Hon. George M. Hollenback, of Aurora, Ill. The last picture made of the old Chief, during the first week of July, 1859, just prior to his death. 166

THE BLACK HAWK WAR.

SHELLEDY, COL. STEPHEN B. From old photograph owned by Margaret I. Vance, of Cresco, Iowa.. 192
SHULL, JESSE W. One of the oldest traders of Northern Illinois. Went to the lead mines in 1819. From old photograph owned by Col. E. C. Townsend, of Shullsburg, Wis., of which city Shull was founder. He was a private in Capt. Enoch Duncan's Company.. 140
SIMPSON, CAPT. GIDEON. From oil portrait owned by Mrs. J. H. King, a granddaughter, of Collinsville, Ill.. 125
SMITH, CAPT. HENRY, U. S. A. From old portrait, made in 1831, owned by his sister, Katharine Smith Sewall, of Watertown, N. Y.................. 113
SMITH, COL. T. W. From the oil painting in the rooms of the Chicago Historical Society 196
SNELLING, COL. JOSIAH. From Appleton's Cyclopedia of American Biography. Used by permission... 77
SNYDER, CAPT. ADAM W. From a rare ivory miniature owned by his son, Dr. J. F. Snyder, of Virginia, Ill... 179
STAHL, SERGEANT FREDERICK. From "History of Jo Daviess County.".......... 139
STAPP, COL. JAMES T. B. From photograph owned by Mr. Guy Stapp, of Chicago 122
STAPP, WYATT B. From oil painting furnished for this book by Mr. Guy Stapp, of Chicago... 133
STEPHENSON, MAJOR JAMES W. From oil painting owned by Mrs. William Hempstead, of St. Louis... 179
STEPHENSON, CAPT. WILLIAM J. From photograph owned by Alexander H. Brown, of Ashley, Ill... 191
STEVENS, FRANK E. From a photograph by Waters, Chicago.......... Frontispiece
STEWART, COL. HART L. From "Kirkland's Chicago."........................ 235
STILLMAN'S BATTLEFIELD. From recent photograph of old cut, by Oliver W. Hall, who was upon the scene the following day. Done in colors for this work by Mrs. Chas. C. Dunlap, of Chicago................................. 134
STILLMAN, COL. ISAIAH. From his only portrait, a daguerreotype, owned by his daughter, Mrs. Mary E. Barber, of Libertyville, Iowa, and now first published 133
STRAWN, JEREMIAH. From photograph owned by Susan S. Dent, his daughter, Chicago 160
STRAWN, COL. JOHN. From photograph furnished by Mr. J. S. Thompson, of Lacon, Ill.. 159
STREET, GEN. JOSEPH M. From the "Annals of Iowa," furnished by Mr. Chas. Aldrich, of Des Moines, Iowa.. 100
STRODE, COL. JAMES M. From a rare ivory miniature, owned by his daughter, Mrs. Luella Strode Howe, of London, Eng. Copied especially for this work, and now first published.. 139
STUART, MAJ. JOHN T. From the first daguerreotype brought to Illinois, owned by his widow—now deceased—and loaned by her to the author..... 94

TAYLOR, MAJOR ZACHARY. From the engraving made by the Bureau of Printing and Engraving at Washington.. 54
TAYLOR, LIEUT. COL. His headquarters at Fort Crawford.................... 128
THOMAS, COL. JOHN. From steel plate in "History of St. Clair County."...... 122

THE BLACK HAWK WAR. 15

THOMAS, CAPT. WILLIAM. From daguerreotype owned by his daughter, Mrs. Belle Flynn, of Carmi, Ill... 194
THOMAS, COL. WILLIAM. From photograph owned by H. E. Rusk, of Jacksonville, Ill 95
THOMPSON, CAPT. JAMES. From an old photograph owned by a son in Chester, Ill... 197
TOWNSEND FAMILY. Early settlers in the lead mines, and all of them, brothers, served in the Black Hawk War in Dodge's squadron. Three of them served in the Winnebago war of 1827. H. S. Townsend, only recently deceased, was at the battle of the Pecatonica............................ 144
TWIGGS, MAJ. D. E. From a photograph obtained from Hon. A. J. Turner, of Portage, Wis., and now owned by the Wis. Hist. Society, at Madison..... 120

VAUGHAN, JAMES W. From photograph owned by his son, G. W. Vaughan, of Sullivan, Ill... 125
VERNOR, Z. H. In the campaign of 1831, under Capt. William Moore. From oil painting owned by his son, Hon. George Vernor, of Nashville, Ill...... 96

WA-BO-KI-E-SHIEK, the PROPHET. From oil painting from life by R. M. Sully while imprisoned at Fortress Monroe. Now owned by the Wisconsin Historical Society, at Madison... 115
WAKEFIELD, JOHN A. Distinguished for services in the war and for writing in 1834 (published at Jacksonville, Ill., the same year), the first history of the same. From his only portrait, owned by his daughter, Mrs. Emily Terry, of St. Paul, Minn., and now first published...................... 139
WALKER, CAPT. GEORGE E. First Sheriff of La Salle County. From photograph made by W. E. Bowman, of Ottawa, and now first published....... 166
WA-PEL-LO, or WAU-PE-LA, CHIEF. From "McKenney and Hall's Indians.".... 308
WESTBROOK, REV. SAMUEL, of Capt. Holliday's Company. Still alive, and who has furnished much information for this book.......................... 193
WARREN, CAPT. PETER. From a very rare tintype, owned by a grandson, W. W. Warren, of Windsor, Ill... 126
WAU-BAN-SE, or WAU-BAN-SEE. From "McKenney and Hall's Indians."...... 166
WHEELER, CAPT. ERASTUS. From old tintype owned by his daughter, Mrs. W. W. Erwin, of Minneapolis, Minn.................................. 97
WHISTLER, MAJOR WILLIAM. From "Kirkland's Chicago.".................. 246
WHITESIDE, GEN. SAMUEL. From the only picture ever made of him—a very rare tintype—owned by his daughter, Mrs. J. A. Henderson, of Mt. Auburn, and now first published.. 115
WHITLOCK, MAJOR JAMES. From a beautiful ivory miniature owned by Mrs. Eliza A. Greenough, of Marshall, Ill.................................. 124
WILLIAMS, ARCHIBALD, of Capt. Flood's Company. One of Illinois' most distinguished men. From old portrait owned by his son, John H. Williams, of Quincy, Ill.. 127
WILLIAMS, GEN. JOHN R. From oil painting in rooms of Michigan Pioneer and Historical Society, at Lansing.. 255
WILSON, LIEUT. GEORGE, chum of Lieut. Jefferson Davis, who carried the note from Lieut. Davis to Miss Taylor which arranged for their marriage. From portrait owned by son, Capt. George Wilson, of Lexington, Mo..... 293

PAGE

WINTERS, CAPT. NATHAN. From photograph owned by grandson, G. L. Winters, of Trenton, Mo.. 126

WISCONSIN HEIGHTS, BATTLEFIELD. From the picture owned by the Wisconsin Historical Society, at Madison.. 216

WISCONSIN HEIGHTS—Plan of the battlefield. From the "Life of Henry Dodge," by William Salter.. 216

WOOD, JOHN. Later Governor of Illinois. Private in Capt. Flood's Company. From photograph owned by D. C. Wood, of Quincy, Ill.................. 217

WOOD, MAJ. JOHN D. From photograph furnished by Hon. George Vernor, of Nashville, Ill......... 197

BLACK HAWK.

CHAPTER I.

BIRTH—PERSONAL DESCRIPTION AND CHARACTER OF BLACK HAWK—NOT A CHIEF—MADE A BRAVE—EXPEDITIONS AGAINST THE OSAGES—DEATH OF PY-E-SA—PERIOD OF MOURNING—EXPEDITION AGAINST THE OSAGES—EXPEDITION AGAINST THE CHEROKEES—EXPEDITION AGAINST THE CHIPPEWAS, OSAGES AND KICKAPOOS—THE FIRST APPEARANCE OF THE AMERICANS.

Black Hawk's name, as given in his autobiography, was Ma-ka-tai-she-kia-kiak,[1] and, without reference to the many renditions of it by various writers, is the version that will be adopted in this work as nearest authentic. He was born in the year 1767 at the Sac or Sauk village, located on the north bank of Rock River in the State of Illinois, about three miles above its confluence with the Mississippi. His father, Py-e-sa, a grandson of Na-na-ma-kee or Thunder (a descendant of other Thunders), was born near Montreal, Canada, where the Great Spirit was reputed in Indian lore to have first placed the great Sac nation. Black Hawk was a full blood Sac, five feet eleven inches tall in his moccasins; of broad but meager build[2] and capable of great endurance. His features were pinched and drawn, giving unusual prominence to the cheek bones and a Roman nose, itself pronounced. The chin was sharp. The mouth was full and inclined to remain open in repose. His eyes were bright, black and restless, glistening as they roamed during a conversation. Above these rested no eyebrows. The forehead was given the appearance of unusual fullness and height from the fact that all hair was plucked from the scalp, with the single exception of the scalp lock, to which, on occasions of state, was fastened a bunch of eagle feathers. In his later years it was his boast that he had worn the lock with such prominence to tempt an enemy to fight for it and to facilitate its removal should he be slain in the encounter. This statement, however, must be received as a boast and nothing more, because among the Sacs the custom of plucking from the scalp all hairs save the scalp lock was general and not confined to Black Hawk's redoubtable person, as he would have us believe. J. C. Beltrami, the Italian traveler, who ascended the Mississippi in 1823, stopping at all the Indian

---

[1] Occasionally rendered in early life "Black Sparrow Hawk."
[2] His weight is commonly placed at 140 pounds.

villages, particularly Black Hawk's upon Rock River, which he reached May 10th, has this to say, which is interesting: "The faces of the Saukees, although exhibiting features characteristic of their savage state, are not disagreeable, and they are rather well made than otherwise. Their size and structure, which are of the middle kind, indicate neither peculiar strength nor weakness. Their heads are rather small; that part called by French anatomists *voute orbitaire* has in general no hair except a small tuft upon the pineal gland, like that of the Turks; this gives the forehead an appearance of great elevation. Their eyes are small and their eyebrows thin; the cornea approaches rather to yellow, the pupil to red; they are the link between those of the orang-outang and ours. Their ears are sufficiently large to bear all the jewels, etc., with which they are adorned; two foxes' tails dangled from those of the Great Eagle. I have seen others to which were hung bells, heads of birds and dozens of buckles, which penetrated the whole cartilaginous part from top to bottom. Their noses are large and flat, like those of the nations of eastern Asia; their nostrils are pierced and ornamented like their ears. The maxillary bones, or pommettes, are very prominent. The under jaw extends outwards on both sides. Their mouths are rather large; their teeth close set, and of the finest enamel; their lips a little inverted. Their necks are regularly formed; they have large bellies and narrow chests, so that their bodies are generally larger below than above. Their feet and hands are well proportioned. Except the tuft on the head, which we have already remarked, they have no hair on any part of the body. Books which deal greatly in the marvelous convert this into an extraordinary phenomenon, but the fact is that, from a superstition common to all savages, they pluck it out, and, as they begin at an early age and use the most perservering means for its extirpation, nothing is left but a soft down."

With this personal description of Black Hawk, it may be well to add the following, published in the "Annals of Iowa," 3rd series, Vol. 4, page 195: "Bones of Black Hawk.—These bones, which were stolen from the grave about a year since, have been recovered and are now in the Governor's office. The wampum, hat,[1] etc., which were buried with the old chief, have been returned with the bones. It appears that they were taken to St. Louis and there cleaned; they were then sent to Quincy to a dentist to be put up and wired previous to being sent to the East. The dentist was cautioned not to deliver them to anyone until a requisition should be made by Governor Lucas. Governor Lucas made the necessary requisition and they were sent up a few days since by the Mayor of Quincy and are now in the possession of the Governor. He has sent word to Na-she-as-kuk, Black Hawk's son, or to the family, and some of them will probably call for them in a few days. Mr. Edgerton, the phrenologist, has

---

[1]This statement, written at the time, would seem to warrant the assertion by friends that Black Hawk's old and disfigured "plug" hat was buried with him, instead of a military cap, as contended by a few claiming knowledge.

taken an exact drawing of the skull, which looks very natural, and has also engraved it on a reduced scale, which will shortly appear on his new chart. Destructiveness, combativeness, firmness and philoprogenitiveness are, phrenologically speaking, very strongly developed. Burlington Hawk Eye, Dec. 10, 1840."[1]

An intimate knowledge of Black Hawk is denied us. The little known of him prior to 1832 is derived from less than a dozen sources, the most important being his autobiography;[2] the others, nearly all military, are to be found in treaties and the records of the war department. A few settlers only knew him, because settlers about his haunts in those days were exceedingly scarce. And so it has come to pass that his character has been universally judged by the contact with him during the last five or six years of his long life, while he was in a sense a captive, brooding over his fallen estate, while the drapery of an eternal evening was fast falling about him. At such an age, shorn of power, chafing under restric-

---

[1] Much has been written of the perfection of Black Hawk's head; so much that it may not be inappropriate to refer to an article to be found in the American Phrenological Journal for November, 1838, Vol. I, No. 2, page 51 et. seq. On page 60: "We are much pleased with the following extract from the pen of the editor of the U. S. Literary Gazette, Philadelphia: 'We found time yesterday to visit Black Hawk and the Indian chiefs at the Congress Hall Hotel. We went into their chamber, and found most of them sitting or lying on their beds. Black Hawk was sitting on a chair and apparently depressed in spirits. He is about sixty-five, of middling size, with a head that would excite the envy of a phrenologist—one of the finest that Heaven ever let fall on the shoulders of an Indian.'

1. Amativeness, large.
2. Philoprogenitiveness, large.
3. Adhesiveness, large.
4. Inhabitiveness, large.
5. Concentrativeness, large.
6. Combativeness, very large.
7. Destructiveness, very large.
8. Alimentativeness, average.
9. Acquisitiveness, large.
10. Secretiveness, very large.
11. Cautiousness, full.
12. Approbativeness, very large.
13. Self-esteem, very large.
14. Firmness, very large.
15. Conscientiousness, moderate.
16. Hope, small.
17. Marvelousness, large.
18. Veneration, very large.
19. Benevolence, moderate.
20. Constructiveness, small.
21. Ideality, moderate.
22. Imitation, small.
23. Mirthfulness, full.
24. Individuality, very large.
25. Form, very large.
26. Size, very large.
27. Weight, large.
28. Color, large.
29. Order, large.
30. Calculation, large.
31. Locality, very large.
32. Eventuality, very large.
33. Time, uncertain.
34. Tune, uncertain.
35. Language, large.
36. Comparison, large.
37. Causality, average.

Measurements from his bust:

Circumference of the head, around philoprogenitiveness, secretiveness and eventuality .... 23 inches
From ear to ear, over firmness .... 14 6-8 "
    "   "   veneration .... 14 6-8 "
From the meatus auditoris to firmness .... 6½ "
    "   "   veneration .... 6½ "
    "   "   benevolence .... 6½ "
    "   "   comparison .... 6⅞ "
    "   "   individuality .... 5½ "
    "   "   philoprogenitiveness .... 5½ "
    "   "   self-esteem .... 6⅝ "
From destructiveness to destructiveness .... 6⅝ "
From secretiveness to secretiveness .... 6⅝ "
From combativeness to combativeness .... 5⅝ "
From cautiousness to cautiousness .... 5⅛ "
From ideality to ideality 5   "

"These measurements are taken with callipers, from the bust of Black Hawk, which was taken in plaster of Paris from the living head and face, by the Messrs. Fowler, in 1837, at New York. As his head was mostly shaved, they are probably as perfect and accurate, by making allowance of about half an inch for integuments, as though measured directly on the skull itself."

[2] That book was dictated by Black Hawk in 1833, interpreted by Antoine Le Claire to J. B. Patterson, who wrote it down in English and assisted materially in securing its publication the following year. Mr. Patterson was a private in Captain Maughs' company of Jo Daviess County volunteers.

tions, disgruntled at the supremacy of his ancient enemy Keokuk, who had answered for his good behavior, the old man's ambitions crushed, he was naturally a distressing object, evoking that pity which so universally appeals to an American and is so surely allowed to cover a multitude of sins. Those few last years have been thus carelessly permitted to become the monument to the man, and those who drove him from power have been harshly judged or jocularly denominated "carpet soldiers," as much as to say the pioneers had never suffered hardships nor endured wrongs. Justice to those whose wives and children had been butchered, whose fathers and brothers had been burned at the stake, demands that all the truth be told and the reason given why those settlers, infuriated at the loss of two successive crops from Black Hawk's perfidy, finally drove his band into the Mississippi River at the mouth of the Bad Axe and almost annihilated it.

It has been written that he possessed a mind of unusual strength, but slow and plodding, with little genius and few talents to manage a great enterprise in war.[1] The influence to sustain such a paradox, as well as kindred irregularities and disorders of the man's mind, may be attributed to the fact that he was a confirmed hypochondriac, morbidly regarding as frivolous everything save war. He was discontented and reckless, envious of others with greater influence or name, and in meeting questions in or out of the council with such men as Keokuk he was churlish to a degree unless his individual will ruled. While it must candidly be owned that the whites have been guilty of the most revolting injustices to other Indians, notably Shabona, the same cannot be pleaded for Black Hawk. He was found making and breaking engagements and treaties[2] the greater part of his very long life, and then, when retribution was imminent, he hoisted flags of truce down to August 2d, 1832, when his power for further mischief was forever crushed.

The reputation which he has established in Indian annals comes not from any sacrifice he made for his people, for never in his life did he make one. Neither comes it from his struggles for an oppressed race, for he never conceived a solitary scheme for its amelioration. He had never a lofty aspiration for his nation. His every venture was made for personal aggrandizement or popularity. Tecumseh dreamed of a great confederation; not to become a leader. Cornstalk, Logan and Pontiac were ambitious for their people, but Black Hawk never. Black Hawk said of Keokuk that the latter was a groveling sycophant, but Keokuk was the most powerful orator of his race, and, penetrating the inevitable destiny of the whites,

---

[1] Reynolds, "My Own Times," p. 320; Perkins and Peck, Annals of the West; Hist. Des Moines Co., Iowa. Brown's Hist. of Illinois, p. 377: "Black Hawk compared with Philip of Pokanoket, Pontiac, Little Turtle or Tecumseh, was but an ordinary man—inferior vastly to either. That he was brave is probable. Mere bravery is but a common virtue in the savage. That he was politic beyond others can scarcely be pretended. He evinced no particular talents in any of his plans, nor did he exhibit extraordinary skill in their accomplishment."

[2] Hist. of Des Moines County, p. 345.

he conformed to it and used his great genius to gain for his people the greatest good. While Black Hawk was stolidly plotting for war, Keokuk was planning to secure for his people good homes and larger annuities, and these he secured, to their very great benefit. Black Hawk's prominence comes from notoriety alone.

In his various conflicts with the whites he was invariably the aggressor. The unfortunate affair which resulted in the death of his so-called adopted son cannot be, by any conceivable logic, tortured into an exception, as we shall presently see. After the treaty of 1804 he and his band were permitted to remain unmolested upon the ceded lands year after year and decade after decade, a license rarely allowed and, as it proved, a thoroughly mistaken policy. He received his yearly annuities and retained the lands for which the annuities were given, literally eating his cake and keeping it. His passions were many, but the consuming passion of his life was hatred of the Americans, a hatred without cause and as unjustifiable and unreasonable as man's baser passions are always found to be. Yet this may not be surprising, fed as he was by his devouring gloom and restless, war-like spirit. The mantle of charity has many a time before and since covered graver faults; so let it be with Black Hawk's, for it is said of him that in his domestic life he was a kind husband and father, and in his transactions with his people he was upright and honest,[1] if he was not ambitious for their elevation.

Black Hawk was not a chief of the Sac nation.[2] He was simply a brave. His father was the tribal medicine man, and whatever standing Black Hawk may have secured was derived from his personal bravery and daring as a warrior, which have never been questioned. Possessed, as we have seen, of a martial spirit, he was ever ready and eager to lead war parties of young companions to battle, and one or two engagements alone were sufficient firmly to establish him in that leadership which bravery fitted him to hold over his followers in war.

At fifteen, having distinguished himself by wounding an enemy, he was permitted to paint and wear feathers and join the rank of the Braves.[3] About the year 1783 he united in an expedition against the Osages and had the fortune to kill and scalp one of the enemy, for which youthful act of valor he was for the first time permitted to mingle in the scalp-dance. As one exploit followed another his desire for blood became insatiable, and from his own account, the number of the enemy slain by him staggers credulity.

A short time after the '83 tragedy—"a few moons," as he puts it— Black Hawk was leader of a party of seven which attacked a band of one

---

[1] Reynolds, "My Own Times;" Hist. of Des Moines County, p. 339.
[2] Perkins and Peck, "Annals of the West," p. 795, Ed. of 1850; Thwaite's "Story of Black Hawk;" Hist. of Des Moines County, Iowa; Fulton's "Red Men of Iowa," and letters from Agents Forsythe and St. Vrain.
[3] Drake.

hundred Osages, killed one of their number and retreated without loss, Black Hawk taking the credit for this fatality to his personal valor. His taste for war, coupled with his prowess, attracted notice from others, and very presently he was found marching at the head of one hundred and eighty braves against the Osage village on the Missouri. Finding it deserted, the greater number of his young followers became dissatisfied, abandoned the enterprise and returned home, but Black Hawk continued, and, with but five followers, came upon the Osages, killed and scalped one man and a boy and then returned home. In consequence of this mutiny he has told us he was not again able to raise sufficient force to move against the Osages until his nineteenth year, during which interim, it was claimed, the Osages committed many outrages on his nation.

In 1786 his restless spirit had planned another attack of a retaliatory nature against the Osages. Setting out with two hundred followers, he met a party of the enemy about equal in strength, which for a time stubbornly resisted Black Hawk's attack, but, unable to maintain an unequal contest with the fierce Sac fighters, the Osages were finally routed and the band almost annihilated. One hundred of them were killed outright and the remnant which remained was left to be scalped while helplessly wounded, or driven from the country, while, on the other hand, Black Hawk's loss was but nineteen men. Six of the enemy were killed by Black Hawk—five men and one squaw—and in alluding to this he adds these words: "I had the good fortune to take all their scalps." In recording his glorious enterprise his interpreter doubtless insisted that the murder of a female by a great warrior was not creditable, for, once the enormity of his offense is cited, he pleads in extenuation that the squaw was accidentally killed; yet he scalped her.

The severe cost to the Osages of this battle brought about a treaty of peace between the belligerents which lasted for a considerable period, as peaceful times between Indian nations seem then to have been reckoned.

The stormiest periods of Black Hawk's life were all born of tranquil times, and this interval of peace served to incubate a plan of campaign against his ancient and inveterate enemy, the Cherokees, which was to be fraught with consequences more serious than all his former campaigns together.

Py-e-sa, Black Hawk's father, the hereditary medicine man of his tribe, had held the medicine bag for many years and his ability as a discreet, fearless and upright man cannot be controverted. Regarding a campaign by the young men so far from home as hazardous in the extreme, he joined this expedition, and with his people paddled his canoe night and day down the Mississippi River until the enemy was reached upon the Merameg River, south of St. Louis, in vastly superior forces. The battle which followed was stubbornly waged, but in it, as in so many others, the ferocity of the attack put the Cherokees to flight, leaving twenty-eight of their number dead upon the field, while the Sacs lost but seven braves. But one of those seven was Py-e-sa, whose loss was never thereafter supplied to the great Sac nation. Had he been spared to treat of subsequent questions with the whites, his moderation had unquestionably sustained Keokuk's position and the campaigns of 1831 and 1832, with their trains of slaughter, would have been averted. In this engagement Black Hawk himself killed three outright and wounded many more.

By the death of Py-e-sa, Black Hawk fell heir to the medicine bag, with its attendant responsibility. He immediately returned to his village, blackened his face and remained tranquil for the succeeding five years of his life, with no more stimulating employment than hunting, fishing and meditation. During this period of inaction, Black Hawk maintains, the Osages were constantly harassing his people by incursions into his country, carrying with each invasion a predatory warfare extremely distressing and galling. These became so frequent and offensive that, as Black Hawk has told us, "the Great Spirit took pity on them" (the Sacs), upon which event he took to the field. Here, at the head of a small party, he overtook a few struggling Osages, so feeble that he simply made them prisoners and handed them over to the Spanish father at St. Louis. With this famous act of clemency he continued his plan of total destruction of the offending Osages.

About the year 1800, the Iowa nation, having accumulated many grievances against the Osages, made common cause with the Sacs for the purpose of waging a war of extermination. Raising a force of about one hundred, which joined the Sac forces, numbering now about five hundred more, the two allies marched upon the unsuspecting Osages, who were unarmed and wholly unprepared for defense. They valiantly defended their homes and families and fought with the desperation known only to those who have waged such defenses against overpowering odds. One by one and dozen by dozen and score by score fell dead before the terrific attacks of the most terrible of Indian fighters, until there was none left to fill the gaps made in their ranks by the tomahawk and spear. Forty lodges were destroyed and every inhabitant save two squaws was put to death. Then, returning home, a great feast was made, at which Black Hawk exploited his personal valor to his friends. In this engagement he killed seven men and two boys with his own hand.

During those five years of meditation following his father's death resentment had but slumbered. They killed his father, 'tis true, but it had been done defending themselves. The Sacs as a nation had no quarrel with the Cherokees. But immediately he returned from his war upon the unsuspecting Osages, Black Hawk collected another party and moved down the river against them. In due season the enemy's country was reached and invaded, but, roam as they would, no more than five unknown people could be found, four men and one squaw. The men, after a short detention, were released, and the squaw was taken back to Black Hawk's village on Rock River.

The futility of this campaign rankled in Black Hawk's heart for a time, and to recoup his lost, or at least suspended reputation, he planned, in the year 1803, about the ninth moon, the most extensive campaign of his life against the combined forces of the Chippewas, Osages and Kaskaskias. No just reason existed for this war; none of the tribes of these nations had trespassed on Sac territory or rights, and none had offended in any other particular. Black Hawk was piqued at his last miscarriage and he simply made war against these people for the sake of war, and bloody indeed it proved to be. During its continuance seven pitched battles were fought, together with numerous skirmishes, in all which more than one hundred of the enemy perished. Here again Black Hawk boasts of personally killing with his own hands thirteen of the bravest warriors in the enemy's ranks. His ferocity in these engagements is the best evidence for the statement that the glory of Black Hawk was placed above every other consideration.

In 1763 France ceded Louisiana to Spain, though Senor Rious, the Spanish agent, did not formally take possession of St. Louis and the upper Louisiana country until 1768, and even then St. Ange, the French Governor, continued to perform official acts until 1770. In 1800 Napoleon took it away again, retaining it until 1803, when it was purchased by the United States.[1] During the Spanish domination Black Hawk had been a periodical visitor to St. Louis, accepting frequent presents and forming what might be termed a devotion to the Governor, whom he designated as his "Spanish Father."

After the conclusion of his last war, he paid this Spanish father a friendly visit at St. Louis. Spanish and French domination had ended and the Americans were just then taking possession of the country, much to his regret and, as might be imagined, disgust. Here are his comments: "Soon after the Americans arrived I took my band and went to take leave for the last time of our father. The Americans came to see him also. Seeing them approach, we passed out of one door as they entered another and immediately started in our canoes for our village on Rock River, not liking the change any more than our friends appeared to at St. Louis. On arriving at St. Louis, we were given the news that strange people had taken St. Louis and that we should never see our Spanish father again. This information made all our people sorry."

---

[1] Treaty concluded April 30, 1803.

CHAPTER II.

BRITISH INTRIGUE AGAINST THE FRONTIERS—HATRED OF THE AMERICANS—TREATY OF 1804.

By the treaty of Paris, Sept. 3, 1783, Great Britain covenanted to surrender certain western forts which were of great strategic importance to the Americans in protecting the frontier from Indian incursions and also in dealing with such as were disposed to treat honorably with the Government. The compact was solemnly made and signed, but, disgruntled from the loss of her colonies, the British government sent secret instructions to its garrisons to retain these forts, and in consequence not one of them was surrendered. Nor was this the only violation by the British of their engagements. Agents were set to work over our vast frontier to foment insubordination among the Indians against American domination. These Indians were supplied with provisions and arms and incited openly to war against the whites and drive them back east of the mountains, and year after year they continued until the sickening horrors of the stake and scalping knife were sweeping the feeble settlements of the West from end to end.

France and Spain, both, with colonial possessions to the west, while gratified to see England stripped of her possessions, were suspected of aiding the design of the British to restrict American settlements to the shores of the Atlantic. Spain claimed exclusive ownership of the Mississippi and commerce upon her waters by Americans was prohibited. The "dark and bloody ground" of Kentucky, long the scene of carnage, was made the first scene of British intrigue, where the atrocities of the Indians were the most frightful in history. The tribes of Ohio and Indiana, which were in the league, penetrated the settlements of the whites, deluging the land with the blood of innocent women and children.

The Government, hopelessly involved with debt and graver questions of state, could offer the struggling settlers no relief, and thus alone they were forced to stand in hourly fear of butchery. They grew to look for no help save in their own resources, and yearly meeting with defiance, a pioneer community of militant husbandmen gradually grew and moved westward; instinctively taught to rush to arms upon the breaking of a twig or the rustle of a leaf in defense of their defenseless loved ones in the cabin. When, therefore, Black Hawk lent a willing ear to the British agent, accepted his presents and performed his murderous behests, which he did, he should have expected the awful consequences of defeat and annihilation which followed his years of hypocrisy, and accepted the Government's final requital with gratitude, or at least Indian stolidity, instead of snarling at his fate and constantly bewailing the elevation of others over him who had loyally stood by the Americans and their Government in perilous times. He invited destruction and was destroyed. The attention of the student is directed to this phase of Black Hawk's character as it develops in these pages down to his defeat, August 2d, 1832.

The Sacs were originally British Indians, domiciled near Montreal. By constant quarrels and wars with their neighbors their tribes, once numerous and powerful, were reduced to a remnant and finally driven from the country altogether. They settled in Wisconsin, where they met the Foxes, similarly driven from Canada, and the two tribes immediately combined, ever after being considered as a confederated nation. They again grew powerful and arrogant and became involved in wars with their neighbors. At the time of the last French and English war they took sides with the English and received from that source presents for many years. This British sympathy was born in Black Hawk, and continued with him, growing in intensity as the Americans expanded and defeated the English, until it became positive hatred.[1] When, therefore, he repeats the statement that he heard bad accounts of the Americans in 1803, and then asserts that all his differences with the Americans date from the signing of the treaty of 1804, he states that which cannot be received with confidence. Prior to 1803 he never had found himself in contact with the Americans to an extent worthy of note, and no cause, real or imaginary, had been given him for a difference, yet on leaving the Spanish father, mentioned in the last chapter, he catches a rumor, adopts a prejudice and dictates for his autobiography the following ill-natured words, false to begin with and as malignant as he was generally found to be in speaking or writing of the Americans: "I inquired the cause and was informed that the Americans were coming to take possession of the town and country, and that we should lose our Spanish father. This news made myself and band sad, because we had always heard *bad accounts* of the Americans from Indians who had lived near them."

During the years 1803 and 1804, Gov. William Henry Harrison of Indiana concluded treaties with the Kaskaskias and the Wabash tribes, obtaining thereby title to a large extent of country south of the Illinois River. Having an immense stretch of country unserviceable for fishing and hunting, many of the Sacs and Foxes considered it desirable to receive

---

[1]The Illinois country, to which the two tribes finally emigrated, was transferred by the French to the English crown in 1765. Thus Black Hawk was born under British rule.

KE-O-KUK.

PA-SHE-PA-HO.

ANTOINE LE CLAIRE.

J. B. PATTERSON.

annuities,[1] after the manner of the Wabash tribes. A bad hunt could thus be recouped in a certain money stipend. Accordingly, slight overtures were thrown out to this effect. The Sacs and Foxes roamed north of the Illinois River, like the fugitive buffalo or lonesome bird of passage. Those broad prairies afforded them no subsistence in hunting or fishing. The bare claim to possession was their sole exercise of it, and that frail tenure had been wrenched by conquest from others without compensation in the smallest degree. Along the streams a few harmless, nondescript Indians and tribal remnants lived, or rather remained, as dependent vassals of the mighty Sacs and Foxes, but these were so inconspicuous and weak as to be ignored by both the whites and Indians in treaties.

There can be no doubt of a knowledge by the Government of this desire for annuities by the Sacs and Foxes. President Jefferson was not the man to simulate the existence of any unfair postulate in treating with the Indians, who were at all times objects of his especial solicitude. Accordingly, on the 27th day of June, 1804, he directed Governor Harrison to treat with the Sacs and Foxes and obtain cessions of lands on both sides the Illinois River, granting as a consideration therefor an annual compensation. Agreeably with his instructions, Governor Harrison called the head chiefs of the consolidated tribes to meet him at St. Louis, which Pashepaho, head chief of the Sacs, Layowvois, Quashquame, Outchequaha and Hashequarhiqua did. Here, on November 3d, the following treaty was solemnly made and signed:

Articles of a Treaty, made at St. Louis, in the district of Louisiana, between William Henry Harrison, Governor of the Indiana Territory and the District of Louisiana, Superintendent of Indian affairs for the said Territory and district and Commissioner plenipotentiary of the United States, for concluding any treaty or treaties, which may be found necessary with any of the Northwestern tribes of Indians, of the one part; and the Chiefs and head men of the united Sac and Fox tribes of the other part.

Article 1. The United States receive the united Sac and Fox tribes into their friendship and protection and the said tribes agree to consider themselves under the protection of the United States, and no other power whatsoever.

Art. 2. The General boundary line between the land of the United States and the said Indian tribes shall be as follows, to wit: Beginning at a point on the Missouri River opposite to the mouth of the Gasconade River; thence, in a direct course so as to strike the River Jeffreon, at the distance of 30 miles from its mouth and down the said Jeffreon to the Mississippi; thence, up the Mississippi to the mouth of the Ouisconsing River, and up the same to a point which shall be 36 miles in a direct line from the mouth of the said river, thence, by a direct line to the point where the Fox River (a branch of the Illinois) leaves the small Lake called Sakaegan; thence, down the Fox River to the Illinois River, and down the same to the Mississippi. And the said tribes, for and in consideration of the friendship and protection of the United States, which is now extended to them, of the goods (to the value of two thousand two hundred and thirty-four dollars and fifty cents) which are now delivered, and of

---
[1] Brown's Hist. of Illinois, p. 381, is emphatic on this point.

the annuity hereinafter stipulated to be paid, do hereby cede and relinquish forever, to the United States, all the lands included within the above described boundary.

Art. 3. In consideration of the cession and relinquishment of land made in the preceding article, the United States will deliver to the said tribes, at the town of St. Louis, or some other convenient place on the Mississippi, yearly and every year, goods suited to the circumstances of the Indians of the value of one thousand dollars (six hundred of which are intended for the Sacs and four hundred for the Foxes), reckoning that value at the first cost of the goods in the City or place in the United States, where they shall be procured. And if the said tribes shall hereafter at an annual delivery of the goods aforesaid, desire that a part of their annuity should be furnished in domestic animals, implements of husbandry, and other utensils, convenient for them, or in compensation to useful artificers, who may reside with or near them, and be employed for their benefit, the same shall, at the subsequent annual delivery, be furnished accordingly.

Art. 4. The United States will never interrupt the said tribes in the possession of the lands, which they rightfully claim, but will, on the contrary, protect them in the quiet enjoyment of the same against their own citizens and against all other white persons, who may intrude upon them. And the said tribes do hereby engage that they will never sell their lands, or any part thereof, to any sovereign power but the United States, nor to the citizens or subjects of any other sovereign power, nor to the citizens of the United States.

Art. 5. Lest the friendship, which is now established between the United States and the said Indian Tribes should be interrupted by the misconduct of individuals, it is hereby agreed that for injuries done by individuals no private revenge or retaliation shall take place, but instead thereof, complaint shall be made by the party injured to the other by the said tribe, or either of them, to the superintendent of Indian affairs, or one of his deputies; and by the superintendent, or other person appointed by the President, to the Chiefs of the said tribes. And it shall be the duty of the said chiefs, upon complaint being made, as aforesaid, to deliver up the person, or persons, against whom the complaint is made, to the end that he or they may be punished agreeably to the laws of the state or territory where the offence may have been committed. And, in like manner, if any robbery, violence or murder shall be committed on any Indian, or Indians, belonging to the said tribes, or either of them, the person or persons so offending shall be tried, and, if found guilty, punished in the like manner as if the injury had been done to a white man. And, it is farther agreed, that the chiefs of the said tribes shall, to the utmost of their power, exert themselves to recover horses or other property which may be stolen from any citizen or citizens of the United States by any individual or individuals of their tribes. And the property so recovered shall be forthwith delivered to the superintendent or other person authorized to receive it that it may be restored to the proper owner. And in cases where the exertions of the chiefs shall be ineffectual in recovering the property stolen, as aforesaid, if sufficient proof can be obtained, that such property was actually stolen by any Indian or Indians belonging to the said tribes, or either of them, the United States may deduct from the annuity of the said tribes, a sum equal to the value of the property which has been stolen, And the United States hereby guarantee to any Indian or Indians of the said tribes a full indemnification for any horses, or other property which may be stolen from them, by any of their citizens; Provided, that the property so stolen cannot be recovered, and that sufficient proof is produced that it was actually stolen by a citizen of the United States.

Art. 6. If any citizen of the United States, or any other white person, should form a settlement, upon the lands which are the property of the Sac and Fox tribes, upon complaint being made thereof, to the superintendent, or other person having charge of the affairs of the Indians, such intruders shall forthwith be removed.

Art. 7. As long as the lands which are now ceded to the United States remain their property, the Indians belonging to the said tribes shall enjoy the privilege of living and hunting upon them.

Art. 8. As the laws of the United States regulating trade and intercourse with the Indian tribes are already extended to the country inhabited by the Sauks and Foxes, and as it is provided by those laws, that no person shall reside as a trader, in the Indian country, without a license, under the hand and seal of the Superintendent of Indian Affairs, or other person appointed for the purpose by the President, the said tribes do promise and agree that they will not suffer any trader to reside amongst them without such license, and that they will, from time to time, give notice to the Superintendent, or to the Agent, for their tribes, of all the traders that may be in their country.

Art 9. In order to put a stop to the abuses and impositions, which are practiced upon the said tribes by the private traders, the United States, will, at a convenient time, establish a trading house, or factory, where the individuals of the said tribes can be supplied with goods at a more reasonable rate than they have been accustomed to procure them.

Art. 10. In order to evince the sincerity of their friendship and affection for the United States, and a respectful deference for their advice, by an act which will not only be acceptable to them, but by the Common Father of all the nations of the Earth, the said tribes do, hereby solemnly promise and agree that they will put an end to the bloody war which has heretofore raged between their tribes and those of the great and little Osages. And for the purpose of burying the tomahawk and renewing the friendly intercourse between themselves and the Osages, a meeting of their respective Chiefs shall take place, at which, under the direction of the above named Commissioner, or the Agent of Indian affairs residing at St. Louis, an adjustment of all their differences shall be made and peace established, upon a firm and lasting basis.

Art. 11. As it is probable that the Government of the United States will establish a Military Post at, or near the mouth, of the Ouisconsing River, and as the land on the lower side of the River may not be suitable for that purpose, the said tribes hereby agree, that a Fort may be built, either on the upper side of the Ouisconsing, or on the right bank of the Mississippi, as the one or the other may be found most convenient; and a tract of land not exceeding two miles square, shall be given for that purpose. And the said tribes do further agree, that they will at all times, allow to traders and other persons traveling through their country, under the authority of the United States, a free and safe passage for themselves and their property of every description. And that for such passage, they shall at no time, and on no account whatever, be subject to any toll or exaction.

Art. 12. This Treaty shall take effect and be obligatory on the contracting parties, as soon as the same shall have been ratified by the President, by and with the advice and consent of the Senate of the United States.

In testimony whereof, the said William Henry Harrison, and the Chiefs and headmen of the said Sac and Fox tribes, have hereunto set their hands and affixed their seals. Done at Saint Louis, in the district of Louisiana, on the third day of November, One Thousand Eight Hundred and Four, and of the independence of the United States the Twenty-Ninth.

ADDITIONAL ARTICLE.

It is agreed that nothing in this treaty contained shall affect the claim of any individual or individuals, who may have obtained grants of Land from the Spanish

Government and which are not included within the general boundary line laid down in this treaty: PROVIDED, that such grant have at any time been made known to the said tribes and recognized by them.

        WILLIAM HENRY HARRISON, [L. S.]
        LAYOWVOIS, *or* LAIYUVA, [L. S.]
         His (X) *Mark.*
        PASHEPAHO, *or* THE STABBER, [L. S.]
         His (X) *Mark.*
        QUASHQUAME, *or* JUMPING FISH, [L. S.]
         His (X) *Mark.*
        OUTCHEQUAHA, *or* SUN FISH, [L. S.]
         His (X) *Mark.*
        HASHEQUARHIQUA, *or* THE BEAR, [L. S.]
         His (X) *Mark.*

    In presence of

        WM. PRINCE, *Sec'y to the Commissioner.*
        JOHN GRIFFIN, *one of the judges of the Indiana Territory.*
        J. BRUFF, *Maj. Art'ry, U. S.*
        AMOS STODDARD, *Capt. Corps of Artillerists.*
        P. CHOUTEAU, *Agent de la haute Louisiana pour le department Sauvage.*
        CH. GRATIOT.
        AUG. CHOUTEAU.
        VIGO S. WARREL, *Lieut. U. S. Artillery.*
        D. DELAUNEY.
  Sworn Interpreters: JOS. BARRON.
        HYPOLITE BOLEN,
         His (X) *Mark.*

CHAPTER III.

TREATY OF 1804, AND BLACK HAWK'S VERSION.

On December 31st, 1804, the President submitted this treaty to the Senate, which ratified it immediately.

In justice to Black Hawk, his relation of all incidents leading up to this treaty, from the departure of French rule to its ratification, which he always insisted was the bone of contention between himself and the whites, will be given, and in justice to the Americans, his inaccuracies, their logical deductions and the manner in which he played the same against the facts will also be given.

In the first edition of his autobiography, published in Boston in 1834, page 25, after concluding his sorrow at the advent of the Americans, he stated:

"Some time afterwards, a boat came up the river, with a young American chief (Lieutenant, afterwards General, Zebulon M. Pike), and a small party of soldiers. We heard of him (by runners) soon after he had passed Salt River. Some of our young braves watched him every day, to see what sort of people he had on board. The boat at length arrived at Rock River, and the young chief came on shore with his interpreter, made a speech, and gave us some presents. We, in return, presented him with meat and such provisions as we could spare.

"We were all well pleased with the speech of the young chief. He gave us good advice; said our American father would treat us well. He presented us an American flag, which was hoisted. He then requested us to pull down our British flags, and give him our British medals, promising to send us others on his return to St. Louis. This we declined, as we wished to have *two fathers*."

"* * * We did not see any Americans again for some time, being supplied with goods by British traders."

"Some moons after this young chief descended the Mississippi, one of our people killed an American and was confined in the prison at St. Louis for the offense. We held a council at our village to see what could be done for him, which determined that Quash-qua-me, Pa-she-pa-ho, Ou-che-qua-ka and Ha-she-quar-hi-qua should go down to St. Louis, see our American father, and do all they could to have our friend released by paying for the person killed; thus covering the blood, and satisfying the relations of the man murdered; that being the only means with us of saving a person who had killed another, and we then thought it was the same way with the whites.

"The party started with the good wishes of the whole nation, hoping they would accomplish the object of their mission. The relatives of the prisoner blacked their faces and fasted—hoping the Great Spirit would take pity on them, and return the husband and father to his wife and children. Quash-qua-me and party remained a long time absent. They at length returned, and encamped a short distance below the village, but did not come up that day, nor did any person approach their camp. They appeared to be dressed in *fine coats,* and had *medals!* From these circumstances we were in hopes that they had brought good news. Early the next morning the Council Lodge was crowded. Quash-qua-me and party came up, and gave us the following account of their mission: 'On their arrival at St. Louis they met their American father, and explained to him their business, and urged the release of their friend. The American chief told them he wanted land, and they agreed to give him some on the west side of the Mississippi, and some on the Illinois side, opposite the Jeffreon. When the business was all arranged, they expected to have their friend released to come home with them. But about the time they were ready to start, their friend was let out of prison, who ran a short distance, and was shot dead. This was all they could recollect of what was said and done. They had been drunk the greater part of the time they were in St. Louis.'

"This was all myself or nation knew of the treaty of 1804. It has been explained to me since. I find by that treaty all our country east of the Mississippi, and south of the Jeffreon, was ceded to the United States for one thousand dollars a year! I leave it to the people of the United States to say whether our nation was properly represented in this treaty, or whether we received a fair compensation for the extent of country ceded by those four individuals. I could say much about this treaty, but I will not at this time. It has been the origin of all our difficulties."[1]

During the years 1803 and 1804, the British were in their ugliest humor toward the Americans, and no effort to aggravate, yea murder, the frontier was spared. In the face of those atrocities and in face of the further fact that on January 9th, 1789, a solemn treaty of friendship was made between the United States and the Sacs, at Fort Harmar, signed by Te-pa-kee and Kesh-e-yi-va, the 14th article of which is as follows: "The United States of America do also receive into their friendship and protection the nations of the Pottiwatimas and Sacs, and do hereby establish a league of peace and amity between them respectively; and all the articles of this treaty, so far as they apply to these nations, are to be considered as made and concluded in all, and every part, expressly with them and each of them,"[2] it would seem in extreme bad taste for Black Hawk to desire a continuance of British paternity and British provisions, and flout British authority in the faces of those Americans who were the sufferers. A sane man would expect something to happen. Black Hawk stated and emphasized the fact that Pike went up the Mississippi and returned before the treaty of 1804 was made, when as a matter of fact he went up the river in 1805 and returned in 1807. Now if he committed such glaring errors in matters of passing importance, what can be expected in matters of graver

---

[1] When the French discovered and took possession of Illinois, neither the Sacs nor Foxes had any claim or existence on the tract of country mentioned in this treaty. Am. State Papers, V, 689, 690, 663. Dawson's Life of Harrison, 59. Perkins and Peck, Annals of the West, 546.

[2] "Public Statutes at Large," ed. 1848, p. 31.

GOV. WILLIAM HENRY HARRISON.

LIEUT. ZEBULON M. PIKE.

COL. AUGUSTE CHOUTEAU.

COL. PIERRE CHOUTEAU.

importance? And where can the intelligent student draw the line between fact and fabrication?

Much else that Black Hawk has said is altogether incorrect as well as preposterous. There can be no excuse for his untruthful statement that but four chiefs signed the treaty, because there were five, as the record itself discloses, and Pash-e-pa-ho, the then principal chief of the Sac nation, was one of them. Nor can it be seen that he strengthened his standing with the public to charge William Henry Harrison, the most upright of men, with giving the Indian emissaries fine clothes and medals as part consideration for their signatures, and with stupefying them with liquor and finally murdering outright the prisoner, and it is certainly regrettable to find in his narrative no mention of the sorrowing wife and weeping children of the murdered American who never returned to his hearthstone.

CHAPTER IV.

TREATY OF 1804.

That the Indian had many wrongs must not be denied, but that such wrongs should be transferred from those who suffered them to the personal account of Black Hawk, either entire or to any great extent, is a proposition too monstrous for sober consideration. The simpering casuist has strenuously endeavored to effect that transfer, even to the extent of adopting his statements about the liquor and the murder. As needless, yea repugnant, to all sense of propriety and truth as the task may be to shore up the reputation of Governor Harrison against Black Hawk's aspersions, it has been thought best to quote the only historical record at hand on the subject of the murder, and dissipate for all time the maudlin sympathy which his contention has raised:

"Some time about the middle of the year 1804, three American citizens, who had settled above the Missouri, were murdered by a party of Sack Indians; and the Governor having learnt this circumstance, as well as the hostile dispositions of the Sacks and Foxes toward the United States, sent them a message by Captain Stoddart, in the month of October, requiring their chiefs to meet him in St. Louis; and on his arrival at that place he learnt the circumstance of the murder, as well as the exertions which were making by some of the old chiefs among them to give up the perpetrators of it, but who were opposed by a majority of the nation, who declared their satisfaction at what had been done, and their determination to protect the murderers at all risk. The Governor dispatched another messenger to the Sack chiefs, to inform them of his arrival at St. Louis, and urge them to make every possible exertion to apprehend, and bring with them, the murderers; but if that could not be effected, he requested that they would come to him at any rate, assuring them of their being permitted to return in safety.

"The Governor, conceiving that if they could be prevailed upon to come to a conference it would be easy to convince them of the necessity of preserving the friendship of the United States, had no doubt that he would prevail upon some of them to remain with him as hostages for the delivery of the murderers. But before his messenger had arrived, the petty chief who headed the war party had surrendered himself to the sachems or head men of the nation, and declared his willingness to suffer for the injury he had done. On the arrival of the chiefs at St. Louis, he was delivered up to the Governor, and a positive assurance given that the whole nation were sorry for the injury which had been done, and that they would never in future lift the tomahawk against the United States."[1]

---

[1]Dawson's "Life of Harrison." (William Henry.)

THE BLACK HAWK WAR.   35

At this same meeting, the treaty was made which has already been set out at length, and while the same authority mentions the fact without comment, it will be quoted, and following it some reasons may be noted why the bargain was not one of particular rigor. At least Black Hawk's argument may be shown to be specious:

"At this meeting with the chiefs of the Sac and Fox Indians, the Government negotiated a treaty by which the Indian title was extinguished to the largest tract of land ever ceded in one treaty by the Indians since the settlement of North America, as it includes all the country from the mouth of the Illinois River to the mouth of the Ouisconsing, on the one side, and from the mouth of the Illinois to near the head of the Fox River on the other side; and from the head of the latter a line is drawn to a point 36 miles above the mouth of the Ouisconsing, which forms the northern boundary, and contains upwards of 51 millions of acres."

Black Hawk offers to leave the question of bargain to the people of the United States. From present day standpoints it might be considered a hard bargain, but from the facts in the case, the reply might be made with an inquiry if the Wisconsin farmer got much of a bargain when he bought from a sharper the Masonic Temple of Chicago for $2,000.

Two-thirds or more of the land ceded was claimed and occupied by the Winnebagoes and Pottowattomies at the time, and Black Hawk knew the fact and admitted it times without number on subsequent occasions. Even down so close to him as the Prophet's village, in the present county of Whiteside, the country was Winnebago territory; the same at Dixon's Ferry, while over on the Illinois River the Pottowattomies had for a great length of time held dominion, and this had never been controverted by the Sacs and Foxes. The fact is that the United States acquired but very little territory by that treaty, when the magnificent proportions are mentioned without regard to the facts.

With his usual carelessness of fact, Black Hawk omitted to mention the payments down in money and trade which were made and which in those days were not regarded as trifling. He made no mention of subsequent and additional payments and annuities, neither did he credit the Government for the use and occupation of those same lands for over a quarter of a century after they had been ceded. He omitted entirely that he had never kept a treaty in his life until he was finally crushed and driven from power at the point of the bayonet, and he forgot to omit the further fact that all the Sac and Fox Indians, save Black Hawk and his immediate followers, recognized that treaty as just in 1808, when a delegation visited Fort Madison to ascertain if its erection was in violation of it. Schoolcraft, Vol. VI, page 393, made a very sensible observation regarding the sales by Indians of their lands: "But while any section of their territories abounded in game, the Indians elected to retire thither, and bestowed but little attention on either grazing or agriculture. There was, therefore, a singular concurrence in the desire of the emigrants to buy and in the willingness of the Indians to sell their lands."

At no time had the Illinois lands been valuable to the Sacs for hunting, the streams and forests of Iowa having always been sought for their annual hunts. There can be no doubt that this feature had its influence exactly as Schoolcraft, the friend always to the Indian, has stated.

FORT MADISON.

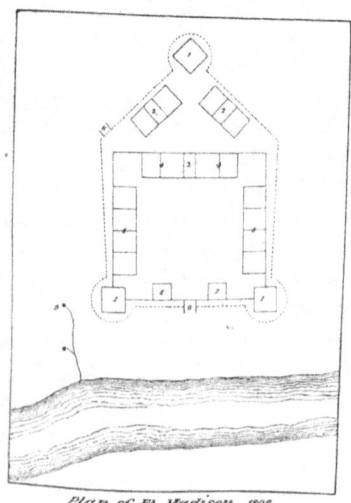

GROUND PLAN OF FORT MADISON.

MAJ. JOHN BEACH.

CHAPTER V.

ERECTION OF FORT MADISON—RUMORS OF INDIAN ATTACK—BLACK HAWK JOINS TECUMSEH—RETURNS TO HIS VILLAGE—ATTACKS FORT MADISON—THE SIEGE.

The object of the expedition of Lieutenant Pike, in 1805-6-7, was, among other things, to select suitable locations for military reservations, Indian posts and forts. One of the last named he located at the head of the Des Moines Rapids, immediately above the mouth of the river of that name, on the west bank of the Mississippi.

In 1808, First Lieutenant Alpha Kingsley, with Captain Ninian Pinckney's company, was sent there from below to construct the fort and garrison it. His work attracted the attention of passing Sacs and excited the suspicion that the act might be a possible infraction of the 1804 treaty. To determine the matter, a party, including Black Hawk, traveled down the river to the scene, where a council or talk was immediately held, at which the intention of the Government was fully discussed. The explanations were satisfactory in every particular to the respective chiefs, who, every one, cheerfully ratified the action of the Government, commending the act as one of prevision for both parties, and with assurances of good feeling returned to their respective homes. Even Drake, the especial champion of Black Hawk, is forced to state, on page 79: "Some of the Indians went down the river, and, after an interview with the officers in charge of the troops constructing it, returned home, satisfied that there was no infraction."

Not so with Black Hawk. He came to the spot bent on mischief, and while the others entered and were engaged in the council, he remained aloof, that no obligation might rest upon him if the talk should result adversely to his wishes, his favorite trick for avoiding the meshes of engagements which might conflict with the arrangements he had made with his British friends, who were furnishing him supplies, as we have seen.

Thus was the construction of Fort Madison permitted to continue, and thus was it in due time completed and garrisoned by seventy-five men; but Black Hawk had studied well its plans and marked it for his vengeance at such a time as stealth should permit him to ambush it and butcher its garrison, lulled into a supine security.[1]

During the winter of 1808-9, the British agents, taking advantage of the suppositious dissatisfaction of the Indians, moved industriously among the tribes, and, through Black Hawk, were able to create among his followers a desire to annoy the Americans. Reports of impending attacks reached the garrison of Fort Madison from time to time. "Upon receiving this information," Lieutenant Kingsley wrote, "I made every exertion to erect the blockhouses and plant my pickets; this we did in two weeks (lying on our arms during the night), and took quarters in the new fort the 14th inst. (April, 1809). Being tolerably secure against an attack, we have been able to get a little rest, and are now making the best preparations for the safety and defense of this establishment."

This letter is dated, "Fort Madison, near River Le Moin, 19th April, 1809." In the same letter Lieutenant Kingsley reported that rumors of an Indian alliance are reaching him frequently, and that any coming trouble may be traced directly to British influence. "The sooner the British traders are shut out of the river," he added, "the better for our Government." Thus was Black Hawk allied, preparing for his part in the war of 1812 with England.

Governor Harrison, in a letter to the Secretary of War, dated Vincennes, July 15th, 1810 (Drake, p. 62), said: "A considerable number of the Sacs went some time since to see the British superintendent, and on the first instant more passed Chicago for the same destination."

General Clark, under date St. Louis, July 20th, 1810, stated in writing to the same department: "One hundred and fifty Sacs are on a visit to the island of St. Joseph, in Lake Huron." John Johnson, the Indian agent at Fort Wayne, under date of August 7th, 1810, said to the Secretary of War: "About one hundred Saukees have returned from the British agent, who supplied them liberally with everything they stood in need of. The party received forty-seven rifles and a number of fusils, with plenty of powder and lead."

In 1811 Black Hawk eagerly accepted British counsel to join the Prophet at Tippecanoe[2] for the purpose of annihilating Governor Harrison. Failing in that effort, he turned westward with a party of Winnebagoes to attack Fort Madison, but the long march homeward must have exhausted his martial spirit, because that attack was not made by him until September 5th, 1812, at 5:30 P. M. However that may be, he considered it unwise to precipitate his contemplated attack without preparation and care. Therefore, he had the ground thoroughly reconnoitered by his spies, who reported that every morning it was customary for the troops to march

---

[1]The exact number employed on this construction was one first lieutenant, Alpha Kingsley; one second lieutenant, Nathaniel Pryor; one surgeon's mate, three sergeants, three corporals, two musicians and sixty privates of Captain Pinckney's company of the First Infantry.—Annals of Iowa, Vol. 3, No. 2, p. 103.
[2]Reynolds, "My Own Times."

out for exercise, leaving no defense behind, and this was the hour finally fixed for his attack.

His British band and about 200 Winnebagoes stealthily marched to the neighborhood, where, after a consultation, the plan of attack was changed into one of assault, which was immediately begun and continued until darkness compelled the Indians to retire. The following morning it was not resumed, as contemplated by the garrison, which lulled it into negligence, for a soldier was permitted to leave the gate. He returned safely, and John Cox, another private, was permitted to go out with less show of caution. This poor fellow was instantly shot and scalped and the Indians, with yells, then recommenced their assault. During the engagement the boat of a Mr. Graham, who had arrived on the 4th, was burned, as were two others belonging to the Government. Soon after fire was thrown upon the blockhouses that stood near the bank of the river, but syringes made from gun barrels were used with such effectiveness that the blaze was confined to little damage. One detachment of the enemy killed the live stock, plundered and burned the house of a Mr. Julian and destroyed the corn. On the 7th the battle was renewed and raged with greater fury, the Indians again throwing fire upon the blockhouses and shooting flaming arrows into the roofs, but the garrison repulsed every attack. In the evening the house of a Mr. Nabb was burned and the blacksmith shop and factory of the garrison threatened. Had these been fired in the prevailing wind, every man of the garrison had been burned alive, but commanding officer Thomas Hamilton, by the most heroic measures, forced the fire away until the wind veered, when he dispatched a soldier to fire the factory, which he successfully did, and in three hours it was consumed without danger to the garrison. During the day, several Indians crept into a stable, and there, harbored from musket balls, shot deadly arrows into the roofs, but a shot from the cannon by Lieutenant Burony Vasquez finally drove them out. On the 8th the attack diminished in ferocity, and on the 9th not an Indian remained to be seen.

Inside the fort only one man was wounded, but the casualties of the Indians were reported as upwards of forty.

Fort Madison, for the purposes of trading, was favorably located, but for purposes of defense it was hopelessly inadequate. Timber, ravines and the bank of the river afforded the enemy positions from which he could not be driven. At the same time a small party could harass the garrison with no great danger to itself unless some of the number became imprudent. During the siege there were but first and second lieutenants Hamilton and Vasquez, two sergeants, two corporals and a few more than thirty privates to defend a fort—a force totally inadequate against a horde of bloodthirsty savages.

After the 9th Black Hawk permitted several days to elapse before resuming hostilities, during which he formed another plan to capture and massacre the garrison. To all appearances they had retired to their homes. Immediately so-called friendly Indians came to trade, including Quash-qua-me and Pash-e-pa-ho, who, while professing friendship under that treaty, could not resist British and Black Hawk intrigue, and were then leagued with Black Hawk to destroy the fort by stratagem. These two were readily admitted to the fort, retired and called again and again, offering finally to entertain the fatigued garrison with a dance. The officers, to oblige the men, signified a willingness to witness the ceremony. Quash-qua-me was to signal Black Hawk, who was to be near by, to rush in upon the men and murder every one while the dance progressed. Early in the day a young woman, who had formed a strong attachment for one of the garrison, appeared before Lieutenant Hamilton as though in great distress. She was taken inside the stockade, and, when free from observation, disclosed the plot of the would-be assassins. Her simple story touched the heart of every man, and, though their long seige had worn them down well nigh to despair, her love and devotion inspired a strength and courage which would only falter when the spirit had fled and left the useless body a clod upon the field.[1] Lieutenant Hamilton caused a six-pounder, loaded with grapeshot, to be masked and ranged full upon the stockade entrance. Sentinels were posted with orders to allow no more than one Indian to enter at a time. Quash-qua-me and his companions duly appeared and were admitted singly. The warriors within, to a considerable number, gathered about the entrance, the designated place, and began their dance, raising with their whoops and yells a din to heaven. Suddenly the dance was suspended by the warriors making a furious rush for the gate, which conveniently opened. Confident that the plot had been successfully carried out by those inside, the others outside madly charged the angle. A lighted fuse, flashed above the unmasked cannon, brought those in front to a sudden halt, while those behind, by reason of it, were plunged headlong into a confused and confounded mass. Aghast at their miserable miscarriage, a general retreat was attempted, but this was not accomplished by Quash-qua-me and his immediate followers, who were made prisoners.

Finding himself in disgrace and fearing condign punishment, Quash-qua-me renounced hostilities against the Americans, was released, and, with slight exception, remained thereafter their faithful friend. His followers, who were imprisoned, finally confessed the plot in its every detail, and when released, as they immediately were, maintained a lasting penitence.

In this episode Black Hawk was at a convenient distance in the bushes, leaving all the danger and obloquy to fall upon Quash-qua-me.

---

[1] Maj. John Beach, agent of Sacs and Foxes, substantiated the story. Fulton and in Hist. Lee Co., Iowa, p. 358.

CHAPTER VI.

BLACK HAWK ENLISTS WITH THE BRITISH IN THE WAR OF 1812—
DESERTS—FOSTER SON STORY—KEOKUK MADE CHIEF.

It was not enough that British intrigue had maintained a reign of terror upon the frontier where the sturdy pioneer was slowly and painfully conquering a few roods of timberland to provide a home for his family. It was not enough that his life, the only protection of that family, should be daily menaced with ambush. British arrogance now menaced the nascent Republic by extending its infamous tactics to the high seas, bullying our infant commerce by exacting the right of search from feebly manned vessels and cruelly impressing into British service American seamen to fight their friends and relatives in case of war. On June 18, 1812, the declaration of war followed; then the fall of Mackinaw, July 17; the Fort Dearborn massacre, August 15, and, finally, the mortifying and distressing surrender of Hull on August 16th.

These disasters opened wide the gates for British influence to promote war upon the feeble frontiersmen, with such allies as Black Hawk, and to him they were buds of mighty promise. The first act of the English trader, Robert Dickson, who had headquarters at Prairie du Chien, was to send La Gouthrie, the trader, by boat to Black Hawk's village on Rock River with presents, money and ammunition for this Indian and his band of mercenaries who did his bidding. The Fort Madison affair followed, after which Black Hawk and 200 of his followers immediately went to Green Bay, Wisconsin, and joined the British expedition fitted out there, and where the commander made him a speech, dubbed him "General Black Hawk" and assigned him the responsible and distinguished position of Aid to the great Tecumseh.[1]

In spite of these calamities, the pioneer hardened his heart, consigned his family to the nearest fort, then, molding his bullets, he shouldered his

---
[1] In 1811, there being a strong probability of war, a deputation of Sacs and Foxes, said to have included Quash-qua-me, visited Washington to tender the services of their tribes to the President; but the members of it were thanked and requested to remain neutral and they returned. Again in 1812, after war had been declared, the same tribes sent deputations to the American agent at St. Louis, renewing their offer of services to fight the British, but again they were urged to remain neutral, which most of them did.

trusty rifle and marched with his brother settler to defend his country, as he had defended his fireside so often before.

To have been assigned to the staff of Tecumseh should have exalted Black Hawk to deeds worthy his renowned superior, but his peevish nature and lack of capacity prevented a comprehension of his just duties. Colonel Dickson admonished him to honest warfare, which was so distasteful to Black Hawk that he wrote: "I told him (Col. Dickson) that I was very much disappointed, as I wanted to descend the Mississippi and make war upon the settlements." This sentiment was, according to his own statement, promptly rebuked by Dickson, as Black Hawk himself recited: "He said he had been ordered to lay the country waste around St. Louis; that he had been a trader on the Mississippi many years; had always been kindly treated and could not consent to send brave men to murder women and children. That there were no soldiers there to fight, but where he was going to send us there were a number of soldiers, and if we defeated them the Mississippi country should be ours!" Here Black Hawk displays his besetting weakness—incapacity to comprehend the ethics of a cause or situation.

Leaving Green Bay immediately, the troops marched past Chicago and without event joined the British forces at Detroit. His first experience in an open fight with the Americans caused surprise, as he stated: "The Americans fought well and drove us with considerable loss. I was surprised at this, as I had been told that the Americans could not fight." He followed the British army until the conclusion of the Battle of the Thames, October 5th, 1813, with its disastrous consequences, when, in the face of defeat to his friends, he, with twenty of his braves, deserted in the night time for home, assigning for his reason: "I was now tired of being with them, our success being bad and having got no plunder." Not a patriotic declaration, to be sure! He arrived home in the spring of 1814, and instead of settling down to peaceful pursuits, endeavoring to make slight amends for his unjustifiable warfare against the Americans, whose country he then occupied, he began a long and bloody series of diabolical raids, inciting others to do the same, until the remotest settlement mourned its dead.

In after years, when conquered, instead of expressing any contrition for his acts, he invented for his autobiography a sympathetic sort of story, but neither fact nor tradition comes to the rescue when it is analyzed. Black Hawk claimed that he had one friend bound closer to him than was usual, and in consideration of this unusual affinity he adopted the friend's only son. When departing to join the British, Black Hawk urged the father to send the son to the war. To this proposition the father protested his declining years, the favor with which the whites had always treated

---

[1]Black Hawk fought at the Battle of Frenchtown, January 22, 1813, and participated in the massacre of the 23d which followed. He was also at Ft. Meigs, April 28, 1813; Ft. Stephenson, July 31, and finally the Battle of the Thames, October 5, 1813.

him, the need of the boy's assistance at home, and refused to allow him to leave.

Returning from the war, Black Hawk said, as he was approaching his village he saw a column of smoke curling over a hilltop near by, which so excited his curiosity that he visited the spot alone (fortunate intuition). There he found his old friend sitting in sorrow upon the ground. Being revived by some water, the old man related to Black Hawk the story of the murder of his son near Fort Madison, whither they had gone to pass the winter and hunt under permission of the commandant. The story continues that the young man started one day, as usual, for a day's hunting. At nightfall he had not returned and the father passed a sleepless night. The following morning the boy had not come back and the father sent the mother to rouse the neighborhood. (Why was she not then present to minister to him?) Footsteps upon the snow soon brought the party to the spot where the boy was found to have shot and skinned a deer and hung it upon a branch. Here tracks indicated the presence of white men who had come upon and taken him prisoner. Following their trail, the body of the boy was soon found, the face shot, the body pierced with dagger thrusts and the scalp removed, while his arms had been pinioned at his sides. As the old man related this story, a great storm rose which lasted for a long time, as though the heavens were angered at the offense and threatening revenge. The old man died, and as the storm subsided Black Hawk wrapped his blanket around the body, and, kindling a fire, sat by it during the night. Were this story true, the act were too dastard to find any explanation, but, as already stated, neither contemporaneous history nor tradition from the many who love to tell such tales confirms this weird invention. On the contrary, Fort Madison had been finally besieged by Indians during the preceding year (1813), the garrison starved to shadows, and only by stratagem were the officers and men enabled to escape, which was accomplished by digging a trench to the river, when, after firing the buildings, they descended the river in boats.[1] Therefore, if the winter just passed, which is the only inference deducible from Black Hawk's account, was the winter referred to, the father and son got no permission from the commandant, because there was no fort remaining and no commandant, and, in view of the hostility of the Indians, no settlers remained about the locality, unprotected as they would have been. If by any juggling of dates the winter referred to had been the one of '12-'13, the peaceful Indians had by their own request been removed far to the southwest, the garrison had just gone through the first long siege before mentioned and only escaped butchery by the plot which the Indian maiden had exposed.

None but hostile Indians were about the fort, and if the young man was unknown and killed as related, he was certainly considered an enemy.

---

[1] Fulton, p. 76. The Annals of Iowa.

If known as the adopted son of Black Hawk, then openly fighting the Americans, it was a fair presumption that he got no permission to hunt and was considered as taken red-handed. The community inside Fort Madison was in a serious mood those days and in no condition to receive Indians with rifles on advantageous terms. Black Hawk arrived at his village filled with indignation, as he has said. He was met by the chiefs and braves and conducted to the lodge prepared for him. After eating, he gave an account of himself and his travels, crediting the Americans with some valor and marksmanship. In turn, the village chief replied that with the absence of Black Hawk and his following, they would have been unable to defend themselves had the Americans attacked them. Not only had they been unmolested, but when Quash-qua-me, the Lance and other chiefs, with their old men, women and children, descended the Mississippi to St. Louis for protection, the Americans received them with every evidence of friendship, sent them up the Missouri River and there abundantly provided for them.

Black Hawk found on his return that Keokuk, during his absence, had been made principal war chief of the Sac nation, which so enraged him that I am forced to believe his attack upon that chief, which followed, was unwarranted, though he magnanimously concluded his philippic with the statement that he was satisfied.

Keokuk, chief of the Sacs, who was above Black Hawk in civil affairs, had, from reasons of polity or preference, maintained close and constant relations of friendship with the Americans and had prospered in the estimation of the latter. His rising fortune created friction from the first, then envy and finally implacable hatred on the part of Black Hawk, who found himself unable to combat the influence of Keokuk, either overtly or covertly, by reason of his incapacity. Instead of meeting Keokuk on terms as nearly equal as his intellect would permit, he invariably grew angry, allowed his baser nature to master him, and left the scene vowing vengeance on the victor. Had he been able to throw off his anger after a brief season, as many impulsive men can do, he might yet have accomplished much, but a yellow streak in his nature forbade it, and, I honestly believe, impelled the man onward to ruinous decisions in spite of himself. His melancholy made him churlish and revengeful, and consequently dissatisfied, unless punishing some real or imaginary wrong.

British agents could not influence Keokuk, whose temper was naturally amiable and gentle, and, if one wishes to adopt Black Hawk's sarcasm, politic, too. He favored peace always. In a sense he was luxurious for an Indian, fond of pomp, and those attributes might in a measure have superinduced his love of peace; but peaceful he was after the fire of youth had somewhat succumbed to the influence of the whites, and so he continued unto his dying day. His oratory was so perfect, his logic so convincing, his person so magnetic and his pleas so engaging, that poor

Black Hawk made a sorry figure against him, and, after a few attempts, dared never again appeal to the reason of his people against the invincible Keokuk.¹ As an orator, Keokuk had no equal among the red men, and the influence it acquired for him so rankled in the heart of Black Hawk that the latter could never overcome his hatred of Keokuk. Even down to the very last speech he ever made, at Fort Madison, he could not repress an unfortunate fling at his rival; and too bad it was that he allowed his passion to sway him from a plain and simple talk upon past or present events. The words and sentiments of that little talk were truly beautiful and had reflected much credit had he resisted the temptation to speak ill of Keokuk. His life was then ebbing away, and had that offensive portion of his talk been omitted, very many of his evil acts could have been pardoned and forgotten. His melancholy and his temper were his undoing.

¹Their final contest was in April, 1832.

CHAPTER VII.

EXPEDITION OF GOVERNOR CLARK TO PRAIRIE DU CHIEN—LIEUTENANT CAMPBELL'S BATTLE.

During the absence of Black Hawk, in 1812 and 1813, Fort Madison fell and considerable trouble was encountered from Indians, but, whether Sacs or others,[1] the Sacs were never molested by the Americans. That the Sacs were unprepared to stand an attack was freely told him on his arrival, and Wash-e-own, who paid him a visit, was warm in his praises of American kindness, upon which Black Hawk scornfully commented: "I made no reply to these remarks, as the speaker was old and talked like a child."

Such perverse assertions as this one, constantly recurring throughout his autobiography, are irritating to one who desires candor, and in the face of them it is difficult to deal justly in the premises without appearing almost savage. He constantly asserts that he never fought the Americans without being first attacked, yet who can say that the Americans had attacked or disturbed him up to this point? And how had the Americans disturbed him after his arrival home in 1814? His village had never been molested, though on his account it might have been with good cause. He was still enjoying the use and occupation of it, but, notwithstanding that fact, he was no sooner back to it but he began an organized campaign of bloodshed on the frontier. Like the torch applied to the dried grass of the prairie, the Sacs and Winnebagoes, under him, spread their ravages in 1814. British agents again had material to work on, and their machinations produced results, as the journals of the day recite.

Black Hawk stated that he, with thirty braves, *immediately* on his return in 1814, out of revenge for the murder of his supposed adopted son, descended the Mississippi, and that the battle of the "sink hole" followed. This would need to be early in 1814, whereas the fact is that the battle of the "sink hole" was fought nearly a year and a quarter after that time, and, what is more, after peace had been declared between the United States and Great Britain. Now if we cannot believe Black Hawk's asser-

---

[1] The moment Black Hawk returned, the Sacs of his village became unusually active in their depredations.

tion in that important matter, which is refuted by the record, then when can he be believed? Indian depredations made necessary the rehabilitation of the fort at Prairie du Chien,[1] long since allowed to fall into a state of decay by the British, and, by reason of the need of troops further to the east, Dickson had removed the garrison to Green Bay. For the purpose of capturing and repairing it, Governor Clark of St. Louis prepared an expedition to ascend the river, which was duly chronicled in the prints of the day:

"A military expedition, of about 200 men in five barges, under the command of Gov. Clark, left St. Louis on the 1st of May, for Prairie du Chien, supposedly with a view of building a fort there and making a station to keep in check the Sioux, Winnebagoes and Falsavoine, lately stirred up to hostility by the infamous British agent, Dickson. There have been several murders by them."[2]

Another dispatch showing the success of the venture is as follows:

"St. Louis, June 18.—On Monday evening last a barge arrived here from Prairie du Chien, with Gov. Clark and a few gentlemen who accompanied him on his expedition to that place. We are very happy in being able to announce the fortunate result of that hazardous enterprise.

"Nothing worthy of remark attended the flotilla from the time they left St. Louis until they reached Rock River. Such of the disaffected Sacs and Foxes as appeared on the approach of the boats were fired on; some canoes were taken with the arms of the affrighted savages, who sued for peace on any terms. Peace was granted them on condition they would join against the enemies of the United States and immediately commence hostilities against the Winnebagoes. The Foxes, who lived above Rock River at Deboque's mines, were willing to come into the same arrangement.

"Twenty days before the arrival of the Governor at Prairie du Chien, Dickson left that place for Mackinaw with 85 Winnebagoes, 120 Falsavoine, and 100 Sioux, recruits for the British army on the lakes. He had information of the approach of Gov. Clark, and had charged Captain Deace, commanding a body of Mackinaw fencibles, with the defense of the place; but Deace and his party ran off, the Sioux and Renards having refused to oppose the Americans. As soon as the troops landed at the town, notice was sent to the inhabitants (who had fled into the country) to return. All came back, but a few scoundrels who knew they deserved a halter.

"Every attention was then directed to the erection of a temporary place calculated for defense. Sixty rank and file of Major Taylor's company of the Seventh Regiment, under command of Lieutenant Perkins, took possession of the house formerly occupied by the old Mackinaw company, and a new fort was progressing on a most commanding spot, when the Governor left the Prairie.

* * *

"Two of the largest armed boats were left, under the command of Aid-de-Camp Kennedy and Captains Sullivan and Yeizer, whose united force amounted to 125 dauntless young fellows from this county. The regulars, under the command of Lieutenant Perkins, are stationed on shore, and are assisted by the volunteers in the erection of the new fort. * * *"[3]

[1]This was one of the posts the British solemnly stipulated in the treaty of Paris to turn over to the U. S., but which they retained.
[2]Niles Register, Vol. 6, p. 242.—June 11, 1814.
[3]Niles Register, Vol. 6, p. 242.—June 11, 1814.

During this celebrated voyage Black Hawk and his British Sacs were busy to undo, at the first favorable moment, all the good work done by Governor Clark, as may be seen by an article which appeared in the Missouri Republican:

"St. Louis, July 16.—Platoff, the Hetman Cossack in the service of Russia, offered 100,000 ducats and his daughter to any person who would assassinate Bonaparte. Alexander discountenanced the affair as infamous and dishonorable. How will the English Government and their agent, Robert Dickson[1] (a native of Scotland), appear to the world when it is announced that he suborned a Sac warrior to assassinate Governor Clark while in council at Prairie du Chien? The affair rests on the testimony of the Indians; the fellow left Rock Island for the diabolical purpose, was admitted to the council, but found the Americans armed at every point and all possibility of escape cut off; he therefore prudently declined the attempt. A gentleman who was at the Prairie and in the council informs us that this Indian rose and occupied the attention of the assembly with a harangue of trifling import; that his eyes were fixed on the Governor as if riveted to the object. At that moment the Governor shifted his sword from an unhandy position to one across his knees, when the savage retired to his seat. * * *"[2]

It may be of interest, though not connected with Black Hawk, to note here that one very strong reason for the subsequent surrender of the fort was the decimation of its garrison:

"St. Louis, July 2.—On Sunday last, an armed boat arrived from Prairie du Chien, under the command of Capt. John Sullivan, with his company of militia and 32 men from the gunboat Governor Clark, their time of service (60 days) having expired. Captain Yeizer, who commands on board the Governor Clark, off Prairie du Chien, reports that his vessel is completely manned, that the fort is finished, christened Fort Selby, and occupied by the regulars. * * *"[3]

But Fort Selby could not spare the withdrawal of the militia mentioned, and on July 21, 1814, the fort surrendered to Colonel McKay after a four days' siege.

Weakened as the garrison was by the withdrawal of the militia, General Howard, on his return from Kentucky, advised that immediate steps be taken to reinforce it. He quickly perceived the danger from an attack and the inability of the small force to defend the post, and he as quickly brought into the field a relief expedition.

Following is the best account extant upon the subject, repeated verbatim:

From the Missouri Gazette, July 30, 1814.

DISASTER.

"As soon as Gov. Clark returned from his successful expedition to Prairie du Chien, it was thought proper by Brigadier-General Howard, commanding in this district (who had in the interim returned to this place from Kentucky), to

---

[1]History generally records Dickson as a trader of good parts and not so savage as pictured during this war.
[2]Niles Register, Vol. 6, p. 426.—Aug. 20, 1814.
[3]Niles Register, Vol. 6, p. 390.—Aug. 6, 1814.

send a force to relieve the volunteers, and preserve the acquisition so important to the welfare of our country. For this purpose, Lieut. John Campbell of the first regulars, acting as brigade major, was entrusted with the command of 42 regulars and 65 rangers, in three keel boats, the contractor's and sutler's boats in company. The whole party, including boatmen and women, amounting to about 133, reached Rock River, within 180 or 200 miles of the Prairie, without any accident. As soon as they entered the rapids they were visited by hundreds of Sacs and Foxes, some of the latter bearing letters from the garrison above to St. Louis. The officers, being unacquainted with Indian manners, imagined the savages to be friendly; to this fatal security may be attributed the catastrophe which followed. It appears that the contractor's and sutler's boat had arrived near the head of the rapids and proceeded on, having on board the ammunition, with a sergeant's guard; the rangers, in two barges, followed, and had proceeded two miles in advance of the commander's barge; the latter inclined to the east side in search of the main channel, and being now on a lee shore, proceeded with much difficulty, and as the gale increased were drifted into shoal water within a few yards of a high bank covered with grass, waist high; a few steps from the bow and stern an umbrage of willows set out from shore.

"In this position the commanding officer thought proper to remain until the wind abated; sentries were placed at proper intervals, and the men were occupied in cooking, when the report of several guns announced an attack. At the first fire all the sentries were killed, and before those on shore could reach the barge, 10 or 15 out of 30 were killed and wounded. At this time the force and intentions of the Indians were fully developed. On each shore the savages were observed in quick motion; some in canoes crossing to the battleground; others were observed running from above and below to the scene of attack; in a few minutes from five to seven hundred were assembled on the bank and among the willows within a few yards of the bow and stern of the barge; the Indians gave the whoop, and commenced a tremendous fire; the brave men in the barge cheered, and returned the fire from a swivel and small arms. At this critical juncture, Lieuts. Riggs and Rector of the rangers, who commanded the two barges ahead, did not hear the guns, but saw the smoke, and, concluding an attack was made, dropped down. Riggs' boat stranded about 100 yards below Campbell's, and Rector, to avoid a like misfortune and preserve himself from a raking fire, anchored above; both barges opened a brisk fire on the Indians, but as the enemy fired from coverts, it is thought little execution was done.

"About one hour was spent in this unequal contest, when Campbell's barge was discovered on fire, to relieve which Rector cut his cable and fell to windward of him, and took out the survivors. Finding he could not assist Riggs, having a number of wounded on board, and in danger of running on a lee shore, he made the best of his way to this place, where he arrived on Sunday evening last.

Killed and Wounded.

"There were 3 regulars killed and 14 wounded; 2 died on their passage to this place; 1 ranger killed and 4 wounded on board Lieut. Rector's barge. Brig.-Maj. Campbell and Dr. Stewart are severely wounded. Two women and a child were severely wounded—one of the women and the child are since dead. Just as we had finished detailing the above unfortunate affair, we received the glad tidings of the arrival of Lieut. Riggs at Cap au Gray; he lost 3 men killed and 4 wounded. Would to Heaven we could account for the remaining 2 barges."

CONSOLATORY.

"As we were preparing the foregoing for press, gunboat Gov. Clark, commanded by Capt. Yeizer, arrived here, in nine days from Prairie du Chien, with the contractor's and sutler's barges, which were fortunately relieved at the moment the Indians were about to board them. From the officers of the Gov. Clark we have received the following very important news from the Prairie: On the 17th inst. the long-expected British force appeared in view. Marching from the Ouisconsing toward the village, the line of the regular troops, militia and Indians extended about 2 miles, with 24 flags flying. A British officer arrived at the fort, demanding its surrender. Lieut. Perkins returned for an answer that he was able and prepared to defend the post entrusted to his charge. Before the return of the flag, the British commenced a fire upon the Gov. Clark from a small battery of 1 or 2 three-pounders, which was immediately answered from a six-pounder from the boat. Soon after firing commenced, a large body of Indians and white troops crossed to the island which fronts the village, and enabled them to fire on the boat at pistol-shot distance, and screen themselves behind trees from the grape which incessantly poured from the boat. In this manner the contest continued for two hours, until the gunboat received several shot between wind and water, when it was concluded to move down the river; by this movement down the narrow channel they had to run the gauntlet through a line of musketry nearly nine miles. On approaching the rapids, Capt. Yeizer sent his skiff with nine men down to reconnoiter, who discovered Riggs' boat engaged with the Indians and Campbell's barge on fire. These appearances induced the boat's crew to return, and the Indians to call to them to come on shore, raising to their view the English flag, believing them to be Mackinaw voyageurs. Before dispatching the reconnoitering boat, the Gov. Clark joined the contractor's and sutler's boats. Those on board were ignorant of the fate of the boats below, and would, within half an hour, have been in the power of the savages, if they had not thus been providentially snatched from destruction.

"Seven were wounded on board the Gov. Clark, namely, Lieut. Henderson and Ensign St. Pierre, severely. Five privates were wounded; one died on the way down the day after his leg was amputated.

"Every account of the attack on Campbell's detachment reflects highest encomium on the skill and undaunted bravery of Lieuts. Rector and Riggs of the rangers. The former, after a contest of two hours and twenty minutes, withdrew to a favorable position, which enabled him to save the few regular troops as well from the flames which surrounded them as the fury of the savages. The high wind which then prevailed, and the loss of his anchors, prevented his rendering a like assistance to Lieut. Riggs. The latter, though stranded and in a hopeless situation, kept up an incessant fire on the Indians, and by a ruse de guerre afforded his party an opportunity of making the savages feel some of the consequences of their perfidy. He ordered his men to cease firing for about ten minutes, and at the same time ordered howitzers to be well loaded with grape, and the small arms to be in readiness. The Indians, believing the rangers to be all killed, or that they had surrendered, rushed down the bank to extinguish the fire on board Lieut. Campbell's barge and to board Riggs'. Our hero then opened upon them a well-directed fire, which drove them in all directions, leaving several of their dead behind."

When Campbell reached Rock River he called upon Black Hawk with a handful of men as an escort—so ridiculously small that Black Hawk repeatedly stated he could have captured and put them all to death with little or no effort. Campbell made the Indians presents, and in return received from Black Hawk a solemn promise that no effort to assist the British or disturb him in his ascent would be made by the Indians, but during the night some powder arrived from the British, who had in the meantime driven the Americans from Fort Selby, and sent it to Black Hawk with instructions to use the same in case any Americans attempted to pass his village to succor the garrison at Prairie du Chien.

Black Hawk had a very facetious way of putting that request into his biography. He stated on page 56 that Campbell and his aids, after holding a council with him, remained all day, and then after receiving word during the night (along with the powder), that Prairie du Chien had fallen, and that the British wished him to join them again: "I immediately started with my party by land in pursuit, thinking that some of their boats might get aground, or that the Great Spirit would put them in our power if he wished them taken and their people killed."

It is astonishing to note how frequently he confused the behests of the British with those supposed to emanate from the Great Spirit!

While the men were helplessly floundering in the mud to extricate their boat, which had run aground, Black Hawk was pouring a murderous fire into their exposed ranks, and that, too, after promising the day previous to be friendly. To reduce the hapless wretches still more, fire was thrown by arrows into the sails, and the boat, likely to be consumed, was abandoned; then the Indians plunged into the water and drew it ashore. At this stage Black Hawk virtuously knocked in the heads of all the kegs of whisky which he found in the hold, yet when he retired down the river to the Fox village, opposite the mouth of Rock River, he hoisted the British flag and when, immediately after, the British came along with a keg of rum, Black Hawk and his band had a great feast and dance,[1] ending the scene in a protracted and hilarious spree. A refinement of the ethics of liquor-drinking quite abstruse—this difference between whisky and rum!

Those British brought the Indians a gun which was used on the defenseless Americans under Zachary Taylor a little later as Black Hawk stated: "We were pleased to see that almost every shot took effect."

---

[1] His autobiography.

CHAPTER VIII.

MAJOR TAYLOR'S BATTLE—BATTLE OF THE SINK HOLE—VARIOUS MURDERS—BRITISH AGENTS WITHDRAWN FROM ROCK RIVER COUNTRY.

Disturbances by the Sacs now followed so frequently that Major Zachary Taylor, with a detachment of troops, was sent against that one disturbing and bandit element of Indian population located near the mouth of Rock River, Black Hawk's village.

Black Hawk attacked and repulsed Major Taylor in a manner which made the pulse of every settler throb with fear for the safety of his family. He had, without the least provocation, been constantly and successfully engaged in warfare the most stubborn and unrelenting, and backed by his British friends, the safety of the country, after Taylor's defeat, hung in the balance. Major Taylor's report, a temperate and dignified document, is as follows:

"Sir:—In obedience to your orders, I left Fort Independence on the 2d ult. and reached Rock River, our place of destination, on the evening of the 4th inst., without meeting a single Indian or any occurrence worthy of relation.

"On my arrival at the mouth of Rock River, the Indians began to make their appearance in considerable numbers; running up the Mississippi to the upper village and crossing the river below us. After passing Rock River, which is very small at the mouth, from an attentive and careful examination, as I proceeded up the Mississippi, I was confident it was impossible for us to enter its mouth with our large boats. Immediately opposite its mouth a large island commences, which, together with the western shore of the Mississippi, was covered with a considerable number of horses, which were doubtless placed in those situations in order to draw small detachments on shore; but in this they were disappointed, and I determined to alter the plan which you had suggested, which was to pass the different villages as if the object of the expedition was Prairie du Chien, for several reasons. First, that I might have an opportunity of viewing the situation of the ground to enable me to select such a landing as would bring our artillery to bear on the villages with the greatest advantage. I was likewise in hopes a party would approach us with a flag, from which I expected to learn the situation of affairs at the Prairie, and ascertain in some measure their numbers and perhaps bring them to a council, when I should have been able to have retaliated on them for their repeated acts of treachery; or, if they were determined to attack us, I was in hopes to draw them some distance from their towns towards the rapids, run down in the night and destroy them before they could return to their defense. But in this I was disappointed. The wind, which had been in our favor, began to shift about at the time we passed the mouth of Rock River, and by the time we reached the head of the island, which is about a mile and a half long, it blew a perfect hurricane, quarterly down the river, and it was with great difficulty we made land at a small island, containing six or eight acres, covered with willows, near the middle of the river, and about sixty yards from the upper end of the island. In this situation I determined to remain during the night if the storm continued, as I knew the anchors of several of the boats in that event would not hold them, and there was a great probability of their being drifted on sandbars, of which the river is full in this place, which would have exposed the men very much in getting them off, even if they could have prevented their filling with water.

"It was about 4 o'clock in the evening when we were compelled to land, and large parties of Indians were on each side of the river, as well as crossing in different directions in canoes; but not a gun was fired from either side. The wind continued to blow the whole night with violence, accompanied with some rain, which induced me to order the sentinels to be brought in and placed in the bow of each boat. About daylight, Capt. Whiteside's boat was fired on at the distance of about fifteen paces, and a corporal, who was on the outside of the boat, was mortally wounded. My orders were, if a boat was fired on, to return it; but not a man to leave the boat without positive orders from myself. So soon as it got perfectly light, as the enemy continued about the boat, I determined to drive them from the island, let their numbers be what they might, provided we were able to do so. I then assigned each boat a proper guard, formed the troops for action and pushed through the willows to the opposite shore; but those fellows who had the boldness to fire on the boats cleared themselves as soon as the troops were formed by wading from the island we were encamped on to the one just below us. Capt. Whiteside, who was on the left, was able to give them a warm fire as they reached the island they had retreated to. They returned the fire for a few moments, when they retreated. In this affair we had two men badly wounded. When Capt. Whiteside commenced the fire, I ordered Capt. Rector to drop down with his boat to ground and to rake the island below with artillery, and to fire on every canoe he should discover passing from one shore to the other which should come within reach. In this situation he remained about one hour, and no Indians making their appearance, he determined to drop down the island about sixty yards and destroy several canoes that were laying to shore. This he effected, and just on setting his men on board, the British commenced a fire on our boats with a six, a four and two swivels, from behind a knoll that completely covered them. The boats were entirely exposed to the artillery, which was distant three hundred and fifty paces from us. So soon as the first gun fired, I ordered a six-pounder to be brought out and placed, but, on recollecting a moment, I found the boat would be sunk before any impression could be made on them by our cannon, as they were completely under cover, and had already brought their guns to bear on our boats, for the round shot from their six passed through Lieut. Hempstead's boat and shattered her considerably. I then ordered the boats to drop down, which was done in order, and conducted with the greatest coolness by every officer, although exposed to a constant fire from their artillery for more than half a mile.

"So soon as they commenced firing from their artillery, the Indians raised a yell and commenced firing on us from every direction, whether they were able to do us any damage or not. From each side of the river, Capt. Rector, who was laying to the shore of the island, was attacked the instant the first gun was fired, by a very large party, and in a close and well contested action of about fifteen minutes, they drove them, after giving three rounds of grape from his three-pounder.

"Capt. Whiteside, who was nearest to Capt. Rector, dropped down and anchored nigh him, and gave the enemy several fires with his swivel; but the wind was so hard down stream as to drift his anchor. Capt. Rector at that moment got his boat off, and we were then exposed to the fire of the Indians for two miles, which we returned with interest from our small arms and small pieces of artillery whenever we could get them to bear. I was compelled to drop down about three miles before a proper place presented itself for landing, as but few of the boats had anchors sufficient to stop them in the river. Here I halted for the purpose of having the wounded attended and some of the boats repaired, as some of them had been injured by the enemy's artillery. They followed us in their boats until we halted on a small prairie and prepared for action, when they returned in as great a hurry as they followed us.

"I then collected the officers together and put the following question to them: 'Are we able, 334 effective men, officers, non-commissioned officers and privates, to fight the enemy with any prospect of success and effect, which is to destroy their villages and corn?' They were of opinion the enemy was at least three men to one, and that it was not practicable to effect either object. I then determined to drop down the river to the Lemoine without delay, as some of the ranging officers informed me their men were short of provisions, and execute the principal object of the expedition, in erecting a fort to command the river. This shall be effected as soon as practicable with the means in my power, and should the enemy attempt to descend the river in force before the fort can be completed, every foot of the way from the fort to the settlements shall be contested.

"In the affair at Rock River, I had eleven men badly wounded, three mortally, of whom one has since died. I am much indebted to the officers for their prompt obedience to orders, nor do I believe a braver set of men could have been collected than those who compose this detachment. But, sir, I conceive it would have been madness in me, as well as a direct violation of my orders, to have risked the detachment without a prospect of success. I believe I should have been fully able to have accomplished your views if the enemy had not been supplied with artillery and so advantageously posted as to render it impossible for us to have dislodged him without imminent danger of the loss of the whole detachment.

"I am, sir, yours, etc.,

"ZA. TAYLOR, *Brev. Maj.*,
"*Com. Detachment.*"[1]

Emboldened by his successes, Black Hawk continued his warfare, and in the murder of inoffensive settlers there was no abatement. Through the year 1814 they continued, and notwithstanding the treaty made between the two nations, we find the English agents and Black Hawk still pursuing their depredations in the spring of 1815.

"Traitors.—The undernamed gentry were residents within this and the neighboring territories previous to the war, and always claimed the rights of citizens of the United States; but as soon as war was declared they, to a man, took part against us, and were active agents in the British interest in different parts of the Indian country:

"Robert Dickson, James Aird, Duncan Graham, Francois Boutillier, Edward La Gouthrie, Brishois, of the Prairie du Chien, Jacob Franks, the brothers Grigneaus

---

[1]Copy of letter to Gen. Howard, Niles Reg., Sup. to Vol. 7, p. 137.

MAJ. ZACHARY TAYLOR.

GEN. ANDREW JACKSON.

GOV. NINIAN EDWARDS.

GEN. (OR GOV.) WILLIAM CLARK.

of Green Bay, Joseph La Croix and Lassaillier of Milwaukee, Joseph Bailly and his cousin Barrott of St. Josephs, Mitchell La Croix, Louis Buisson, Louis Benett, formerly of Peoria.

"It is ascertained that in the unsuccessful attack made by the unfortunate Lieut. M'Nair, four men were killed. M'Nair was wounded and taken prisoner and conveyed two days on his march to Rock River; but, being unable to travel, was tomahawked. A man taken up from the river at Carondelet a few days ago was recognized to be one of the four missing of the name of Best.

"By late news from Rock River, we learn that the Kickapoos have abandoned the British and demanded peace, agreeably to the treaty. It is further said that the Sacs, Winnebagoes and Fallsavoine are determined to prosecute the war."[1]

Here, long after the treaty of Ghent, signed December 24th, 1814, Black Hawk formulated and made his dastard attack on Fort Howard, known as the "sink hole affair." Note how puerile, yea, preposterous, his adopted son fiction appears in the light of contemporaneous reports and his continued war upon the Americans! This affair, unprovoked and mean, occurred in May, 1815, and I take the liberty to copy the account of it as published immediately after its occurrence.

"St. Louis, May 20 (1815).—Every day affords a new proof that the Rock River Sacks intend to continue the war. They have been notified of the pacification by the military commander of this district, as well as by Governors Clark and Edwards; yet they still continue their war parties on the frontiers of St. Charles, and murder all those who are so unfortunate as to come within their reach.

"On Wednesday, the 10th inst., at Cap aux Gre, a party of rangers were detached to procure wood. Whilst proceeding on this duty, a man by the name of Bernard, who was in advance of the squad, was fired on and mortally wounded. Lieut. Massey, with a reinforcement from the fort, attacked the Indians, and, after a rapid exchange of several shot, the savages precipitately retreated.

"On the Friday following, a young man, an inhabitant of Portage des Sioux, was pursued by four Indians. He was returning from the village of St. Charles on horseback, and had reached the Portage fields, when he discovered the Indians in full speed after him. Being well mounted, he escaped.

"An express arrived here on Wednesday last from Capt. Musick of the rangers stationed near Cuivre, informing him that a number of the rangers' horses are stolen by the Indians, who are becoming very troublesome. The extraordinary rise of the waters of the Mississippi, overflowing its banks in many places, and filling up the lakes and rivulets in the neighborhood, enables the Indians to attack and to baffle pursuit."

Extract of a letter from Lieut Drakeford, of the United States Rangers, to Col. Russell, dated Fort Howard, May 25, 1815.

"Sir:—Yesterday, about 12 o'clock, five of our men went to some cabins on the bluff, about one-quarter of a mile below the fort, to bring a grindstone. The backwater of the Mississippi rendered it so that they went in a canoe. On their return they were attacked by a party of Indians, supposed to be about fifty in number. They killed and tomahawked three and wounded one mortally. While about this mischief, we gave them as good a fire from a little below the fort as

[1] Niles Reg., Vol. 8, p. 311.—June 10, 1815.

the breadth of the breakwater would permit of. Captain Craig and myself, with about forty men, waded across the water and pursued them. In going about half a mile we came on them and commenced a fire, which continued about one hour, part of which time at a distance of about forty steps, and no part of the time further than one hundred and fifty steps. Shortly after the commencement of the battle, we were reinforced by Capt. Musick and twenty of his men. The enemy now ran; some made their escape, and others made to a sinkhole that is in the battleground, and from there they returned a most rapid fire. It being very dangerous to approach nearer than fifty steps of the sink, we at length erected a breastwork on the two wheels of a wagon, and resolved on moving it up to the edge of the sink to fire from behind, down into the sink, and preserve us from theirs.

"We got the moving battery finished about sunset and moved it up with a sufficient number of men behind it, whilst all other posts round were sufficiently guarded in case they should be put to the rout.

"We had not moved to within less than ten steps of the sink before they commenced a fire from the sink, which we returned at every opportunity and all possible advantages. Night came on and we were obliged to leave the ground and decline the expectation of taking them out without risking man for man, which we thought not a good exchange on our side. During the time of the battle, another party of Indians commenced a brisk fire on the fort. Captain Craig[1] was killed in the commencement of the battle; Lieutenant Edward Spears at the moving of the breastwork to the sink. The morning of the 25th we returned to the ground and found five Indians killed and the sign of a great many wounded that had been taken off in the night. The aggregate number of killed on our part is one captain, one third lieutenant; five privates killed, three wounded, one missing; one citizen killed and two wounded mortally."[2]

Concerning the same affair, Captain David Musick, of the St. Louis county rangers, in a letter or report to Col. William Russell, commander of that district, dated Lower Cuivre Ferry, May 25, 1815, had this to say:

"About 11 o'clock yesterday we were alarmed by the firing of guns in the direction of Fort Howard, and immediately mounted such horses as were within reach and proceeded in full speed to the assistance of Captain Craig, whom we found closely engaged with the Indians and pretty equally matched with respect to number.

"Having arrived in good season, just on the rear of the Indians, who immediately broke and ran, a part of them retreated into a sinkhole and baffled every art to get them out, as they had a better chance to kill than be killed."[3]

To which battle a Mr. Archambeau added the finishing touches:

"St. Louis, Missouri, June 3.—The Indians must have suffered considerably in their late attack on the rangers near Fort Howard. Two more dead Indians have been discovered some distance from the battleground, and a vast quantity of blood marked their retreat to their canoes. Indeed, I think the rangers behaved extremely well in this affair; only their ardor to get at the enemy exposed them too much, which was the cause of our loss. Craig and Spears would have done better in combat with regular troops; they evinced such a contempt of danger

---

[1] Black Hawk claimed the credit of being in the sink and also of killing Capt. Craig, "the leader," which, of course, could not be true.
[2] Niles Reg., Vol. 8, p. 311.—July 1, 1815.
[3] Niles Reg., Vol. 8, p. 312.—July 1, 1815.

THE BLACK HAWK WAR. 57

and death that they despised the devious mode of Indian warfare. I am informed Lieutenant Spear's family are by no means opulent. His widow should receive his pay without delay. I am informed from good authority that the Indians of Rock River have declared they are willing to bury the tomahawk if *their friends*, the English, will only say the word. The last war parties sent to our frontiers were mustered by the *British* and sent to murder our women and children *since* they received an official account of the ratification of the late treaty. The bulk of the Kickapoo nation have separated from the hostile bands, and I am at a loss to imagine how the redoubtable Duncan Graham can subsist so many of his Majesty's allies at this time. The village at Rock River and the straggling camps on this side, above and below the Lemoine, must amount to 1,200 or 1,500 warriors—Sacks, Foxes, Ioways, Winnebagoes and Fallsavoins."[1]

The most atrocious of his murders may be found in the following:

"The house of Mr. Robert Ramsay of St. Charles County, Missouri Territory, about 50 miles from St. Louis, was recently attacked by the *British allies*. Three of his children were horribly butchered, his wife so mangled as to leave no hope of her recovery, and he himself dangerously wounded. Hard the necessity that may compel the extermination of these miserable beings excited to murder by the nation that has been impudently called the 'bulwark of religion.' We trust decisive measures will be taken to give security to our frontiers. It is probable that, as in 1794, many *Englishmen* are among the savages, exciting them to these horrid deeds. If any such are found, they ought to be capitally punished on the spot without mercy."[2]

In a later communication, this same revolting crime is more particularly related:

"A letter received at St. Louis, Missouri, has the paragraphs below. Why does British influence lead the deluded savages to extermination? In the South as well as the West, it appears that the war in which the Indians were involved on British account is not yet closed. Is the alliance to be dissolved only by the destruction of one of the parties? What murders has the 'bulwark of religion' to account for! Merciless Englishmen, let the wretched Indians have peace!

"You have no doubt heard of the butchery of Robert Ramsey and his family by the savages.

"Mrs. Ramsey was attending the milking of her cow and their pretty little children were amusing themselves feeding the poultry and assisting their mother. Mr. Ramsey, who, you know, has but one leg, was near his wife at the moment the first shot was fired. He saw his wife fall and proceeded to lead her into the house; but as he reached the door he received a wound which prevented him going to the relief of his children, who were caught by the Indians and cut to pieces in the yard. Mr. and Mrs. Ramsey are dead; both were shot through the abdomen. Mrs. R. was far advanced in pregnancy."[3]

Matters in the West had assumed such a tragic phase that heroic measures were projected at the seat of government, and Gen. Jackson was given command of the military district which embraced the seat of hostilities.

---
[1] Niles, Vol. 8, p. 312.—July 1, 1815.
[2] Niles, Vol. 8, p. 271.—June 17, 1815.
[3] Niles, Vol. 8, p. 348.—July 15, 1815.

He at once assigned Brig.-Gen. Smith to command the post at Prairie du Chien and Gen. Scott to the command of military districts 8 and 9, being Tennessee, Kentucky, Illinois and Missouri, while Jackson himself was placed under orders to conduct a western campaign. Col. Miller with 500 men was encamped at Portage des Sioux and the regiment of riflemen under Lieut.-Col. Hamilton was directed by Jackson to immediately organize and march to Prairie du Chien. The fact that Jackson was to settle with Black Hawk and his braves at once stimulated the people with new hope, as will be seen by the following:

"It is determined to scourge the *allies* of our late enemy in the Missouri Territory, etc., into a respect for the lives and property of our frontier fellow citizens. Their depredations are constant and distressing. The commissioners to settle a peace with them have effected nothing. The deputations from most of the tribes were 'insufficient,' and from those most desirable to have met there were no representatives at all. The detail of proceedings is interesting and shall be preserved; but at present the flood of news from France bears down everything. It appears that General Jackson will open a new *negotiation* with them upon the 'last resort of reason.' We understand he will soon proceed from Nashville to St. Louis, where a handsome body of regulars will be collected, and that he will be accompanied by a militia force from Kentucky and Tennessee. In obedience to his request, Governor Clark of the Missouri Territory has, in genral orders, directed the militia of that state to hold itself in readiness to march at a moment's notice; and we have every prospect that British influence among the northern will receive the same reward that befell it among the southern Indians. *It must be eradicated.*"[1]

Doubtless British influence recollected a little adventure with Jackson the preceding 8th of January, for immediately the expedition by him was to become a reality, overtures for peace were made and commissioners to make a treaty were substituted for the person of Jackson, as will be seen by the following from the Missouri Gazette of June 17th, 1815.

The following letters were received by Governor Clark on Wednesday last:

"It appears that Messrs. Turcot and Lagoterie (who were employed by the commissioners to proceed to Rock River and announce to the Indians the object of the treaty to be held at Portage des Sioux) were fortunate in reaching Little Mascoutille, some distance below their place of destination, without any accident. At this place they met with a party of Fox Indians, bearing letters from the British commandant of Prairie du Chien to Governor Clark, who informed them of the departure of Captain Duncan Graham, deputy scalping master general, from Rock River, after bestowing on his worthy comrades, the Sacks, 10 barrels of gunpowder and 20 fuses as a reward for their services in butchering the helpless women and children on the frontiers.

"As usual, the Sacks received the news of peace with 'unbounded joy,' and even sent a British flag to protect our messengers on their return. They acknowledged they had 200 warriors on the frontiers, but could not tell the number of

[1] Niles, Vol. 8, p. 436.—Aug. 19, 1815.

their killed and wounded. They said they would attend the treaty and bury the tomahawk."[1]

A treaty of peace was finally in sight—the treaty of Portage des Sioux! And now up to this time, it must be owned by the impartial mind that rather than receiving any wrong from the Americans, Black Hawk, without any provocation and contrary to his promises, had waged a merciless war on the feeble settlements simply because he hated the Americans —the enemy of his friends, the British. Drake, to condone those atrocities, has stated on page 90 of his "Life of Black Hawk:" "Some palliation for these outrages may be found in the fact that the British on the northwest frontier, long after they were officially notified of the peace, continued to excite the Indians to acts of violence against the United States, and, indeed, participated in them likewise." This statement, from a man snugly ensconced in an upholstered chair, must be regarded as magnanimous! We have found here Black Hawk the cold-blooded aggressor and murderer, and when he subsequently stated that the treaty signed by him in 1816 was not made known to him, can he be believed? Armstrong, another apologist for the "poor Indian," stated that Black Hawk was a truthful Indian, though he "withheld facts that were material."[2] The frightful plight of the settlers can never be realized by the present generation; neither can the actions of the British be justly comprehended in the face of present amity. Plotting destruction, Black Hawk was invariably found to the front, and while successful, he found no fault with the defense of the Americans. That remained for the time when he felt the heel of the conqueror, resenting his years of blood-shedding. Where one man is invariably the offender, it is safe to pronounce him an incorrigible quarreler. Black Hawk was this and more—he was a British mercenary.

---

[1] All these Indian troubles dated from Black Hawk's return, it must be noted. Prior to it, no record is to be found of hostile Sacs.
[2] Armstrong's, "The Sauks, etc.," p. 126.

CHAPTER IX.

TREATY OF PORTAGE DES SIOUX, 1815—TREATY OF ST. LOUIS, 1816.

At the close of hostilities with England, a quietus to the horrors of Black Hawk's raids was demanded. The treaty with that power provided for it. As shown in the preceding pages, all efforts had failed to get the Indians together for that purpose until it was learned that Jackson was on their trail. Then Duncan Graham fled from Rock River and the Indians generally became suddenly impatient at the delay of the few days necessary for notifications to meet the commissioners, William Clark, Ninian Edwards and Auguste Chouteau, at Portage des Sioux, the place designated for treaty negotiations. Promptly on the day, all the principal Sacs and Foxes met and participated in this council save Black Hawk and a few of his immediate followers. This Indian, dissatisfied, sullen, malignant, declined to participate, and, lurking in the woods near by, where he might spy upon his neighbors, sulked, claiming to be an English citizen and subject, and notwithstanding the peremptory nature of the provision in the treaty of Ghent for just such a council as the present, he neither appeared in council nor signed the treaty which followed.

Separate treaties were made, one with the Sacs and another with the Foxes. That with the Sacs was signed on the 13th day of September, 1815, and that with the Foxes the following day, and to forever silence all objection and cavil to the treaty of 1804, an article was inserted in each emphasizing and expressly ratifying it.

That with the Sacs was as follows:

"A Treaty of Peace and Friendship, made and concluded between William Clark, Ninian Edwards and Auguste Chouteau, Commissioners Plenipotentiary of the United States of America, on the part and behalf of the said States, of the one part; and the undersigned Chiefs and Warriors of that portion of the Sac Nation of Indians now residing on the Missouri River, of the other part:

"Whereas, The undersigned, chiefs and warriors, as well as that portion of the nation which they represent, have at all times been desirous of fulfilling their treaty with the United States, with perfect faith; and for that purpose found themselves compelled, since the commencement of the late war, to separate themselves from the rest of their nation, and remove to the Missouri River, where they have continued to give proofs of their friendship and fidelity; and,

"Whereas, The United States, justly appreciating the conduct of said Indians, are disposed to do them the most ample justice that is practicable; the said parties have agreed to the following articles:

"Article 1. The undersigned chiefs and warriors, for themselves and that portion of the Sacs which they represent, do hereby assent to the treaty between the United States of America and the united tribes of Sacs and Foxes, which was concluded at St. Louis, on the third day of November, one thousand eight hundred and four; and they, moreover, promise to do all in their power to re-establish and enforce the same.

"Art. 2. The said chiefs and warriors, for themselves and those they represent, do further promise to remain distinct and separate from the Sacs of Rock River, giving them no aid or assistance whatever, until peace shall also be concluded between the United States and the said Sacs of Rock River.

"Art. 3. The United States, on their part, promise to allow the said Sacs of the Missouri River all the rights and privileges secured to them by the treaty of St. Louis, before mentioned, and, also, as soon as practicable, to furnish them with a just proportion of the annuities stipulated to be paid by that treaty; provided they shall continue to comply with this and their former treaty.

"In witness whereof, the said William Clark, Ninian Edwards and Auguste Chouteau, Commissioners, as aforesaid, and the aforesaid Chiefs and Warriors, have hereunto subscribed their names and affixed their seals, this thirteenth day of September, in the year of our Lord one thousand eight hundred and fifteen, and of the Independence of the United States the fortieth.

      Wm. Clark.
      Ninian Edwards.
      Auguste Chouteau.
      Shamaga, the lance.
      Weesaka, the Devil.
      Catchemackeseo, the big eagle.
      Chekaqua, he that stands by the tree.
      Kataka, or sturgeon.
      Mecaitch, the eagle.
      Neshota, the twin.
      Quashquammee, the jumping fish.
      Chagosort, the blues' son.
      Pocama, the plumb.
      Namachewana Chaha, the Sioux.
      Nanochaatasa, the brave by hazard.

"Done at Portage des Sioux, in the presence of R. Wash, Secretary of the Commission; Thomas Levers, Lieut-Col., commanding 1st reg't. I. T.; P. Chouteau, agent; T. Paul, C. C. T.; Jas. B. Moore, capt.; Samuel Whiteside, capt.; John W. Johnson, U. S. factor and Indian agent; Maurice Blondeaux, Samuel Solomon. Noel Mograine, Interpreters; Daniel Converse, 3d lieut. To the Indian names are subjoined a mark and seal."[1]

This treaty was ratified December 26th, 1815.

The treaty with the Foxes, made on the following day by the same commissioners, and ratified December 16, 1815, while not affecting Black Hawk in particular, was so intimately connected with him that it may be

---

[1] Vol. 7, Pub. Statutes at Large, U. S., p. 134, ed. 1848.

well to repeat it here. After the caption and the recital of a desire to re-establish peace it ran as follows:

"Article 1. Every injury or act of hostility by one or either of the contracting parties against the other shall be mutually forgiven and forgot.

"Art. 2. There shall be perpetual peace and friendship between the citizens of the United States of America and all the individuals composing the said Fox tribe or nation.

"Art. 3. The contracting parties do hereby agree, promise, and oblige themselves reciprocally, to deliver up all the prisoners now in their hands (by what means soever the same may have come into their possession), to the officer commanding at Fort Clark, on the Illinois River, to be by him restored to their respective nations as soon as it may be practicable.

"Art. 4. The said Fox tribe or nation do hereby assent to, recognize, re-establish and confirm the treaty of St. Louis, which was concluded on the third day of November, one thousand eight hundred and four, to the full extent of their interest in the same, as well as all other contracts and agreements between the parties; and the United States promise to fulfill all the stipulations contained in the said treaty in favor of the said Fox tribe or nation."[1]

This document, with its trifling exactions, was signed by twenty-two Fox chiefs and warriors without protest or comment, forcibly demonstrating the anxiety of all for peace when removed from ulterior influences. Everyone who participated therein appeared gratified that hostilities were ended; but an insecurity was still sensible which nothing but the signature of Black Hawk could quiet. In the face of the many murders so lately committed by Black Hawk's band and the English, the statement by Black Hawk that he was still an English subject and his refusal to treat brought an issue squarely between the United States and him, and the authorities at Washington were in no humor to allow that dissembler to dictate the policy of the Indians and continue his crusade of crime against helpless settlers. He was urged to sign and when pressed, preferring plunder to peace, declined and stalked to his canoe in dudgeon. Was he to be peacefully subdued?

While the United States authorities were actively planning to bring him to terms, the leading men from the other Sac tribes and from the Foxes continued their persuasions, and on meeting constant refusal, finally, with some of his personal followers, unitedly demanded that he sign a treaty, and then, fearing the possible loss of his influence, he reluctantly consented. Another convention was at once called to meet at St. Louis May 13, 1816, which Black Hawk attended and there "touched the goose quill," as he has stated. This treaty, more important than the other two, because it bound the leader of all the insurgent Indians, was signed on the 13th day of May and ratified December 30 of the same year and is as follows:

[1] Vol. 7, Pub. Stat. at Large of U. S., p. 135.

THE BLACK HAWK WAR. 63

"*A TREATY OF PEACE AND FRIENDSHIP, made and concluded between William Clark, Ninian Edwards and Auguste Chouteau, commissioners plenipotentiary of the United States of America, on the part and behalf of the said states, of the one part, and the undersigned chiefs and warriors of the Sacs of Rock River and the adjacent country, of the other part.*

"Whereas, By the ninth article of the treaty of peace, which was concluded on the twenty-fourth day of December, eighteen hundred and fourteen, between the United States and Great Britain, at Ghent, and which was ratified by the President, with the advice and consent of the Senate, on the seventeenth day of February, eighteen hundred and fifteen, it was stipulated that the said parties should severally put an end to all hostilities with the Indian tribes, with whom they might be at war, at the time of the ratification of said treaty, and to place the said tribes inhabiting their respective territories, on the same footing upon which they stood before the war; provided, they should agree to desist from all hostilities against the said parties, their citizens or subjects respectively, upon the ratification of the said treaty being notified to them, and should so desist accordingly; and,

"Whereas, The said United States being determined to execute every article of treaty with perfect good faith, and wishing to be particularly exact in the execution of the article above alluded to, relating to the Indian tribes: The President, in consequence thereof, for that purpose, on the eleventh day of March, eighteen hundred and fifteen, appointed the undersigned William Clark, governor of Missouri territory, Ninian Edwards, governor of Illinois territory, and Auguste Chouteau, Esq., of the Missouri territory, commissioners, with full power to conclude a treaty of peace and amity with all those tribes of Indians, conformably to the stipulations contained in the said article, on the part of the United States, in relation to such tribes; and,

"Whereas, The commissioners, in conformity with their instructions in the early part of last year, notified the Sacs of Rock River, and the adjacent country, of the time of the ratification of said treaty; of the stipulations it contained in relation to them; of the disposition of the American government to fill those stipulations, by entering into a treaty with them, conformably thereto; and invited the Sacs of Rock River, and the adjacent country, to send forward a deputation of their chiefs to meet the said commissioners at Portage des Sioux, for the purpose of concluding such a treaty as aforesaid, between the United States and the said Indians, and the said Sacs of Rock River, and the adjacent country, having not only declined that friendly overture, but having continued their hostilities, and committed many depredations thereafter, which would have justified the infliction of the severest chastisement upon them; but having earnestly repented of their conduct, now imploring mercy, and being anxious to return to the habits of peace and friendship with the United States; and the latter being always disposed to pursue the most liberal and humane policy towards the Indian tribes within their territory, preferring their reclamation by peaceful measures, to their punishment by the application of the military force of the nation; now,

"Therefore, The said William Clark, Ninian Edwards and Auguste Chouteau, commissioners, as aforesaid, and the undersigned, chiefs and warriors, as aforesaid, for the purpose of restoring peace and friendship between the parties, do agree to the following articles:

"Article 1. The Sacs of Rock River, and the adjacent country, do hereby unconditionally assent to recognize, re-establish, and confirm the treaty between the United States of America, and the united tribes of Sacs and Foxes, which was concluded at St. Louis, on the third day of November, one thousand eight hundred and four; as well as all other contracts and agreements heretofore made between the Sac tribe or nation and the United States.

"Art. 2. The United States agree to place the aforesaid Sacs of Rock River on the same footing upon which they stood before the war; provided, they shall, on or before the first day of July next, deliver up to the officer commanding at cantonment Davis, on the Mississippi, all the property they or any part of their tribe, have plundered or stolen from the citizens of the United States, since they were notified, as aforesaid, of the time of the ratification of the late treaty between the United States and Great Britain.

"Art. 3. If the said tribe shall fail or neglect to deliver up the property aforesaid, or any part thereof, on or before the first day of July aforesaid, they shall forfeit to the United States all right and title to their proportion of the annuities which, by the treaty of St. Louis, were covenanted to be paid to the Sac tribe; and the United States shall forever afterwards be exonerated from the payment of so much of said annuities as, upon a fair distribution, would fall to the share of that portion of the Sacs who are represented by the undersigned chiefs and warriors.

"Art. 4. This treaty shall take effect and be obligatory on the contracting parties, unless the same shall be disapproved by the President and Senate of the United States, or by the President only; and in the meantime all hostilities shall cease from this date.

"In testimony whereof, the said William Clark, Ninian Edwards, and Auguste Chouteau, commissioners as aforesaid, and the undersigned chiefs and warriors as aforesaid, have hereunto set their hands and affixed their seals this thirteenth day of May, one thousand eight hundred and sixteen."

"WM. CLARK,
"NINIAN EDWARDS,
"AUGUSTE CHOUTEAU."

"ANOWART, or, the one who speaks,
"NAMAWENANE, Sturgeon Man,
"NASAWARKU, the Fork,
"NAMATCHESA, the Jumping Sturgeon,
"MATCHEQUAWA, the Bad Axe,
"MASHCO, Young Eagle,
"AQUAOSA, a Lion coming out of the water,
"MUCKETAMACHEKAKA, Black Sparrow Hawk,
"SAKEETOO, the Thunder that frightens,
"WARPALOKA, the rumbling Thunder,
"KEMEALOSHA, the Swan that flies in the rain,
"PASHEKOMACK, the Swan that flies low,
"KEOTASHEKA, the Running Partridge,
"WAPALAMO, the White Wolf,
"CASKUPWA, the Swan whose wings crack when he flies,
"POINAKETA, the Cloud that don't stop,
"MEALESETA, Bad Weather,
"ANAWASHQUETH, the Bad Root,
"WASSEKENEQUA, Sharp-faced Bear,
"NAPETAKA, he who has a Swan's throat around his neck,
"MASHASHE, the Fox,
"WAPAMUKQUA, the White Bear."

"St. Louis, May 13th, 1816. Done in the presence of R. Wash, Secretary to the Commission; R. Paul, C. T. of the C. J. Bt. Caron, Samuel Solomon, Interpreters; Joshua Norvell, Judge Adv. M. M.; Joseph Perkins, Joseph Charless,

THE BLACK HAWK WAR. 65

B. G. Tavar, Charles Wm. Hunter, Cerré, M. La Croix, Guyol de Guirano, Boon Ingels, Moses Scott, James Sawyer."

"To the Indian names are subjoined a mark and a seal."[1]

After all the trouble given the Americans by Black Hawk, it is not to be presumed that this treaty was lightly considered, or that the Americans neglected to explain every line of it fully, thereby allowing opportunity for future contention from one only too apt to contend; yet Black Hawk later had the audacity to claim that he did not know his village passed by that treaty when it became time for him to enjoy another war with his ancient enemy, the Americans. Line upon line and section upon section the treaty was carefully read and interpreted by men whose names were above reproach, that no future claim of misunderstanding could be alleged, and to that solemn treaty Black Hawk placed his mark and declared and promised thereby that he would no longer torment the whites with his aggressions. The preamble of the document should forever have estopped Black Hawk from alleging ignorance of its provisions; with respect to all the others who signed that treaty, the facts recited in it were so truthfuly stated, and they were so well satisfied with its provisions, that not one of them was ever heard to complain.

[1] Vol. 7, Pub. Stat. (U. S.) at Large, p. 141.

CHAPTER X.

FORT ARMSTRONG BUILT—BLACK HAWK AS A FAULT-FINDER—ANNIHILATION OF THE IOWAS.

Black Hawk's intermittent promises of good behavior and declarations of future tranquility were justly distrusted by the War Department, and rather than remain open to future disadvantage, it resolved to erect near his haunts a fort. Accordingly, on the 10th day of May, 1816. Gen. Thomas A. Smith and Brev. Lieut. Col. W. Lawrence, with a detachment of men, landed on Rock Island and soon thereafter, under the direction of the latter, began the construction of Fort Armstrong[1]—so called in honor of Gen. John Armstrong, then late Secretary of War.

Black Hawk witnessed these movements with dissatisfaction. The Indians had a superstitious veneration for the island, claiming, as will be seen from Black Hawk's words:[2] "A good spirit had care of it, who lived in a cave in the rocks immediately under the place where the fort now stands, and has often been seen by our people. He was white, with large wings like a swan's, but ten times larger. We were particular not to make much noise in that part of the island which he inhabited, for fear of disturbing him. But the noise of the fort has since driven him away, and no doubt a *bad spirit* has taken his place." And in further contemplation of the beauties of the place and pleasures of this island to the Indians, Black Hawk was made to utter many fine sentiments, of a character to command our stanchest support and evoke a sympathy from one cover of this history to the other, had they been ingenuous and free from the suspicion that Col. Patterson may have allowed his generous nature to tint them a color not to be found in that Indian's nature.

Though hampered by various annoyances, the troops eventually completed Fort Armstrong and occupied it; their presence serving a healthy object lesson to quiet those British Sacs who were too fierce to be pacified while life lasted, and to stimulate a healthy and satisfactory trade between the remote points of the north and northwest and those to the south. It frequently has been alleged that Black Hawk and his people

---

[1] Flagler's Rock Island Arsenal, p. 15.
[2] Auto., p. 70.

FORT ARMSTRONG.

never received their annuities. This is untrue as the record of the time has disclosed.¹

In November, 1820, we find the Sacs were drawing their annuities and had been on the 3d of each November; in fact, those annuities had been made permanent, and while bickerings about a fair division at times had been noticeable, the tribes and head men were satisfied.²

It may be well to add here, that when Rev. Jedediah Morse made the report just cited, he was a commissioner appointed by the President for the purpose of ascertaining the actual state of the Indian tribes of the northwest, and having visited Fort Armstrong in the summer of 1820, he found British flags still floating and English medals still worn almost exclusively in Black Hawk's village. An exchange of these for American flags and medals had been recommended in a letter written to him November 20, 1820, from that post, and he adopted the suggestion in his report;³ but the flags and medals continued in evidence, notwithstanding Morse's report.

Following those manifestations, hostility to American rule was also expressed in mutterings and quiet threats in 1823, when Beltrami stopped there, and which he expressed in his books as follows: "For, both from instinct and from feelings transmitted from father to son, they cordially despise and hate them'"⁴ (the Americans), which certainly did not indicate that the treaty of 1804 was responsible for their hatred; it indicated also that the treaty of 1816 rested very lightly upon their shoulders and that the erection of Fort Armstrong was a wise precaution. If it may be thought that the treaty of 1804 made Black Hawk a fault-finder with the Americans, it may be well to introduce a specimen of his chronic affliction, found in the papers of Capt. T. G. Anderson, British Indian Agent, in Vol. 10, Wis. Hist. Coll's., pp. 145, 146.

"Speeches of Black Hawk and Na-i-o-gui-man, at Drummond's Island, July 12, 1821.

"Present, Lieut.-Col. Wm. McKay, British Indian Superintendent; Capt. Thos. G. Anderson, Clerk; Maj. James Winnett, and other officers of the Sixty-eighth British Regiment, together with Lieut. L. Johnston.

"The Black Hawk, Speaker:

"'Father, I am not very able to speak—probably I may say something improper. I may have something to reproach my father with. I could not get any of my chiefs to come with me.⁵ One of the Reynard or Fox chiefs accompanied me, and some of the Menominees who reside among us. My mind has been entirely taken up since I left home with the idea that every stroke of my paddle carried me nearer to my Great Father's fire, where his soldiers, the red coats, would be charitable to me and cover my naked skin; and that in consequence of my not

---

¹Journal of Maj. Thomas Forsythe, the Indian agent, who called June 24, 1819, at Black Hawk's village to pay the installment due, as all previous ones had been paid. Vol. 6, Wis. Hist. So. Colls., p. 191.
²Morse's Report to Secretary War, pp. 130, 377, etc.
³Morse's Report, p. 59.
⁴Beltrami's Pilgrimage, Vol. 2, p. 165.
⁵A circumstance demanding notice.

having been able for three years to step across the barriers, which separate us from them, I would receive a double proportion of my Great Father's bounty.

"'The Americans, my father, surround us, but we are ever ready to meet them. Now, my father, as we see you but seldom, I hope you will open your stores and give us more presents than you do to other Indians who visit you annually. Now I speak to you, my father, in hopes you will be charitable to us, and give us something to take to our wives and children. They are expecting to be warmed by the clothing of their Great Father.'

"Taking some strings of wampum, he added: 'Father, I got this from the White Elk (Capt. McKee), to open a smoother path from our country to all your fires. I spoke to the Pottawattomies with it, and they were happy to accede to our proposals of friendship. Now, my father, we have always obeyed your voice and will ever listen to your counsels. With regard to the Indians, we have a good road from our country to your fires; but there are whites who appear strong, and tell us they will not allow us to see you any more. Should that be the case, we will be miserable. But if the road continues good, as Capt. McKee told us it would, we will see you every day' (year). Delivered the wampum.

"Answer of the Superintendent:

"'Children, I have listened to your discourse. Every word has entered into my ears. When you came here three days (years) ago, I gave you of your Great Father's bounty a much greater proportion than I did to other Indians, and told you your presents would in future be given you at Amherstburg. You were displeased. You went away dissatisfied. I have again this year treated you well. You appear dissatisfied still, and want more. I now tell you that your presents are at Amherstburg, and that in future you must go there if you wish to receive your Great Father's bounty. I have done everything in my power to please you and render you happy; but my efforts appear to have been thrown away upon you. Go home, and I do not wish to see dissatisfied children about me again. With respect to the road being stopped up as you say, that is news to me. I do not know that any steps have been taken to effect that; and, indeed, if you behave yourselves, as I have always recommended you to do, I do not believe you will be hindered from seeing your Great Father's fires.'"[1]

It will be seen from that meeting with his friends that Black Hawk was a hard man to get along with, even with his friends. He returned home; but instead of behaving himself he joined Pash-e-pa-ho in a war which robbed the Iowas of their lands and exterminated their tribes, so that thereafter their nation became a tradition. If Black Hawk should be heard to complain of the loss of his lands to the Americans for a trifling price, how much more should others whom he had wantonly robbed and whose kin he had murdered be heard? Old men, young men, old women, young women and children in swaddling clothes were murdered in the most brutal manner; their homes were confiscated and their tribal name effaced from history, to be no more known of men. Aye, upon that bloody battlefield it was decreed that Black Hawk should be buried and from it a ghoulish hand should steal his body; a fitting retribution, one might justly say!

---

[1] If he had behaved himself as advised, there had been no Black Hawk campaigns in 1831-2 and no occasion for this history. The admonition contains more food for thought than four volumes of comment could supply.

THE BLACK HAWK WAR.

On the first day of May, 1823, the Iowas were celebrating their return from a successful hunt by feasts, games and horse-racing. The mellow sun had just arisen to witness their mock jousts and races. Intent upon the harmless tournament, none had noticed the gradual gathering in the neighboring grass and woods of the vicious Sacs during the night. The women and children had been left at the village, while the men, discarding their arms, gathered some distance away to enjoy their frolic, unarmed and unsuspecting. A race had been appointed for the most famous, and thus, while all were eagerly preparing for its issue, the murderous Sacs pounced upon them.

All that day the unequal struggle waged; the unarmed Iowas against their armed and powerful foes. Man after man went down before the fury of the victors. Home after home was made desolate from the blow of the tomahawk, the thrust of the spear and the ugly gash of the knife in the hands of the hideous, howling Sacs; very devils incarnate. Parties of twenty-five armed Sacs sought out a similar number of unarmed Iowas whose strength had been well nigh spent and slaughtered them. Fresh bands of the same number from the reserves did the like with other tired and spent defenders until evening approached, when, unsupported by the arms which had been left back at the village, and fighting against hopeless odds, the Iowas could no longer sustain an honest cause; then, and then only, as the mantle of evening fell upon that gory battlefield, with a few scattered exceptions, the last of the Iowas was sent to the hunting grounds of his dreams. The victorious Sacs fell upon the women, children, invalids and cripples and murdered all save a pitiful handful, which Black Hawk piously offered afterward to adopt into his tribe.

No one can estimate the number of dead. Pashepaho and Black Hawk have attempted the task, but when it is known that the ordinary wild Indian cannot comprehend numbers, we must leave all calculation open to conjecture. Suffice it to say, the Iowa nation was annihilated, its lands confiscated, and a scene of desolation was upon the land for many years thereafter.

Following the account of Fulton, we find on page 120 *et seq.* the following:

"When Mr. Jordan first saw the battleground in 1828, the graves of the slain still appeared fresh, as if they had not been made more than a year or two before. Black Hawk had often detailed to him the plan of the attack and the incidents of the engagement. Contrary to the usual Indian custom, this battle was brought on in the daytime. The battlefield is a level river bottom prairie, about four miles in length and two miles wide near the middle, narrowing to points at either end. The main area of the bottom rises about twenty feet above the river, with a narrow strip of lower land skirting the margin of the stream, covered with trees. The river bank was fringed with a dense growth of willows. Near the lower end of the prairie, and extending up to the bank of the river, was situated the

Iowa village. Two miles above the town, near the middle of the prairie, was situated a small natural mound which was then covered with a growth of small trees and shrubs. In the rear of this mound lay a belt of wet prairie which was covered with a rank grass. Bordering this on the north, the land rises abruptly into broken bluffs covered with a heavy forest many miles in extent. It was through this forest that the Sac and Fox war party approached in the night before the attack, and secreted themselves in the tall grass mentioned, intending to remain in ambush through the day, and make observations to aid them in the attack which they contemplated making on the following night. From this position their spies could take a full survey of the situation of the village and watch the movements of the Iowas.

"Near the mound mentioned, the Iowas had their racecourse, where they were frequently wont to resort to engage in the amusement of horse-racing. Unfortunately for them, this day they had selected for their sports. Unconscious of the proximity of a lurking foe, they repaired to the racing ground, leaving most of their arms in the village with the old men, women and children, unprotected. The Sacs and Foxes, under the leadership of their wily old chief, Pash-e-pa-ho, perceived their advantage. He directed his subordinate in command, Black Hawk, with a band of young warriors to file off through the tall grass and avail themselves of the cover of the timber along the river bank, to reach the village with the utmost speed and there commence the battle. This movement was successfully executed, while Pash-e-pa-ho with his division made a simultaneous assault from their ambush upon the unarmed Iowas, who were engaged in their amusements at the racecourse. Black Hawk, with his warriors at the village, poured a furious volley upon the defenseless inhabitants, completing the slaughter with tomahawk and scalping knife. The unarmed Iowas at the racecourse attempted to reach the village, two miles distant, but most of them were slain in their flight by Pash-e-pa-ho's warriors. The survivors reached their village only to find it in flames and to behold their slaughtered friends in the midst of the devouring element. So great was the advantage of their assailants that the Iowas could make but a feeble resistance. Their enemies, however, accorded to them the credit of making a brave but hopeless resistance and of yielding only because of the advantage their enemies had taken. The Iowas asked a parley and submitted their fate to the will of their conquerors. For a time they lived in the country as an integral part of the Sac and Fox nation. This condition of a conquered people they felt to be a galling one, and they complained of the tyranny of the Sacs and Foxes."

CHAPTER XI.

TREATIES OF 1822-24-25—WINNEBAGO OUTBREAK—ATTACK ON THE BOATS—ARREST AND DISCHARGE.

The Sacs and Foxes were also trespassers upon Illinois soil, dispossessing by conquest, after the manner just related, the Santeaux, who claimed the soil from which they were driven.[1] Black Hawk was always strenuously insistent for the principle that land could not be alienated, therefore his nation could not, by treaty, legally have alienated their lands. If lands were inalienable by grant, how, then, could they have been alienated by conquest? The difference was in instance and not principle with Black Hawk, and he no doubt argued that the case was different with Santeaux and Iowas, because his was a party in interest. And so with the treaty of 1804; it was good if it helped Black Hawk and very bad if it contained anything good for the Americans.

That the Americans were intent on doing the best for the Indians which then could be done under all circumstances is everywhere apparent in the several treaties with the Sacs and Foxes. On September 3d, 1822,[2] another treaty was negotiated with them, which also recognized the 1804 compact, and doubtless Black Hawk thought this all right, because it gave to them an additional $1,000.00 for the privilege of being relieved from the obligation of building a factory as that treaty had provided. This 1822 affair bears the signature of Black Hawk.

Again on August 4th, 1824, a treaty was made between the Sacs and Foxes recognizing the former treaties.[3]

On August 19th, 1825, another treaty for the purpose of suspending the constant internecine wars of the Indians was made at Prairie du Chien, wherein all former treaties were recognized.[4] With all these various ratifications one would naturally infer that the treaty of 1804 was pretty thoroughly understood by the Indians, and particularly by Black Hawk, yet in the face of them all he continued his hostility to the Americans whenever the possibility of making them trouble arose, and if it did not

---
[1] Annals of the West, Perkins & Peck Edition, pp. 713, 795.
[2] U. S. Stat., p. 223, and comment in above Annals, p. 796.
[3] U. S. Stat., p. 229.
[4] U. S. Stat., p. 272.

71

arise from the efforts of others, he was ever alert to set it in motion on his own account. The Winnebago outbreak, coming along in 1827, afforded him the next opportunity to display his genius for war, and he was quick to place himself against his ancient foe, the Americans. The unfriendly attitude of certain unruly Sioux, sometimes called or classed as the Dakotas in the prints of those days, was quickly brought to his attention, and without delay he was on the road north to find trouble in which to participate.

In those days there were good and bad Dakotas, as with the Sacs, and the malcontent element of the former was generally finding itself in trouble. Upon two notable occasions parties of Dakotas wantonly murdered unoffending Chippewas, the latest offense being under the very walls of Fort Snelling and at a time when the Chippewas were dispensing a liberal hospitality to them—a most atrocious crime![1]

These deeds were so revolting that Col. Josiah Snelling, the commandant, very properly applied the custom prevalent among the Indians by turning the four captured culprits over to the injured Chippewas for punishment. Each Dakota was given thirty paces law, and a chance to run for his life; but Chippewa bullets were swifter, and four vicious Dakotas were speedily forwarded to their fathers. Revenge toward the whites for the part they played in that affair rankled within the breasts of the friends of the dead Dakotas and they diplomatically set about settling the grudge in a most civilized and sensible manner, at the expense of their friends, the Winnebagoes. Red Bird, a Winnebago chief of note, contemporaneously, or soon thereafter,[2] led a losing enterprise against the Chippewas, returning to his camp crestfallen and sullen. It was at this fecund moment that emissaries from the Dakotas fell upon him with all manner of adroit badinage for his fallen estate, impressing upon his mind, with much innuendo, to what belittled influence his parts had been reduced in the estimation of his people and to what distressing ridicule he was being subjected by the laughter of the Americans. While in the receptive mood to which these tactics had driven his mind, he was in the same perverted manner made to believe that the four guilty Dakotas turned over to the Chippewas and killed were Winnebagoes. Thus was the foundation laid for the "Winnebago war" of 1827! The murder of one Methode, with his wife and five children, was discovered. Following this, on the 26th of June, 1827, Red Bird, with We-kau and Chic-hon-sic, called at various places in Prairie du Chien (the garrison and its stores having been removed just previously to Fort Snelling), obtained from a trader ammunition and, as some have said, whisky, and left for the cabin of one Registre Gagnier, who resided with his wife, young son, baby daughter and an old discharged American soldier named Solomon

---

[1] Vol. 5, Wis. Hist. Colls., p. 130, et seq.
[2] P. 143, above.

Lipcap some two miles from the village. The three entered, begged and received food, and, taking advantage of their entertainers' unguarded condition, shot down and instantly killed Gagnier and Lipcap. Madam Gagnier, in the frenzy of her excitement, seized the gun of her dead husband, and while protecting her son finally drove the savages into the yard, where they scattered. She then ran to the village with her boy, forgetting the infant daughter, which had been lying upon the bed when the Indians entered. The posse which immediately returned found Gagnier and Lipcap scalped, but the girl baby, alive, was discovered under the bed, though scalped and savagely cut in the neck. Stranger yet, she recovered and grew to woman's estate.

Thomas L. McKenney, who gained the woman's story from her own lips, has narrated it in a manner worthy so illustrious a writer, disclosing a heroism sufficient to warrant the erection to her memory of a monument more than a little pretentious. In the order of mundane things, however, heroines fare very badly when burly heroes can be found or manufactured to consume the contributions of a hero-loving public, and probably Madam Gagnier will get no monument.

Next evening a keel-boat, its sides literally filled with leaden balls, arrived from Fort Snelling, bearing the dead bodies of two of its crew and four wounded members, two mortally and two slightly; also the body of a dead Indian, the result of a conflict of unusual fierceness and inequality with Sac and Winnebago Indians at the mouth of the Bad Axe about sunset of the 26th. This boat, the Oliver H. Perry, with its consort, had gone up to Fort Snelling, under the command of Captain Allen Lindsay, some time before, and meeting on the route[1] with many exactions and exasperating and suspicious ovations from the Dakotas whose villages were along the river, asked and received at Fort Snelling thirty-two muskets and a quantity of powder and ball.

Arriving on the downward passage[2] at the the last of their villages, Wa-ba-sha, now Winona, Minnesota, the Dakotas were found dancing a war dance and making threats, but, offering no resistance (the Winnebagoes and Sacs present having assumed that dangerous function), Captain Lindsay very naturally considered all danger over and allowed the boats, which had been lashed together for protection, to separate. That which sat deeper in the water, having the advantage of the river's undercurrents, gained several miles' advantage. This boat, commanded by a Sac half-breed named Beauchamp, was manned by a crew of sixteen, officers and men. The Frenchmen of the party, growing suspicious of the actions of new bands of Indians gathering as the boat approached the Bad Axe, urged the crew to caution, but the usual contempt for Indian prowess and

---
[1] Vol. 5, Wis. Hist. Colls., p. 144.
[2] Vol. 5, Wis. Hist. Colls., p. 147.

the thought that all danger had been passed caused a foolhardy disregard of the Frenchmen's warning. Naturally a supine security followed.

The wind had sprung into unusual strength from the east and, in the face of continued admonition, some of the crew were for tying up for the night then and there, river crews in those days being much used to the enjoyment of their own wishes.

A large body of Indians had collected on an island to the west of the channel near to which the boat must pass, and as it reached this point was rapidly drifting toward the bar on the island's edge. Suddenly the trees and rocks reverberated with blood-curdling war-whoops and a volley of bullets rained upon the deck, wounding a negro named Peter so desperately that he afterward died. The crew instantly sought shelter by lying flat below the water line, because the bullets penetrated the bulwarks. The second volley resulted in the instant death of an American named Stewart, who had risen to return the first fire through a loophole. The exposure causing a target to be made of his head, he fell back dead, his finger still upon the trigger of his undischarged gun. No further attempt was made to return the Indians' second volley, and they, encouraged by this non-resistance, rushed to their canoes with intent to board. The men who had remained flat recovered in a measure from their panic and the boarders were received with a disastrous fire and repulsed. One canoe in particular was severely received, two of its crew being killed, and in the death struggle overturned, compelling the others to swim for their lives.

Presently a voice in the Sac tongue hailed the boat, demanding to know if the crew were English. Beauchamp, who was a half-breed Sac, answered in the affirmative.

"Then," replied the querist, "come on shore and we will do you no harm, for we are your brethren, the Sacs."

"Dog," retorted Beauchamp, "no Sac would attack us thus cowardly. If you want us on shore, you must come and fetch us."

Confident that it was impossible to storm the boat with success, the plan was abandoned by all save two daring Indians, who leaped aboard. One seized the steering oar and strove to run the boat aground, while the other discharged some guns found abandoned on the deck, wounding one white. After this exploit, he hastened to the bow of the boat and, lying upon the deck, endeavored to assist his companion in stranding the boat. Succeeding in this, he dropped the pole, and with supreme contempt for danger began loading and firing, passing unscathed through the return volley. In the general fusillade Beauchamp succeeded in shooting the Indian at the steering oar, who dropped dead upon the deck and was carried into Prairie du Chien, but in retaliation the savage in the bow, with his third fire, shot Beauchamp and he fell upon the deck mortally wounded. At this critical loss of the commander, some of the crew were for an immediate surrender, but the suggestion was quickly vetoed by Beauchamp, who cried: "No, friends, you will not save your lives so. Fight to the last, for they will show no mercy. If they get the better of you, for God's sake throw me overboard. Do not let them get my hair." In the meantime Jack Mandeville, a powerful member of the crew, with the heart of a lion, jumped into the breach, and as Beauchamp was cheering him with cries of "fight on," Mandeville shot the Indian through the head and he, with his gun, fell overboard. Bullets from the shore continued to pour into the boat, and one party of the crew favored attempting an escape in the skiff, but Mandeville, who now assumed command, threatened death to the first man who suggested anything but fight.

He routed out the timid and skulkers. Darkness was approaching, which boded evil for the crew. The bullets were falling with painful precision, and if the boat was allowed to remain aground it was clear that every man must die by the most refined torture.

With the judgment and determination of a brave man, Mandeville jumped overboard and began the use of his herculean strength to dislodge the boat from the bar.

The savages rushed upon him, but with an armored club he beat them back. Only warily and at intervals could the whites fire in their efforts to protect Mandeville. Seeing the futility of this style of warfare, four of the crew resolutely jumped upon the bar to their leader's assistance, and in a space too brief for the relation the boat was put afloat and the crew quickly and safely working her down stream, the gathering gloom assisting their escape from the bullets which followed.

The battle had raged for three hours with a fierceness which no Indian but Black Hawk could precipitate, and there he was, directing a cause which was none of his own, he and his British band, notwithstanding his pledges and protestations, fighting the Americans with the ferocity of a wild beast. The casualties were two of the crew killed outright and four wounded, two mortally and two slightly, while the loss of the Indians was variously estimated at from seven to twelve killed and many wounded.

The other boat, which had aboard William J. Snelling, son of Colonel Snelling, followed, but the darkness saved it from any damage, the volley which was fired passing harmlessly overhead.

It has been said the Indian force numbered thirty-seven, but these figures appear ridiculous when parties at Prairie du Chien, present when the boat landed, reported over five hundred bullet holes in the craft, and Mr. Snelling reported 693, which would allow eighteen bullets to the Indian and leave no reckoning for the many which missed the boat entirely. As this conflict occurred on the same day which saw the Gagnier family murdered by Red Bird and his companions, it is not conceivable how Red Bird could have been present. In fact, he was not, as Black Hawk admitted after his acquittal. He was the leader and he said so.[1]

It should be noted in this place that the miserable rumor mentioned by Reynolds in his "My Own Times" and by other writers, of the action of the crew upstream in debauching certain Winnebago squaws, had no foundation whatever.

Black Hawk was subsequently arrested for this attack, but the lack of evidence allowed him to escape an indictment. When discharged he made no secret of his participation in the affair, but prior thereto he was the most discreet Indian the imagination can portray. The only reference to the court proceedings made by the newspapers at the time is to be found in the Miner's Journal of Galena for Saturday, September 13, 1828, and is as follows:

"A gentleman who was present at the time of the arraignment and trial of these Indians at Prairie du Chien has given us the following particulars:

"A special term of the United States Circuit Court for the county of Crawford, sitting as a court of oyer and terminer for the trial of seven Indian prisoners (Winnebagoes), confined at Prairie du Chien, was held at that village on the 25th ult., by the Hon. James D. Doty, additional U. S. Judge for Michigan. Wan-i-ga, or 'the Sun,' and Chick-hong-sic, or 'the Petit Boeuff,' were tried severally on two indictments, one for the murder of Registre Gagnier, as accomplices of Red Bird, deceased. On the second indictment, Chick-hong-sic was tried for the murder of Solomon Lipcap, and Wan-i-ga was also tried on the same as his accomplice. On the third indictment, Wan-i-ga was tried for scalping Louisa Gagnier, with intent to kill. On first indictment, defendants were found guilty. On second, Chick-hong-sic guilty, Wan-i-ga acquitted. On third, Wan-i-ga found guilty; the others acquitted. In the case of the United States vs. Wau-koo-kah and Mah-na-at-ap-e-kah, for the murder of Methode and family, a *nolle prosequi* was entered and the prisoners discharged.

"There being no bills found against Kanon-e-kah, or 'The youngest of the Thunders,' and Kara-zhon-sept-kah, or 'The Black Hawk,' imprisoned for attacking and firing on the keel boat last year, nor against the son of Red Bird, they were discharged.

"Counsel for the prosecution, John Scott, Esq., of Ste. Genevieve, Mo.; for the defense, assigned by the Court, Charles S. Hempstead, Esq., of St. Louis.

"Wan-i-ga and Chick-hong-sic were sentenced to be executed on the 26th of December."

---

[1] Annals of the West, pp. 796-7; Brown's Hist. of Illinois, p. 357.

FORT SNELLING.

COL. JOSIAH SNELLING.

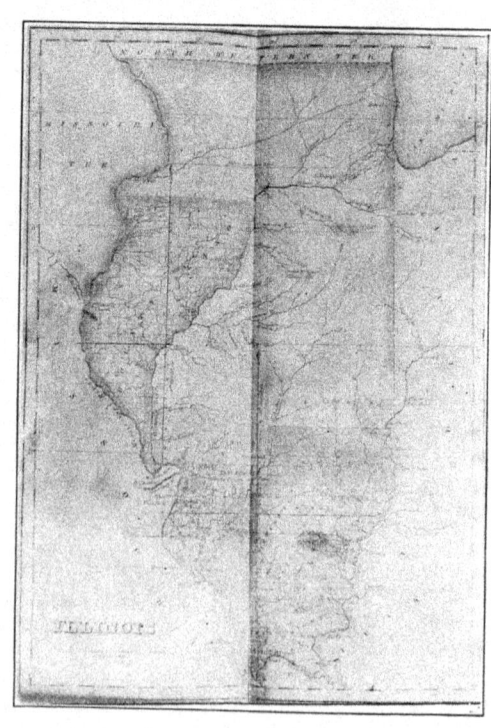

MILITARY TRACT OF ILLINOIS.

CHAPTER XII.

THE MILITARY TRACT—PERILS OF FRONTIER LIFE—GATHERING SETTLEMENTS ABOUT BLACK HAWK'S VILLAGE—FRICTION—ATTEMPTED COMPROMISE—CORRESPONDENCE—GAINES AT FORT ARMSTRONG.

It may be possible that this fresh outbreak was superinduced by the gradual appearance of the hated American further and further northward toward Black Hawk's village, but, if true, the act was indefensible as it was meddlesome. He deliberately assisted in precipitating the trouble between Red Bird (who was a remarkably decent Indian) and the Americans, without the slightest provocation.

By acts of Congress[1] bounty land warrants were voted to the soldiers of the war of " 'twelve," and for their especial benefit the so-called "Military Tract" was erected in the State of Illinois, comprising the territory between the Illinois and Mississippi rivers, 169 miles north to a line drawn from the great bend of the river above Peru to the Mississippi, containing 5,360,000 acres.[2] Into this, two classes of settlers poured—as Catlin aptly put it, "the overwhelming torrent of emigration to the 'Far West.'"

From the conclusion of the first peace with Great Britain, the native white population increased at a ratio astonishing to the observer and writer of those days, particularly James Hall, and with the advent of the "twenties" the overflow was moving into this "Military Tract." One class comprised the soldier, who was the beneficiary, with his family, while the other was composed of families from Kentucky and Tennessee, the purchasers of those warrants, which had been gradually working northward from the beginning of the century, and which up to this time largely predominated in the population of Illinois. In both of these classes were the Indian fighters; men whose homes had been desolated or whose fathers and mothers had been murdered by blood-thirsty savages; men whose bodies carried lead placed there by Indian muskets, and who, from sad

---

[1] December 24, 1811; January 11, 1812, and December 10, 1814.
[2] Peck's Gazeteer for 1825. The land was surveyed in 1815 and 1816.
 By letter of the Surveyor-General, August 10, 1815, we are informed that lands were selected in Southern Michigan, Northern Ohio, the military tract in Illinois and in Missouri, but by reason of Indian hostility the first two selections could not be surveyed that year.—Niles Reg., Vol. 9, p. 15.

experience, were not likely to receive with composure the raids of bandit Sacs. These men were tired of tilling the soil with rifles lashed to the plowbeam and of being constantly called away from the field to awful scenes of carnage, where perhaps neighbor or wife or child had just been burned at the stake. Gen. A. C. Dodge, who was a pioneer by birth, a man whose honesty of purpose and soundness of judgment on Indian questions have never yet been questioned, forcibly illustrated those conditions in a speech at the semi-centennial of Burlington, Iowa: "In the settlement of Kentucky five of my father's uncles fell under the Indian hatchet. Among the incidents of his very earliest recollection was to have seen the dead and bleeding body of one of those uncles borne in the arms of another on horseback to the stockade fort in which they lived. My own brother, Henry LaFayette Dodge, * * * was captured and burned to death at the stake."

James Hall, the friend and defender of the Indian, has pictured the vicissitudes of the pioneers who blazed the way for later generations to follow. Among other things, we find, on page 152, Vol. 2, "Sketches of the West," the following:

"They left behind them all the comforts of life. They brought but little furniture, but few farming implements, and no store of provisions. Until their lands were cleared and brought into culture, and their domestic animals became productive, they depended for subsistence chiefly upon the game of the forest. They ate their fresh meat without salt, without vegetables, and in many instances without bread; and they slept in cabins hastily erected, of green logs, and in which they were exposed to much of the inclemency of the weather. To their other sufferings that of sickness was often added; and they found themselves assailed, in situations where medical assistance could not be procured, by diseases of sudden development and fatal character.

"While thus overburthened by toil and assailed by disaster, the settler found employment for all the energy of his character and all the inventive powers of his mind. The savage was watching, with malignant vigilance, to grasp every opportunity to harass the intruder into the hunting grounds of his fathers. Sometimes he contented himself with seizing the horses or driving away the cattle of the emigrant, depriving the wretched family of the means of support, and reserving the consummation of his vengeance to a future occasion; sometimes, with a subtle refinement of cruelty, the Indian warrior crept into a settlement by stealth, and created universal dismay by stealing away a child, or robbing a family of the wife and mother; sometimes a father was the victim, and the widow and orphans were thrown upon the protection of the friends who, on such occasions, were never deaf to the claims of the unfortunate, while as often the yelling band surrounded the peaceful cabin at the midnight hour, applied the firebrand to the slight fabric, and murdered the whole of its defenseless inmates."

Exhausted by such scenes, these men had come to Illinois with their children, whose tender memories had gathered material never to be effaced, to enjoy peaceful pursuits and erect homes for their families. When, therefore, Black Hawk sought to renew such tactics, he trod the mine which exploded and tore his power to shreds. The final conflict was inevitable, and though during the first portion of the campaign, for want of discipline, those spirited, independent and unrestrained young fellows brought no great honor to their arms, when the iron hand of Gen. James D. Henry brought them to reason, they marched with a grim determination to avenge the murders of their ancestors by hurling Black Hawk forever from the power to molest them more, and they did it in a manner sufficiently decisive.

In 1829[1] these settlers, observing the fertility of the lands at the mouth of Rock River, the protecting influence of a Government fort, pushed over to that point and squatted upon the lands there. Settlements multiplying by the reputation of the land, the President was persuaded that the time had come to survey and open them up for sale, and he issued his proclamation accordingly. This survey included the village occupied by Black Hawk.

It has been urged by some that there was no necessity for opening up this tract for settlement, because the nearest settlements were far away, leaving an extensive belt between, which should first have been occupied. Who is to judge of man's choice in the public domain but the man himself? The fort and public buildings made a respectable settlement by themselves. Add to these the traders and a garrison with all the hangers-on, and the neighborhood became an inviting one for settlers. The mines to the north were booming; the river boats were carrying great numbers of passengers, who always stopped at this point, and one must repeat, why should it not be attractive?

When requested, Keokuk and the other chiefs issued proclamations, and, with most of their people, removed to the west side of the river.[2] Wapello, the head chief of the Foxes, and Pash-e-pa-ho of the Sacs, making the decision almost unanimous, also went over, but Black Hawk, finding it possible to annoy the Americans, refused, claiming that when he signed the treaty of 1816 he had been deceived and never knew that his village had been included in its terms. His offenses had been condoned so many times by the indulgent Americans that he had grown to consider himself above danger from them, and doggedly remained, in defiance of the wish of the President and the proclamations of Keokuk and Wapello. The promotion of Keokuk to be chief of the Sacs had its influence, for any proclamation Keokuk might make would certainly be defied by Black Hawk. Keokuk urged him to avoid friction by peaceably removing with the others, but this appeal only strengthened his determination to remain, and he sat back upon his haunches like the bull before the locomotive,

---

[1] Annals of the West, p. 797. In 1828 the President issued his proclamation opening this land, which had been previously surveyed, and the following year was occupied, and later sold.

[2] In 1828 some few lingered, but by May all but Black Hawk's band and Quash-qua-me remained.

und, to carry the simile to a logical conclusion, was very naturally annihilated.

The disposition to quarrel may be seen from the following extract from a letter written to Governor Clark by Agent Forsythe:

Rocky Island, 17th May, 1829.

Sir:—Some time early in the spring, a number of settlers came to the Sac village on Rock river and enclosed nearly all the Sac Indians' corn fields. The Indians, on their arrival, were surprised at this, as also the destruction committed by the settlers by tearing down many of their lodges. The settlers who reside at the Sac village have called on me frequently, wishing me to drive the Indians away; that they must go, ought to go, pointing out the necessity of sending them away, etc., etc.

I yesterday had a meeting with a number of Indians, and had a very long talk with them on the subject of all the Indians moving onto their own lands.

Quash-qua-me denying that he ever sold any land above Rock river, etc., the Black Hawk also saying that the white people were in the habit of saying one thing to the Indians and putting another on paper; and both those Indians made use of every argument they were masters of to convince me that they never had sold the land above Rock river, etc.

I acquainted all the Indians with the provisions of the treaty of 1804, where Quash-qua-me's name is, as one of the chiefs who sold the land in question (the other chiefs being dead). I also reminded the Black Hawk of the treaty of 1816, when the commissioners refused to smoke with him and the other Sac chiefs (who accompanied him down to St. Louis), to make peace, until they signed the treaty, etc.

The Black Hawk denied that any mention was made to him about land in making the treaty of 1816; but that the commissioners must have inserted in the treaty what was not expressly explained to him and friends.

The Indians and myself had a great deal of talk at this meeting, the most of which was quite unnecessary, at the winding up of which I told the Indians I would not listen to any complaints that might come in future from any Indians who would remain at Rocky river.

The chief Keokuk inquired of me in private if he and some of his friends could remain at Rocky river to raise the corn they had planted,[1] saying at the same time that most of the principal chiefs and braves had gone to reside at a place a few miles within the mouth of Ioway river, and that more than one-half of those now at Rocky river would also go shortly to the same place.

I told Keokuk that he had heard what I had said to the Indians in council, and that it was out of my power to give any Indians such permission as he asked for.

It is my opinion that but few Indians will remain at Rocky river this summer, but yet I am fearful that some difficulties will take place among them and the settlers during the ensuing summer. All the Fox Indians formerly residing in this vicinity have gone and made a new village at the Grand Mascatin.

As has been stated, Black Hawk was not a chief, and was never recognized as such. He was simply a brave who had gathered around him a party of disaffected spirits, eager to foment strife; being no Pontiac or Tecumseh, and having no call upon him by his nation or his tribe to

---

[1] The planting of the corn in 1829 by the squaws was done to feed those who had gone to the Iowa River and were there preparing new fields, which could not then be used.

THE BLACK HAWK WAR.   81

rectify any wrongs, his controversies in 1830 had degenerated into petty quarrels with the incoming settlers.

He refused to cross the Mississippi because he was meanly jealous of Keokuk and his influence and because of his hatred of the Americans, and not because of fealty to any principle. He considered every argument of his friends to mean that his removal meant his absorption as an attraction. Removal west, with Keokuk above him, meant desuetude and dry rot for his schemes. He preferred being a small quarreler to being none at all, and he remained.

The Indian inclosures were made with stakes driven into the ground, to which poles were transversely laid and tied with strips of bark. When the crop of 1830 had been planted within these enclosures, or otherwise, the Indians left for a summer hunt. Returning when the corn was in the milk, it was gathered and their horses were turned into the fields. The aftermath of those meagerly cropped fields was uninviting while the ripening grain of the whites was near at hand, and, without any ceremony, the slight fences were trampled down and the grain of the white man more or less consumed or destroyed. A casual glance at this state of things would disclose no premeditation on the part of the Indians to molest the whites, but the whites complained and seem to have proven beyond all doubt that the Indians, finding they could harass the whites by these tactics, carried them a little further, until they secretly drove horses into the fields and upon various occasions killed the live stock of the whites. The correspondence entire upon the subject, as found in public document No. 2 of the proceedings of the Twenty-second Congress, first session, is scattered along through this chapter. These depredations continued until autumn, when Black Hawk and his band departed on their winter's hunt.

By way of experiment, a compromise for the year 1830 was attempted whereby the whites and Indians were to try to live together in peace, but the antagonistic natures of both made success impossible and the attempt was abandoned, with the determination by the whites that if Black Hawk annoyed them in their future efforts to develop their farms his actions would be met with resistance and his removal by force demanded of the authorities. In the spring of 1831 the Indians returned to find the whites prepared to resist them. Black Hawk's wick-a-up was occupied. This act brought his contention to a climax, as might have been expected, by openly attempting the destruction of property. This he did without molesting the owner, adroitly provoking the Americans to menace and possibly force him to assume an attitude of defense of Indian rights and the "graves of his fathers." On April 30, 1831, the following letter was sent to Governor Reynolds, setting forth grievances, and signed by a numerical force which should command attention from any executive:

THE BLACK HAWK WAR.

"April 30, 1831.

"His Excellency, the Governor of the State of Illinois:

"We, the undersigned, being citizens of Rock River and its vicinity, beg leave to state to your honor the grievances which we labor under, and pray your protection against the Sac and Fox tribe of Indians, who have again taken possession of our lands near the mouth of Rock River and its vicinity. They have, and now are, burning our fences, destroying our crops of wheat now growing, by turning in all their horses. They also threaten our lives if we attempt to plant corn, and say they will cut it up; that we have stolen their lands from them, and they are determined to exterminate us, provided we don't leave the country. Your honor, no doubt, is aware of the outrages that were committed by said Indians heretofore. Particularly last fall, they almost destroyed all our crops, and made several attempts on the owners' lives when they attempted to prevent their depredations, and actually wounded one man by stabbing him in several places. This spring they act in a much more outrageous and menacing manner, so that we consider ourselves compelled to beg protection of you, which the agent and garrison on Rock Island refuse to give, inasmuch as they say they have no orders from government; therefore, should we not receive adequate aid from your honor, we shall be compelled to abandon our settlement, and the lands which we have purchased of government. Therefore, we have no doubt but your honor will better anticipate our condition than it is represented, and grant us immediate relief in the manner that to you may seem most likely to produce the desired effect. The number of Indians now among us is about six or seven hundred. They say there are more coming, and that the Pottawattomies and some of the Winnebagoes will help them, in case of an irruption with the whites. The warriors now here are the Black Hawk's party, with other chiefs, the names of whom we are not acquainted with. Therefore, looking up to you for protection, we beg leave to remain yours, etc."[1]

"John Wells,	"Erastus Kent,	"G. V. Miller,
"B. F. Pike,	"Levi Wells,	"Edward Burner,
"H. McNiel,	"Joel Wells,	"Joel Thompson,
"Albert Wells,	"Michael Bartlet,	"Joel Wells, Jr.,
"Griffith Ausbury,	"Huntington Wells,	"J. W. Spencer,
"Thomas Gardiner,	"Thomas Davis,	"Joseph Danforth,
"J. Vandruff,	"Thomas Lovitt,	"William Brazher,
"S. Vandruff,	"William Heans,	"Jonah H. Case,
"John L. Bain,	"Charles French,	"Samuel Wells,
"Horace Cook,	"M. S. Hulls,	"Charles French,
"David B. Hail,	"W. Wells,	"Benjamin Goble,
"John Barrel,	"Asaph Wells,	"Gentry McCall."
"William Henry,		

Receiving no reply to that request, the citizens waited until the 19th of May, when they fancied they would have to send a personal embassy to Reynolds, which they did, in as much haste as possible, as they were expecting momentary trouble from those Indians. They accordingly drew up the following petition and sent it by one of the most respectable of their citizens, who in person laid it before the Governor:

[1] Wakefield, Appendix, Note 1, pp. 107-116.

THE BLACK HAWK WAR.

"Farnhamburg, May 19th, 1831.
"To his Excellency, the Governor of the State of Illinois:
"We, the undersigned, citizens of Rock River and its vicinity, having previously sent a petition to your honor, praying your protection against these Sac Indians, who were at that time doing every kind of mischief, as was set forth and represented to your honor; but feeling ourselves more aggrieved, and our situation more precarious, we have been compelled to make our distress known to you by sending one of our neighbors, who is well acquainted with our situation. If we do not get relief speedily, we must leave our habitations to these savages, and seek safety for our families by taking them down into the lower counties and suffer our houses and fences to be destroyed, as one of the principal war chiefs has threatened, if we do not abandon our settlement, his warriors should burn our houses over our heads. They were, at the time we sent our other petition, destroying our crops of wheat, and are still pasturing their horses in our fields, burning our fences, and have thrown the roof off one house. They shot arrows at our cattle, killed our hogs, and every mischief.

"We have tried every argument to the agent for relief, but he tells us they are a lawless band, and he has nothing to do with them until further orders, leaving us still in suspense, as the Indians say, if we plant we shall not reap, a proof of which we had last fall; they almost entirely destroyed all our crops of corn, potatoes, etc. Believing we shall receive protection from your excellency, we shall go on with our farms until the return of the bearer; and ever remain your humble supplicants, etc.,"

Which petition was signed by nearly the same citizens as the first. Benjamin F. Pike, the bearer of the above petition, and also Hiram Sanders and Ammyson Chapman, made oath to the truth of the allegations contained in it, as follows:

"State of Illinois, St. Clair County.
"Present, Benjamin F. Pike, before me, a Justice of the Peace in and for the said county, and made oath and deposed, that he has resided in the vicinity of Rock River, in the State of Illinois, for almost three years last past; that he is well acquainted with the band of the Sac Indians whose chief is the Black Hawk, and who have resided and do now reside near the mouth of Rock River, in this State; that he understands so much of the said Indian language, as to converse with the said Indians intelligibly; that he is well satisfied that said Indians, to the amount of about three hundred warriors, are extremely unfriendly to the white people; that said Indians are determined, if not prevented by force, to drive off the white people, who have some of them purchased land of the United States, near said Indians, and said Indians to remain the sole occupiers of the said country.

"That said Indians do not only make threats to this effect, but have, in various instances, done much damage to said white inhabitants, by throwing down their fences, destroying the fall grain, pulling off the roofs of houses, and positively asserting that if the whites do not go away, they would kill them; that there are about forty inhabitants and heads of families in the vicinity of said Indians, who are immediately affected by said band of Indians; that said Pike is certain that said forty heads of families, if not protected, will be compelled to leave their habitations and homes from the actual injury that said Indians will commit on said inhabitants. That said band of Indians consists, as above stated, of about three hundred warriors, and that the whole band is actuated by the same hostile feelings towards the white inhabitants; and that, if not prevented by an armed force of men, will commit murders on said white inhabitants. That said Indians have said, that they would fight for their country where they reside, and would not permit the white people to occupy it at all. That said white inhabitants are desirous to be protected, and that immediately, so that they may raise crops this spring and summer.

"BENJAMIN F. PIKE.

"Sworn and subscribed before me, this 26th May, 1831.
"JOHN H. DENNIS, J. P."

"The deposition of Hiram Sanders and Ammyson Chapman, taken before Stephen Dewey, Esq., a Justice of the Peace for Fulton County.

"State of Illinois, Fulton County.

"Personally appeared before me, Stephen Dewey, an acting Justice of the Peace in and for said county of Fulton, and State of Illinois, Hiram Sanders, and Ammyson Chapman, of the aforesaid county and State, and made oath that some time in the month of April last, they went to the old Indian Sac town, about thirty miles up Rock River, for the purpose of farming and establishing a ferry across said river, and the Indians ordered us to move away, and not to come there again and we remained there a few hours.

"They then sent for their chief, and he informed us that we might depart peaceably, and if we did not that he would make us go.

"He therefore ordered the Indians to throw our furniture out of the house; they accordingly did so, and threatened to kill us if we did not depart. We therefore discovered that our lives were in danger, and consequently moved back again to the above county.

"We supposed them to be principally Winnebagoes.

"H. SANDERS,
"A. CHAPMAN.

"Sworn and subscribed this 11th. day of May, 1831.
"STEPHEN DEWEY, J. P.

There were several other petitions sent to the Governor from Henderson River and elsewhere; likewise a number of depositions were taken, the substance of which will be found in General Gaines' report to the Secretary of War.

For almost twenty-seven years, much over an average Indian's lifetime, the Government had faithfully observed its compact of 1804 to allow the Sacs and Foxes the privilege of remaining on the ceded lands until surveyed and thrown upon the market. With each new treaty acknowledging that one, additional annuities had been granted them, until the annual distribution amounted to $27,000.00: "The Sacs and Foxes are already drawing an annuity of twenty-seven thousand dollars for thirty years to come, in cash, and by the present treaty that amount will be enlarged to thirty-seven thousand dollars per annum.'" The last named treaty, mentioned by Catlin, brought these Indians seventy-five cents per acre for their lands. Yet Black Hawk, regardless of the obligation of his lawful superiors and his own, under those repeated treaties and payments,

[1]Catlin.

lingered and quibbled and quarreled, thinking, no doubt, by this time that he could not or would not be removed at all.

The little band of whites, unable to contend successfully against the overwhelming numbers of Indians and their exasperating thefts and annoyances, applied to the agent and got no relief and, as it seemed to the settlers, almost no thought. The United States authorities, particularly Governor Clark, Superintendent of Indian Affairs at St. Louis, were the ones to furnish protection, *vi et armis* or otherwise. Governor Reynolds was very unwilling at first to send the militia to the scene without invitation from those army officers; therefore, when he received the first petition, instead of replying at once to it, he applied to the Indian agents at Rock Island and to General Gaines. Failing of receiving any consideration, the second message from the citizens, who thought he had ignored them, compelled the "Old Ranger," as the Governor was called, to take the initiative by calling out the militia to the number of 700, which he did on May 26th, with instructions to rendezvous at Beardstown June 10, 1831.[1] On the day of issuing that call, he wrote Governor Clark a letter, calculated to leave no room for doubt as to the course he should pursue and the manner of his treatment of the Indians if they did not move.

"Belleville, 26th May, 1831.

"Sir:—In order to protect the citizens of this State, who reside near Rock River, from Indian invasion and depredations, I have considered it necessary to call out a force of militia of this State of about seven hundred strong, to remove a band of the Sac Indians who are now about Rock Island. The object of the government of the State is to protect those citizens, by removing said Indians, peaceably, if they can, but forcibly if they must. Those Indians are now, and so I have considered them, in a state of actual invasion of the State.

"As you act as the public agent of the United States in relation to those Indians, I considered it my duty to inform you of the above call on the militia, and that in or about fifteen days a sufficient force will appear before said Indians to remove them, dead or alive, over to the west side of the Mississippi; but to save all this disagreeable business, perhaps a request from you to them, for them to remove to the west side of the river, would effect the object of procuring peace to the citizens of the State. There is no disposition on the part of the people of this State to injure those unfortunate and deluded savages if they will let us alone; but a government that does not protect its citizens deserves not the name of a government. Please correspond with me to this place on this subject.

"Your obedient servant,

"JOHN REYNOLDS.

"GEN. CLARK, Supt., etc."

Reynolds' letter hastened the following reply, which clearly indicated that much had really been done by Governor Clark to remove the Indians:

"Superintendency of Indian Affairs,
"St. Louis, May 28, 1831.

"Sir:—I have the honor to acknowledge the receipt of your letter of the 26th inst., informing me of your having considered it necessary to call out a force of

---

[1] "My Own Times," p. 328.

militia of about seven hundred for the protection of the citizens of Illinois who reside near Rock Island from Indian invasion and for the purpose of removing a band of Sac Indians who are now about Rock Island, etc.

"You intimate that to prevent the necessity of employing this force, perhaps a request from me to those Indians to remove to the west side of the Mississippi would effect the object of procuring peace to the citizens of your State. In answer to which, I would beg leave to observe, that every effort on my part has been made to effect the removal of all those tribes who had ceded their lands. For the purpose of affording you a view (in part) of what has been done in this matter, I enclose you herewith extracts from the reports of the agents for the Sacs and Foxes, by which it will be seen that every means, short of actual force, has been employed to effect their removal.

"I have communicated the contents of your letter to Gen. Gaines, who commands the western division of the army, and who has full power to act and execute any military movement deemed necessary for the protection of the frontier. I shall also furnish him with such information regarding the Sacs and Foxes as I am possessed of, and would beg leave to refer you to him for any further proceedings in relation to this subject. I have the honor to be, with great respect,
"Your obedient servant,
"WM. CLARK.

"His Excellency, JOHN REYNOLDS, Governor of Illinois."

The fact that Governor Reynolds did not immediately hear from General Gaines or the Indian agents led him into the mistaken belief that they were entirely inactive and unsympathetic as to the fate of the settlers. The contrary is the truth, as the following letters, mentioned in the foregoing, from Agent St. Vrain, a most courteous and conscientious man, will disclose. This same good man was subsequently butchered in a most shocking manner by the Indians:[1]

"Rock Island, May 15, 1831.

"Respected Sir:—I have again to mention to you that the Black Hawk (a Sac chief) and his party are now at their old village on Rock River. They have commenced planting corn and say they will keep possession. I have been informed that they have pulled down a house and some fences, which they have burned. They have also turned their horses in wheat fields and say they will destroy the wheat, so that the white people shall not remain among them.

"This is what I expected from their manner of acting last fall, and which I mentioned to you in my letter of the 8th October last. I would not be at a loss were it not for the 7th article of the treaty with the Sacs and Foxes of 3d November, 1804.

"I respectfully ask, would it not be better to hold a treaty with those Indians and get them to remove peaceably, than to call on the military to force them off? None of this band has as yet called on me for information. A few have been at my agency to have work done at the smith's shops. I have the honor to be,
"Your obedient servant,
"FELIX ST. VRAIN, Indian Agent.

"GEN. WILLIAM CLARK, Supt. Ind. of St. Louis."

"St. Louis, May 28, 1831.

"Respected Sir:—Since my last of the 15th inst. on the subject of the band of Sac Indians, etc., the Indian village on Rock River near Rock Island, I have

---
[1] See page 170, post.

heard from the Indians and some of the whites, that a house had been unroofed instead of pulled down and burned and that the fence had caught fire by accident. As regards the destroying of the wheat, etc., the Indians say that a white man hauled some timber through a field and left the fence down, by which means their horses got into the field. This, however, has been contradicted by the white inhabitants of that place. They say that the Indians are constantly troubling them by letting their horses into their fields and killing their hogs, etc., etc. This, however, I am confident is occasioned in a great measure by whisky being given to the Indians in exchange for their guns, traps, etc.

"I had a talk with the principal chief and braves of that band of Indians. I spoke to the Black Thunder, who is the principal of that band. The Black Hawk is only a brave, but has considerable influence with them. I told them that they had sold those lands to the government of the United States, and that they ought to remove to their own lands. They then said that they had only sold the lands south of the river. I then produced the treaties and explained to them that they had relinquished their right as far as the Ouiscosin. Quash-quam-me (the jumping fish) then said that he had only consented to the limits being Rock River; but that a Fox chief agreed (as he understands, afterwards) for the Ouisconsin; that he (Quash-quam-me) had been deceived, and that he did not intend it to be so. I had considerable talk with them on this subject, and could discover nothing hostile in their disposition, unless their decided conviction of their right to the place could be construed as such. I have been informed that a white man and his family had gone to an Indian village on the borders of Rock River, about forty miles from Rock Island, for the purpose of establishing a ferry, and that the Indians at that place had driven them away, at the same time saying to them that they would not hurt them, but they should not live there. This village is occupied by a mixture of Winnebago, Sac and Fox bands and headed by the Prophet, a chief. I have the honor to be
"Your obedient servant,
"FELIX ST. VRAIN, Indian Agent.
"GEN. WILLIAM CLARK, Supt. Indian Affairs, St. Louis."

That General Clark was more active than credited by Reynolds will also be learned from the ensuing letter, which he at once dispatched to General Gaines:

"Superintendency of Indian Affairs,
"St. Louis, May 28, 1831.

"Sir:—I have the honor to inclose to you a copy of a letter of 26th inst. just received from the Governor of Illinois, by which you will perceive he has thought it necessary to call out a force of about 700 militia for the protection of the citizens of that State, who reside near Rock River, and for the purpose of removing a band of Sacs which he states are now about Rock Island.

"As the commanding General of this division of the army, I have thought it my duty to communicate to you the above information; and for the purpose of putting you in possession of the views of the Government in relation to this subject, as well as to inform you of the means which have been heretofore employed for the removal of the Sacs now complained of, I enclose to you herewith copies of my correspondence with the War Department and with the agent for those tribes, also extracts from such of their reports as had immediate relation to the subject.[1]

---
[1]Forsythe's letter of 1829. *ante,* was one of them.

"The Sacs and Foxes have been counseled with on the subject of their removal from the lands which they had ceded to the United States. The prospect of collisions with the white settlers who were then purchasing those lands, and the interminable difficulties in which they would be involved thereby were pointed out, and had the effect of convincing a large majority of both tribes of the impropriety of remaining at their old villages. They, therefore, acquiesced in the justice of the claim of the United States and expressed their willingness to comply with my request to remove to their new village on Ioway river, west of the Mississippi, all but parts of two bands headed by two inconsiderable chiefs, who, after abandoning their old village, have, it appears, returned again, in defiance of all consequences.

"Those bands are distinguished and known by the name of 'The British Party,' having been for many years in the habit of making annual visits at Malden in Upper Canada for the purpose of receiving their presents, and it is believed to be owing in a great measure to the counsels they have there received, that so little influence has been acquired over them by the United States agents.

"In justice to Keokuk, Wapello, The Stabbing Chief, and, indeed, all the other real chiefs and principal men of both tribes, it should be observed that they have constantly and zealously co-operated with the Government agents in furtherance of its views, and in their endeavors to effect the removal of all their property from the ceded lands.

"Any information in my possession which you may deem necessary in relation to this subject will be promptly afforded. With high respect, I have the honor to be

"Your most obedient servant,

"WILLIAM CLARK.

"MAJOR-GEN. EDMUND P. GAINES, Commanding Western Department, U. S. A."

"P. S. The agent for the Sacs and Foxes (Mr. St. Vrain) has received his instructions and will perform any service you may require of him with the Sacs and Foxes."

Reynolds must have received General Clark's letter on the date of writing, since he concurrently addressed General Gaines as follows:

"GENERAL GAINES. "Belleville, May 28, 1831.

"Sir:—I have received undoubted information that the section of this State near Rock Island is actually invaded by a hostile band of the Sac Indians, headed by Black Hawk; and in order to repel said invasion, and to protect the citizens of the State. I have, under the provisions of the Constitution of the United States and the laws of this State, called on the militia, to the number of seven hundred men, who will be mounted and ready for service in a very short time. I consider it my duty to lay before you the above information, so as you, commanding the military forces of the United States in this part of the Union, may adopt such measures in regard to said Indians as you deem right.

"The above-mentioned mounted volunteers (because such they will be) will be in readiness immediately to move against said Indians, and, as Executive of the State of Illinois, I respectfully solicit your co-operation in this business. Please honor me with an answer to this letter.

"With sincere respect for your character,

"I am, your obedient servant,

"JOHN REYNOLDS."

THE BLACK HAWK WAR.   89

To which rather tart epistle General Gaines replied instanter:

"H. Q. Western Department, May 29, 1831.
"His Excellency, GOVERNOR REYNOLDS.

"Sir:—I do myself the honor to acknowledge the receipt of your letter of yesterday's date, advising me of your having received undoubted information that the section of the frontier of your State near Rock Island is invaded by a hostile band of Sac Indians, headed by a chief called Black Hawk. That in order to repel said invasion, and to protect the citizens of the State, you have called on the militia to the number of seven hundred militiamen, to be in readiness immediately to move against the Indians, and you solicit my co-operation.

"In reply, it is my duty to state to you, that I have ordered six companies of the regular troops stationed at Jefferson Barracks to embark to-morrow morning and repair forthwith to the spot occupied by the hostile Sacs. To this detachment I shall, if necessary, add four companies. With this force I am satisfied that I shall be able to repel the invasion and give security to the frontier inhabitants of the State. But should the hostile band be sustained by the residue of the Sac, Fox and other Indians, to an extent requiring an augmentation of my force, I will, in that event, communicate with your Excellency by express, and avail myself of the co-operation which you propose. But, under existing circumstances, and the present aspect of our Indian relations on the Rock Island section of the frontier, I do not deem it necessary or proper to require militia, or any other description of force, other than that of the regular army at this place and Prairie du Chien.

"I have the honor to be, very respectfully,
"Your obedient servant,
"EDMUND P. GAINES,
"Major-Gen. by Brevet, Commanding."

Dignifying Black Hawk's return with the term invasion was a misnomer, at least an exaggeration, on the part of Reynolds, but Gaines promptly set out for Fort Armstrong, where he quickly absorbed the situation and communicated it to Reynolds.

"Headquarters, Rock Island, June 5, 1831.
"JOHN REYNOLDS, Governor of Illinois.

"Sir:—I do myself the honor to report to your Excellency the result of my conference with the chiefs and braves of the band of Sac Indians settled within the limits of your State near this place.

"I called their attention to the facts reported to me of their disorderly conduct towards the white inhabitants near them. They disavow any intention of hostility, but at the same time adhere with stubborn pertinacity to their purpose of remaining on the Rock River land in question.

"I notified them of my determination to move them peaceably if possible, but at all events to move them to their own side of the Mississippi River, pointing out to them the apparent impossibility of their living on lands purchased by the whites without constant disturbance. They contended that this part of their country had never been sold by them. I explained to them the different treaties of 1804, '16 and '25, and concluded with a positive assurance that they must move off, and that I must as soon as they are ready assist them with boats.

"I have this morning learned that they have invited the Prophet's band of

Winnebagoes on Rock River, with some Pottawattomies and Kickapoos, to join them. If I find this to be true, I shall gladly avail myself of my present visit to see them well punished; and, therefore, I deem it to be the only safe measure now to be taken to request of your Excellency the battalion of mounted men which you did me the honor to say would co-operate with me. They will find at this post a supply of rations for the men, with some corn for their horses, together with a supply of powder and lead.

"I have deemed it expedient under all the circumstances of the case to invite the frontier inhabitants to bring their families to this post until the difference is over.

"I have the honor to be, with great respect,
"Your obedient servant,
"EDMUND P. GAINES,
"Major-Gen. by Brevet, Commanding."

"P. S. Since writing the foregoing remarks, I have learned that the Winnebagoes and Pottawattomie Indians have actually been invited by the Sacs to join them. But the former evince no disposition to comply; and it is supposed by Colonel Gratiot, the agent, that none will join the Sacs, except, perhaps, some few of the Kickapoos. E. P. G."

The situation had developed such symptoms, to the mind of General Clark, that, after writing Governor Reynolds and urging Gaines forward, he made the following report to the Secretary of War:

"Superintendency of Indian Affairs,
"St. Louis, May 30, 1831.

"Sir:—On the 28th inst. I had the honor of receiving a letter from the Governor of Illinois dated the 26th, informing me of the measures which he had considered it necessary to pursue for the protection of the citizens of his State from Indian invasion and for the purpose of removing a band of Sacs then about Rock Island. A copy of his letter and my answer is herewith enclosed.

"Deeming the information received from the Governor of Illinois important, I immediately communicated it to General Gaines, who happened to be in this place at the time; and shortly after was called upon by Governor Reynolds himself, to whom I gave such information respecting the Sacs complained of as had come to my knowledge, and also furnished him with such of the reports of the agent for those tribes as had relation to the subject. To the commanding General I furnished similar information; and also for the purpose of possessing him of the views of the Government on that subject, I gave him copies of such of my correspondence with the War Department as had any relation thereto.

"I also enclose to you copies of two reports of the agent for the Sacs and Foxes of the 15th and 28th inst. By the first it will be seen that the band complained of is determined to keep possession of their old village;¹ and it is probable from a knowledge of the disposition evinced in the matter by the Sacs and for the purpose of dispossessing them, that the commanding General has thought proper to make a display in that quarter of a part of the force under his command, six companies of which are now leaving this place for Rock River. The expedition (be the result what it may) cannot fail of producing good effects, even

---

¹See letter Col. Henry Gratiot, next following.

should the Indians be disposed to move peaceably to their own lands; and if not, their opposition should, in my opinion, be put down at once.

"I have the honor to be, with high respect,

"Your most obedient servant,

"WILLIAM CLARK."

"THE HON. JOHN H. EATON, Secretary of War."

"Rock Island, June 12, 1831.

"Sir:—I have the honor to report to you that, agreeably to my intimation to you, I visited the village of Sac Indians near this place yesterday for the purpose of persuading off the Winnebago Prophet and some young men of his band whom I knew had previously been there, and, I believe, with an intention to support the Sac Indians. I found that the Prophet had just left there for his village, which is within my agency upon Rock River, and although he had previously promised that he would return home and remain there, I have reason to believe that his object is to get as many of his band and of the other bands of the Winnebagoes (who reside at Rock River, within my agency) as he can, for the purpose of joining the Sacs and of supporting them in their present pretensions.

"I have recently been at some of the principal villages of Winnebagoes within my agency, and have ascertained from unquestionable authority that, although they had been invited to join the Sacs, they had refused to do so. I think it will be prudent for me to follow the Prophet, to prevent him from influencing any of the Indians up the river to join him. Should I, however, find that any of the warriors have left before my arrival amongst them, I will (if you think it best) return immediately to this place, bringing with me three or four influential chiefs who can be relied on and who will, with my assistance, I think, be able to control them.

"In my opinion there are at least 400 warriors at the Sac village which I visited yesterday, apparently determined to defend themselves in their present position. On the receipt of your letter of the 4th instant, I immediately hastened to this place with a view to give you the most satisfactory information upon the subject of it and tender my services in any way you may think useful.

"I am, respectfully yours,

"HENRY GRATIOT, Sub-Agent, etc."

"MAJ.-GEN. GAINES."

CHAPTER XIII.

COUNCIL—MILITIA ORGANIZED—MARCH TO BLACK HAWK'S VILLAGE—FLIGHT—VILLAGE BURNED—TREATY OF 1831.

Once awakened, General Gaines lost no time in bringing about a convention with the Indians, to avoid, if possible the trouble of a demonstration, but Black Hawk was fired with hatred and unprepared to accept any terms whatsoever. A council or talk was had in the council chamber at Fort Armstrong, which Black Hawk and his British sympathizers attended in numbers, and all fully armed. General Gaines opened the council by stating that the great father at Washington desired only what was right, and closed by insisting that the Indians should remove peaceably. Black Hawk replied that the Sacs had never sold their lands and were determined not to give up their village. General Gaines then asked: "Who is Black Hawk? Is he a chief? By what right does he appear in council?" To these questions Black Hawk that day made no reply, but on the following morning he was again in his seat. When the council opened he arose and, addressing General Gaines, said: "My father, you inquired yesterday, 'Who is Black Hawk? Why does he sit among the chiefs?' I will tell you who I am. I am a Sac; I am a warrior, and so was my father. Ask those young men who have followed me to battle, and they will tell you who Black Hawk is; provoke our people to war and you will learn who Black Hawk is."[1] It is further recorded of this meeting that in the heat of passion Black Hawk called General Gaines a liar and made demonstrations to kill him, which were only averted by the coolness of Gaines in parrying his threats by words of calmness. In this delicate affair Antoine LeClaire, the interpreter, was a powerful factor in smothering the threatened disturbance. The situation has been briefly set out in fortieth of Niles Register, page 310, as follows:

"Encampment, Rock Island, June 8th.

"We yesterday had a talk with the Indians, and from their determination not to leave the white settlements, and from their numbers, we shall have pretty serious work; that is, we shall have no play. They came into the council house yesterday with their spears, hatchets and bows strung. I have no doubt, from

---

[1]Fulton's "Red Men of Iowa," p. 194; Davidson & Stuvé Hist. Ill., p. 377.

GEN. EDMUND P. GAINES.

GOV. JOHN REYNOLDS.

MR. FRANCIS ARENZ.

COL. SAMUEL C. CHRISTY.

the extreme agitation of the interpreter, that there was more danger than most were aware of, as our troops were near a quarter of a mile off and they were about ten for one of us."

If any proof of hostility had been theretofore wanting, that demonstration supplied it and determined General Gaines to act heartily in conjunction with Governor Reynolds, and hastily as well.

Men left their plows, and, with little or no preparation, hastened to Beardstown, where twice the number of volunteers asked assembled. In bringing this expedition about, with as little hardship as possible, Governor Reynolds summoned none south of St. Clair or east of Sangamon counties.

None brought provisions and many failed to bring firearms, as requested in the call, but through the unusual resourcefulness of Colonels Enoch C. March and Samuel C. Christy, who were appointed quartermasters, supplies were quickly and abundantly provided, and by the good fortune of finding with Mr. Francis Arenz, a merchant of Beardstown, a consignment of brass guns, designed for the South American trade, but not so used, arms for all were provided. Governor Reynolds seemed determined not to conform to the punctilio of bureau fighting.

To organize the army, Governor Reynolds appointed as his aids James D. Henry and Milton K. Alexander. The task was difficult, but it was done satisfactorily. It must be remembered that the men were unaccustomed to subordination; many aspiring politicians whose appeals could not be ignored clamored for recognition; many more troops than were needed appeared, and to turn any number back might have jeopardized the success of the expedition, yet all conditions were met and harmoniously adjusted.

Joseph Duncan of the state militia, afterward Governor, was appointed Brigadier General, to assume immediate command of the brigade,[1] and William Thomas was appointed Brigade Quartermaster; William G. Brown, Paymaster General, and A. Atkins, Isom M. Gillham and Enoch B. Wethers, aids to General Duncan. E. D. Taylor was his Adjutant and J. J. Hardin Inspector General on his staff.

The brigade was divided into two regiments, a minor odd battalion and a spy battalion. The First Regiment was composed of seven companies, commanded by Captains Adam Smith, William F. Elkin, Achilles Morris, Thomas Carlin,[2] John Lorton, Samuel C. Pierce or Pearce and Samuel Smith, the staff officers being James D. Henry,[3] Colonel; Jacob Fry, Lieutenant-Colonel; John T. Stuart, Major; Thomas Collins, Adjutant; Edward Jones, Quartermaster; Thomas M. Neale, Paymaster.

The Second Regiment was composed of seven companies, commanded by Captains H. Mathews, John Haines, George Bristow, William Gillham,

---
[1]Reynolds' "My Own Times," p. 334.
[2]Subsequently Governor of Illinois.
[3]On the election of Henry to be colonel, John Dement was made aide to Reynolds.

Hiram Kincaid, Alexander Wells and William Weatherford; the staff officers, so far as known, being: Daniel Lieb, Colonel; Nathaniel Butler, Major, and W. Jordan, Quartermaster.

The odd battalion was composed of three companies, commanded by Captains William Moore, John Loraine and Solomon Miller, with the staff made up of Nathaniel Buckmaster, Major; James Semple, Adjutant; David Wright, Quartermaster; Joseph Gillespie, Paymaster; Charles Higbee, Surgeon, and John Krupp, Armorer. Richard Roman was Surgeon's Mate; John H. Blackwell, Quartermaster Sergeant.

The spy battalion, first mentioned, was composed of four companies, commanded by Captains Erastus Wheeler, William B. Whiteside, William Miller and Solomon Preuitt, with the staff officers as follows: Samuel Whiteside, Major; Samuel F. Kendle, Adjutant; John S. Greathouse, Quartermaster, and P. H. Winchester, Paymaster;[1] John F. Gillham, Armorer.[2]

Thus organized, the little army left camp near Rushville for Fort Armstrong, June 15,[3] 1831, about 1,600 strong, reaching a point on the Mississippi about eight miles south of Black Hawk's village, called Rockport, after a pleasant and prosperous march of four days. E. C. Berry, Adjutant-General of the State, accompanied the army, which was met at Rockport by General Gaines, who had brought on a steamboat loaded with provisions, secured by the General Quartermasters March and Christy, and here Major John Bliss, First U. S. Infantry, mustered it into the United States service.

At that point the army encamped for one night, where a plan of operation was concerted. The following morning the army moved forward with an old regular soldier for a guide, the steamboat at the same time starting, with General Gaines, up the river[4] for Vandruff's Island, where it was expected the Indians would concentrate, opposite their village, to pick off the soldiers as they approached. It was planned that the volunteers should cross the slough to this island, rout the enemy and ford the main river to the village, where the regular troops were to meet them from Fort Armstrong. The island was covered with bushes and vines, so thick as to render them impenetrable to the sight at a distance of twenty feet. General Gaines ran his steamboat up to the south point of the island and fired several rounds of grape and canister into the bushes to test the presence of the enemy. The spy battalion formed in line of battle and swept the island until it was ascertained that the ground rose so high and so suddenly that General Gaines' shot could have taken no effect one hundred yards from shore. The main body of volunteers, in three columns, came

[1]Wakefield.
[2]The name of George F. Kennedy has at times been confused with that of Samuel F. Kendle.
[3]40 'Niles, 341, says June 19.
[4]Ford, 112.

BRIG. GEN. JOSEPH DUNCAN.

GOV. THOMAS FORD.

GOV. THOMAS CARLIN.

MAJ. JOHN T. STUART.

CAPT. W. F. ELKIN.

COL. WILLIAM THOMAS.

COL. J. J. HARDIN.

COL. JACOB FRY.

THE BLACK HAWK WAR. 95

following, but before they could reach the northern border of the island the troops became so indiscriminately mixed, officers and men together, that no man was able to distinguish his own company or regiment. Gaines had ordered the artillery of the regulars to be stationed on a high bluff which looked down on the contemplated battlefield half a mile distant, from which, had the expected battle ensued, more friends than foes had been killed, many times over.

When the army finally reached the main body of the stream it was found bold and deep, fordable at no place nearer than half a mile and with no means of transportation convenient to carry the troops across. There, within sight of the enemy's village, they were compelled to waste much time in idleness until scows could be brought to ferry them over.

After unusual effort the volunteers reached the village, only to find it abandoned, the Indians having quietly withdrawn to the west side of the Mississippi that morning. A most abortive and humiliating campaign!

Whilst in camp down the river the previous evening a canoe filled with friendly Indians, bearing a white flag, called upon General Gaines to inform him of their neutrality, and ascertain a place of safety to which they might remove from the dangers of the anticipated battle of the morrow. Had Gaines desired to pursue a tactful course and punish the Indians, he might have learned definitely the position of the enemy and planned a successful campaign, but he gruffly told them to be gone, and that night they returned to the village, where preparations were immediately made to abandon it, as they did the following morning.

Governor Ford, who was a private of Whiteside's battalion in this expedition, has been especially severe with Gaines in his narration of the lack of preparation and the frightful confusion which ensued, together with the peril in which the troops found themselves by Gaines' disposition of the cannon on the heights above. It always is easy to plan an enterprise after it has been concluded and all its details fathomed by experience; much easier than before, with its uncertainties and possible failure. The Indians left; no blood was shed; no accidents happened to man or beast, and so long as the wish became a fact, though somewhat ingloriously done, there should be no cause for such acrimonious comments as Ford saw fit to record.

The enemy having escaped, the volunteers were determined to leave behind them a record of their displeasure. The rain descended in torrents, and though shelter might have been found for many in the frail houses, the Indian village was put to the torch and soon consumed with flames.

The volunteers then marched for Fort Armstrong the following morning and encamped several days on the left bank of the Mississippi, where the city of Rock Island now stands. The island, Rock Island, was then a most romantic bit of nature. To this landscape Governor Ford in his narrative did ample justice: "It was then in a complete state of nature—

a romantic wilderness. Fort Armstrong was built upon a rocky cliff on the lower part of an Island near the center of the river. ** The shores on each side, formed of gentle slopes of prairie, extending back to bluffs of considerable height, made it one of the most picturesque scenes in the western country. The river here is a beautiful sheet of clear, swift-running water, about three-quarters of a mile wide; its banks on both sides were uninhabited, except by the Indians, from the lower rapids to the fort, and the voyagers upstream, after several days' solitary progress through a wilderness country on its borders, came suddenly in sight of the whitewashed walls and towers of the fort, perched upon a rock, surrounded by the grandeur and beauty of nature, which, at a distance, gave it the appearance of one of those enchanted castles in an uninhabited desert, so well described in the Arabian Nights Entertainment."[1] Reynolds, in his "My Own Times," page 338, mentions a supposition that Gaines purposely retained the troops in camp at Rockport over night to allow the Indians to escape, and that he and Duncan knew of their flight when the brigade moved upon the village. If he did, then his arrangement of the contemplated battle was justified. But whether he knew of the departure or not, his measures for pursuit were prompt, vigorous and effective, and Black Hawk realized the fact. When demanded to return for a "peace talk," some of the Indians appeared at the fort without Black Hawk. Immediately Gaines sent word down to the camp, twelve miles below, that unless the remaining warriors came in at once and sued for peace he would chastise them. Very soon these recalcitrants, five or six hundred in number, appeared upon the river, picturesquely dotting it with their canoes for the whole distance.

On the 30th of June, 1831, in full council, Black Hawk and twenty-seven chiefs and warriors signed a treaty with Governor Reynolds and General Gaines, which was faithfully interpreted, word by word, by Antoine LeClaire, and is as follows:

"ARTICLES OF AGREEMENT AND CAPITULATION made and concluded this thirtieth day of June, one thousand eight hundred and thirty-one, between E. P. Gaines, Major-General of the United States Army, on the part of the United States; John Reynolds, Governor of Illinois, on the part of the State of Illinois; and the chiefs and braves of the band of Sac Indians, usually called the 'British Band of Rock River,' with their old allies of the Pottawatomie, Winnebago and Kickapoo nations:

"WITNESSETH: That, Whereas, the said British Band of Sac Indians have, in violation of the several treaties entered into between the United States and the Sac and Fox nations in the years 1804, 1816 and 1825, continued to remain upon and to cultivate the lands on Rock River, ceded to the United States by the said treaties, after the said lands had been sold by the United States to individual citizens of Illinois, and other states. And, Whereas, the said British Band of Sac Indians, in order to sustain their pretensions to continue upon the said Rock River lands, have assumed the attitude of actual hostility towards the United

---

[1]Ford, 115.

Z. H. VERNOR.

JAMES SEMPLE.

JOSEPH GILLESPIE.

SURGEON RICHARD ROMAN.

CAPT. ERASTUS WHEELER.

CAPT. SOLOMON PREUITT.

MAJ. JOHN BLISS.

MAJ. NATHANIEL BUCKMASTER.

THE BLACK HAWK WAR.

States, and have had the audacity to drive citizens of the State of Illinois from their homes, to destroy their corn, and to invite many of their old friends of the Pottawatomies, Winnebagoes and Kickapoos to unite with them (the said British Band of Sacs) in war, to prevent their removal from said lands: And, Whereas, many of the most disorderly of these several tribes of Indians did actually join the said British Band of Sac Indians, prepared for war against the United States, and more particularly against the State of Illinois, from which purpose they confess that nothing could have restrained them but the appearance of force far exceeding the combined strength of the said British Band of Sac Indians, with such of their aforesaid allies as had actually joined them; but being now convinced that such a war would tend speedily to annihilate them, they have voluntarily abandoned their hostile attitude and sued for peace.

"First—Peace is therefore given to them upon the following conditions, to which the said British Band of Sac Indians, with their aforesaid allies, do agree; and for the faithful execution of which the undersigned chiefs and braves of the said band, and their allies, mutually bind themselves, their heirs and assigns forever.

"Second—The British Band of Sac Indians are required peaceably to submit to the authority of the friendly chiefs and braves of the United Sac and Fox nations, and at all times hereafter to reside and hunt with them upon their own lands west of the Mississippi River, and to be obedient to their laws and treaties; and no one or more of the said band shall ever be permitted to recross this river to the place of their usual residence, nor to any part of their old hunting grounds east of the Mississippi, without the express permission of the President of the United States or the Governor of the State of Illinois.

"Third—The United States will guarantee to the united Sac and Fox nations, including the said British Band of Sac Indians, the integrity of all the lands claimed by them westward of the Mississippi River pursuant to the treaties of the years 1825 and 1830.

"Fourth—The United States require the united Sac and Fox nation, including the aforesaid British Band, to abandon all communication, and cease to hold any intercourse with any British post, garrison, or town; and never again to admit among them any agent or trader who shall not have derived his authority to hold commercial or other intercourse with them by license, from the President of the United States or his authorized agent.

"Fifth—The United States demand an acknowledgment of their right to establish military posts and roads within the limits of the said country guaranteed by the third article of this agreement and capitulation, for the protection of the frontier inhabitants.

"Sixth—It is further agreed by the United States, that the principal friendly chiefs and head-men of the Sacs and Foxes bind themselves to enforce, as far as may be in their power, the strict observance of each and every article of this agreement and capitulation; and at any time they may find themselves unable to restrain their allies, the Pottawatomies, Kickapoos, or Winnebagoes, to give immediate information thereof to the nearest military post.

"Seventh—And it is finally agreed by the contracting parties, that henceforth permanent peace and friendship be established between the United States and the aforesaid band of Indians.

"In Witness Whereof, we have set our hands, the date above mentioned.
"Edmund P. Gaines,
"Major-General by Brevet, Commanding.
"John Reynolds,
"Governor of the State of Illinois."

CHIEFS.

Pash-e-pa-ho	Stabbing Chief	his X mark
Washut	Sturgeon Head	his X mark
Cha-kee-pax-he-pa-ho	Little Stabbing Chief	his X mark
Chick-a-ka-la-ko	Turtle Shell	his X mark
Pem-e-see	the one that flies	his X mark

WARRIORS AND BRAVES.

Ma-ca-la-mich-i-ca-tak	the Black Hawk	his X mark
Men-a-con	the Seed	his X mark
Ka-ke-ka-mah	all Fish	his X mark
Nee-peek	Water	his X mark
A-sam-e-saw	the one that flies too fast	his X mark
Pan-see-na-nee	Paunceman	his X mark
Wa-wap-o-la-sa	White Walker	his X mark
Wa-pa-qunt	White Hare	his X mark
Ke-o-sa-tah	Walker	his X mark

FOX CHIEFS.

Wa-pa-la	the Prince	his X mark
Kee-tee-see	the Eagle	his X mark
Pa-we-sheek	one that sifts through	his X mark
Na-mee	one that has gone	his X mark

FOX BRAVES AND WARRIORS.

Al-lo-tah	Morgan	his X mark
Ka-ka-kew	the Crow	his X mark
She-she-qua-nas	Little Gourd	his X mark
Koe-ko-skee		his X mark
Ta-ko-na	the Prisoner	his X mark
Na-kis-ka-wa	the one that meets	his X mark
Pa-ma-ke-tah	the one that stands about	his X mark
To-po-kia	the Night	his X mark
Mo-lan-sat	the one that has his hair pulled out	his X mark
Ka-ke-me-ka-peo	sitting in the grease	his X mark

WITNESSES.

Joseph M. Street, U. S. Indian Agent at Prairie du Chien.
W. Morgan, Colonel 1st Infantry
J. Bliss, Brevet Major 1st Infantry.
Geo. A. M'Call, aid-de-camp to Maj.-Gen. Gaines.
Sam'l Whiteside.
Felix St. Vrain, Indian Agent.
John S. Greathouse.
M. K. Alexander.
A. S. West.
Antoine LeClaire, Interpreter.
Jos. Danforth.
Dan S. Witter.
Benj. F. Pike.[1]

---

[1] Ex. Doc. B, 1st Sess. 22d Congress, p. 187.

THE BLACK HAWK WAR.

During the progress of this treaty the women and children remained encamped on the west bank of the river, reduced by the improvidence of the men to the extremity of starvation. In many cases they had nothing to cover their nakedness, presenting a spectacle so appealing to Gaines and Reynolds that the former took from the general store of provisions and delivered to Black Hawk and his band a quantity sufficient to tide them over until another crop should have been gathered. Black Hawk accepted them and went his way with many protestations of satisfaction.

Black Hawk in his book has stated that at this time he was perfectly willing to remove to the west bank of the river for a cash consideration of $10,000 to himself, and thus abandon his village and the graves of his fathers. Rather a sordid ultimatum for a patriot!

The regular troops reached Jefferson Barracks on their return, July 6th, and the volunteers, in riding to their various counties, required a little more time. The latter, who had hoped to end the controversies with Black Hawk in an open fight, were loud in their protests when they discovered that instead of bullets the Indians were to receive provisions, calling the expedition a corn war and other names of ridicule, but the sober judge of all the circumstances will render his opinion in favor of the justness of Gaines' and Reynolds' actions.

CHAPTER XIV.

UNREST—MESSENGERS AND WAR PARTIES SENT OUT—ATTACK ON THE SIOUX—THEY RETALIATE—ATTACK ON THE MENOMINEES—A COUNCIL.

The Sioux and Sacs and Foxes had been enemies for generations. Predatory excursions by each nation into the other's country had decimated the ranks of both, until the Government found it necessary to interfere and demand a treaty of peace between them. Accordingly, on the 19 of August, 1825, William Clark and Lewis Cass, as commissioners on behalf of the United States, met representatives from the Chippewas, Sacs and Foxes, Sioux, Menominees, Winnebagoes, Iowas and portions of the Ottawas and Pottowattomies at Prairie du Chien, where the first step toward a general peace was taken by making a treaty wherein it was finally agreed (Article 2) that the United States should run a boundary line between the Sioux on the north and the Sacs and Foxes on the south, as follows: Commencing at the mouth of Upper Iowa River, on the west bank of the Mississippi, and ascending said Iowa River to its left fork; thence up the fork to its source; thence crossing the fork of Red Cedar River in a direct line to the second or upper fork of the Des Moines River; thence in a direct line to the lower fork of the Calumet (Big Sioux) River, and down that river to its junction with the Missouri River.[1]

Article 1 provided for a perpetual peace between the Sioux and Chippewas and confederated tribes of Sacs and Foxes and between the Iowas and Sioux.

Article 7 determined the boundaries of the Winnebago country in Illinois and Wisconsin, most of which, including the lead mines, the Sacs and Foxes had claimed and ceded by the treaty of 1804, and which fact, when considered, brings the consideration for the lands actually acquired within reason.

Article 9 defined the boundaries of the territory of the Ottawas, Chippewas and Pottowattomies, none of which the Sacs and Foxes ever owned, though they conveyed it by the treaty of 1804.

This treaty of 1825, recognizing the right of the United States to

---
[1]Peters' U. S. Stat. at Large, Vol. vii, p. 272.

GEN. JOSEPH M. STREET.

GEN. LEWIS CASS.

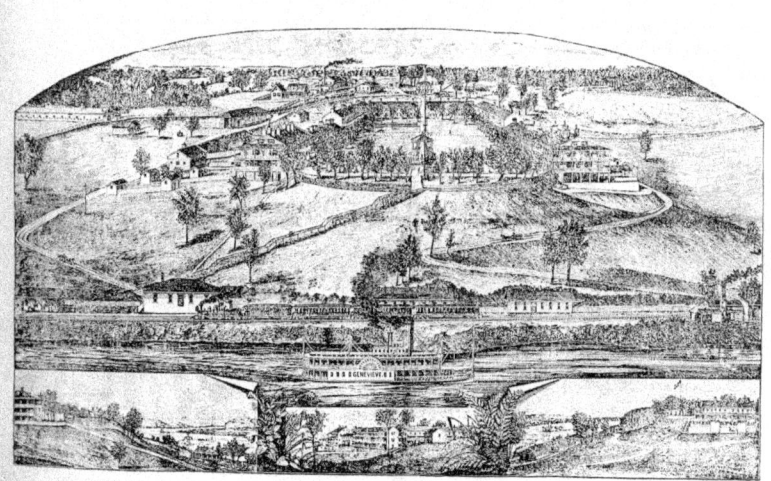
JEFFERSON BARRACKS.

sundry other lands theretofore ceded by the Sacs and Foxes, over which they had some shadow of authority, drew the line immediately north of the Black Hawk village,[1] and this fact may have caused the impression by some of the Indians, designedly or otherwise, that the treaty of 1804 contained the same stipulation.

By Article 10 "all the tribes aforesaid acknowledge the general controlling power of the United States, and disclaim all dependence upon and connection with any other power."

Evidently the pact relating to peace between the Sioux and Sacs and Foxes had been avoided or disputed by one or both the subscribing parties, for on July 15th, 1830, at Prairie du Chien, it became necessary to call another council and make another treaty whereby the Sacs and Foxes ceded to the United States a strip of country twenty miles in width, lying south of the line established by the treaty of August 19, 1825, and extending along on the south side of said line from the Mississippi to the Des Moines. In the same treaty the Sioux ceded to the United States a like strip twenty miles wide, extending along the north side of said line from the Mississippi to the Des Moines. This forty-mile trip was known as the "Neutral Ground," into which the tribes on either side of the line were allowed to enter and hunt and fish unmolested.

Unmindful of these treaties, however, we find a war party of Sacs and Foxes, in 1831, near the headwaters of Blue Earth River, pouncing upon some unoffending Sioux and murdering two of them in cold blood,[2] as will be seen by the following:

"Indian Agency, St. Peters,
"August 8, 1831.

"General:—What I have always feared and what has been predicted by me, in the most decided form, has recently taken place. The Sac or Fox Indians, about forty, invaded the Sioux territory on or about the 25th of last month (July). These were *mounted men*, who penetrated the country as far as Cintajah, or the Grey Tail, near the headwaters of the Terre Blue River, which is a tributary of the St. Peter's, and contiguous to this post. *There is no mistake; the Sac Indians have killed* two of the most respectable men of the Wahpakoota Sioux, at the time and place above stated, and this, too, at least *sixty miles from the ceded territory*, as concluded upon at the treaty of July, 1830, at Prairie du Chien. The Wahpakootas ask for immediate redress, and I beg leave to assure you that the sooner their *just* expectations in this important matter be met, the better for *me* and for this country. I mean after what was promised by the Government, through the commissioners, at the treaty of 1830, in presence of the assembled tribes. The Sacs lost one man in their attack upon the Sioux, who were in sight of their encampment at the time.

"I have written to Col. Morgan, or officer commanding the troops at Prairie du Chien, a copy of which letter is herewith enclosed. I have not gone much into detail, as the matter in question does not admit of delay. The *traders* must lose $20,000 worth of credits already given for the country in possession of the

---

[1]See same in map of "Military Tract."
[2]Vol. 2, Wis. Hist. Colls., p. 170.

Wahpakootas, if the present difficulty be not very speedily adjusted. I have the honor to be, with the highest respect, sir, your obedient servant,

"LAW. TALIAFERRO,
"Indian Agent, St. Peters.

"GENERAL WILLIAM CLARK,
"Superintendent of Indian Affairs."

"Indian Agency, St. Peters, August 12, 1831.

"General:—I declined sending off my express on the 8th inst., understanding that one of the Wahpakoota chiefs would be here in a day or two. Tah-sau-gah-now, the principal chief, reached this place last night, and confirms the statement made to you on the 8th as to the attack of the Sac Indians upon his people. He desires me to say to you, that in a few days you may expect to hear of a number more of his people losing their scalps, as there was considerable firing heard in the direction of the camp of the second chief, from whom he had separated but the day previous. The Sacs scalped the two Sioux, after which their bodies, together with the Sac killed in the conflict, were buried by the Wahpakootas. The chief wishes me to state further to you, that it is his intention, at my earnest request, to remain quiet until the first of October, when, if the Government settles the difficulty as declared at the treaty of Prairie du Chien, his people will be satisfied; otherwise, they will, with all their force, carry the war into the Sac country to protect themselves. He also states that he has a heart, and it is hard for him to see his people shot down like the buffalo on the lands acknowledged by all nations to belong to them. I have the honor to be, with high respect, sir, your obedient servant,

"LAW. TALIAFERRO,
"Indian Agent, St. Peters.

"GENERAL WILLIAM CLARK,
"Superintendent of Indian Affairs at St. Louis."

Notwithstanding the promise to wait, this unprovoked attack aroused other bands of the Sioux, who lost no time avenging the act in the following manner: A band of the Foxes living near the Dubuque mines had made an engagement to meet the agent at Prairie du Chien. Learning of this contemplated visit, one John Marsh informed the Sioux of the time and place thereof. Between midnight and the morning of the day fixed for the approach of the Foxes, a band of Sioux, which had been joined by a few young Menominees, passed down the river some twelve or fifteen miles below Prairie du Chien, where a thick growth of bushes afforded ample opportunity for an ambush. The channel there was narrow, with less current than a broader, and was the one always selected by Indians for voyaging upon the river. Kettle, the Fox chief, was leading his party up the channel in person, when, passing the point of bushes there, the Sioux and Menominees opened fire, killing Kettle and several of his followers. The frightened Foxes fled to their Dubuque village, while the Sioux and Menominees returned home to dance over the event.

No action was taken against them by the authorities, for the reason, perhaps, that the act was retaliatory, *lex talionis* being the law of the Indian, treaty or no treaty.[1]

---

[1] Keokuk, as will be seen later, said the matter was "made all good and even," but no record of the transaction is to be found.

Black Hawk, after his fiasco of 1831, had retired to the west side of the Mississippi. He had agreed to remain tranquil; his people had been provided with enough to maintain a provident band through the ensuing winter, but no sooner had the soldiers dispersed than he began fomenting trouble, and trying, as he had tried in 1831, to form a confederacy to fight the whites. War parties of various sizes were soon on foot to stir up trouble with those Indians then known to be on good terms with the whites, as will be set forth in the correspondence which I have seen fit to copy in full rather than make extracts.

"Cantonment Leavenworth, July 29, 1831.

"Sir:—Last night two young men of the Ioway tribe arrived at this post on express for the purpose of informing me that about 120 Sacs from the Mississippi, in three different war parties, were on the way up the Mississippi in search of the Ottoes, Omahas or Sioux. I immediately sent off a runner to apprise all the Indians above this, and put them on their guard. One of these parties passed the Ioway village, proceeded on, and crossed the Missouri at the Black Snake Hills, and are now on this side somewhere above this place. Four men of this last party turned back from the Ioway village and bore off with them two horses belonging to one of our citizens in Clay county. I understand the whites have pursued them.

"On the 21st instant, 32 Sacs from Rock River passed this point on their way to the Osage towns. They were accompanied by two Osages, one of whom called himself the son of Clament. I think it highly probable that these Rock River Sacs will give us much trouble in this quarter. I have the honor, etc.,

"JOHN DOUGHERTY,
To GEN. WM. CLARK, "Indian Agent.
Supt. Indian Affairs."

On July 30th, 1831, a band of Menominees, having business with the agent at Prairie du Chien, was assembled on an island almost under the guns of the fort. Menominees loved whisky, and these Indians drank themselves socially full, carrying their revels far into the night, when further drinking put them entirely *hors de combat*. About two hours before daylight of the 31st a war party of Sacs and Foxes, which had been watching the debauch, fell upon the helpless Menominees, killed twenty-five of them outright and wounded others. A few, less confused by liquor, roused themselves and pursued the Sacs and Foxes a short distance without doing more damage than wounding a few. The women, fearing possible harm to each other, had hidden all the firearms to be found, thus leaving the Menominees doubly insecure.

The Sacs and Foxes fled direct to Black Hawk's camp, and about that individual secreted themselves beyond discovery.

Those Menominees, while lovers of whisky, were pronounced by Hon. James H. Lockwood, who was present at Prairie du Chien at the time, and who was intimately acquainted with Menominee character, to be, with surprisingly few exceptions, a quiet, peaceable race, Tomah, the then acting chief, occupying in Menominee annals a high character for ability and exemplary enterprises.

"United States Indian Agency,
At Prairie du Chien, August 1, 1831.

"Sir:—One year had scarcely elapsed after the sealing of the treaty of 1830 at this place, before one of the parties has broken its solemn engagements, and dyed the scene of the ratification in the blood of those Indians whom they took by the hand in the presence of their great father's commissioners.

"Two or three hours before day, on the morning of the 31st July, a party consisting of 80 or 100 Sacs and Foxes surprised a Menominee camp, three or four hundred paces above old Fort Crawford, on the east side of the Mississippi, and killed twenty-five of the latter, and wounded many who may probably recover. There were about thirty or forty Menominees, men, women and children, in the camp, most of whom were drunk, and the women had hidden their guns and knives, to prevent their hurting each other. The Sacs and Foxes, though so greatly superior in numbers, and attacking by surprise a drunken and unarmed encampment, lost several men who were seen to fall in the onset, and retreated in less than ten minutes, with only a few scalps, pursued by four or five Menominees, who fired on them until they were half a mile below the village. I received information, and was on the ground in an hour and a half after the murders were committed. The butchery was horrid, and the view can only be imagined by those acquainted with savage warfare.

"At seven o'clock a. m., I addressed the letter marked 'A' to the officer commanding at Fort Crawford, giving him the first intimation of the massacre, and received in answer his letter of this date, marked 'B'. Lieut. Lamotte, stationed on the west bank of the Mississippi, two miles below Prairie du Chien, saw the Indians pass up about 9 o'clock p. m. the night the murders were committed and again saw them descend with great rapidity at daylight the next morning.

An express was dispatched by the commanding officer here to Rock Island at two o'clock on the day of the murders; but no other steps to arrest these daring violators of the provisions of the treaty of July, 1830, have, as I believe, been taken.

"To-day, the remaining Menominees asked to speak to me, and I met them accordingly. They complain of the violation of the treaty, and say they have fallen victims to their confidence in the security that was promised them under the sanctions of a treaty made in the presence of their fathers, Gen. Clark and Col. Morgan. That Col. Morgan promised them a free and secure path to this place, and that if they were struck, he would march an army of his warriors into the country of those who struck them with their warriors, and take man for man of their enemies. They say they have lost many of their bravest men. 'One of our chiefs has lost all his family; his wife and his children and his brother were all murdered, and he is left alone. He is not here; he is in his lodge mourning.' They added, 'Take pity on our women and our orphan children, and give us something to console us, and we will wait a while to see if our great father, whom you tell us is strong, will help us to punish those Sacs and Foxes, who shake hands and smoke the pipe of peace to-day, and to-morrow break it and kill those they smoked with.' Under existing circumstances, I deemed it prudent and humane to give them a few things and to provide some necessaries for their destitute children, the amount of which I will forward by mail. I also promised to lay the affair before their great father, the President, and ask him to have justice done for them agreeably to their treaty, if they would go into their country and remain quiet. They have promised to do so a short time, yet I learn from other sources that runners have been dispatched to Green Bay and among the Sioux.

The Menominees also complain that they were promised that if they would be quiet, their great father would see justice done between them and the Chippeways. That nothing is done, nor are their dead covered. They remarked, 'Shall we remain quiet on the faith of our great father until we are all killed? When will our great father answer us?'

"They inform me that a white man (a discharged soldier from St. Peters) had killed a Menominee a few days past. On inquiry I learned that the white man had a fight with two Indians, and in the fight he struck the Indian on the head with a stick and fractured his skull, and he died the day after. There is no white person who can testify anything about it, and the white man has gone off, I know not where.

"I have received no answer to my letters respecting the murder of the Menominees by the Chippeways, and am unable to satisfy them on that subject. I now hope that on the present representation of facts, the Government will feel the necessity of a prompt interference, to save this fort from a general rupture.

"The pacification of July, 1830, has been violated under the guns of Fort Crawford, and if some immediate course is not taken to chastise those violators of that solemn arrangement, the influence of the officers of the United States will be destroyed and the power of the Government disregarded by the Indians.

"Respectfully, etc., etc.,

"Jos. M. STREET, Indian Agent.

"GEN. WILLIAM CLARK, Superintendent of Indian Affairs at St. Louis."

"U. S. Indian Agency at Prairie du Chien,
July 31, 1831, 7 o'clock A. M.

"Sir:—After a personal inspection of the scene of massacre, I hasten to inform you that last night the Sacs and Foxes struck the Menominees, encamped on the east side of the Mississippi, about three or four hundred paces above old Fort Crawford, and killed twenty-four[1] of the latter, butchering them in a most shocking manner.

"The Sacs and Foxes came up and left their canoes just above the old fort and completely surprised the Menominees, who, under the sanction of the peace of 1830 at this place, and their vicinity to the fort, were unsuspicious of danger.

"The attack was made about two hours before daylight, and the assailants were gone before light.

"So daring a violation of the treaty of July, 1830, made at this village, and within cannon shot of the fort, evinces a spirit little in accordance with its humane and pacific object.

"I am also this moment informed that runners will be immediately dispatched by the Menominees to Green Bay and to the Sioux.

"I shall be at Judge Lockwood's during the day.

"Respectfully yours, etc.,

"JOSEPH M. STREET, U. S. Indian Agent.

"To CAPT. G. LOOMIS, Commanding Fort Crawford."

"Superintendency of Indian Affairs,
"St. Louis, Sept. 12, 1831.

"Sir:—I have the honor to acknowledge the receipt of your letter of the 26th ult. on the subject of the late violation of the treaty of Prairie du Chien by the

---

[1] Twenty-five.

Fox Indians; and have, in accordance with your instructions, given the necessary directions to the agent at Rock Island to convene the chiefs of the Fox tribes, etc., at that place, to meet, if possible, on the 26th inst. Col. Morgan will, agreeably to the directions of Gen. Atkinson, be present at the council and will make the necessary demand of a surrender of the principal men connected with the outrage complained of; and I have reason to believe that if the requirements of the act of intercourse of 1802, as well as the stipulations of the treaty of 1825, shall be strictly complied with, it will be owing to the prompt and decisive measures pursued by the department. The result of this council shall be promptly communicated.

"I take the liberty of enclosing to you herewith two letters from Major Taliaferro, of the 8th and 12th August, and one from Gen. Street, received by the last mail, charging the Sacs with another violation of the treaty of 1825. The facts, however, in relation to this last affair have been differently stated by the Sacs, who were the first (it appears) to commence them. They say that the affair took place on their own land, on the waters of the Ioway River; that a party of the Sioux, in a buffalo chase, fired upon some of their people and killed a Sac, and that the rest of their people coming up, pursued the Sioux, and killed two of them.[1] I have the honor to be, with high respect, Your most obedient servant,

"WM. CLARK.

"The HON. LEWIS CASS, Secretary of War."

"Rock Island Indian Agency,
"September 10, 1831.

"Respected Sir:—I have been informed, and it is currently reported, that two Sioux and three Sac Indians met in a prairie, within the limits of the Sac and Fox lands; that one of the Sacs went up towards the Sioux with the intention of shaking hands with them; but the Sioux refused and threw off their blankets and breech cloths, evidently showing an unfriendly disposition towards the Sacs; the Sac still continued approaching them until they shot him dead. The other two Sacs, who had been concealed from the view of the Sioux, pursued them until they killed both the Sioux. This is the report of the Sac Indians.[2]

"I, in concert with Major Bliss, called a council of the principal chiefs of the Sac and Fox Indians for the purpose of demanding the leaders of the band which were concerned in the massacre at Prairie du Chien. The result is as contained in the enclosed journal, which was kept for the purpose. The Indians remained at this place about four days; they got credit from their traders and departed with the intention of making an immediate move to their hunting grounds. I presume that you have heard of the death of Morgan, the Fox brave. One of his followers, after hearing of the circumstance, said that it was useless for him to live any longer, now that Morgan was no more. He took his rifle and went out and shot himself.

"Since writing the above, Captain Low told me that the Menominees were preparing to march against the Sacs and Foxes, and that they would listen to no one, but were determined to take revenge. Should I get any further information on the subject, I will immediately inform you of it. I have the honor to be Your obedient servant,

"FELIX ST. VRAIN, Indian Agent.

"GENERAL WILLIAM CLARK,
"Superintendent Indian Affairs, St. Louis."

---

[1] Untrue in every respect. Every Sac who attempted an explanation had a widely different version.

[2] Substantially different from the other version and painfully unreal.

"JOURNAL OF A COUNCIL HELD WITH THE CHIEFS AND WARRIORS OF THE SAC AND FOX INDIANS AT FORT ARMSTRONG ON THE FIFTH SEPTEMBER, 1831, BY MAJOR BLISS, FIRST INFANTRY, COMMANDING, AND FELIX ST. VRAIN, THE U. S. AGENT.

"At about 12 o'clock the council was opened by the commanding officer, as follows:

'Chiefs and Warriors of the Sacs and Foxes: By the treaty of Prairie du Chien, made at the request of the President of the United States with the Sioux, Menominees and other Indian tribes, you solemnly promised and agreed that there should be peace between you and those tribes. You also agreed that if either tribe should attack either of the other tribes, that the persons of those who should be concerned in the outrage should be delivered up to the officers of the United States. About four or five nights since a war party of Foxes and some Sacs, led on by Pash-qua-mee, attacked a peaceable party of Menominees near Fort Crawford and killed 26 men, women and children. Wrong has been done and the treaty of Prairie du Chien has been violated.

"It becomes our duty, therefore, as officers of the United States, to demand that you, the chiefs and warriors of the Sac and Fox Indians, deliver and surrender to us Pash-qua-mee and all the principal Indians of the Sacs and Foxes who were engaged in this late massacre of the Menominees near Fort Crawford, and we do demand them. We wait for your answer. We hope it may be such as to convince the President, the Great Council and the citizens of the United States that the Sacs and Foxes are not liars; that they always speak truth and perform as they promise.'

"After a short delay, Tiornay (the Strawberry), a Fox chief, replied: 'My Father: I have heard you and the commanding officer. We were all at the treaty at Prairie du Chien. We have the talk in our minds. All the chiefs you see here have told the young men left behind all that was said at that time. It is because you do not know our manners that you think ill of this. When we hear of a war party going out, we do all in our power to stop it. You have heard what I say. We did not tell them to go to war.

"'My Father and Commanding Officer: How can we stop our men, when your white men cannot stop the whites from committing crimes? Both of our cases are hard; our young men will not do what we wish, and yours act in the same way. This is all I have to say.'

"Kottekennekak, the Bald Eagle, a Fox brave, then said: 'My Father: Though we were all at Prairie du Chien, how can we stop our young men? They go off while we are asleep and we know nothing of it. It was not by our consent that the young men struck the Menominees at Prairie du Chien. We have done all we could; but the young men will not listen to us.'

"Quash-quah-ing, the Jumping Fish, a British chief: 'My Father and my Friends: All the chiefs are dead and the young men have told me to speak for them. You tell the truth about the treaty at Prairie du Chien, but the Menominees struck us first and we struck back. The chiefs have said, "Do not let us strike first." What do you expect us to do? We only do what our old chiefs have told us. The chiefs that have spoken told the truth; but what can we do when our young men will not listen?'

"Keokuk, he that has been everywhere, a Sac brave:

"'You tell the truth about the treaty at Prairie du Chien. I was there myself; but you tell a little more. After the treaty was concluded at Prairie du Chien, I and four chiefs went to General Clark and Colonel Morgan and said to them, "What will you do with those that strike first?" They told us that the principal men should be delivered. This is what I mean when I say "a little more." It was then discovered and explained that the word "principal" had not been interpreted.

"'My old man (pointing to Quash-quah-ing) did not understand. After the affair of last year we went to General Clark and Colonel Morgan and, notwithstanding the attack of the Menominees, they made all good and even. But now, if what they did and what we have now done was put in scales, it would balance. I expect it is because our names are Sacs and Foxes that you make a noise about it. When we do the least thing, you make a great noise about it. Last winter I went to the Missouri. There an Ioway killed an Omaha. Why was he not hung? They were at the treaty. The reason I say so much against you is because our hearts are good. Our chiefs were killed with the pipe of peace and the wampum in their hands. This is all I have to say. As for my chiefs and braves, they will do as they please. I have said all that I have to say; but why do you not let us fight? Your whites are constantly fighting. They are now fighting way east. Why do you not interfere with them? Why do you not let us be as the Great Spirit made us, and let us settle our difficulties?'"

As this speech of Keokuk's was received by the Indians with applause for its ingenuity, the commanding officer thought it proper to add that such treaties as were made at Prairie du Chien were frequently made between the white nations at the east and enforced.

That it was not because they were Sacs that the present demand was made, but because it was not wished that the Sacs would become liars. That as it regarded the Omahas, whenever they demanded redress for the murder from the United States, it would then be time to interfere. That the affair did not concern the Sacs.

James H. Lockwood, Vol. 2, p. 170, and John H. Fonda, Vol. 5, p. 256, in writing of these events from memory for the Wisconsin Historical Collections, fixed upon the year 1830 for the murders of the Sioux and Kettle's Foxes, Fonda including the Menominee affair in the same year. A. R. Fulton, in his "Red Men of Iowa," inferentially used the same year for the three events; all agreed that the three followed in *rapid* succession. Lockwood has made so many glaring errors in other parts of his narrative that it is easy to believe that he was wrong in placing any of them in 1830. The three affairs did occur with unusual propinquity of succession, but in 1831, as the contemporaneous reports herein given have shown, and which must be believed against memory. L. C. Draper, usually accurate, fell into Lockwood's mistake in his note to Fonda's letter, by not taking time to investigate.

CHAPTER XV.

NE-A-POPE'S MISSION—KEOKUK'S VILLAGE—COUNCIL—BLACK HAWK MOVES DOWN IOWA RIVER AND UP THE MISSISSIPPI TO ROCK RIVER —ATKINSON MOVES UP TO FORT ARMSTRONG.

With these contentious spirits, Black Hawk, restless Black Hawk, employed his genius, sending out runners to all points of the compass, some going as far as the Gulf of Mexico, to rally round him the confederacy which Tecumseh attempted, but who, with his transcendent genius for organization and war, failed, and so did Black Hawk, much more ingloriously, though assured by his runners of an irresistible force to join him the moment he rose to strike the whites. He had in 1831 sent his lieutenant, Ne-a-pope,[1] to the British in Canada to solicit aid. That Indian, inauspiciously returning through the village of Wa-bo-ki-e-shiek, the crossbred Winnebago prophet, who lived at his village on the left bank of Rock River forty miles from its mouth, told the latter vicious meddler of the object of the Canadian trip. The unscrupulous prophet, delighted at the possibility of making trouble for the whites, performed for Ne-a-pope numerous incantations, received a few visions, and made a prophecy that if Black Hawk would take up the hatchet once more against the whites he would be joined by the Great Spirit and a great army of worldlings, and in no time at all he would vanquish the whites and be restored to his ancient village. It is more than probable that this hocuspocus had great influence with Black Hawk, which, added to Ne-a-pope's falsehoods, determined Black Hawk to open another campaign against the whites without delay. To begin with, his followers had wantonly wasted their provisions, and even before winter had set in he had inaugurated nightly raids upon the storehouses of the whites, stealing the grain and vegetables there stored with a devilish glee. These raids continued with exasperating frequency and regularity all winter and spring. He even brought himself to believe that he could easily create dissension among the followers of Keokuk and overthrow his power entirely.

Emissaries from the camp of Black Hawk had been busy in Keokuk's village on the Iowa River,[2] and, by insidious industry, murmurs began arising upon all sides. Seizing this supreme moment, while Keokuk's

---
[1]Pronounced Naw-pope.
[2]Fulton's Red Men, 233.

reputation, influence and life, perhaps, were quivering in the balance, Black Hawk threw off the mask and defiantly marched with his entire force to Keokuk's village to dispute the supremacy of Keokuk, steal away his warriors and wage war upon the whites.

There at the village all was bustle and confusion. The rifle was loaded and the knife and the hatchet strapped about the warriors' loins. They had importuned Keokuk to lead them to battle, and so subtle had been the work of Black Hawk's men that those importunities could not be ignored. The torrent of a mighty and heedless anger raged and carried conservatism, treaties, sentiment and every motive before it. Menaced now by Black Hawk, who had so recently solemnly promised to behave himself for all time, every frontier family stood in danger of the tomahawk. Had the united Sacs and Foxes levied war against the whites, the wavering tribes from Illinois north might have joined them and devastated the country and desolated every hearth.

Black Hawk harangued the Indians with all his energy, firing them to a pitch of excitement he had not expected and compelling Keokuk then and there to promise to lead them to war; but in promising he, like Antony, was permitted to make a speech—and like Antony's it swayed the mob—against Black Hawk.

"Kill your old men and squaws and children," cried he, "for never will you live to see them more,"[1] and haste was urged in doing it. An electric wave from the skies never could have stricken those howling beasts of the moment before as did that condition precedent. "You have been imposed upon by liars," he shouted, and when he had finished speaking, he stood, a conqueror, in a silence inspired by awe, and Black Hawk and his band moved sullenly down the river to war upon the whites once too often.

It has been said, and no doubt truly, that one Josiah Smart,[2] the representative of George Davenport, was present to learn of Black Hawk's success and was so secreted as to overhear every word of those memorable proceedings, and for their truth he has vouched.

On April 1, 1832, Gen. Henry Atkinson, then in command at Jefferson Barracks, received an order dated March 17th, announcing the determination of the Government to interfere and demand from the Sacs and Foxes at least eight or ten of the principal murderers of the Menominees. In obedience to that order, General Atkinson started on April 8th for the upper Mississippi with six companies of the Sixth Infantry (220 men) and the following officers of the expedition, in the steamboats Enterprise and Chieftain:,

Brig.-Gen. Henry Atkinson, Commanding.
Brev. Maj. Bennet Riley, Commanding 6th Regiment.

---

[1] Almost identical with the speech of Cornstalk at Chillicothe, just after the battle of Point Pleasant.
[2] Armstrong.

THE BLACK HAWK WAR. 111

Capt. Zalmon C. Palmer, 6th Regiment.
Capt. Henry Smith, 6th Regiment.
Capt. Thomas Noel, 6th Regiment.
Capt. Jason Rogers, 6th Regiment.
Capt. George C. Hutter, 6th Regiment.
First Lieut. Asa Richardson, 6th Regiment.
First Lieut. J. Van Swearengen, 6th Regiment.
Second Lieut. Albert Sidney Johnston, 6th Regiment, Asst. to Adjt. Gen.
Second Lieut. Joseph D. Searight, 6th Regiment.
Second Lieut. Nathaniel J. Eaton, 6th Regiment, Acting Commissary of Subsistence.
Brevet Second Lieut. T. L. Alexander, 6th Regiment, Adjutant of Detachment.
Brevet Second Lieut. Thomas J. Royster, 6th Regiment.
J. S. Van Derveer, 6th Regiment.
J. S. Williams, 6th Regiment.
Second Lieut. W. Wheelwright, 1st Artillery, Ordnance Officer.
Will Carr Lane, Surgeon.
Maj. Thomas Wright, Paymaster.

On April 10th the expedition arrived at the rapids of the Des Moines about 2 P. M., where General Atkinson was informed that Black Hawk on the 6th had crossed to the east bank of the Mississippi, near the mouth of the lower Iowa, with 400 or 500 horsemen, beside others to portage canoes, making a total force able to bear arms of over 500 men, the whole band, men, women and children, amounting, as then estimated, to about 2,000 souls,[1] and going, as Black Hawk has told in his book, "to make corn."

---

[1] Life of A. S. Johnston, p. 33.

CHAPTER XVI.

COUNCIL—ATKINSON'S CALL FOR TROOPS—REYNOLDS' PROCLAMATION—BLACK HAWK DEFIANT—GRATIOT'S JOURNEY.

What the intentions of General Atkinson might have been, above his actual instructions, when leaving St. Louis, are entirely conjectural. The same may be said with reference to the 10th, but when he arrived at Fort Armstrong, during the night of the 12th, they are plainly evident.

On the 13th, at 10 A. M., he called a council, at which Keokuk and his head men, some seventy in number, including Wapello, attended, and there he demanded the surrender of ten of the principal men concerned in the murders. Keokuk replied that he was unable to deliver them up because some had joined the Prophet's band at his village, toward which Black Hawk was then rapidly marching along the left bank of Rock River, and the others were with Black Hawk.

When first the demand was made the Indians retired to the plain close by to consult. On determining on the foregoing statements among other things, Keokuk returned and finished his talk as follows: "You wish us to keep at peace and have nothing to do with the Rock River Indians. We will do so. In token of our intentions, you see we have laid our spears there together. While you are gone to Prairie du Chien we will endeavor to speak to Black Hawk's band and try to persuade them to go back. If we do not succeed, I can do no more; then we will go home and try to keep our village at peace. The one who has raised all this trouble is a Winnebago called the Prophet." Wapello spoke to the same effect.

As it was evident that Keokuk, by reason of his continued acts of friendship, might lose much of his influence if too much were exacted of him, all demands, including hostages, which were first asked, were waived and the council adjourned to the 19th of April.

General Atkinson immediately started up the river for Fort Crawford, where he secured all the reinforcements which could be spared from that garrison; at the same time he sent messengers to Fort Winnebago and the lead mines district to admonish the settlers to place themselves in a state of defense.

Lieut.-Col. Zachary Taylor, with two companies of the First Infantry, returned with Atkinson to Fort Armstrong, which was reached

GEN. HENRY ATKINSON.

CAPT. HENRY SMITH, U. S. A.

GEORGE DAVENPORT, ASSISTANT QUARTERMASTER.

LIEUT. N. J. EATON, U. S. A.

LIEUT. M. L. CLARK, U. S. A.

on the 19th. Immediately after the conclusion of the council on the 13th, General Atkinson dispatched a letter to Governor Reynolds, who had not been idle, asking the latter for the assistance again of his militia, to drive Black Hawk and his band from the State once more. Promptly on the 16th, the Governor responded with a call for an indefinite number of men, accompanied by this appeal:

"To the MILITIA OF THE NORTHWESTERN SECTION OF THE STATE.

"FELLOW CITIZENS:

"Your country requires your services. The Indians have assumed a hostile attitude and have invaded the State in violation of the treaty of last summer.

"The British band of Sacs and other hostile Indians, headed by Black Hawk, are in possession of the Rock River country, to the great terror of the frontier inhabitants. I consider the settlers on the frontiers to be in imminent danger.

"I am in possession of the above information from gentlemen of respectable standing, and also from General Atkinson, whose character stands high with all classes.

"In possession of the above facts and information, I have hesitated not as to the course I should pursue. No citizen ought to remain inactive when his country is invaded and the helpless part of the community are in danger. I have called out a strong detachment of militia to rendezvous at Beardstown on the 22d inst.

"Provisions for the men and food for the horses will be furnished in abundance.

"I hope my countrymen will realize my expectations and offer their services as heretofore, with promptitude and cheerfulness in defense of their country."

Meantime, to protect the frontier, he on the same day called for a battalion of 200 militia under Major Isaiah Stillman of Fulton County, to patrol the country to the north and westward. On the 20th Judge Richard M. Young, Col. James M. Strode and Benjamin Mills wrote from Dixon's Ferry to the Governor, urging haste in protecting the settlements along that part of Kellogg's trail between Peoria and Dixon's Ferry, and at once another battalion of 200 men, under Major David Bailey of Tazewell County, was called out for the purpose, and both battalions quickly responded.

On the 19th, General Atkinson met the friendly Sacs and Foxes, who in the meantime had brought in three young men engaged in the Menominee murders. Wapello, who delivered them up, said: "There are the young men who have taken pity on the women and children. There are three of them. These are my chiefs. These are the men who went into the braves' lodge to give themselves up. Father, I have received these young men. I now deliver them to you."

Keokuk spoke in the same strain, and received assurances that the young men should receive generous treatment.[1]

Until the 24th, General Atkinson had sent embassies to Black Hawk to dissuade him from his enterprise, but hearing nothing from them, he

[1] Life of A. S. Johnston, p. 35.

dispatched two young Sacs with a *mild talk*. On the 26th they returned, bringing Black Hawk's answer that "his heart was bad and that he was determined not to turn back."

During these negotiations occurred one of the most daring and heroic incidents of the campaign. Col. Henry Gratiot, father-in-law to the late Hon. E. B. Washburne, had early established smelting works at Gratiot's Grove, just over the line into the present county of LaFayette, Wisconsin. By his humane and honorable treatment of the Winnebagoes he had secured their unbounded confidence, and the Government had made him agent for the Winnebagoes, under the celebrated John Kinzie, then at Fort Winnebago. Upon him General Atkinson relied as the one man above all others who could gain the ear of the Winnebago "Prophet," who was in his agency, and Black Hawk's evil genius, and turn the deluded British band back to its Iowa reservation. From Fort Crawford General Atkinson had dispatched a[1] request to undertake this perilous mission. Colonel Gratiot received the same April 16 and started, taking one white man. On the 19th he arrived at the Turtle village of the Winnebagoes, where, in order to secure a hearing, he was delayed until the 22d. There twenty-four Winnebago chiefs and head men were added to his embassy, including Broken Shoulder, Whirling Thunder, White Crow, Little Medicine Man and Little Priest among the number.[2] He hurriedly rode to Dixon's Ferry, where canoes were taken and the journey completed to the Prophet's village on the 25th. There, despite his flag of truce, Colonel Gratiot was surrounded by hostile Sacs, who, with every demonstration of violence,[3] made him prisoner, Black Hawk himself, who had hoisted the British flag in camp, supervising the incident, and evil times had certainly fallen upon the head of Colonel Gratiot had not the Prophet, seeing the danger of his agent, rushed to his rescue, crying, "Good man, good man, my friend. I take him to my wigwam. I feed him. He be good friend of my Indians."

When the Prophet had him securely in the wigwam, Colonel Gratiot explained the peaceful object of his mission and the perfidy of the Indians if they refused to deal honorably with him. He further sought, with all the eloquence and logic he could master, to dissuade the Prophet and Black Hawk from their unrighteous expedition. The Prophet listened attentively, but if any impression had been made upon him it was not noticeable in word or action, and neither could he be persuaded to try to influence Black Hawk to give up his mad enterprise. However, as a friend, the Prophet was determined to save Colonel Gratiot's life, if such a thing were possible. He kept him in the wigwam for two or three days, watching an opportunity to free them. The ferocious Sacs clam-

---
[1] Wakefield, p. 10.
[2] Wis. Hist. Colls., Vol. x, p. 253.
[3] Life A. S. Johnston, p. 35.

COL. HENRY GRATIOT.

WA-BO-KI-E-SHIEK, THE PROPHET.

HENRY EDDY.

GEN. SAMUEL WHITESIDE.

ored louder each hour for scalps, and no doubt would have succeeded in taking them had not the Prophet seduced them away temporarily by promises until the desired opportunity should arrive. Returning hastily on the 27th, he said to Colonel Gratiot: "Chouteau,[1] you have always been my friend and the friend of my people, and you and your party must not be harmed, but there is great trouble. My young men will never consent to give you up and so you must leave without their knowledge. Your canoes are on the shore; go to them at a moment when I shall indicate and leave instantly, and go with all speed—like wild fire—for the young men will give you chase. All will depend on the strength of your arms."

The signal was given, and scarcely had the canoes been launched when an alarm in the village brought the Sacs and young Winnebagoes to the river, where a wild war-whoop was sounded and an exciting chase down Rock River was begun to capture and kill Colonel Gratiot. Gratiot's men pulled for their lives, first losing and then gaining. The maddened Sacs whooped and shrieked with anger at the possible miscarriage of their plans as they lent renewed vigor to their strokes, but a sense of their overwhelming danger put courage and strength into the oars of the pursued and they finally distanced their pursuers, arriving safely at Fort Armstrong on April 27th, unnerved and exhausted, to report that nothing could be done by moral suasion to prevent the advance of Black Hawk and that nothing but force would avail.

While captive in the Prophet's tent Black Hawk came to see him, and in response to the appeal of Gratiot to return, replied that his heart was bad; that he was going sixty miles up the river, and if molested would fight.[2]

[1] The Colonel's Indian name.
[2] Wakefield. There are many versions of Col. Gratiot's trip; but the one given is considered the most authentic, as it came through Hon. E. B. Washburne, son-in-law of Col. Gratiot.

CHAPTER XVII.

THE MILITIA MOVES TO ROCK RIVER.

At Beardstown the forces rapidly gathered. Colonels March and Christy were again placed in charge of the commissary department, but Christy, unable to give the service that attention which it demanded, resigned, leaving March to go alone to St. Louis for supplies, with instructions to have them at Yellow Banks (now Oquawka), on the Mississippi River, by the time the army reached that point. Col. E. C. Berry, Adjutant-General, and Col. Henry Eddy, Quartermaster-General of the State Militia, accompanied the expedition clear through. Gen. Samuel Whiteside was appointed Brigadier-General and the other field officers were elected by the troops.

Two companies of foot appeared, which were formed into a battalion under the command of Major Thomas Long, and though infantry was not asked for in the call for troops, it was deemed impolitic to decline them, and they were disposed of by the following order:

"Headquarters, Beardstown, April 29, 1832.

"Special Order.—Major Thomas Long, commanding the odd battalion of infantry.

"Sir:—You are hereby commanded to repair forthwith on the steamboat employed in the service of the United States to the mouth of Henderson's River, and there await further orders. And you will strictly prohibit all shooting and other disorderly conduct in your command, and use all military precaution to protect the steamboat upon which you are conveyed, and use every exertion to meet the army at the point designated on the 2d of May next.

"By order of Brig.-Gen. Whiteside.

"NATHANIEL BUCKMASTER, Brigade Major."

On the 30th Governor Reynolds had received a message from Atkinson stating that the Indians had begun that day a movement up Rock River. Had the order to Major Long not been issued, the army might have been ordered to Peoria or Hennepin and Black Hawk could easily have been headed off at Dixon's Ferry, saving thereby much blood and treasure, but Reynolds feared he could not overtake March and divert him to the course up the Illinois River, therefore the circuitous march to

Yellow Banks was undertaken. We have fortunately preserved to us an account of that march, made by Private O. H. Browning, later United States Senator, and later Secretary of the Interior.

"Minutes of an expedition undertaken to the northern part of the State of Illinois, in the spring of 1832, against the hostile bands of Sac and Fox Indians, who, it was rumored, had invaded that portion of said State which lies contiguous to and upon both sides of Rock River.

"Sunday, April 22, 1832.

"About 12 o'clock an order from John Reynolds, Governor of the State of Illinois, reached Quincy, requiring the colonel commandant of the militia of Adams County to raise a company of fifty mounted men and march them without delay to Beardstown on the Illinois River, the place appointed for the rendezvous of the army.

"Monday, 23.

"Militia of county convened at Quincy. Second order received from Governor increasing the requisition from 50 to 100 men, all of whom volunteered. Elected William G. Flood captain of Quincy company, Ed. L. Pearson first lieutenant and Thomas Crocker second lieutenant. Philip W. Martin elected captain of Bear Creek company, Howard first and Lillard second lieutenant. Elam S. Freeman chosen to take command as major until we reached Rushville, to which place we were directed to march instead of Beardstown.

"Tuesday, 24.

"Spent in making preparations to march.

"Wednesday, 25.

"Convened in Quincy and between 11 and 12 o'clock marched with 80 or 85 mounted volunteers. Three miles from Quincy heavy fall of rain. Continued our march 15 miles and encamped at Lasley's.

"Thursday, 26.

"Marched from Lasley's to west bank of Crooked Creek in Schuyler County and encamped 11 miles from Rushville.

"Warm and sultry. Encampment much infested with rattlesnakes. Killed several. At 8 o'clock commenced raining and continued without intermission during the night. Had no tents. Could not sleep. Stood in mud ankle deep till day.

"Friday, 27.

"Morning cold and rainy. Decamped early. Crossed Crooked Creek in boat and marched through mud knee deep to our horses to Rushville. Stopped and took some refreshments. Got merry and continued our march three miles east of Rushville on the road to Beardstown and encamped.

"Saturday and Sunday, 28 and 29.

"Remained at the encampment, troops collecting from various places coming up from headquarters at Beardstown.

"Monday, 30.

"Whole army, consisting of 1,300 horses and some foot, removed seven miles and again encamped four miles north of Rushville. The two companies from Adams were now attached to the Greene, Montgomery and Bond troops and formed into a regiment to the command of which Col. Jacob Fry of Greene County was elected. Major Gregory commanded the battalion of Greene troops and Capt. Philip W. Martin of Adams was elected to the command of the battalion composed of the Adams, Bond and Montgomery troops. David Crow succeeded Martin in the command of the Bear Creek Company of Adams troops. E. S. Freeman of Adams was appointed adjutant to the regiment, Hiram Bennett of Montgomery quartermaster, E. L. R. Wheelock of Adams paymaster, Dr. Dulaney of Greene surgeon and Calvert Roberts of Montgomery sergeant-major. A brigade had been formed previous to the troops leaving Beardstown, to command which General Samuel Whitesides was appointed by Governor Reynolds, who accompanied the army on its march. Mr. Nathaniel Buckmaster of Madison County received the appointment of brigade major, after having been a candidate for the command of the regiment, consisting in part of the troops from his own county, and after having been rejected by them.

"Tuesday, May 1.

"Took up line of march for Yellow Banks, 70 or 75 miles distant; traveled about 25 miles and encamped in McDonough County.

"Wednesday, May 2.

"Continued our march successfully and encamped at night, by order of Mr. Buckmaster, in a large prairie, two miles from timber or water. Night cold and tempestuous—much dissatisfaction and murmuring among the troops. All cursing Buck for keeping them in the prairie.

"Thursday, May 3.

"About 12 o'clock reached Henderson River; not fordable—no boats or canoes. No pioneers had been sent forward to construct bridges. Army crossed in great disorder by felling trees into the river at different places, making thereby a show of bridges upon which the troops crossed with difficulty and swam their horses—two or three horses drowned. Continued our march to the Yellow Banks in Warren County, which we reached before night and encamped. Provision scarce. Hogs shot by the soldiers. Supplies brought up Mississippi River by steamboat William Wallace. No guard placed out at night."

Private Browning was evidently a fair weather soldier and not at all disposed to accept camp life in a soldier-like way, like his superior, Major Buckmaster. Governor Reynolds is authority for the statement that after separating the army into two divisions the 2,000 horses, with their riders, crossed the swollen Henderson River in less than three hours, with the loss of but one horse. The boat with provisions had not yet arrived, which caused Governor Reynolds much anxiety. Neither did it appear on the fourth nor the morning of the fifth, when Reynolds in despair dispatched three pioneers, Messrs. Hewitt, Luther Tunnell and Orestus Ames, to go to Fort Armstrong, some fifty miles distant, for provisions. Before night they reached Atkinson's headquarters, and by the morning of the sixth a boat, the William Wallace, hove to with ample supplies.[1] The times were trying and should have been met as bravely and patiently as soldier life demands.

The spirit of unrest in the pioneer breast when in restraint must, of

---

[1] In command of March from St. Louis.

MAJ. THOMAS LONG.

O. H. BROWNING.

COL. WILLIAM ROSS.

CAPT. BENJAMIN BARNEY.

course, be considered and many extenuations allowed, but Private Browning, a lawyer, should not have been so critical. This spirit of unrest and insubordination was responsible for Stillman's defeat and the unhappy and futile ending of this campaign. It should be noticed, too, in this connection that in the face of the Indian Creek massacre, when all were bound by every principle of humanity to avenge it, Major Buckmaster re-enlisted and fought to do it, while Private Browning did not.

From Yellow Banks Reynolds desired to move with all speed on to Dixon's Ferry to overtake Black Hawk, if possible at that late date, but with the provisions sent by Atkinson, which arrived just at dark on the 6th, came a message that Black Hawk was returning down the river and that the volunteers were needed at the mouth of Rock River. Therefore camp was broken the following morning and the march to that point made in one day, arriving May 7th, about nightfall.[1]

The report of Black Hawk's descent proved untrue and added another important factor to the Stillman miscarriage, because Reynolds, by marching direct to Dixon's Ferry, could have followed the hypothenuse of the triangle on solid ground and had an easy journey. As it followed, however, he was forced to pursue both sides of the triangle, over swampy ground and through almost impassable bogs and bayous, until the strength of the troops was spent and their temper turned. But, above all, time was lost. While the rains made bad marching and bad tempers, they likewise promised great returns to the husbandman, and the fact that many were forced to leave their plows contributed to imperil the good disposition of the troops. The probable loss of a crop meant much to them that year, for the reason that the two preceding years had been failures and destitution was abroad in the land.[2] Men dropped their plows when the call came, without asking questions, but under delays and hardships, while they cursed Black Hawk, they murmured.

A fine illustration of the alacrity with which those men responded was written in the history of Pike County.

"On Friday, the 20th day of April, 1832, in response to Governor Reynolds' call for volunteers to fight Black Hawk, the following order was issued: 'Company Orders—The volunteer company of Pike County will meet at Atlas on Monday the 23d, ready to take up the march by sunrise, except such part of the company as are living on the east side of the county, which part will meet the company at the house of William Hinman, about four miles this side of Phillips' Ferry, on the same day, all with a good horse, and rifle, powder horn, half pound of powder and one hundred balls, with three days' provisions. The commanding officer of said company flatters himself that every man will be prompt to his duty.

"'W. Ross,
"'Capt. 1st Rifles, Pike Co.'"

---

[1] Note:—The Indian scare having reached Ft. Dearborn, a company of 40 men pledged themselves to defend it and elected Gholson Kercheval Captain, George W. Dale First Lieutenant and John S. C. Hogan Second Lieutenant, May 3d.

[2] Edwards, Hist. of Ill., 368.

THE BLACK HAWK WAR.

The Captain called upon Benjamin Barney at his blacksmith shop and told him of the nature of the order he had received and asked him forthwith to mount a horse and start out to notify the settlers to assemble immediately. Benjamin Barney was engaged at his forge at the time, making a plow, but he at once laid down his hammer and tongs, untied his leathern apron, left his fire to smoulder and die, and started immediately upon his mission. The men responded, and, bidding their families good-by, went forward, leaving their work to languish. Beardstown, then Yellow Banks, and finally the mouth of Rock River were reached, and at the latter place the troops were met by the officers and men of the regular army, and here the volunteers were sworn[1] into the United States service by Gen. Henry Atkinson on the 8th day of May. Lieut. I. R. B. Gardenier, then on detached service at the Dubuque lead mines, was ordered to Galena at this time by request of its citizens, to assist in its defense. There he was placed at the head of a volunteer company to drill them, and there he remained, with a brief exception, until July 14th, when he was superseded by Nicholas Dowling.

While mentioning members of this celebrated old Sixth regiment, it will be of interest to copy the roster complete from the official army register:

Colonel, Henry Atkinson, Brevet Brigadier General.
Lieutenant-Colonel, Daniel Baker.
Major, William Davenport.
Captains, Bennet Riley, I. Clark, Jr., Jacob Brown, Zalmon C. Palmer, W. N. Wickliffe, **Henry Smith**, Thomas Noel, Jason Rogers, George C. Hutter and Clifton Wharton.
First Lieutenants, R. Holmes, G. W. Waters, Levi M. Nute, M. W. Batman, George Andrews, Asa Richardson, John Nichols, G. H. Crossman, J. Van Swearengen and Joseph S. Worth.
Second Lieutenants, H. St. J. Linden, Gustavus Dorr, Albert S. Johnston, Joseph D. Searight, F. J. Brooke, P. St. George Cooke, Nathaniel J. Eaton, Robert Sevier, Gus S. Rousseau, Thomas F. Drayton, William Hoffman, Albert Cady, Jonathan Freeman, M. L. Clark, T. L. Alexander, J. S. Van Derveer, Thomas J. Royster, J. S. Williams and John Conrod
Of the First Infantry and participating were Lieut.-Col. Zachary Taylor, Major John Bliss, the mustering officer of 1831.
Captains William S. Harney,[2] William R. Jouett, E. A. Hitchcock, who, with the junior officers and men, went to Rock Island and then to Dixon, and Capt. R. B. Mason. First Lieut. W. M. Boyce, Second Lieut. Levin Gale and Captain Thomas Barker and First Lieut. W. L. Harris, who remained at Fort Crawford.
With the first named captains of the First were First Lieutenants Albert S. Miller, J. W. Kingsbury, J. J. Abercrombie; Second Lieutenants E. G. Mitchell, Jefferson Davis and J. K. Greenough.
Second Regiment, Col. Hugh Brady.
Fourth Regiment, Lieut.-Col. David E. Twiggs, Capt. James H. Hook, First Lieut. W. M. Graham, Second Lieut. F. D. Newcomb.

---
[1]Gen. Order No. 8.
[2]Harney's company was then stationed at Ft. Armstrong.

CAPT. W. S. HARNEY, U. S. A.

LIEUT. JOHN S. C. HOGAN.

GEN. HUGH BRADY.

MAJ. D. E. TWIGGS.

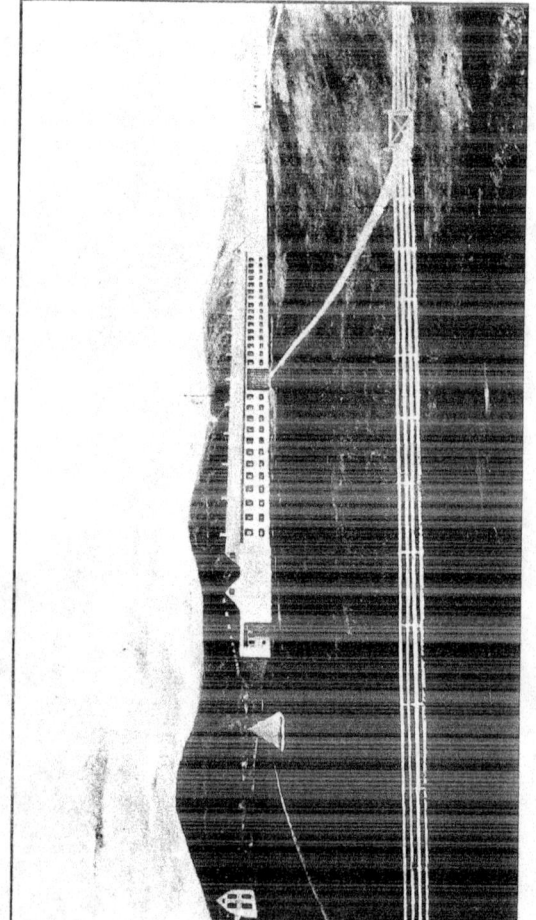

FORT CRAWFORD.

Fifth Regiment, Lieut.-Col. Enos Cutler, Capt. Gideon Lowe, First Lieut. James Engle and Second Lieut. Amos Foster.

At the breaking out of hostilities in 1832 Major John Bliss, of the First Regiment, was in command of Ft. Armstrong; Lieut.-Col. Zachary Taylor, of the First, was in command of Ft. Crawford; Col. Henry Atkinson, of the Sixth, was in command of Jefferson Barracks; Major William Davenport, of the Sixth, was in command of Canton Leavenworth, and Lieut.-Col. Enos Cutler, of the Fifth, was in command of Ft. Winnebago, the five Government forts prominent in this war.

MAJ. ALEXANDER BEALL.

GEORGE OREAR.

CAPT. W. G. FLOOD.

SAMUEL HORNEY.

J. A. Blackwell, Quartermaster.
William G. Brown, Paymaster.
Richard Roman, Surgeon.
J. M. McTyre Cornelius, Surgeon's Mate.
Samuel Sybold, Quartermaster's Sergeant.
Alexander Shields, Sergeant-Major.

SECOND REGIMENT.

Jacob Fry, Colonel.
Charles Gregory, Lieutenant-Colonel.
Philip W. Martin, Major.
Elam S. Freeman, Adjutant.
Hiram C. Bennett, Quartermaster.
James Durley, Quartermaster's Sergeant.
E. L. R. Wheelock, Paymaster.
William H. Dulaney, Surgeon.
John F. Foster, Surgeon's Mate.
Calvin Roberts, Sergeant-Major.

THIRD REGIMENT.

Abraham B. DeWitt, Colonel.
William Weatherford, Lieutenant-Colonel.
Alexander Beall, Major.
Murray McConnel, Adjutant.
George Orear, Quartermaster.
Andrew Mackitee, Paymaster.
Samuel M. Prosper, Surgeon.
James Morrison, Surgeon's Mate.
Levin N. English, Quartermaster's Sergeant.
Robert Davis, Sergeant-Major.

FOURTH REGIMENT.

Samuel M. Thompson, Colonel.
Achilles Morris, Lieutenant-Colonel.
Moses G. Wilson, Major.
John B. Watson, Adjutant.
Samuel Horney, Quartermaster.
William Carpenter, Paymaster.
Jacob M. Eddy, Surgeon.
Adams Dunlap, First Surgeon's Mate.
William Constant, Second Surgeon's Mate.
Edward Doyle, Sergeant-Major.
A. McHatton, Sergeant-Major (Successor).
William Fitzpatrick, Quartermaster's Sergeant.
William Sprouce, Gunsmith.
Richard Jones, Color Bearer.
James Baker, Wagon Master.

SPY BATTALION.

James D. Henry, Major.
William L. E. Morrison, Adjutant.

Montgomery Warrick, Quartermaster.
Robert Blackwell, Paymaster.
Joseph C. Woodson, Surgeon.
Peter Randall, First Surgeon's Mate.
Benjamin Birch, Second Surgeon's Mate.
M. E. Rattan, Sergeant-Major.
John F. Posey, Quartermaster's Sergeant.
Jesse M. Harrison, Paymaster's "Sergeant."
William Cook, Color Bearer.

Spy Battalion.

Thomas James, Major.
James Moore, Adjutant.
James Whitlock, Quartermaster to May 15th. Resigned.
Scipio Baird, Quartermaster.
Michael Horine, Paymaster.
William Headen, Surgeon.
George Gordon, Surgeon's Mate.
N. C. Johnston, Sergeant-Major. Resigned May 5th.
John James, Sergeant-Major.
James W. Vaughan, Armorer.
Moses Haskins, Bugleman.
J. Milton Moore, Color Bearer.

Foot Battalion.

Thomas Long, Major.
John Summers, Adjutant.
Vawter Henderson, Quartermaster.
J. L. Thompson, Paymaster.
Matthew Duncan, Surgeon.
Jonathan Leighton, Surgeon's Mate.
Sion R. Green, Sergeant-Major.
Thomas J. (or I.) Marshall, Quartermaster's Sergeant.
Benjamin Howard, Fife Major.
Thomas Burton, Drum Major.

The First Regiment consisted of six companies, commanded by the following captains: Julius L. Barnsback and Josiah Little of Madison County and Gideon Simpson, William Moore,[1] John Winstanley and John Tate of St. Clair County. Thomas was first elected Captain of Simpson's company, but on being promoted to Colonel, Simpson was elected to succeed him. Preuitt was elected Captain of Little's company, but upon his promotion to Lieutenant-Colonel, Little was elected.

The Second Regiment was composed of nine companies, commanded, respectively, by Captains Thomas Chapman, Samuel Smith,

---

[1] From Risdon Marshall Moore of San Antonio, Texas, the following information is gathered: His father, Jonathan Moore, a brother of the Captain, was a private in this company. The grandfather, Risdon Moore, was Speaker of the Territorial Legislature of Illinois in 1814 and in 1822 signed the celebrated protest against slavery.
Capt. William Moore, besides being a member of the Ninth and Tenth General Assemblies, occupied many positions of prominence. See also "Historical Encyclopedia of Illinois."

WILLIAM HEADEN.

WILLIAM CARPENTER.

ROBERT BLACKWELL.

JAMES WHITLOCK.

JAMES W. VAUGHAN.

CAPT. J. L. BARNSBACK.

CAPT. GIDEON SIMPSON.

LIEUT. STARKEY R. POWELL.

THE BLACK HAWK WAR. 125

Thomas McDow and Jeremiah Smith of Greene County, Levi D. Boone of Montgomery County, Benjamin James of Bond County, William G. Flood and David Crow of Adams County, and James White of Hancock County. Gregory was first elected Captain of Chapman's company and Fry of Samuel Smith's company, but both were promoted.

The Third Regiment consisted of six companies, commanded, respectively, by Captains Benjamin Barney and Elisha Petty of Pike County, John Harris of Macoupin, and William B. Smith, William T. Givens and Nathan or Nathaniel Winters of Morgan County. William Ross was first elected Captain of Barney's company, but upon his promotion to the staff Barney was elected.

The Fourth Regiment consisted of four companies, commanded by Captains Samuel Hollingsworth and William C. Ralls of Schuyler County and Abraham Lincoln and Levi W. Goodan of Sangamon County. Moses G. Wilson was first elected Captain of Hollingsworth's company, but upon his promotion to Major, Hollingsworth was elected.

Henry's Spy Battalion was composed of four companies, commanded by Captain John Dawson of Sangamon, Captain Thomas Carlin of Greene, Captain John Dement of Fayette and Erastus Wheeler of Madison.

James' Spy Battalion was composed of three companies, commanded by Captains Daniel Price and Peter Warren of Shelby County and Thomas Harrison of Monroe.

Long's Foot Battalion was composed of three companies, commanded by Captains Jacob Ebey, Japhet A. Ball and Seth Pratt of Sangamon.[1]

In addition to these troops, the battalions of Stillman and Bailey, ordered to range the country and concentrate at Dixon's Ferry, which they did on the 10th, were considered, of course, a part of the army, though not then sworn in.

The battalion of Major Isaiah Stillman was composed of three companies, commanded by Captains David W. Barnes and Asel F. Ball of Fulton County and Abner Eads of Peoria County.

Major David Bailey's Battalion was composed of four companies, commanded by Captains M. L. Covell and Robert McClure of McLean County, Captain John G. Adams of Tazewell and Captain James Johnson of Macon County. On the 16th, however, after Stillman's defeat, the new Fifth Regiment was organized from these two commands, and I. C. Pugh was elected captain of the company commanded by Captain James Johnson, who was elected Colonel. No staff officers were appointed for the two battalions prior to their merger into the Fifth Regiment.

While dwelling on the composition of the Fifth Regiment, it may be

---

[1]This roster will be found to materially differ from the "Record of the Services of Illinois Soldiers," published by the Adjutant General in 1882, which is shamefully inaccurate in many particulars. I fortunately came into possession of the original "rank roll," so called, made by General Whiteside and Maj. Buckmaster, which has permitted me to be accurate.

well to name its officers as I find them on the original roster in my possession:

James Johnson, Colonel.
Isaiah Stillman, Lieutenant-Colonel.
David Bailey, Major.
James W. Crain, Adjutant.
Hugh Woodrow, Quartermaster.
David C. Alexander, Paymaster.
Samuel Pillsbury, Surgeon.
Daniel McCall, Sergeant-Major.
Joshua C. Morgan, Quartermaster's Sergeant.

On the 9th of May, with not a man on the sick list, General Atkinson isued the following orders:

"Headquarters, Right Wing, West. Dept.
"Mouth of Rock River, 9th May, 1832.

"Order No. 12.

"The mounted volunteers will move in the morning under Brig.-Gen. Whiteside, by the route of Winnebago Prophet's village, with a view of reaching the hostile band of Indians assembled on Rock River, near or above Dixon's Ferry. The regular troops will move by water and meet the mounted troops at Prophet's village. Should General Whiteside, however, on reaching Prophet's village, be of opinion that it would be prudent to come up with the enemy with as little delay as possible, he will move upon him, and either make him surrender at discretion, or coerce him into submission.

"Order No. 13.

"Colonel Taylor, First Regiment, will assume the command of the Infantry of Illinois at this place. They will move by water in conjunction with the U. S. Infantry now under his orders, and will be assigned to the charge of transporting a portion of the munitions, supplies, etc., for the troops.

"Order No. 14.

"Lieut. Robert Anderson, Third Regiment Artillery, will, till further orders, perform the duties of Assistant Inspector General of the troops now in the field."

By order No. 9 Colonel Taylor was also given command of the regular troops under orders for active service, viz.: Six companies of the Sixth Regiment Infantry, under the command of Major Riley, and the companies of the First Regiment Infantry from Fort Crawford, and Captain Harney's Company of the First Infantry of the garrison of Fort Armstrong. Lieutenant Burbank,[1] Acting Quartermaster of the post, was ordered to store such clothing, provisions and stores as should be left by the troops under marching orders. Major Beall[2] was further charged with the safe-keeping of the three Indian prisoners then in confinement, which completed all arrangements for marching.

The volunteer army set out on the 10th and reached the Prophet's village in the afternoon. Near that place the spies which Governor

---

[1] Of the First Inf. Sidney Burbank.
[2] Thomas J. Beall, of the First Inf.

CAPT. LEVI D. BOONE.

CAPT. W. T. GIVENS.

CAPT. NATHAN WINTERS.

CAPT. PETER WARREN.

CAPT. DANIEL PRICE.

CAPT. ISAAC C. PUGH.

ARCHIBALD WILLIAMS.

W. A. RICHARDSON.

Reynolds had sent out on the 8th to reconnoiter and locate the enemy[1] met the army and reported that they had captured an Indian, who had truly informed them that Black Hawk was on Rock River, above Dixon's Ferry, as had been previously reported. Disappointed at such a delay as the march to Black Hawk's camp would incur, the men fired the Prophet's village and burned every vestige of it—an act wholly unwarranted and useless. About twelve miles above the Prophet's village the army camped, and, for reasons utterly inconceivable at this late day, decided to abandon all the cumbersome baggage and provisions and force a march to overtake the Indians. Whether the troops, who considered it part of their duty to dictate policies to their superior officers, clamored for such a move, or whether it emanated from the officer in command, has never been explained to this day, either in books or personal interviews had by the writer. Whiteside got all the blame for it, but I believe that his action was governed by pressure from the headstrong militia, who desired to accomplish too much in a limited time, and the passion of Governor Reynolds to manage the campaign to a rapid and glorious finish. It was an unfortunate act at best. Perishable property was piled up to waste, unprotected and regardless of future needs. With scarcely enough to last them in a forced march to another base, where abundance might await them, these impatient men marched into a wilderness where defeat might overtake them, with only rations enough to last for a period of three or four days. This criminal indiscretion was the first cause of dissatisfaction among the men. The commander should have known that those who urge the most haste have for all time been first to find fault when the first evidence of its indiscretion appears and at once vetoed the foolhardy move.

Whiteside was a famous old Indian fighter; brave as a lion and ready and eager at all times to meet an enemy; but he had never before handled a large body of men, and in this case at least it may be said that bravery alone was not an indisputable qualification for leadership. It rarely is. It later remained for James D. Henry, in a case almost forlorn, to terminate further moves like this injudicious one, and thereby end the war, as he did. After writing General Atkinson of the action, Governor Reynolds, with the troops, moved rapidly for Dixon's Ferry, which was reached on the 12th, where James W. Stephenson, James M. Strode and others were found, all of whom stated that from scouts just returned it was ascertained beyond doubt that the Indians, who had fixed upon a point of rendezvous about thirty miles up the river, were at that time scattered over a large area, securing food, and in all probability recruits, and that an attempt to march against them would be useless at that moment. Governor Reynolds at once realized the force of the point and abandoned his projected attack and agreed to rest until Atkinson appeared,

---

[1] Col. John Ewing, Maj. John A. Wakefield and a Mr. Kinney, who understood the Sac language and who served as guide.

which he hoped would be very soon. The scouts sent out, and hereafter noticed, were sent to Shabbona's village, and had it not been for the unfortunate action of Stillman, there probably had been no trouble in ending the campaign without loss of time or blood. But the country was covered with water, the ground was swampy and almost impassable to footmen, the river was high, and only by the most heroic efforts was it made possible to navigate the keel boats and Mackinaw boats upstream.[1] Men waded up to their middle to pull them along, and then only a snail pace could be accomplished. A change to the other side of the river was attempted, with no better results, and finally Atkinson was compelled to issue the following order:

"Headquarters, Right Wing, West. Dept.,
"Near Marie de Ogee, Rock River, 11th May, 1832.
"Order No. 15.

"The troops on foot will move in ascending the river, in the following order: The First Infantry will march in front, the Sixth Infantry in the center and the Illinois Infantry in the rear. An advance guard from the First Infantry will precede the column from 400 to 1,000 yards; a flank guard from the Sixth Infantry will be thrown out from 200 to 400 yards, and more, if necessary, according to the ground. The Illinois Infantry will march in the rear and furnish the rear guard, which is not at any time to leave any of the boats in the rear. The river will be crossed to avail the troops of the best ground for navigation and marching; the troops will encamp in the order of march. In case of attack the troops will form to the front, the rear or upon the flank as circumstances may demand."

The march was slow and toilsome, but made with decency and, considering the surface of the country, dispatch. But it was necessarily so difficult to make progress that Atkinson did not reach Dixon's Ferry until the 17th, when all was confusion and the men loud in their demands to be discharged. So utterly unmanageable had they become that it became necessary on that day to issue the following order, and which, by the by, was rigidly enforced by Col. Zachary Taylor:

"Headquarters, Right Wing, West. Dept.,
"Dixon's Ferry, Rock River, 17th May, 1832.
"Order No. 16.

"The frequent unauthorized firing of arms in and about the vicinity of the encampments of the different corps of the army, composed of the U. S. Infantry and the State troops now in the field, compels the Commanding General to forbid a practice so dangerous to the individual members of the different corps and derogatory to the military character of well-organized troops. No officer or private, therefore, will fire again in camp or on the march without permission or an order from the commanding officer of his regiment or company."

From the mouth of the river the soldiers had indulged this boisterous pastime, with no restraint whatever, and it is said that this abridgment of their pioneer prerogative provoked much indignation, but firing at once ceased.

---

[1]The U. S. Infantry and Long's foot battalion left on the 10th. The Prophet's village was reached on the 14th.

CAPT. GIDEON LOWE, U. S. A.

LIEUT. COL. ZACHARY TAYLOR'S HEADQUARTERS AT FORT CRAWFORD.

JOHN DIXON.

DIXON'S FERRY.

CHAPTER XIX.

DIXON'S FERRY—PLIGHT OF REYNOLDS' MESSENGERS—STILLMAN'S DEFEAT.

Dixon's Ferry, now Dixon, Illinois, at the period of this campaign consisted of a ferry, the simple flat-bottomed affair of those days, and a 90-foot log cabin, built in three sections, both owned by John Dixon. The patriarchal appearance of this old pioneer had brought to him the title "Na-chu-sa" from the Indians, meaning in the Winnebago dialect "Long hair white," and from the whites "Father Dixon." By his kindness, gentleness, honesty and courage he had won the love of every person, white and red, who had ever met him, and to those in the land who had not met him his reputation had extended, so that the mention of his name meant an overture for peace.

In the spring of 1827 his brother-in-law, O. W. Kellogg, broke a trail through the country from Peoria to Galena, to facilitate the rapidly increasing overland travel to the lead mines. "Kellogg's trail," as it was then called, crossed Rock River at this place, and in 1828, when Father Dixon received the contract for carrying the mails from Peoria to Galena and Gratiot's Grove, he took with him from Peoria to Rock River a halfbreed named Joseph Ogee,[1] who established a permanent, though unlicensed, ferry. Prospective competition or a friend must have suggested his *laches* in this respect, for on December 7, 1829, he received from Jo Daviess County, whose jurisdiction embraced all that section of country, the statutory license to operate the same. But by 1830 the restraint of a ferryman's life had become so exceedingly irksome to one of his nomadic nature that Father Dixon was constrained to take it off his hands and remove his family thence, which he did, arriving there April 11, 1830.

When Ogee established his ferry he built a hut of logs, unfit for habitation to any but a rover like himself. The needs of Father Dixon's family and increasing travel required something better, and this improvement he at once supplied by making additions, so that he soon had the comfortable house-store-hotel displayed in the illustration. He, with his family of wife and five children, from that time forward entertained travelers and

---
[1]Pronounced Ozha.

traded with the Indians until the Indians were no more and travel many years later had become diverted to bridges and other thoroughfares made by the new and ever-multiplying settlements. He was made postmaster, and thenceforth Dixon's Ferry was of commanding prominence in Illinois travel and Illinois geography. At this period, however, Father Dixon's was the only family on Rock River above the old Black Hawk village.

On his march up the river Black Hawk camped one night near the Dixon cabin, and with Ne-a-pope and the Prophet ate with the family, Mrs. Dixon waiting upon them in a manner so courteous as completely to captivate Black Hawk and command from him thereafter his highest admiration. During this stop the family, after a careful observation, estimated the number of able-bodied warriors with the expedition to be 800, and that number was reported to the troops, which arrived there May 12. Under the order of April 16th from Governor Reynolds, Majors Stillman and Bailey recruited to their battalions the companies already named.

Leaving Pekin May 8th,[1] Bailey's battalion reached Boyd's Grove the first night out, where Stillman, with his three companies, joined them and all camped for the night. The following day, at Bureau Creek, another detachment under a Captain Bowman, which had been ranging through the country toward Dixon's Ferry, joined these forces, reporting the theft of many of their horses by the Indians. At Dad Joe's Grove the combined forces camped the second night, marching the following day (the 10th), across the present county of Lee to Dixon's Ferry, where Reynolds and the militia joined them on the morning of the 12th.

The first act of the Governor was one of circumspection. Selecting from his ablest and most discreet officers Captain John Dement, Colonel James T. B. Stapp, Wyat B. Stapp, Major Joseph M. Chadwick and Benjamin Moore, and Louis Ouilmette, a French trader, thoroughly familiar with those parts and with Indian character, and who, with others, was waiting at Dixon's Ferry, they were directed to start for Paw Paw Grove,[2] some forty miles to the southeast, in the present confines of Shabbona township, DeKalb County, and there have a "talk" with the Pottowatomies, whose village was at that place, and assure themselves of the positive neutrality of that nation.

The prairies were covered with water, there were no roads, the day was dark and threatening, and, to frustrate their mission completely, a large party of Black Hawk's band overtook them. The enemy undertook by every art known to savage tactics to lure the men into an ambush. To refute Black Hawk's constant protestations of peace, this scouting party of his was discovered to be actively recruiting among the Pottowatomies

---

[1] James Haines, still living at Pekin, remembers the circumstances well. His two older brothers, Alfred and Jonathan, were members of Capt. Adams' company.
[2] Shabbona's village.

CAPT. J. A. BALL.   LIEUT. EDWARD D. BAKER.

OTTAWA AT THE TIME OF THE WAR.

THE BLACK HAWK WAR. 131

and Winnebagoes. The attempts to decoy the messengers into the Indian camp were diplomatically avoided, and so was a pitched battle, which could only have resulted in annihilation of the whites. After forty-eight hours of ceaseless endeavor, without food, the party finally succeeded in reaching headquarters. By this time the forces of Stillman and Bailey were marching up the river on their ill-fated expedition.

There were at Dixon's Ferry, when Reynolds arrived, several prominent men from the mining country, including Colonel James M. Strode, commander of the militia of Jo Daviess County, James W. Stephenson, William S. Hamilton, son of Alexander Hamilton, Col. Henry Gratiot and Louis Ouilmette, the trader. Colonel Henry Dodge of Michigan territory had organized a company to protect the frontier until he could communicate with Reynolds and systematically organize the mining district forces in a manner materially to assist the latter. James H. Gentry was captain of this company; Henry L. Dodge, son of Colonel Dodge, was elected first lieutenant; Paschal Bequette, a son-in-law, was elected second lieutenant, while Charles Bracken was aid to the colonel. The file consisted of some fifty men. This company of rangers, leaving Mineral Point May 8th, covered the northwestern frontier until Whiteside's Brigade reached Dixon's Ferry, and was camped on the north side of Rock River, not far from Black Hawk's camp, when Whiteside and his troops reached that point. Here Colonel Dodge was keeping a watchful eye on Black Hawk's every movement and warily awaiting the moment he could pounce down upon the old Indian if he saw fit to offer war,[1] an emergency which the intrepid little band was fully equal to.

Dodge saw the frightful consequences of an ill-advised expedition up Rock River and urged against it. Failure meant active co-operation with Black Hawk by the neutral and undecided Winnebagoes and Pottowatomies, and this in turn meant that the entire northwest frontier would be overrun with maurading bands and murderers.

But the impatient troops of Stillman and Bailey were ambitious to fight and would listen to no restraint. They had enlisted to kill "Injuns." Nothing but a valorous conquest would receive their attention, and General Whiteside and Governor Reynolds were constrained to allow the following order to be issued:

"Headquarters Camp No. 10, Dixon's Ferry,
"12th May, 1832.

"The troops under the command of Major Stillman, including the battalions of said Major Stillman and Major Bailey, will forthwith proceed with four days' rations to the head of Old Man's Creek, where it is supposed the hostile Sac Indians are assembled, for the purpose of taking all cautious measures to coerce said

[1] Note:—Dodge's command (May 8) proceeded by way of Apple River to Buffalo Grove, at which an Indian trail led to Rock River, at a point nearly opposite the mouth of the Kish-wau-kee and only a few miles from Stillman's battle, and where the troops were encamped at that time. Smith's Hist. Wis., Vol. 1, p. 266.

Indians into submission, and report themselves to this department as soon thereafter as practicable.

"By order of Brigadier Samuel Whiteside, commanding brigade of mounted volunteers.

"N. BUCKMASTER,
"Brigade-Major."

Writers upon this subject have so stated before, and others have told the writer that such was the case here. Furthermore, a rankling jealousy existed between Stillman and Bailey, each contending that he should be the other's superior and allowed the command of the combined troops. Governor Reynolds did his very best to harmonize the men by recognizing Stillman, but the rancorous hatred which existed among the troops for their rivals destroyed, in a great measure, their effectiveness.

On the morning of Sunday, the 13th of May, the two brigades marched up from Dixon's Ferry for Old Man's Creek. Many adventurous spirits from the main army were permitted to accompany the troops, as were a few others, like Colonel Strode, who wanted to see the "fun" which was promised. A baggage train of six wagons, drawn by oxen, guarded by about fifty men, under Mr. Hackelton of Fulton County, and bearing the four days' rations, followed in the rear. The day was black and threatening, and before the battalions had proceeded ten miles a pelting rain compelled them to halt and camp for the night.[1] All through the night the rain continued, holding the troops there until the morning of the 14th was well advanced, when the march was resumed. About dark of the same day Old Man's Creek was reached and crossed and the troops dismounted to camp for the night. The creek, then much swollen by recent rains, formed on the south side a disagreeable swamp. The object of crossing to the north side was to avoid this morass and also avail themselves of the natural advantages which the north side afforded for protection, as well as the more solid ground for camping.

The creek was lined on both sides with tall willows, while just a little to the north the ground was covered with a growth of small black oak trees, denominated generally scrub oak. These same "scrub oak," grown to thrice the thickness of a man's body, stand to this day, and, judging from a present-day standpoint, one can easily see how a handful of resolute men could defend themselves there against overwhelming odds. To the willows the horses were tied, fires were made, coffee pots put to boiling and a general preparation for supper was going forward, when three Indians appeared in camp bearing a white flag.[2] They were taken in, but in the haste of supper preparations and the absence of an interpreter, their mission, if for peace, was not discovered at once. As a matter of fact, however, Black Hawk had in his lifetime disregarded so

---

[1]Wakefield.
[2]Col. Wm. S. Hamilton and many other usually reliable authorities claimed the flag was red, indicative of war; but that contention cannot be credited.

DAVID HAACKE.

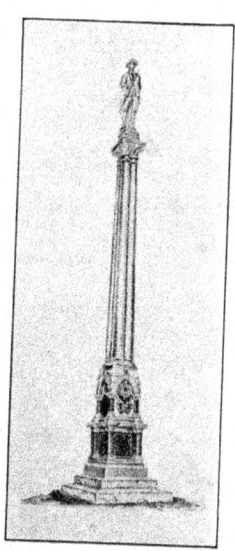

MONUMENT ON STILLMAN'S BATTLEFIELD.

ORDER MAY 25.

MAJ. ISAIAH STILLMAN.

MAJ. DAVID BAILEY.

WYATT B. STAPP.

OLIVER W. HALL.

many treaties and flags of truce, that it is no small wonder some of the men were for dispatching them on the spot. An abiding sense of his many misfeasances, no doubt, prompted him to station five other Indians on a neighboring hill, some three-quarters of a mile to the north, where they might watch and report the manner in which his flag was received. The presence of these five Indians on the hill, unexplained, may rightfully be styled a misprision, and sufficient to set the camp into a spasm of turmoil. About twenty of Eads' men mounted their horses to charge the five Indians, who in turn wheeled to run away. This action was taken by the excited and undisciplined troops to mean a retreat, and Eads' men immediately began firing upon their retiring foe. Other small squads joined the haphazard pursuit, in the course of which two of the five Indians were killed.

The camp became a bedlam, and while Stillman, Bailey, Adams, Eads and other officers tried desperately to restrain the troops and restore order, as well might they have commanded the rains to cease and the sun to return for half an hour as to have expected obedience from those raw and independent spirits. They were having the "fun" for which they had enlisted.

Black Hawk the while was at the mouth of the creek with half a hundred warriors, where he had been giving a dog feast to Shabbona, Waubansee and other influential Pottowatomies in his frantic efforts to secure reinforcements against the whites.

The interchange of shots ahead led those in camp to believe that a general engagement was upon them, whereupon Thomas B. Reed of Eads' company shot down in cold blood one of the three bearers of the flag of truce, an offense so dastardly as to permit of no excuse. It may be urged that the troops were frenzied by excitement or dazed with the thought that the 800 Indians were coming down upon them like an avalanche, but such was not the case; it was part of the program of "fun" which impelled it. The confusion which followed permitted the two remaining Indians of the party of three to escape and join in the massacre of the whites which followed soon after. Squads of two, three and more continued to leave camp to join the chase, presenting in the twilight a thin and irregular line, without order and without a head, until nearly four miles were covered by these stragglers.

As had been adroitly arranged, no doubt, by the survivors of the party of five, the foremost of the pursuers were suddenly plunged into Black Hawk's presence, behind a growth of chaparral at the mouth of the creek, where this wily old savage had arranged his braves, few in number, but many more than the first white arrivals, and the instant the whites appeared the Indians sent up whoops, shrieks and howls calculated to frighten even a brave man. As the savages dashed headlong into the advance column, or rather squad, of the whites, with the spirit and suddenness of an electric shock, the reckless pursuers realized their awful temerity, and the futility of fighting, even under careful protection and with the full strength of the battalions, what might be the 800 warriors known to belong to Black Hawk's command.

Stunned by the sudden and furious onslaught of Black Hawk, the troops wheeled to retreat, yelling as they fled "Injuns! Injuns!" (like the madmen they now truly became), that their approaching comrades might in turn retreat to safety. In no time at all the cry had reached camp, which became as panic-stricken as the returning troopers.[1]

At the foot of the hill on which the five Indians had rested James Doty of Eads' company was killed, and while many of the horses became mired in the mud of the creek, Gideon Munson, a Government scout, was also slain. As the troops came headlong on, Captain Adams,[2] than whom no braver man ever lived, attempted to make a stand with a handful of companions upon the brow of the hill which lies about half a mile to the south of the creek, to cover the retreat of the fugitives. Darkness was upon them and they had no reason to believe that less than the full force of 800 was upon them, yet they stood their ground to sell their lives as dearly as possible to save those who by the delay might reach points of safety.

The moonlight was only sufficient to confuse the panic-stricken troops still more, and in that heroic fight unto death which Captain Adams and his men made, he scarcely knew whether he was fighting friend or foe. In the gloaming the conflict went on, and in the darkness of the night, while the scattering forces were safely fleeing on to Dixon's Ferry, Captain Adams and his little band fell one by one, until the last man bit the dust, and then a scene of malignant deviltry almost incredible was perpetrated.[3] Mr. Oliver W. Hall of Carlinville, Illinois, who was present on the field the following day, wrote a brief description of it as follows:

"We were camped at Dixon's Ferry at the time of Stillman's defeat. Now Stillman had about two hundred and seventy-five well-mounted men, with baggage wagons, and he started out on his own accord, camping late in the evening on the north side of that little creek. The ford was just above, where the willows stood thick on each side of the creek. While Stillman's men were cooking supper, three or four Indians on their ponies rode up on that high hill just north of Stillman's camp, about sundown, and five or six of Stillman's men caught their horses and ran them to where the Indians were in camp, in the timber, about a mile and a half from Stillman's camp, north. The Indians killed one of our men and ran the balance of them into camp. The first that Stillman knew of any danger was when the Indians came yelling over that high hill just north of

---

[1] All survivors interviewed by the author stoutly maintained that Black Hawk so disposed his troops as to make it appear that the whites were surrounded.
[2] The father and mother of Capt. Adams were killed by Indians.
[3] Wakefield, p. 21, is authority for the statement that Dr. Donaldson was surgeon of Stillman's Battalion.

Stillman's camp, and it was a perfect stampede with Stillman's men. Some of them got their horses, but lots of them got away on foot, and after the Indians had killed eleven of our men they went back to Stillman's camp and cut the spokes out of the wagons and poured out a barrel of whisky. Well, we lay on our arms the next night on the south side of the creek, for we had left our tents at Dixon's Ferry, as we had to go back to meet the boat to get our rations. There were twenty-five hundred of us with shotguns and rifles and muskets, all flintlocks, and we were mounted, all but two or three companies. We picked up nine dead men as we came up from Dixon's Ferry on a forced march the next morning after Stillman's defeat. The last two that we found were Major Perkins and Captain Adams,[1] with both their heads cut off and their heads skinned all over and left by them. We found them on that descent as you go down to the creek from the high land, about half way down, and we buried nine men in one grave about two hundred yards southwest of those willows, just below the ford and on sideling ground, not as far south as the top of the hill. We buried one young man about three-quarters of a mile north of Stillman's camp (if true, this was James Doty), where he was found, and another young man about one-half a mile east, where he was found. (This was Gideon Munson.)

"Now the road crossed the creek just east of those willows, where there were a few scattering, scrubby trees. The nine men were buried about two hundred yards southwest of those willows and on the west side of the road leading to Dixon's Ferry. We never knew how many Indians there were."

If the statement concerning Doty and Munson is true, then but eight men could have been buried in the common grave, because but twelve were killed, and two were buried to the south. The fact is, Munson was buried in this one grave.

The names of Captain Adams' companions were David Kreeps, Zadock Mendinall and Isaac (nicknamed Major) Perkins, of Captain Adams' company; James Milton of Captain Pugh's company; Tyrus M. Childs, Joseph B. Farris and Corporal Bird W. Ellis of Captain David W. Barnes company, and Sergeant John Walters of Captain Ball's company.

Joseph Draper of Captain Covell's company was also shot and his body found five miles due south of the battlefield, on what is now known as Mrs. George F. Smith's farm, where it was buried.

Young Ellis, who was but a boy in years, was able to crawl two and a half miles south of the battlefield, where his body was found beside a strapping Indian, who had demanded his life, though it was then ebbing away. In this enfeebled condition he fought and killed his antagonist,

---

[1] The shock to Mrs. Adams on learning of her husband's horrible fate deprived her of reason, which was never recovered.

sinking into death soon after. Ellis was buried on the spot, now the farm of Mr. A. C. Brown.

The death of Private Joseph Draper was particularly pathetic, and is narrated in the historical records of McLean County as follows:

"In the confusion resulting from Black Hawk's attack, Draper lost his horse. A comrade, John Lundy, took Draper onto his horse. While retreating they found a stray horse which Draper insisted upon mounting. It had no saddle or bridle, but it was supposed it would follow the other horses; instead, it turned and ran toward the Indians, who shot Draper. He fell from the horse, crawled off into the underbrush, where his body was found by the burial party. He had written on his canteen an account of his wounds. No copy of the writing on his canteen has been preserved."

It would scarcely seem credible that a man in full possession of his faculties would remain on a horse running toward the enemy instead of dropping off to seek the shelter of the bushes and secrete his sound body, especially in the light of the fact that he was able securely to hide himself when wounded, but so it must have been in that fearful panic, because his comrade, Lundy, has vouched for the first part of the story and the man's canteen told the rest; and the words of a dying man cannot be doubted, particularly when alone in the night, miles away from friends and ministering care, with the raw and desolate prairie for a bed, howling wolves and Indians prowling near and the rough winds of spring about to blow his spirit into eternity.

After five miles' pursuit, the Indians abandoned it to return to mutilate the bodies, as described by Mr. Hall, but the whites continued their flight, running, riding, yelling, crying, hopelessly crazed, until Dixon's Ferry was reached in the early hours of the morning of the 15th. Others who became confused in the darkness, and deflected to the south, never stopped until the Illinois River had been reached at a point near the present city of Ottawa. From here they scattered (some forty) for their homes.

It was a clear case of panic. Men were crazed. They who in a sober moment would have walked straight to death without a protest; they who would bend to no command of a superior officer; they who would not obey or follow, were driven as easily as a flock of panic-stricken sheep. It has been said and written that whisky was the cause of this unfortunate rout, but this is hopelessly improbable in the face of the fact that but two casks were taken with the baggage train to be consumed by 275 men, who lived in a whisky drinking age, when five or ten drinks, more or less, made little difference in a daily average. Mr. John E. Bristol, of Eads' company, who at ninety-one is alive and hearty to-day, vouches for the truth of this assertion and the other one that but two small casks were taken along. Mr. Hall specifically states that *one* cask was emptied by the

STILLMAN'S BATTLEFIELD.

JOHN E. BRISTOL.

ALFRED HAINES.

JONATHAN HAINES.

LIEUT. ASAHEL GRIDLEY.

Indians, and Black Hawk makes the same statement, therefore it is certain that whisky cut no figure in the panic.

In justice to Stillman, his version of the affair, published in "The Missouri Republican" of July 10th, 1832, should be given:

"To the Editors of the Missouri Republican: Gentlemen—I have this day discovered in your paper of the 22d ult. an account of the engagement between the men under my command and the hostile Sac and other Indians on the Rock River. Finding that statement altogether incorrect, I take the liberty to give an outline of the transaction, which I am compelled to do in the utmost haste.

"On the 12th I received orders from His Excellency, John Reynolds, Commander-in-Chief, etc., to march immediately from Dixon's Ferry to what is commonly known as Old Man's Creek, about 30 miles distant, and coerce the said hostile Indians into subjection. We took up our march on the 13th, and on the 14th, at 2 o'clock, one of our spies discovered two Indians on our left. The Indians immediately fired on him, and undertook to make their escape by swimming Rock River; this, however, they did not succeed in; our spy brought his gun to bear on the forward one, who was tumbled into the river—the horse immediately turned his course and swam back, the surviving Indian being, from the unmanageable disposition of his horse, compelled to follow until he shared the fate of his companion. Both horses were brought in. We reached our camping ground on the north side of Old Man's Creek about 6 o'clock, after having used every precaution to guard against being deceived by the Indians, having kept out the most experienced spies and a very strong guard front, rear and flank, during the day. Soon after our arrival we discovered a small party of men in our advance, supposed at this time to be a part of our front guard. Lieutenant Gridley being then mounted, passed up a ravine for the purpose of ascertaining. It was soon after, however, ascertained that our spies with the whole of our advance guard had come in. Captain Covell with a party detached, followed. On the approach of Lieutenant Gridley, while rising the bluff, the Indians faced and leveled their guns. When prudence directed a return, the Indians pursued and were met by Captain Covell at nearly the same moment, when the fire was exchanged without effect. The Indians retreated and were pursued. Three were killed and three taken, with a loss of one of our men (as supposed). Our men were all immediately formed and took their march in the direction of Sycamore Creek, five miles above. After marching about three miles an Indian appeared and made signs of peace. I was informed of the fact, and orders were given for a halt. Myself, together with most of the field and staff officers advanced with Captain Eads as interpreter. We were soon informed that the Indians would surrender in case they would be treated as prisoners of war. This was promised them, and they returned with the intelligence, after promising to meet us at a specified point. On arriving at that point, however, no Indians appeared to make the proposed treaty, which convinced us of treachery.

"Directions were immediately given for our men to advance, while Captain Eads proceeded a few yards alone to make further discoveries. On reaching Sycamore Bluff, the Indians were discovered in martial order; their line extended a distance of nearly two miles, and under rapid march. Their signals were given for battle—war-whoops were heard in almost every direction—their flanks extending from one creek to the other. Orders were given for a line of battle to be formed on the south of the marsh between the two creeks, while the Indians were advancing with the utmost rapidity; their fire was tremendous, but on account of the distance, of little effect. Night was closing upon us in the heart of an Indian country, and the only thing to brighten our prospects, the light of our guns. Both officers and men conducted themselves with prudence and deliberation, until compelled to give ground to the superior foe, when the order for a retrograde movement was given, and our men formed in Old Man's Creek. Here a desperate attempt was made by the Indians to outflank us and cut off our retreat, which proved ineffectual, some clubbing with their fire-locks, others using their tomahawks and spears.

"A party of our men crossed the creek, and with much difficulty silenced their fire, which made a way for the retreat of our whole party, which was commenced and kept up, with few exceptions, in good order.

"Many of our officers and men having been in the battles of Tippecanoe, Bridgewater, Chippewa and Ft. Erie, have never faced a more desperate enemy. Having had the advantages of ground, the enemy being on an eminence, operated much in our favor. In passing Old Man's Creek many of them got their guns wet and were deprived of the use of them. Our force consisted of 206 men; that of the Indians not known, but consisting of a whole hostile band. Eleven of our men were killed, 5 wounded, with a loss of 34 to the enemy. From report, their encampment consisted of 160 lodges. Our men mostly arrived at Dixon's Ferry about 3 o'clock a. m., and it is to be hoped that in a short time the number of troops stationed at that point and elsewhere will be able to bring them into subjection, and relieve our frontier from a much dreaded foe.

"I am, with much respect, your obedient servant,

"I. STILLMAN,
"Brig.-Gen. 5 Brig., Ill. Mil. and Act. Maj. N. Ill. Vol.
"In Camp, 19 June, 1832"

It cannot be said of this explanation that it offers any extenuating circumstances for that inglorious retreat or that abandonment by Stillman's men of gallant Captain Adams and his men to fight it out alone and die.[1]

[1] On June 14, 1902, the State of Illinois dedicated a monument costing $5,000 on the hill where Capt. Adams made his stand. The officers of the association to whom the credit of securing that monument is due are Lovejoy Johnson, Pt.; L. Dickerman, V. Pt.; John A. Atwood, Secy.; John A. White, Treas.; Wallace Revell, Trustee.

ELISHA DIXON.

WILLIAM DIMMETT.

LEVI DANLEY.

JAMES BENSON.

THOMAS O. RUTLEDGE.

MRS. E. B. BAKER.

LEWIS ROSS.

REV. REDDICK HORN.

WILLIAM McCULLOUGH.

JAMES K. ORENDORF.

WILLIAM COPES.

WILLIAM McKEE.

JOHN A. WAKEFIELD.

COL. JAMES M. STRODE.

SERGT. FRED STAHL.

CAPT. MILTON M. MAUGHS.

CHAPTER XX.

CALL FOR ADDITIONAL TROOPS—BURIAL OF THE DEAD—ARRIVAL OF ATKINSON—LEAD MINES MILITIA—ERECTION OF FORTS—DODGE'S MARCH TO THE FOUR LAKES COUNTRY.

The straggling arrival of the panic-stricken troops into camp at Dixon's Ferry, from three o'clock to daylight of the morning of May 15th, threw Whiteside's camp into confusion. The force of Dodge's warning had now a depressing, yea, disastrous effect on the army, and the conduct of the men was most humiliating to Governor Reynolds. With one accord the officers flocked to his tent to hear the exaggerations of the runaways and plan a possible maneuver to counteract the fleeting fortune of their volunteer arms.

The catastrophe, instead of inspiring the troops with resolution to revenge their fallen comrades, spread disaffection, and demands arose from all sides to be discharged from a campaign which promised nothing but trouble and a long absence from home. The Governor, foreseeing the plight likely to visit him, at once, by the light of a solitary candle, wrote out the following call for 2,000 more volunteers to rendezvous at Hennepin on the 10th of June:

"Dixon's Ferry, on Rock River, May 15, 1832.

"It becomes my duty to again call on you for your services in defense of your country. The state is not only invaded by the hostile Indians, but many of our citizens have been slain in battle. A detachment of mounted volunteers, about 275 in number, commanded by Maj. Stillman, were overpowered by hostile Indians on Sycamore Creek, distant from this place about thirty miles, and a considerable number killed. This is an act of hostility which cannot be misconstrued. I am of the opinion that the Pottawatomies and Winnebagoes have joined the Sacs, and all may be considered as waging war against the United States. To subdue these Indians and drive them out of the state, it will require a force of at least 2,000 mounted volunteers, in addition to troops already in the field. I have made the necessary requisition of proper officers for the above number, and have no doubt that the citizen soldiers of the state will obey the call of their country. They will meet at Hennepin, on the Illinois River, in companies of 50 men each, on the 10th of June next, to be organized into brigades.

"JOHN REYNOLDS, Commander in Chief."

John Ewing of Franklin County and John A. Wakefield and Robert Blackwell of Fayette County were the trusted messengers selected to carry this call over the state. At the same time, Col. James M. Strode, colonel and commander of the Jo Daviess County militia, was empowered and requested to organize his county for immediate action.

Governor Reynolds also sent word of the defeat to Colonel Dodge at the camp of the latter on the north side of the river some distance above, with the request that he forthwith take measures to protect the frontier of Michigan Territory (now Wisconsin).

Major Horn[1] of Reynolds' staff was dispatched to St. Louis with a message to Colonel March, who was at that place, to forward the supplies for the new levy to Hennepin. With his conspicuous vigor the order was executed, but not by leaving the provisions at Hennepin. Fort Deposit, or later Fort Wilbourn, so-called from Captain John S. Wilbourn of the militia from Morgan County, was a point on the south bank of the Illinois River about midway between the present cities of Peru and LaSalle. It was nearer the seat of action at Dixon's Ferry and was accordingly chosen by Major Horn, and there he deposited the provisions. Thither, too, the troops marched, and, as Albert Sidney Johnston wrote in his journal on June 12, 1832: "General and staff arrived at this place this evening. The Illinois volunteers having arrived here in great numbers, the General decided upon organizing them at this point, supplies for the troops having been placed in depot at this place, and the route to Dixon's quite as good and as near as the mouth of Fox River."

That explains the erection of this base, and in the same connection it may be said that the old army trail subsequently became known as the "Peru road," was the one traveled by Abraham Lincoln on his return home via Peoria, and was the route traversed by Colonel John Dement, Receiver of the Dixon Land Office, when subsequently he carried the public moneys from Dixon to Peru to be shipped by boat to St. Louis, the industrial and financial center of the times.

Another message was sent to General Atkinson, not yet arrived from Fort Armstrong, and finally Major Adams[2] was dispatched to Quincy to procure corn for the horses. By daylight the various expresses were hurrying on their respective ways over the state.

With the abandonment of the baggage and supplies down the river, the improvidence of the troops with the provisions brought along and the destruction and confiscation of Stillman's by Black Hawk, there was imminent danger of a famine, but Mr. Dixon came to the rescue by slaughtering his oxen, milch cows and young stock, which the troops devoured without bread or salt. After a hasty breakfast, a general march for the battlefield to bury the dead was begun, and by evening finished.

The sight of the mangled remains of their comrades did not inspire the majority of the men with a wish to prolong their service. Dissatis-

---

[1] Reddick Horn.
[2] 2d Sergeant Parker Adams, of Gideon Simpson's Company.

CAPT. S. H. SCALES.

SURGEON HORATIO NEWHALL.

JESSE W. SHULL.

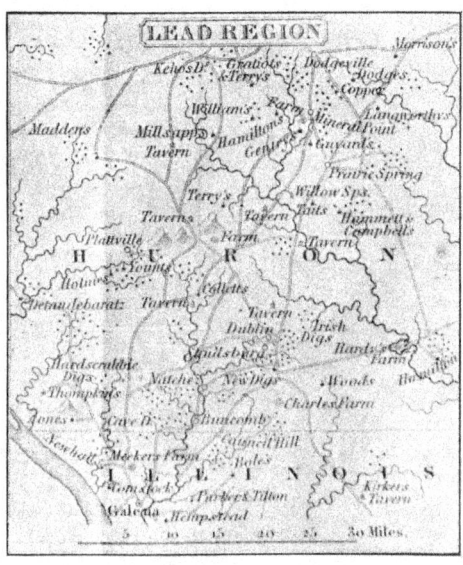

THE LEAD MINES DISTRICT.

COL. HENRY DODGE.

COL. HENRY DODGE AS A U. S. RANGER.

CAPT. JAMES CRAIG.

CAPT. J. R. B. GRATIOT.

THE BLACK HAWK WAR.   141

faction, much of it unexplained, prevailed, and nothing but a demand for a discharge from further service was heard.

Gathering the fragments of the mutilated bodies together, they buried Captain Adams and his faithful companions that evening, the 15th. The dismantled baggage wagons, ruined saddlebags, dead horses, destroyed provisions and the whisky keg, said by Black Hawk to have been emptied by his direction, were found upon the field.

The army camped that night upon the south bank of the creek, with little to disturb it save the casual firing of small arms in the distance, which might have indicated the presence of the enemy, but Major Henry and his battalion of spies, detached to scour the country and test the presence of the Indians, returned to camp at an early hour of the morning without discovering a sign of them.

On the morning of the 16th the army began its return march for Dixon's Ferry for provisions, presuming, of course, that Atkinson's forces would be there against their arrival in the evening, but the progress of the keel boats up the river had necessarily been very slow, and when the army reached Dixon's Ferry the regulars had not yet arrived. This caused a storm of protest to reach the ears of the officers, which demanded decisive action. The unplanted crops, the futility of the enterprise and innumerable other reasons were urged for disbanding. The "fun" of an Indian campaign had proved too serious for the younger generation.

In this dreadful state of insubordination the Governor held the troops until the morning of the 17th, when, after a fervid appeal to their patriotism to continue their service to protect the exposed frontier until the new levies arrived, the remaining troops of Stillman and Bailey, recovering their lost senses, immediately consented, whereupon the Fifth Regiment was organized, as before mentioned. Delaying for a few hours the decision, which must inevitably have come in favor of the other men, hopeful that Atkinson would come, Governor Reynolds was happily relieved by the arrival of Atkinson's forces and Major Long's foot battalion about noon, with stores, which momentarily quieted the clamoring of the volunteers. With these reinforcements came Captain W. S. Harney and Lieutenant Jefferson Davis, each of whom had been absent on furlough, but who, on the crossing of Black Hawk into Illinois, had returned to his regiment at Fort Armstrong in time to march up the river with Atkinson.

Before dark of the 15th, Strode, Captain J. W. Stephenson and others from the mining district reached Galena with the intelligence of Stillman's defeat, and the possibilities of immediate and general Indian hostilities created the greatest excitement among the people. The notes of a bugle at once called the settlers and miners together on the old race course on the bottom near the river,[1] and by reason of his popularity, Captain Stephenson quickly organized a company of mounted rangers, which

---
[1]Hist. Jo Daviess County, p. 284.

elected him captain. Strode, however, could not manipulate his militia, as he had confidently expected and promised. Candidates for office contested the supremacy of Strode, then a candidate for State Senator (and later elected), with suggestions that he should get out of the way. With this conflict among leaders, men did not respond as expected, and to still more complicate Reynolds' already distressing plight, Strode's troubles reached Dixon's Ferry. Resolving upon asking the advice of Atkinson, he started an express for Atkinson's camp at 3 o'clock in the morning of Saturday, May 19th, consisting of Sergeant Fred Stahl and William Durley, Vincent Smith, Redding Bennett and James Smith, who bore dispatches for Atkinson and who took John D. Winters, the mail contractor, for guide. On Sunday, 20th, Stahl returned and added to the alarm by reporting that his party had been ambuscaded by the Indians just on the edge of Buffalo Grove (now Polo, Illinois), fifty miles from Galena, about 5 o'clock of Saturday afternoon, and that Durley was instantly killed and left on the spot.

Strode was in despair. He declared martial law, and had not Atkinson, on his arrival at Dixon's, anticipated his troubles and sent relief, poor Strode might have been discomfited. As it was, Lieutenant Jefferson Davis and a small detachment was ordered to hasten to his assistance. Arrived there, Davis, with the co-operation of H. Hezekiah Gear, a man of strong personality, great force of character and of commanding influence with the sturdy miners, smoothed the ruffled tempers of the miners and softened them into an eager desire for enlistment, and the organization of the Twenty-seventh Regiment followed.

This regiment, organized on the 19th and 21st, was composed of the companies of Captains Milton M. Maughs, Nicholas Dowling, Clack Stone, Charles McCoy, Benjamin J. Aldenrath, H. Hezekiah Gear, Samuel H. Scales, Jonathan Craig, L. P. Vansburgh, all from Jo Daviess County. It was commanded by Colonel Strode, ranged the northwestern part of the state and was mustered out at Galena, September 6th. Owing to the careless manipulation of the records in those days, it is impossible to state the remaining officers of the regiment, except to note the name of Dr. Horatio Newhall as surgeon and the casual use of the name of Captain Stephenson as major, but as he was subsequently attached to Dodge's squadron as major, and acted almost entirely with Dodge thereafter, his should be classed as an independent company, not in Strode's regiment.[1]

In addition to the Twenty-seventh Regiment, Jo Daviess organized two independent companies, which later became permanently attached to Dodge's squadron and were mustered out September 14 at Galena by Lieut. J. R. B. Gardenier, who for the most part acted as commandant of the company of Nicholas Dowling. One of those two companies was commanded by Capt. James Craig and the other was the company of Captain

---
[1]William Campbell was later made Major of the Twenty-seventh Regiment.

A. L. CHETLAIN.

LOUIS CHETLAIN.

LIEUT. CHARLES GRATIOT.

NATHANIEL T. PARKINSON.

MAJ. THOMAS JAMES.

CAPT. J. H. ROUNDTREE.

EDWARD D. BOUCHARD.

CAPT. HIRAM ROUNDTREE.

Stephenson, until he was elected major. On that date Enoch Duncan was elected captain, vice Stephenson.

Of the body called Dodge's squadron, Henry Dodge was Colonel, James W. Stephenson was Major and later Lieutenant-Colonel, W. W. Woodbridge, Adjutant, Addison Philleo, Surgeon, and John Bivens, Surgeon's Mate. The moment Dodge received word from Reynolds of Stillman's disaster, he lost not one minute in returning to the mining district to quiet the Winnebagoes, who might and probably would have risen with the Pottowatomies and overwhelmed the settlers over the entire northwestern country, but Dodge and Henry Gratiot gave them no time to formulate a plan. The Winnebagoes were the natural friends and allies of the Sacs and the constant and unscrupulous enemy of the whites when the least opportunity arose, but since the affair of 1827 they feared Dodge.

His public position in 1832 was Colonel of Michigan Militia,[1] to which command was added, immediately on the commencement of hostilities, the command of the mounted volunteers of Iowa County and the Galena volunteers in Illinois, when they served by companies in Michigan Territory. Starting before dawn of May 15th for the lead mines settlements, he in an incredibly short time had preparations moving for the safety of every settler in southwestern Michigan. In a week's time stockades made of logs ten or twelve feet high, buried end up, in forms of squares or parallelograms, with blockhouses inclosed and lookouts at one or more corners, were finished and ready for occupation at the following places, after which all persons so disposed were comfortably "forted," as the expression was in those days:

Fort Union (headquarters), Colonel Dodge's residence near Dodgeville. Colonel Dodge commanding.

Fort Defiance, at the farm of Daniel M. Parkinson, about five miles southeast of Mineral Point. Captain Hoard commanding.

Fort Hamilton, at William S. Hamilton's diggings, later Wiota.

Fort Jackson, at Mineral Point. Capt. John F. O'Neal commanding.

Mound Fort, on the high prairie about a mile and a half south of Ebenezer Brigham's residence at Blue Mounds. Capt. John Sherman commanding.

Parish's Fort, at the residence of Thomas J. Parish, later Wingville.

And forts, unnamed, at Cassville, Platteville, Gratiot's Grove, under command of J. R. B. Gratiot, Diamond Grove, White Oak Springs, Old Shullsburg and Elk Grove, at the farm of Justus DeSeelhorst.

About the 22d or 23d of May, Colonel Dodge and Col. Henry Gratiot, sub-agent of the Winnebagoes, assembled a company of fifty mounted volunteers, commanded by Captains James H. Gentry and John H. Roundtree, and marched to the head of the Four Lakes, where, on the 25th, the assembled Indians were asked to declare their intentions. If they decided

---
[1] Vol. 1, p. 265, Smith's Hist. of Wis.

to aid, counsel or abet the Sacs, or harbor them in their country, such acts would be received as a declaration of war and would be visited with condign punishment. Dodge emphatically proclaimed the Sacs liars and traitors, who wished only to draw the Winnebagoes into a war to distract attention from their own actions, while they might escape when hostilities went against them, thus leaving the Winnebagoes to bear the brunt of the punishment which must follow in blood and uncomfortable peace conditions.

So vigorous, yet so diplomatic, were Dodge and Gratiot, that peaceful relations were at once assured and, with slight exception, maintained by all.[1]

---
[1] The "talk" had at this meeting given in full note A, p. 416, Smith, Vol. I.

THE TOWNSEND FAMILY; ALL THE ABOVE BROTHERS SERVED IN THE WAR.

CHAPTER XXI.

ATKINSON'S MOVEMENT UP ROCK RIVER—INDIAN CREEK MASSACRE—NARRATIVES.

On the 18th, after ten days' rations had been issued, Atkinson, by order No. 17, directed Whiteside to be in readiness to move up the river the following morning, while Col. Johnson was to remain with his battalion at Dixon's as a corps of reserve until the return of the main army, which contemplated a movement after the Indians the following morning, or until further orders. Later in the day rumors of possible attacks caused Atkinson, for better security of the post, to order the company of Capt. James White to be in readiness to move to Fort Armstrong at any moment. The necessity for departure that day was not, however, apparent, but early the following morning the alarm along the frontier had grown to such proportions that not only was Capt. White ordered to proceed at once, but Capt. Seth Pratt's company was added to the detail, under orders of Capt. White, to proceed at once down the river in the "large" keel boat with the sick and wounded, to report to Major Thomas J. Beall, then in command of Fort Armstrong, Major John Bliss being left at Dixon's in charge of that post.

While many wild rumors were constantly afloat, no positive danger of attack was apprehended up to this time, but when a delegation of influential and reputable men from the settlements on the Fox and Du Page rivers met the army the follwing day, some distance up the river, and reported actual attacks and more in prospect, another order, No. 20, directed Col. Johnson, with Major Bailey and the four companies of Captains Covell, McClure, Pugh and Adams (then commanded by First Lieutenant Benjamin Briggs, who succeeded to the command), to proceed at once to those scenes, after first securing from Col. Taylor, while marching, two kegs of rifle powder and one hundred pounds of lead. This disposition left the three companies of Captains Eads, Barnes and Ball, under Lieut-Col. Stillman at Dixon's Ferry.

To ascertain the route pursued by the Indians after Stillman's defeat, a party composed of Elijah Iles and four others was ordered out. These men passed around the late camp a distance of eight or ten miles. A trail was found going in the direction of the Illinois River, which was followed some distance without results. The second night out they were alarmed by evidence which clearly proved the presence of Indians; pony tracks, leaves turned up by the feet of the ponies and other indisputable indications, which were followed by the sight of three Indians, evidently searching for them. These were eluded and the second night passed without event. Continuing the next morning a course down Rock River, Black Hawk's late camp on that river was found about noon, deserted, with many canoes and other articles of Indian property left behind. Again striking out for the army, the little party reached it about night, when news of the murders at Indian Creek was received.

This scouting party learned that the trail toward the south was a ruse to divert the army from intercepting their march to the north, which the Indians covered with remarkable cleverness, a few of them going on to Indian Creek to participate in the murders, while the others returned north.[1]

On the 19th the army, ostensibly to pursue the Indians, moved twelve miles up the river from Dixon's Ferry and there camped for the night. The following morning the march was resumed with more vigor, and by dark Stillman's battlefield was reached almost simultaneously with an express bearing tidings of the murder of fifteen persons at the Davis settlement, twelve miles above Ottawa, on Indian Creek, which empties into the Fox about ten miles above its mouth. The effect of this staggering news was immediately to place the army in the best possible state of defense against attack, which might be made by the confederated tribes of Sacs, Foxes, Winnebagoes and Pottowatomies at any moment, as was then feared. Accordingly general order No. 21 was fulminated, and detachments were sent to Dixon's Ferry and other points, as will be noticed hereafter:

"The order of encampment and the order of march observed by the mounted volunteers will be continued. Should the brigade be attacked in front on its march, the advance guard will, as far as practicable, maintain its ground until the line can be formed and come up to its assistance. Col. DeWitt and Col. Fry's regiments will move up and form line to the front, 100 paces in rear of the advance guard and dismount; the regiments having been previously told off in squads of seven, the fourth man of each squad will take charge of the horses. The two regiments will then be formed on foot and advance to the attack. In an attack on the right flank, Col. DeWitt's and Col. Fry's regiments will form line on the right flank, with the battalion of spies on their right. In case of an attack in the rear, Col. Fry's regiment, Col. James' odd battalion, and Col. Thomas' regiment will form line, facing to the rear.

"In the several formations directed, those regiments not named will remain in position, and be held in readiness to support the point of attack when ordered. Brig.-Gen. Whiteside will cause these dispositions for battle to be practiced as often

---

[1] Iles' Early Life and Times, p. 43. The author claimed the presence of Col. William S. Hamilton in his party, but in that he was mistaken, as Col. Hamilton returned to Galena with Strode.

as he may deem necessary. The piece of artillery will be brought into action as circumstances may require. Should the camp be attacked, they will be formed in front of their tents and in rear of the fires. The regiments thus posted will remain in their respective positions until otherwise directed by the commanding officer. The Spy Battalion will occupy the center of the camp, and be held in reserve, to be directed upon any point that may require support. At night, the fires will be made 40 yards in front of the line of tents; the guard will consist of four companies, one to be posted on the center of each front, 150 to 200 yards in advance. The sentinels will be posted at a proper distance, which will be varied according to the nature of the ground. If the guard should be attacked, it will maintain its position as long as practicable, and if forced to retire, will do so in good order under the direction of the officer of the day, who will instruct the guard when mounted as to its disposition in this event.

"By order of Brig.-Gen. Atkinson.

"A. S. JOHNSTON, A.-D.-C.—A. A. A. Gen."

This massacre was instigated by three of Black Hawk's braves and executed by them with the assistance of about seventy disaffected Pottowatomies and Winnebagoes.[1]

In the spring of the year 1830 William Davis had made a claim on "Big Indian Creek," erecting a cabin, blacksmith shop (being a blacksmith by trade), and later a mill. When Black Hawk invaded the state in 1832, Davis was finishing a dam for the purpose of furnishing power to run the mill, preventing thereby the running upstream of the fish, as was claimed by the Indians. A numerous band of Pottowatomies, under their chief, Meau-eus, lived in their village on this creek, six miles above the dam, subsisting largely on the fish caught in that little stream. Meau-eus, having been always a fine hater of the whites, grew excessively angry at this obstruction, and in an attempt to destroy it resistance followed, in which the Indians claimed one of the band was unmercifully flogged by Davis, a man of powerful physique. For final adjustment, the controversy was carried before Shabbona, who, in conjunction with Wau-ban-se, concluded an arrangement whereby the Indians were persuaded for the future to fish below the dam, which involved but little additional labor and which they did for a time with apparent good will, but beneath the surface a hatred lodged, only to be spent when, through the assistance of Black Hawk's braves, the settlement perished.

John and J. H. Henderson, Allen Howard, William Pettigrew, William Hall and others, with their families, had from time to time settled near the place, until the settlement had grown to be one of the most promising in northern Illinois.

After Black Hawk passed Dixon's Ferry, it was not long before his emissaries discovered the situation and made the best of it by recruiting to his ranks the entire band, the very thing the Governor attempted to prevent when he sent out his express from Dixon's. The Indians at once

---

[1] The statement by Matson that one Mike Girty was connected with the Indian Creek massacre is incorrect.

ceased to fish, a circumstance which Davis and J. H. Henderson proceeded to investigate by visiting the village. They found it abandoned, as they had feared, as was that of Wau-ban-se, who, by the advice of Shabbona, had taken his men to the village of the latter after both had sent their women and children to Ottawa for protection.

Stillman's defeat followed, and then came Shabbona's famous ride to warn the settlements of the dangers which he too well realized were in store for the Davis settlement. Never lived there a more devoted and upright Indian than Shabbona! From the day he left the fortunes of Tecumseh he neglected no opportunity to manifest his friendship for the whites, and never was a more perilous ride projected in a frontier country than the one he took with his son, Pype-gee, and his nephew, Pypes, that memorable day down the Fox River Valley, on to Holderman's settlement, and, separating, thence on to Bureau Creek, passing through the Indian Creek settlement on the route, missing none in all that vast territory.

Howard and the two Hendersons took their families to Ottawa and then returned to work their farms. Pettigrew likewise took his wife and two children to the same place, but finding no trouble in sight at the end of a few days, he brought them all back again, reaching Davis' house at noon of the day of the massacre. Robert Norris and Henry George, young men from the neighboring settlements, were also at the Davis house, so on that particular day Davis naturally thought their numbers sufficient to resist any attack; in fact, he had urged against any member of the settlement removing to Ottawa for protection.

Pypes, or Pipe, as he was sometimes called, carried his messages safely on down as far as Rochelle's village, below the Illinois River, where he tarried, as we are told, to urge his suit with a maid of great beauty at that village. Returning home by way of the Indian Creek settlement, he discovered, toward dark of the 19th, a large band of Indians entering the timber, which fact he reported to Shabbona so soon as he reached the latter's village, about midnight.[1]

Once more the grand old chief mounted his pony and rode out into the night, as he had before done so many times, to spread a warning. By sunrise, every person in the settlement had again been notified and given a chance to flee to Ottawa, but Davis, again protesting, prevented.

As Shabbona subsequently told the story, these Indians camped near the head of the timber on the creek, while reconnoitering parties surveyed and learned the exact location and pursuit of each settler and determined on a propitious moment for the assault. These did their work thoroughly, leaving no possibility for escape by any number of the intended victims. About 4 o'clock of May 20th the scattered settlers were suddenly confronted by seventy Indians, led there by two Pottowatomies named To-qua-mee and Co-mee, all of whom had so adroitly covered their movements

---

[1] Matson's "Memories of Shau-be-na."

as to be able to reach the very dooryards before discovery. The barking of a dog attracted the attention of Mrs. Davis, who exclaimed, on looking out the door: "My God! Here they are now."

Mr. Pettigrew attempted to barricade the door, but was shot down amidst shrieks and whoops, signals for the slaughter which followed. The men at the blacksmith shop were so completely surprised that no opportunity for defense was offered. Hall was instantly dispatched. Norris attempted resistance, but his gun was seized and in another instant he, too, was dead. Davis, the strongest of the party, fought desperately by clubbing his rifle, but to no purpose against such frightful odds, for no sooner would he dispose of one antagonist than others would take his place with added ferocity, for Davis was the man they most of all hated and feared, and well he earned the distinction of being a fighter on that dreadful day. The ground about his dead body was torn and bloody, indicating a conflict second only to the hand-to-hand contest of gallant Captain Adams at Stillman's defeat. The brains of children were dashed out against a stump; the women were butchered, and, after the most revolting mutilations, their bodies were hanged, heads downward, to neighboring trees.[1] Young William Davis and John W., a son of William Hall, made their escape after desperate chances. Henry George, in attempting to escape, jumped into the mill pond, but a bullet quickly disposed of him. Spears, knives, tomahawks and rifles performed their bloody and deadly offices, and the fiends afterward confessed they relished the sight because the women squawked like ducks as the steel penetrated their flesh. Mrs. Davis, in her fright, threw both arms about Rachel Hall, and when shot down the muzzle of the rifle had been so close as to burn the flesh to a blister. Aside from the few who escaped, but two, Sylvia and Rachel Hall, aged, respectively, seventeen and fifteen years, were spared, whether from a sentimental demand made by the two Indians, To-qua-mee and Co-mee, before consenting to act as guides, or for the purpose of ransom, cannot be definitely determined, but from subsequent developments it is probable that both reasons were factors in their preservation.

These two Indians, who subsequently confessed their part in the affair to Louis Ouilmette, after their acquittal, insisted that it was agreed the two young ladies should be spared because of the infatuation of those young red men for them. They had been frequent visitors at the Hall home, and endeavored, after the fashion of the Indian, to purchase the girls from Mr. Hall.

Following is the narrative of the captivity of the Hall girls, reduced to writing by them and John W. Hall, the manuscripts being now in possession of Hon. James H. Eckles of Chicago, and by him loaned to be used herein. Mrs. Eckles is a granddaughter of Mrs. Munson.

"A short and concise account of the capture, treatment and rescue of

---

[1] Matson.

the two Misses Hall. The capture occurred on the 20th of May, 1832, in the afternoon, by the Sacs and Foxes, and the rescue on the 1st of June following.

The following is a statement of the two girls, made in the presence of William Munson and W. S. Horn, their husbands:

"In the afternoon of the 20th day of May, 1832, we were alarmed by Indians rushing suddenly into the room where we were staying. The room or house was situated on the north bank of Indian Creek, in the county of LaSalle, State of Illinois, about 12 miles north of Ottawa. Here our father and family, consisting of father, mother, four sisters and three brothers, were stopping a few days. Father's name was William Hall, about 45 years old. Mother's name was Mary Jane Rebecca, aged 45. The eldest sister's name was Temperance Cutright, who was living in McLean County, Illinois, at the time, and was about 27 years old; eldest brother's name was John W., who was at home, aged 23; Edward H. Hall, aged 21; Greenbury Hall, aged 19 (these two last named were not at the house at the time when the Indians made the attack); Sylvia Hall, aged 17; Rachael Hall, aged 15; Elizabeth, aged 8. The house in which we were belonged to Wm. Davis, who, with his family, contained nine members. Mr. Pettigrew's family, consisting of four members, were also at the house, where those families were stopping together, in order to protect each other in case of danger from the Indians. John H. Henderson, Henry George and Robert Norris also were stopping at the same house.

"John H. Henderson, Alexander Davis, Edward and Greenbury Hall, Allen Howard, Wm. Davis, Jr., were in the field, about 100 rods south, at the time when the Indians approached the house. Wm. Hall, Wm. Davis, John W. Hall, Norris and George were at the time in a blacksmith shop about sixty or eighty steps from the house, rather down the creek, and near the bank and not far from the north end of a mill dam, which was being built.

"Mr. Pettigrew was in the house, when all of a sudden the Indians came to the door of the house. Pettigrew, with a child in his arms, flew to the door and tried to shut it, but failed to accomplish his object, being shot, and fell in the house. Then commenced a heart-rending scene. Mrs. Pettigrew had her arms around Rachael at the time she was shot, and the flash of the burning powder blew in her face. We were trying to hide or get out of the way, while there was no place to get. We were on the bed when the Indians caught us, and took us out into the yard, two Indians taking each of us by the arms and hurrying off as fast as possible, and while going, we saw an Indian take Pettigrew's child by the feet and strike its head against a stump, and Davis' little boy was shot by an Indian, two other Indians holding the boy by each hand.

We passed on to the creek, about 80 steps, when they dragged Rachael into the creek and about half way across, when they turned back and went near half way to the house, where Sylvia and Rachael got together and were hurried up the creek on the north side, being the same side the house stood upon, to where the Indians had left their ponies, about 1½ miles from the house. Here we found the Indians with father's horses and some of the neighbors tied up with their ponies. We were then placed on a pony apiece, on an Indian saddle, and placed near the center of the procession, each of our ponies being led, and occasionally the ponies we were riding received the lash from someone behind.

"We supposed that there was somewhere about 40 warriors, no squaws being in this party. In this way we traveled until late in the night, when the party halted about two hours, and the Indians danced a little, holding their ponies by the bridles. We rested during this time on some blankets, and both permitted to sit together. Then we were remounted and traveled on in the same order until one or two o'clock the next day, when they halted again near some bushes, not far from a grove of timber (on our right). Just before we stopped, Rachael made signs to them that she was tired, and was allowed to get off her pony and walk awhile, and while walking we came to a stream of water some three feet deep, and she was compelled to wade through the water. Here we rested one or two hours while the ponies picked a little, and some beans were scalded by the Indians and some acorns roasted, and the Indians ate heartily, and we tried to, but it was very hard to get much down while expecting all the time to fare like our beloved friends, or worse. After thus resting, we were packed up as usual, and traveled on a while, when some of the Indians left us for some time. When they returned we were hurried on at a rapid rate some five miles, while the Indians that were following had their spears drawn, and we expected that the party while absent had seen some whites, and that if we were overtaken they would destroy us.

"After having rode at this rapid rate for about one hour, they slacked or checked their speed and rode on as usual, until near sundown, when the whole party halted for the night, and, having built a fire, the Indians required us to burn some tobacco and corn meal in the fire, which was placed in our hands by them, which we did, not knowing why we did so, except to obey them. We, however, supposed it might be to show that they had been successful in their undertaking. The Indians then prepared their supper, consisting of dried meat sliced, coffee boiled in a copper kettle, corn pounded and made in a kind of soup; they then gave us some of this preparation in wooden bowls, with wooden ladles. We partook of those provisions, but did not relish them, after which the Indians partook of their supper, prepared in the same manner. After supper the warriors held a dance, and after the dance concluded, we were conducted to a tent or wigwam, and a squaw placed on each side of us, where we remained during this night, sleeping what we could, which was but little. The Indians kept stirring round all night. In the morning, breakfast in about the same manner as supper. Breakfast over, the Indians cleared off a piece of ground about 90 feet in circumference, and placed a pole about 25 feet high in the center, and 15 or 20 spears set up around this pole, and on the top of the spears were placed the scalps of our murdered friends. Father's, mother's and Mr. Pettigrew's were recognized by us. There were also two or three hearts placed upon separate spears; then squaws, under the directions of the warriors, as we understood it by their jabbering, painted one side of our faces and heads red and the other black, we being seated on our blankets near the center pole, just leaving room for the Indians to pass between us and the pole. Then the warriors commenced to dance around us with their spears in their hands, and occasionally sticking them in the ground. And now we expected at every round the spears would be thrust through us and our troubles brought to an end, yet no hostile demonstration was made by them toward us.

"After they had continued their dance about half an hour or more, two old squaws led us away to one of their wigwams and washed the paint off our faces, as well as they could, after scrubbing very hard. Then the whole encampment struck tents and started in a northward direction, while the whole earth seemed to be alive with Indians This being the third day of our suffering, we were very much exhausted, and still we must obey the savage murderers, and while traveling now, we were separated from each other during traveling hours, under charge of two squaws to each of us, and being permitted to stay together when not on the march under the direction of our four squaws, we now traveled slowly over rough, barren prairie land until near sundown, when we camped again, being left with our four squaws, with whom we were always in company, day or night, they sleeping on each side of us during the night.

"The warriors now held another dance, but not around us this time, as before. Here we had all the maple sugar we desired, while the Indians seemed to make as good preparations for our accommodation as they could.

"About this time our dresses were changed, the Indians furnishing the dresses. The one furnished Rachael was a red and white calico dress, ruffled around the bottom. Sylvia's was blue calico. The Indians now tried to get us to throw away our shoes and put on moccasins, which we would not do. They also threw away Rachael's comb, and she went and got it again and kept it. We now traveled and camped about as usual, until the seventh day, when the Indians came to where we were and took Sylvia off on to the side of a hill, about 40 rods from where we were before, to where the Indians seemed to have been holding a council, and one of the Indians said that Sylvia must go with an old Indian, which we afterward learned was the chief of the Winnebagoes, and called himself White Crow, and was blind in one eye, and that Rachael was to remain with the Indians we had been with all the time. Sylvia said she could not go unless Rachael went also. He, the White Crow, then got up and made a speech, loud and long, and seemed very much excited and interested. After he had concluded his speech, some Indian, who called himself Whirling Thunder, went and brought Rachael to where Sylvia was, and the chiefs shook hands together, and horses were brought, switches cut to whip them with, and we were both placed on horses, while one of the young Indians stepped up, and with a large knife cut a lock of hair out of Rachel's head over the right ear, and one out of the back of the head and said to the old chief White Crow that he would have her back (as we afterwards learned) in three or four days. One of the Indians also cut a lock of hair out of the front part of Sylvia's head. Then we started and rode at a rapid rate, until the next morning near daylight, when we halted at the encampment of the Winnebagoes, and where a bed was prepared on a low scaffold with blankets and furs, upon which we lay down until after daylight. This was the morning of the ninth day of our captivity. After breakfast the whole encampment packed up and placed us and themselves in canoes, and we traveled all day until near sundown, by water, and camped on the bank of the stream, the name of which we never knew, neither can we now tell whether we traveled up or down; neither can we tell what went with the horses on which we rode the day before.

"On the morning of the 9th we were up and had breakfast as usual with the Indians very early, after which White Crow went round to each camp or wigwam, as far as we could see, and stood at the opening with a gourd with pebbles in it, shaking it and occasionally talking as if he was lecturing, then he went off and was gone all day, while we remained in camp. He came back at night, and for the first time spoke to us in English and asked if father or mother was alive, and whether we had any brothers or sisters. We told him we thought not, for we expected they were all killed. When he heard this he shook his head and looked very sorry, and then informed us that he was going to take us home in the morning.

"Things remained as usual through the night. Next morning, being the 10th, White Crow went through the same performance as on the morning of yesterday. Then 26 of the Winnebagoes went with us into the canoes and crossed over the stream, swimming their ponies by the side of the canoes. After landing on the other shore, all were mounted on the ponies, and we traveled all day through wet land, sloughs and a growth of underbrush, no water being where the underbrush grew.

"At night we came to where there were two or three families encamped. (They expressed great joy at seeing us.) Here we stopped for the night and camped.

At the camp where we staid, White Crow and Whirling Thunder staid. Here we had pickled pork, potatoes, coffee and bread for supper for ourselves and the two chiefs, which we relished better than anything we had since our captivity.

"After all the Indians had laid down, except White Crow, we laid down on the bed prepared for us, and White Crow came and sat down by our bed and commenced smoking his pipe and continued there, smoking the most of the time until morning, never going to sleep, as we believe.

"The next morning, 11th, breakfast about the same as supper. The Indian families with whom we staid bid us good-bye, and the same company of 26 Indians as the day before started with us, and we traveled over land that seemed to be higher than that traveled over the day before, and more barren timber. About 10 a. m. we came to some old tracks of a wagon, and now for the first time we began to have some hopes that these Indians were going to convey us home, as they said they would. And as we passed on we began to see more and more signs of civilization. About three o'clock p. m. we stopped and had some dinner, broiled venison and boiled duck eggs, and if they had not been boiled so soon, the young ducks would have made their appearance, and our stomachs would have revolted at such a mess as this. But the Indians would never starve, if they could always get young ducks boiled in the shell.

After this sumptuous feast, we traveled on until we found we were near the fort at the Blue Mounds. White Crow then took Rachael's white handkerchief, or one that had once been white, and made a flag of it, raised it on a pole, rode on about one-half mile, and halted. There the Indians formed a ring around us, and White Crow and two others went on towards the fort until they came within about one-half mile of the fort, where they halted and remained until an interpreter met him and ascertained what he wanted. When the interpreter learned what was wanted, he returned to the fort, and the Indian Agent, Henry Gratiot, in company with a company of soldiers, returned to where we were enclosed. White Crow then delivered us over to the company of soldiers, and we returned with the troops to the fort and found, to the great joy of our hearts, two of our uncles in the company, Edward Hall and Reason Hall.

"We remained here in the fort two nights and one day; obtained here a change of clothing. It was now about the 1st of June. We started in company with the same 26 Indians and a company of soldiers, with the Indian agent, Henry Gratiot, for Gratiot's Grove, which place we reached at night, and remained over night with a family, the agent and interpreter remaining with us, while the Indians camped near by. Next morning White Crow made a speech to the company, in which he referred to the incidents of our rescue. He also proposed to give each of us a Sac squaw for a servant during life, which we declined, telling him that we did not desire to have them placed in such a situation. Then we, in company with the troops, went on to the fort at the White Oak Springs (the Indians bidding us a final adieu at Gratiot's Grove). Here we remained three or four days, when J. W. Hall, our dear brother, who we supposed murdered, met us, and from whom we learned that all the families that were at the house of Davis, and all the individuals that were present, were killed, himself excepted. Those in the field at the time of our captivity made their escape to the fort at Ottawa, LaSalle County, Illinois, and he, J. W. Hall, after seeing all fall by the hands of the Indians, made his escape by jumping down the bank of the creek and keeping under said bank on the side nearest the Indians, until he could venture out in the prairie and get across to said fort. His statements will be found in this work. There we remained two or three weeks, and while there we were furnished with materials (by the merchants and others, who seemed to take a great interest in our welfare) to make us some clothing, which we made, in order to prepare ourselves to pass through the country honorably, decently and respectably. And we are very sorry we cannot recollect the names of those kind friends, that they might appear upon record as a testimony of their kindness to us in our destitute condition. May the blessings of our Father in Heaven rest upon them all!

"From this place we went, in company with brother John W. Hall and uncle Edward Hall to Galena. Here we staid at the house of Mr. Bells, with whom we had a little acquaintance, some days. While here we received rations from the army. We also found kind friends in abundance, and received donations in clothing and other things, and needed nothing to make us comfortable as we could be under such circumstances. For what was supplied, all those friends have our thanks, and now we take our leave of them and pass down the Fevre River, to the Mississippi, then to St. Louis, Mo. Here we stopped with Governor Clark, where we received all the attention necessary to make us comfortable and happy, that could be bestowed by himself and kind family. We also here received many presents in the way of clothing, and through his (Hon. Gov. William Clark) influence, a sum of money was raised and placed in his hands for our special benefit, amounting in all, we believe, to the sum of four hundred and seventy dollars, to be laid out in land and intrusted to the care of Rev. R. Horn, of Cass County, Illinois, which was done at our request. There were also other smaller sums donated to pay our expenses up the river homeward. Those kind friends also have our thanks for their kindness and liberality. We remained here a few days and took our leave of those kind friends, probably never to meet again in this world. Leaving here, we took boat for Beardstown, Cass County, Illinois, on the Illinois River, where we were safely landed in due time and escorted out in the country five miles east, by brother J. W. Hall and uncle Edward Hall, who had been with us all the time since leaving Blue Mounds, to where we had an uncle, Robert Scott, living here. Here we remained about two months while brother J. W. Hall went up to Bureau County, Illinois, which is about 40 miles from where we were captured, Uncle Edward returning to Galena. About the last of September or first of October, 1832, brother J. W. Hall returned, and in his company we went to Bureau County, Illinois, where we remained with brother J. W. Hall until the next spring.

"Some time in March, 1833, sister Rachael was married to a William Munson. Then sister Sylvia staid part of the time with brother Green and part with Rachael until in May, 1833, sister Sylvia was also married to William S. Horn, and removed to Cass County, Ill.* Thus we have given the circumstances of our captivity and rescue as near as we can recollect at this date, September 7, 1867, in the county of Nemaha, State of Nebraska, where Sylvia Horn lives and where I and my husband have been paying them a visit.

"Rachael Munson,
"Sylvia Horn."

In presence of:
"W. S. Horn,
"W. Munson."

State of Nebraska, }
County of Nemaha. }   September, 1867.

"I, John W. Hall, being requested by my sisters, Sylvia Horn and Rachael Munson, to state what I recollect in reference to the massacre of my father's family, and the captivity of my two sisters, Rachael and Sylvia, would most gladly comply with their request, so far as I can; but after 35 years of toil have passed over my head since that memorable occasion, my memory is in some things rather dim; yet

---

*That part of Morgan County subsequently organized into Cass County in 1837.

MRS. RACHEL HALL MUNSON.

MRS. SYLVIA HALL HORN.

INDIAN CREEK MONUMENT.

Inscribed thereon is: "William Hall, aged 45; Mary J. Hall, aged 45; Elizabeth Hall, aged 8; William Pettigrew, wife and two children; ——— Davis, wife and five children, and Emery George. Killed May 20, 1832."

there are some things that I do remember most distinctly, and shall as long as I have a being (I think).

"It was in 1832, as near as I now recollect, on or about the 15th or 16th of May, Old Shabbona, chief of the Pottawatomies, notified my father and other neighbors that the Sac and Fox Indians were hostile, and would in all probability make a raid on the settlement where we lived and murder us and destroy our property, and advised him to leave that part of the country (LaSalle County, Illinois) and seek a place of safety; but Indian rumors were so common, and some of our neighbors did not sufficiently credit this old Indian, and we were advised by them, in connection with others, to collect together as many as possible and stand our ground and defend each other; so after spending the night and consulting together and hiding all heavy property that we could, my father loaded up his wagon and we started for Ottawa, and meeting Mr. Davis, who lived about two and a half miles west, who had been at Ottawa the day before, and had learned that a company had gone out in a northerly direction, to see what they could learn about the Indian movement, who were to report on their return, to Mr. Davis, in case of danger, he, my dear father, was prevailed on by Davis to abandon his retreat and stop at Davis', where Mr. Pettigrew and family, Mr. Howard and son, Mr. John H. Henderson and two men that were hired by Mr. Davis, Robert Norris and Henry George, were all stopping. On or about the 20th day of May myself and dear father were working under a shed adjoining a blacksmith shop, and on the west side, next to the dwelling house, Mr. Davis and Norris were at work in the shop. Henry George and William Davis, Jr., were at work on a mill dam a little south of the shop. It being a very warm day in the afternoon, someone brought a bucket of cool water from the spring to the shop, and we all went into the shop to rest a few minutes and quench our thirst.

"Brother Edward Hall, Greenberry Hall and Mr. Howard and son, Henderson and two of Mr. Davis' sons were at this time in the field, on the south side of the creek, and in full view of the house, and about one-half mile from the house, planting corn. While we were sitting resting ourselves in the shop, we heard a scream at the house. I immediately said, 'There are the Indians now!' and jumped out of the door of the shop, it being on the opposite side from the house, and the others followed as fast as they could, and as we turned the corner of the shop, I discovered the dooryard full of Indians. I next saw the Indians jerk Mr. Pettigrew's child, four or five months old, taking it by the feet and dashing its brains out against a stump. Seeing Mr. Pettigrew back in the house, I heard two guns, seemingly in the house, and then the tomahawk soon ended the cries of those in the house, and as near this moment as possible they fired about twenty shots at our party of five, neither of us being hurt, that I know of. The next motion of the Indians was to pour some powder down their guns and drop a bullet out of their mouths and raise their guns and fire; this time I heard a short sentence of a prayer to my right and a little behind. On turning my eyes to the right I saw that my dear father was lying on the ground shot in the left breast and expiring in death. On looking around, I saw the last one of the company were gone or going, and the Indians had jumped the fence and were making towards me. Mr. Davis was running in a northeast direction for the timber. Looked back and said, 'Take care,' he having his gun in his hands. I at this time discovered quite a number of Indians on horseback in the edge of the woods as though they were guarding the house, to prevent any escape. Then it flashed into my mind that I would try and save myself. I think there were 60 or 80 Indians. I immediately turned toward the creek, which was fifteen or twenty steps from where I stood. The Indians by this time were within three paces of me, under full charge, with their guns in hand. I jumped down the bank of the creek, about

12 feet, which considerably stunned me. At this moment the third volley was fired, the balls passing over my head, killing Mr. Norris and George, who were ahead of me, and who had crossed the creek to the opposite shore, one in the water and the other on the bank. I then passed as swiftly as possible down the stream, on the side next the Indians, the bank hiding me from them. I passed down about two miles, when I crossed and started for Ottawa, through the prairie, overtaking Mr. Henderson, who had started ahead of me, and we went together until we got within four miles of Ottawa, when we fell into company with Mr. Howard and son and three sons of Mr. Davis and my two brothers, all of whom were in the field referred to, except one of Mr. Davis' sons, who was in the shop when the first alarm was given, and who immediately left when he heard the cry of Indians. We all went to Ottawa together in the short space of one hour or less, it being twelve miles (and the county seat of LaSalle County). Here we aroused the inhabitants and raised a company during the night and started the next morning for the dreadful scene of slaughter and butchery.

"On the way we met with Stillman's defeated troops, who had been defeated a night or two before, they having encamped within four miles of where the bloodthirsty Indians passed the night, after they had killed my dear friends, and instead of going with us and helping bury the dead, they passed on to Ottawa, and we went to the place where the massacre took place. And what a scene presented itself! Here were some with their hearts cut out, and others cut and lacerated in too shocking a manner to mention, or behold without shuddering. We buried them all in great haste, in one grave, without coffin, box or anything of the kind, there to remain until Gabriel's trump shall wake the nations under the ground, and call to life the sleeping dead.

"We then returned to Ottawa and organized a company out of a few citizens and some of Stillman's defeated troops, into which company I enlisted. The next day we were on the line of march, in pursuit of the red savages, to try, if possible, to get possession of my two eldest sisters, who were missing, and who, we were satisfied, had been carried away with the Indians when they retreated, from signs found on the trails. We proceeded up Rock River, above Sycamore Creek, and our provisions failing, we returned to Ottawa and laid in provisions for a second trip. Here I had a conversation with General Atkinson and proposed that some means be used with friendly Indians, in order to purchase my sisters, as I feared the Indians would, in case we overtook them, kill my sisters. He then informed me that he had that morning made arrangements with Winnebago Indians to try to purchase my sisters.

"Now we started the second time in pursuit, and proceeded up Rock River, and fell in with a company of volunteers, under General Dodge, from whom we learned that the friendly Indians had succeeded in obtaining my sisters, and that they were at White Oak Grove or Springs. Then, in company with a company of regulars, under General Atkinson's orders, we marched to a place called the Burr Oak Grove, or Kellogg's old station. Here I, with some others, was detached to guard one of the company, who had stabbed his comrade, to Galena, and we started at midnight. Arriving at Galena, I obtained a furlough, and went to the White Oak Springs, where I found my sisters, and returned with them to Galena, stopping at the house of Mr. Sublets, visiting Mr. Rhodes and Mr. Bells, who were acquaintances of father's.

"Here we remained a week or ten days. Then bidding those kind friends adieu on board the steamer Winnebago, we glided down Fever River to the Mississippi, and down that stream to St. Louis, Mo., and stopped at the Honorable William Clark's mansion (governor of Missouri), where we met and enjoyed the company of his kind family. Here we remained about one week, and were made as comfortable and happy as his family and friends could make us.

"We received presents and money, an account of which has been given by my sisters in their statement, and here I wish to express my thanks to those kind friends for their hospitality, sympathy and love, for I feel that we have been brought under lasting obligations to them.

"Leaving here, we took a steamer for Beardstown, on the Illinois River, in Cass County, near to which we had an uncle Scott living. Arriving safely at Beardstown, we were conveyed to our uncle's, five miles out, where we remained a few days, and, leaving my sisters here, I went up the Illinois River to Bureau County and lived in a camp until I could build me a house. This county adjoins LaSalle on the west. The Indians, having received a dreadful scourging, had become peaceable, and in the fall I returned to Cass County and took my sisters and returned to Bureau County again, where we tried to make ourselves as comfortable as possible. This fall I married, and my sisters lived with me through the winter and in the spring, after which they both married, and now I am at the house of the eldest, Sylvia Horn, and dictated the above lines, while my brother-in-law, W. S. Horn, committed them to paper.

"September, 1867. "J. W. Hall."

In presence of:
"W. S. Horn,
"Sylvia Horn."

Late in the afternoon of the 20th, while Capt. George McFadden, Wilbur Walker and others who had been to ask Governor Reynolds and General Atkinson for the four companies ordered by them to go under Colonel Johnson were passing this point, some two miles distant, on their return trip, the shots of that frightful massacre were heard, but in their haste to reach their own settlements they did not pause to investigate the cause.

The following day the company of Capt. Joseph Naper, from Chicago, which had been ranging the country, reached the scene and buried all the dead except little Jimmie Davis, a lad of seven years, who had been spared at first and taken along, but who, being unable to keep the pace demanded, was shot a short distance out. The scene was awful, but the lad showed a spirit of fortitude attained by none other in this war of brutal slaughter. The two Indians who had him in charge held him between them, one by each hand, while another shot him down in cold blood, and then, before life was extinct, his scalp was lifted and his body left a prey for wolves or carrion birds. The little fellow blanched like marble, but received the fatal shot without a quaver. Later his body was fortunately discovered and buried with the others.

To-qua-mee and Co-mee, who were indicted for complicity in the murders, were brought to bar for the crime, but by reason of the uncertainty of the times and judges to try them, the first term of court passed with nothing done except to admit the culprits to bail on the bond of Shab-bo-na, Shem-e-non, Snock-wine, Sha-a-toe, Mee-au-mese and

Sash-au-quash, chiefs and head men of the Pottowatomie nation. Before the next term of court could be held the tribe had been removed west of the Mississippi, whither went the two defendants. When needed for trial they were sought by Sheriff George E. Walker, who alone journeyed into the Indian country. He gathered together the several chiefs, according to custom, who decided the two must return, which they did, with no effort or inclination to escape. This conduct, together with the lavish use of paint, rendered recognition almost impossible by the Hall girls, who were the chief witnesses for the State, and procured their acquittal by the jury.[1]

A deep scar ran across the face of To-qua-mee, by which the Hall girls easily recognized him at the murder of their parents, and by which they could easily have recognized him on his trial, but, thanks to the ingenuity of counsel, who had him so bedaub his face with paint, recognition was all but impossible. A little later, when he bathed in the Illinois River with his friends, the imposture was discovered and he was forced to flee for his life to escape the wrath of the settlers.

---
[1] Kee-was-see was another defendant, Armstrong 368. Richard M. Young was the judge, Thomas Ford the prosecutor, and Hamilton and Bigelow attorneys for defense at that time.

CAPT. ROBERT BARNES.

CAPT. WILLIAM HAWS.

COL. JOHN STRAWN.

LIEUT. COL. WILLIAM COWEN.

CHAPTER XXII.

GENERAL PANIC—INDEPENDENT COMPANIES RAISED—ATKINSON'S MARCH CONTINUED—INSUBORDINATION—ARMY DISBANDED—INTERIM REGIMENT RAISED.

If Stillman's defeat spread consternation, the Indian Creek massacre created a veritable and universal panic in the West. Counties began the organization of companies and regiments, Putnam alone contributing an entire regiment, called the Fortieth, which was mustered into the field May 21st. It was composed of the companies of Captains George B. Willis, Robert Barnes, William M. Stewart and William Haws, with the following staff: Colonel, John Strawn; Lieutenant-Colonel, William Cowen; Major, Elias Thompson; Adjutant, Henry K. Cassell; Quartermaster, Jeremiah Strawn; Paymaster, Peter Barnhart; Surgeon, B. M. Hayse; Quartermaster's Sergeant, Roland Mosley; Surgeon's Mate, Richard Hunt; Sergeant-Major, William Myers; Drum Major, Ward Graves; Fife Major, Michael Reed.

After ranging that section of the country until June 18th, when all danger was thought to be over, it was mustered out at Hennepin.

Colonel Moore's Vermilion County regiment was another, while ten companies of foot and mounted rangers ranged over territory generally local: Capt. Peter Menard, mounted, of Peoria County, mustered out at Dixon's August 14th;[1] Cyrus Matthews, foot, of Morgan, mustered out at Fort Wilbourn August 1st; Capt. George McFadden, mounted, of LaSalle, mustered out at Ottawa June 29th; Capt. John Stennett, mounted, of Schuyler, mustered out September 4th; Capt. M. L. Covell of McLean, mounted, mustered out at Bloomington August 3d; Capt. John S. Wilbourn, foot, of Morgan, mustered out June 9th; Capt. Solomon Miller, mounted, of St. Clair, mustered out at Belleville August 2d; Capt. William Warnick, mounted, of Macon (ranged that county only), mustered out September 24th at Decatur; Capt. Charles S. Dorsey, mounted, of Tazewell (ranged that county only), mustered out at Pekin July 9th;

---

[1] Also served at Bad Axe.

Capt. James Walker of Will, and, finally, the company of Capt. Earl Pierce, about which nothing can be learned, mustered out August 16th.

The life of Captain Wilbourn's company was ephemeral. Reports reached Beardstown that trouble was imminent at Hennepin and that reinforcements were needed at once. Accordingly twenty-nine men volunteered from Beardstown under Capt. John S. Wilbourn, took the steamer Caroline, Captain Doty commanding, and proceeded forthwith to Hennepin. Captain Doty, for the better protection of those aboard, and also aggressively to deal with the enemy, mounted a field piece upon the boat, where it might do execution at long range. At Hennepin, however, the rumor was found to be false and without delay the company was sent back to Beardstown and mustered out June 9th, and this was all the service that the company of Captain Wilbourn saw.

Neighboring states were also placed in a state of panic, and to escape possible raids, Michigan, Indiana and Missouri called out the militia, the first two actually sending a force to Chicago. The last named, while calling out its militia, did not send it forward. The following general order, made in response to the call of Governor Miller of Missouri, ordering Major-General Gentry to have 1,000 men in readiness to march at a moment's warning to the frontier, appears in the Missouri Republican of June 12th, 1832:

"GENERAL ORDER.

"Columbia, May 31, 1832.

"Sir:—Having been required by General Order to raise and organize the Ninth Brigade, which I have the honor to command, 300 mounted volunteers, for the defense of the frontiers of the State of Missouri, to be held in readiness to march at a moment's warning, you will, therefore, with the least possible delay, cause to be raised and organized in the Twenty-sixth Regiment, Ninth Brigade, and Third Missouri Militia, which you have the honor to command, 100 mounted volunteers.

"You will organize 100 volunteers, to be raised into two companies—50 men each—and cause an election to be held in each for one captain, one lieutenant, and one ensign, and as soon as all the company officers are elected, you will make a return to me, certifying the name and rank of each person elected, etc., that they may be commissioned accordingly. Their services will be accepted for six months, unless sooner discharged; but no pay or compensation need be expected unless ordered by the Governor into actual service. Each volunteer will keep constantly in readiness a horse, with necessary equipment, a rifle in good order, with an ample supply of ammunition, etc., so as to be ready to march at a moment's warning.

"JESSE T. WOOD,

"Brig.-Gen., Commanding Ninth Brigade, Third Div., Mo. Militia."

"THOMAS G. BERRY,

"Col. Commanding Twenty-سixth Reg., Ninth Brig., Third Div., Mo. Militia."

Very naturally the frontier was regarded as a slaughtering pen, where flame and the tomahawk were ravaging the settlements almost to extinction, and one would think such scenes as the Indian Creek massacre would have incited the militia to revenge the atrocities of monsters who could

H. K. CASSELL.

JEREMIAH STRAWN.

CAPT. PETER MENARD.

CAPT. CYRUS MATHEWS.

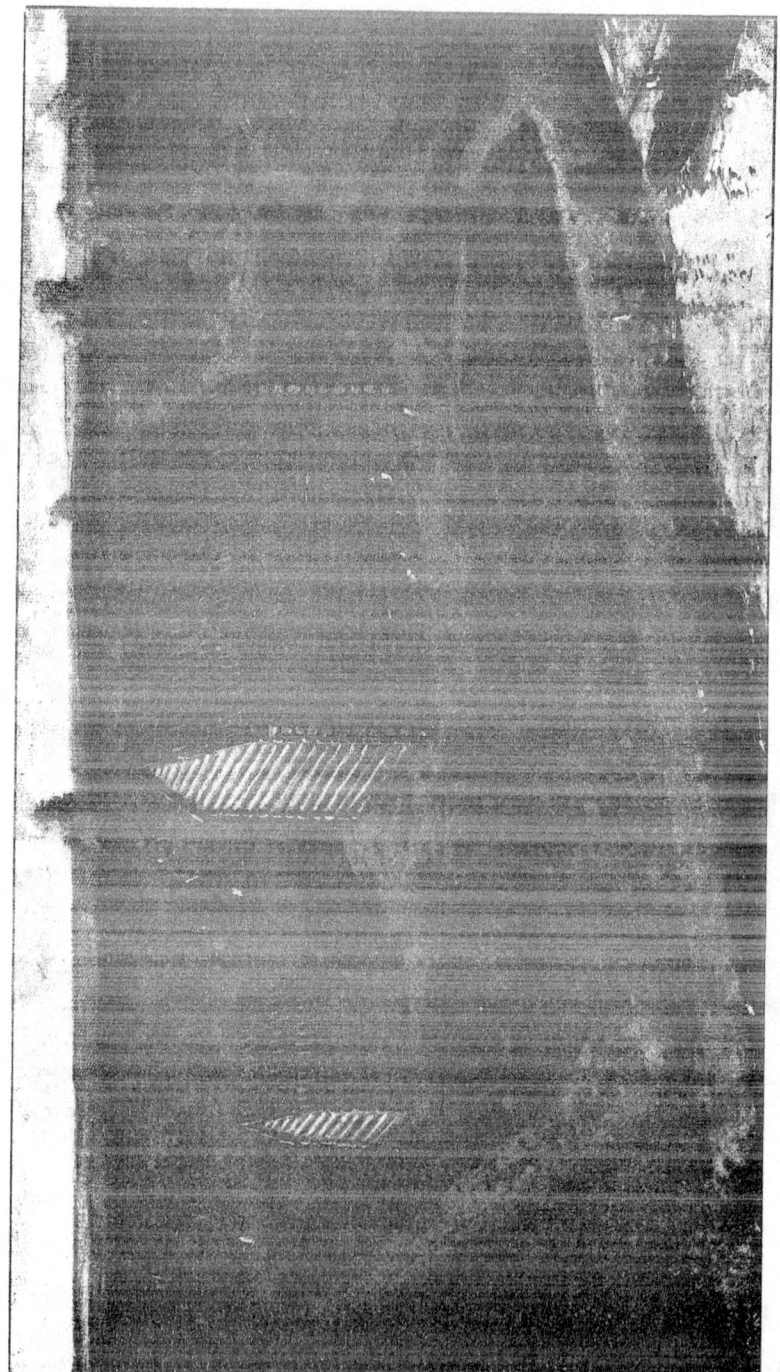

FORT DIXON; ERECTED BY LIEUT. COL. ZACHARY TAYLOR ON THE NORTH SIDE OF ROCK RIVER, WITHIN THE PRESENT CITY OF DIXON, ILL.

butcher women and children; but such was the disorder, lack of organization, dissension and open insubordination among many of the influential that, though they passed scalps, plunder and other evidences of hideous crimes, the troops murmured, and upon one plea and another flatly asked for discharge.

Atkinson did everything a gallant officer could to spur the army on to an early capture of the enemy. On the 22d, at the third camp above Dixon's, he issued the following order:

"Headquarters, Right Wing, West Dept.,
"Third Camp above Dixon's, on Rock River, 22d May, 1832.
"Order No. 22.
"The troops will move this morning as early as practicable. General Whiteside will call on the Commanding General for special instructions as to the operations of the Illinois volunteers. Major Long's Battalion will join General Whiteside's Brigade, and receive his orders. Col. Taylor, First Regiment Infantry, will accompany the volunteers as inspector general of that corps, and will superintend the regularity of its movements, order of encampment, of battle, etc., etc. Capt. Harney of the First Infantry will accompany Col. Taylor as assistant inspector.
"By order of Brig. Gen. Atkinson,
"A. S. JOHNSTON, A. D. C., A. A. A. Gen."

The purpose of these orders was to have such men as Taylor and Harney, who were courageous and tactful fighters, pursue the enemy to the death, and effectually would they have done it had the troops manifested the least disposition for the task.

Further alarming reports of danger to the frontier below Dixon's prompted General Atkinson, on the 23d, to withdraw with the regulars to Dixon's, from which point Stillman was ordered with his three companies to proceed to join the main army for scouting service, leaving Lieutenant Williams of Colonel James' odd battalion in command of the volunteers remaining, while Major Bliss continued in charge of the regulars at that post, which was ordered to be fortified for better security. Accordingly Fort Dixon was erected on the north side of Rock River, opposite.

The special instructions mentioned in the foregoing order were as follows:

"Headquarters Right Wing, Western Department,
"Third Camp above Dixon's Ferry, Rock River, 22d May, 1832.
"Special Order No. 11.
"It being ascertained that the hostile Indians have left Rock River and passed up Sycamore Creek, and probably across to Fox and DuPage rivers, General Whiteside will move with the Illinois volunteers up Sycamore Creek, scour the country in that direction for the enemy, pass from thence to Fox River of the Illinois, and be governed by circumstances as to a further pursuit of him, persevering, however, until he is subdued or driven from the country. As soon as this service is performed and Governor Reynolds may deem the frontier secure, or take other measures for its defense, the Illinois volunteers, in the United States service,

will be mustered by the brigade major and discharged, he taking care to note on the muster rolls all delinquents.

"General Whiteside will, during his operations, inform the commanding general by express, at Dixon's Ferry, which is established as general headquarters and the base of operations, of every occurrence that may require his attention.[1]

"By order of Brig. Gen. Atkinson,
"Alb. S. Johnston, A. D. C., A. A. General."

After three days' vain search, the army reached a Pottowatomie village on Sycamore Creek, where much of the plunder secured from Stillman was found cached, likewise many of the scalps taken from his men and the murdered victims of Indian Creek. All Indian property found there was confiscated by the men, who were becoming audacious. At that point the trail of the Indians lay to the north, while their homes lay to the south. Taylor urged pursuit with his accustomed vigor, but the undercurrent of dissatisfaction was so strong that Governor Reynolds called to his tent all the captains of his army for a conference. A tie vote resulted, whereupon General Whiteside, in his wrath at seeing the scalps of his friends and women and children ignored, declared he would no longer lead them except to be discharged. Therefore the army turned its course southward, a detour being made by some of the troops to rob Shabbona's Paw Paw village of the little plunder remaining, thence over to Fox River, which was reached May 25th, and where the following order was promulgated:

"Headquarters Camp No. ——, Fox River, May 25, 1832.
"Special Order.   Col. DeWitt (and the other officers):

"You are hereby commanded forthwith to cause an inquiry and search of regiments in your line and report the articles of any description taken by the men at the Paw Paw and the Indian villages on Sycamore Creek belonging to the Indians, by whom taken, with the supposed value of such articles, to headquarters this evening.

"By order of Brig. Gen. Whiteside,
"N. Buckmaster, Brigade Major."

Lawlessness was running rampant! Leisurely following Fox River, its mouth was reached on the morning of the 27th, where on that day and the next the volunteers were mustered out of service by Major Buckmaster.[2]

While the mortification which fell upon the gallant "Old Ranger" Governor, Reynolds, was crushing to his fine sense of honor, it was probably best for the dissemblers to go, even at so great a sacrifice of life and personal feeling. An opportunity was given the patriotic and well disposed

---

[1] The direction thought to have been taken by the enemy and mentioned herein was erroneous. He had followed Rock River to a point near its source.

[2] . . . "The muster roll is not on file, but the records show that the company was mustered out at the mouth of Fox River, May 27, 1832, by Nathaniel Buckmaster, Brigade Major, to General Samuel Whiteside's Illinois Volunteers." Letter Gen. R. C. Drum, Adj. Gen. U. S. Army, in Vol. I, p. 96, of Nicolay and Hay's Abraham Lincoln.

Head Qrs Right Wing West Dept
3 Camp above Dixons ferry Rock River
22d May 1832.

Special Order
No. 11.

It being ascertained that the hostile Indians have left Rock River and passed up Sycamore Creek and probably across the Fox an Rock Rg rivers, General Whiteside will move with the Illinois Volunteers up Sycamore Creek scour the Country in that direction for the enemy, pass from thence to Fox river of the Illinois and be governed by circumstances as to a further pursuit of him. Persevering however until he is subdued or driven from the Country. As soon as this service is performed and Governor Reynolds may deem the frontier secure, or take other measures for its defence, the Illinois Volunteers in the United States service will be mustered by the Brigade Major and discharged. He taking care to note on the muster Rolls all delinquents.

General Whiteside will during his operations, inform the commanding General by express, at Dixons ferry which is established as General Head Quarters, and the base of operations, of every occurrence that may require his attention.

By Order of Br. Genl. Atkinson
Alb. S. Johnston
A.D.C. & A.Ag.Genl.

ORDER MAY 22, TO CAUSE INQUIRY.

volunteers to accept a twenty-day service to guard the frontier while the new levy could be brought into the field and finish the campaign. On the 29th General Atkinson reached the scene from Dixon's and established his headquarters opposite the mouth of the Fox, and immediately urged that 1,000 men volunteer for the twenty-day temporary service, which, he hoped, would assure him of 3,000 men when in conjunction with the new levy.

The utter disregard of the troops for discipline; their contempt for superiors; contempt for their period of enlistment, not one-half expired, and almost open insubordination, cannot be appreciated by the present generation, unless the matter has been made the subject of conversation with a survivor who may have opened his mind in confidence. The following order should be a revelation to explain Stillman's defeat. Dislike of Whiteside alone could not have been sufficient to demand such an order:

"Headquarters, May 24, 1832.
"General Orders:
"The great disorder in the brigade occasioned by the men's quitting their places in the line and scattering over the country, renders it absolutely necessary to inflict punishment on everyone who violates orders in that particular.

"Colonels of regiments and majors of separate battalions will require that every man shall keep his place in the ranks if the individual is able to march, and if not, he will obtain permission of his captain to march in the rear of the army.

"All footmen will march with Major Long's battalion. Should any man attempt to pass out of the army on either flank, or should he be found out without permission, he will be taken in custody of the guard and, if he be an officer, will immediately be arrested. The officer of the day will be particularly charged with the execution of this order.

"By order of the Brig. Gen.
"N. Buckmaster, Brigade Major."

There were so many jealousies and irritations, there was such lack of cohesion, and certainly lack of organization and discipline, that men naturally disposed to continue their service lost interest by the contagion of disaffection and wished themselves well rid of it. It may therefore be said that the dispersion of the army was the act of wisdom.

General Whiteside was an energetic and patriotic man, and so it should be said of Governor Reynolds. Both had been rangers in the war of 1812, suffering dangers and fatigues without number. Both had been in responsible military positions and acquitted themselves creditably, but the army was composed of such divergent, discordant, independent and headstrong characters that harmony was impossible.

Crops for the second year were being neglected; business interests left to be resumed at the end of thirty days[1]—as was supposed—were urging many to return. The prospect of a long campaign, complaints for burning the village of the Prophet and the forced march to Dixon's thereafter

---

[1] The enlistment was for sixty days.

—allowing the Stillman expedition, when probably the men favored it at the time—all conspired to raise a state of affairs so disagreeable all round that disintegration was inevitable and proper. Immediately the mustering out was finished, on May 27th, six companies, commanded by Captains Samuel Smith of Greene County, Benjamin James of Bond County, Elijah Iles—with whom Lincoln was a private—Alexander White and Alexander D. Cox of Sangamon, William C. Ralls of Schuyler and Adam W. Snyder of St. Clair, flew to the rescue at this regiment. Jacob Fry, on the 31st, was made colonel; James D. Henry, lieutenant-colonel; John Thomas, major; E. P. Oliphant, adjutant; John W. Scott, paymaster; William Kirkpatrick, quartermaster; H. Dulaney and John B. Rutledge, surgeons; Thomas R. Waldron, quartermaster's sergeant; Jonathan Leighton, surgeon's mate, and William McAdams, sergeant-major.

This regiment, the flower of the first army, was made up of resolute and fearless men, among them Privates Joseph Gillespie, Francis Jarrott, Pierre Menard, Richard Román, James Semple, John T. Stuart, John Dement, John J. Hardin and General Samuel Whiteside—men who would not permit crops, business or any other enterprise to keep them away from the path of duty as they then saw it.

CHAPTER XXIII.

VARIOUS ILLINOIS MURDERS, INCLUDING THOSE OF SAMPLE, PAYNE AND THE ST. VRAIN PARTY.

Before recording the actions of this little regiment, or parts of it, all of them important, time must be taken to consider intermediate incidents of greatest importance and sadness. The first demonstration by the Indians after crossing the Mississippi was blood-curdling to the last degree, and proof positive that the wily old Sac was for war, and had not come for the purpose of "making corn" at all.

In the autumn of 1831 a young Methodist preacher named James Sample took up a claim near Black Hawk's village, built a cabin and was engaged in subduing the land in the spring of 1832, when Black Hawk's approach in April was proclaimed. Sample, with others, fled to the island garrison for refuge. Remaining there some weeks without any overt demonstration coming to notice, all danger was considered past, and Sample and his young wife of a few months determined to dispose of their effects and return to their friends south of the Illinois River. Proceeding for a time along the old Sauk trail, always used by Black Hawk in journeying to Malden to receive his annuities from the British government, it was their intention to remain the first night with Henry Thomas, who lived about one mile north of it on Kellogg's trail, where the same passed West Bureau timber. But the cabin was found vacant and all the doors and windows barricaded against intrusion, which compelled the travelers to journey on. They must have camped for the night in the timber, swam the creek and then set out for Smith's cabin, some six miles distant, only to find it as empty as the first, as was also Elijah Epperson's, a mile to the south. The travelers, weary and faint from hunger, were forced to continue until sixty miles had been covered.[1]

At this time, while picking their way over the prairies, they were astounded to hear whoops from a band of Indians to their rear, who, having discovered their presence at the Epperson cabin, were then giving them chase. Jaded though the horses were, the faithful beasts took heart and were soon rapidly distancing their pursuers, and but for the frightful

---
[1] Matson's Memories of Shau-be-na.

condition of the ground would have carried the Samples to safety, but while attempting the passage of a muddy spot the horse of Mrs. Sample mired in the inextricable mud and could not move. Try as he would, the faithful animal was fast mired. By the time Sample had abandoned further efforts to release the horse, the Indians were upon them, intent upon murder. Resolved to sell life dearly as possible, he fired his pistol and one Indian dropped dead. Others of the band quickly pounced upon the hapless pair, bound them hand and foot, and carried them back to camp, to be disposed of in a manner most revolting and fiendish.

Everything Sample owned he offered them to spare the life of his wife and return her safely to the people at Fort Armstrong, but blood was demanded, and nothing but the blood of both would avenge the death of their comrade, so swiftly both were tied to trees, to watch the fiendish brutes gather faggots to place around them. When these were knee high the torch was applied, and the helpless victims, writhing in the agonies of a lingering death, were reduced to ashes.

These murders were committed in the western part of the state, and, isolated as they were, one might conclude that none others would follow, but as Black Hawk advanced up Rock River the infection to take the lives of white people spread in all directions.

About May 1st, in response to Black Hawk's request to make common cause with him against the whites, the Pottowatomies held a council at the mouth of Rock Creek to consider the question and decide on their course during the conflict which was inevitable. That they anticipated one cannot be denied, and that many wished to join Black Hawk is equally certain, corroborated as the fact was by Shabbona himself, who was present and whose influence dominated the sentiment of the council to a large degree. Billy Caldwell, Robinson and George E. Walker were also present to contribute their influence for the peace party. That sentiment, after a long deliberation, prevailed, with an open and unanimous declaration that any Pottowatomie who joined Black Hawk's forces would be proclaimed a traitor; but notwithstanding the friendly resolutions of the council, Black Hawk prevailed upon a few of them to join him and to carry on the predatory warfare and assist in the murders of Indian Creek, Adam Payne and others through the Illinois, Fox and DuPage river districts.[1]

When Shabbona, Pype-gee and Pypes made their famous ride, the panic-stricken settlers along these rivers generally flocked to the stockades, barricading their homes as best they could. During the raids which followed the store of George B. Hollenback was looted, the Indians drinking of the liquor until too stupid to carry their program of crime further. But for this fact murders without number might have been committed.

[1] Correspondence of Hon. George M. Hollenback.

SHA-BO-NA.

WAU-BAN-SE.

CHIEF ALEXANDER ROBINSON.

SHERIFF GEORGE E. WALKER.

CAPT. JOSEPH NAPER.

REV. STEPHEN R. BEGGS.

FORT DEARBORN.

As it was, the time consumed in sobering up allowed leisure for all who wished to reach the nearest stockade.

In what is now Will County, Plainfield was the designated refuge, and to the little fortification, which was built of logs and fence rails, around the log cabin of Rev. S. R. Beggs, the name of Fort Beggs was given. It was not much of a fortification, but it served the purposes of protection to the people, who placed themselves under orders of Chester Smith as captain until Captain Naper called with his little company, after the Indian Creek murders, and escorted the entire garrison to Chicago for better protection. They went none too soon, for the entire country along the Illinois, Fox, DuPage and Auxplaines (Desplaines) was very soon overrun with murderous bands of Indians, invariably led by prominent Sacs. As their actions became more and more annoying and then distressing, men from Chicago and vicinity, under Capt. James Walker, constituted themselves a band of rangers, doing yeoman service, ranging through to Ottawa as an independent company, until placed under Major Buckmaster when he later came to take charge of the DuPage River district, and under whom the Indians were soon dispersed.

The murder at this time of Rev. Adam Payne, a Dunkard preacher, was as pitiful as it was atrocious. He was a man found at all times sacrificing his personal comforts and his substance to alleviate the distresses and discomforts of his fellowman, and particularly the Indian. His ministrations to their needs had been rewarded by professions of religion from numbers, and among the Pottowatomies he was venerated to the last degree. His family had been stopping at Hollenback's Grove, where he expected to find them at or near the home of Mr. Cummings, his stepson.[1]

On reaching Plainfield he found that they had gone to Ottawa for safety, where, in fact, they were in safety at that moment. He wished to reach them instead of marching to Chicago, as the garrison at Fort Beggs was preparing to do. He was importuned to go along, but by reason of his abiding faith in the Indians' appreciation of his works and his trust in the protection of God, he determined to set out for Ottawa. The fact that he had traveled from Ohio to Illinois, thence by way of Hickory Creek to Plainfield without the least interruption from the Indians, was reason enough to convince him that he would not be disturbed if he continued. Accordingly he started the very morning the garrison set out for Chicago under Captain Naper. He was mounted on a fine bay mare, carried a large spyglass in his saddlebags, and with the aid of the two he was confident he could, if threatened, elude any ordinary foe.

About the middle of the afternoon, as he was skirting Holderman's Grove, unconscious of danger, he was awakened from a reverie by shots fired from a foe concealed in a clump of underbrush. One ball entered his

---
[1]Correspondence of Hon. George M. Hollenback.

shoulder and another inflicted a wound, which soon proved mortal, in the body of his beautiful mare. Realizing that no time was to be lost in garrulous appeals for sympathy and that the only possible chance for escape lay in the old-fashioned way of flight, he pricked his mare forward and for five miles maintained a safe distance ahead of his three pursuers on ponies. But the effect of the mare's wound was now apparent. She staggered and fell dead under her rider. The three pursuers quickly came upon him and leveled their guns, while he simply raised his hands to Heaven and appealed for mercy. The appeal was heeded by two of them, but, so we are told by one of the party, who subsequently removed west, the third pulled his trigger and fired and Mr. Payne dropped dead. If two of these fiends had been so humane in lowering their weapons it is remarkable that they should all have joined in severing the head from the body, as they did. A long black beard flowed from the victim's chin, and by this one of the party seized the head, threw it over his shoulder and together the three returned to camp. At this very moment Mr. Payne's brother Aaron was in the volunteer ranks, and it may not be amiss to relate an incident which occurred at the battle of the Bad Axe. He, too, was a Dunkard preacher, but, being a sensible man, the murder of his brother called every honest human passion into play, one being the desire to revenge his brother's death, though this he subsequently denied.

In pursuing the retreating Indians, he, with others, came upon a squaw and a boy crouched behind a tree, but, under the belief that the pair were harmless, no attention was paid to them. As the last of the rangers passed the boy raised his gun and shot Payne from his horse, two balls entering his back near the spine. The enraged rangers wheeled and riddled both squaw and boy with bullets, an act which might be deplored in a discussion of casuistic questions, but not to be considered in a case so infamous as this. These bullets Mr. Payne carried during a very long life.

General Scott, attracted to this simple man as he was lying in the hospital at Prairie du Chien, had this to say of him:

"While inspecting the hospital at Fort Crawford, I was struck with a remarkably fine head of a tall volunteer lying on his side, and seeking relief in a book. To my question, 'What have you there, my friend?' the wounded man pointed to the title page of 'Young's Night Thoughts.' I sat down on the edge of the bunk, already interested in the reader, to learn more of his history. The wounded volunteer said his brother, Rev. Adam Payne, fell an early victim to Black Hawk's band, and he (not in the spirit of revenge, but to protect the frontier settlements) volunteered as a private soldier. While riding into the battlefield of Bad Axe he passed a small Indian boy, whom he might have killed, but thought him a harmless child. 'After passing, the boy fired, lodging two balls near my spine, when I fell from my horse.' The noble volunteer, although suffering great pain from his wound, said he preferred his condition to the remorse he should have felt if he had killed the boy, believing him to be harmless."

THE BLACK HAWK WAR. 169

Public feeling, by these murders, had been worked to such a pitch that a rumor, no matter how impossible or ridiculous, was sufficient to throw a community into a panic, consequently over in Fulton County occurred the silly "Westerfield scare," which threw the population of the entire county into the improvised fortifications. At such times one Indian might have captured the county without the slightest resistance.

While Dodge was covering Michigan territory (Wisconsin), independent regiments and companies from the south were organized and sent rapidly forward to protect the country between Plainfield and Chicago and Ottawa and the Mississippi, the most important being the Vermilion County regiment organized by Colonel Moore on the 23d of May, the staff officers of which, as near as can be ascertained from the defective records and correspondence, were: Colonel, Isaac R. Moore; Lieutenant-Colonel, Daniel W. Beckwith. It was composed of the seven companies of Captains John B. Thomas, Alexander Bailey, of which Gurdon S. Hubbard was Second Lieutenant, Eliakem Ashton, James Palmer, I. M. Gillispie, James Gregory and Corbin R. Hutt; also of Morgan L. Payne, subsequently transferred to Buckmaster's battalion. Of this Vermilion organization Governor Reynolds learned May 28th. The regiment ranged constantly until June 23d, when, finding its territory purged of the enemy and peace thoroughly conserved by Major Buckmaster's battalion, it was mustered out.

At this period of atrocious murders, the killing of Felix St. Vrain, the Fort Armstrong agent for the Sacs and Foxes, was particularly thrilling as well as pathetic. This man, appointed about a year previous to supersede Agent Forsythe, had always been found the stanch friend of the Indian, and such had been the appreciation of his labors that "The Little Bear" had adopted him as his brother.

Aaron Hawley, John Fowler, Thomas Kenney, William Hale, Aquilla Floyd and Alexander Higginbotham, who had been to Sangamon County to buy cattle, had heard of the Indian troubles, and, abandoning their project, were hurrying home to assist in the protection of their homes. On the 22d of May they left Dixon's Ferry for Galena and traveled as far as Buffalo Grove, where they found the body of Durley, who, as will be remembered, was the murdered member of the Frederick Stahl party. The party immediately returned to Dixon's, reported the murder and remained there over night. As General Atkinson, who had just returned there on the 23d, had dispatches for Fort Armstrong, he detailed Felix St. Vrain, the most competent officer for the service, to travel to Galena with the party and from that point carry the dispatches down the Mississippi to the fort.[1]

At Buffalo Grove the returning party found and buried the body of Durley about a rod from the spot where he fell. The party then resumed

---
[1] Smith's Wisconsin, 418. Hist. Jo Daviess County, 286.

its march, traveling toward Fort Hamilton for a distance of ten miles. Here it halted and camped for the night.

At daylight the little band started out again on its march and proceeded about three miles and then stopped again to cook breakfast. After the meal had been finished and the men were about a mile further on their journey, they fell in with a band of thirty Sacs under the command of "The Little Bear." St. Vrain regarded this as peculiarly propitious and at once assured his companions that no trouble need be feared from his friend, who had many times been an inmate of his house and partaken of his hospitality. Though he approached the Indian with outstretched hand, the overture of peace was spurned, and death to everyone sworn. In vain St. Vrain pleaded for his companions and urged his relations as agent and adopted brother. The Indians attempted in the most methodical and cold-blooded manner imaginable to murder every man present.

Seeing the hopelessness of further parley or an attempt to fight such odds, each man dashed for freedom, trusting to the superior speed of the horses to distance the ponies of the Indians, and the motion of the flight to dodge bullets. But first Fowler was shot down, a few yards distant, then St. Vrain, a little further out, and Hale about three quarters of a mile from the scene of the parley.

Exulting in the glory of their deeds of blood, the Indians, after scalping the three, cut off the head and hands and feet of St. Vrain and took out his heart, which was cut up and passed in pieces to the braves to eat,[1] that they might take pride in the statement that they had eaten of the heart of one of the bravest of Americans. After these ghoulish acts, the pursuit of the survivors was resumed, and in it Mr. Hawley was killed, though his body was never recovered and nothing ever definitely heard thereafter concerning it. However, as Black Hawk himself was subsequently found in possession of his coat, it can be easily conjectured that Hawley's horse mired in the mud, and then, while helpless, the rider was shot down, his body spirited away and his clothing used by his murderers.

The three other fugitives directed their course toward Galena, pursuing it successfully for three or four miles, when they met part of the same band of Indians, who gave them another chase of five or six miles, after which the pursued evaded them altogether. The men then crossed Brush Creek, and, sighting another band, immediately back-tracked six or eight miles to Plum River, where they camped in a thicket until night. Traveling all that night and the succeeding night, resting the intervening day, the three survivors reached Galena the morning of the third day.

Aaron Hawley's horse being the fastest, was the first to get away, and it was always supposed that he was cut off by another party of the same band of Indians and killed, as stated. When last seen by the other three he was making his course toward the Pecatonica.

---

[1] Account of George W. Jones, his brother-in-law.

THE BLACK HAWK WAR.   171

On the 8th of June the bodies of St. Vrain, Fowler and Hale were recovered[1] and buried four miles south of Kellogg's Grove, "old place." A bill for the relief of the widow and heirs of St. Vrain was passed by Congress January 6th, 1834. His tragic death was deplored the country over by reason of his unusual acquaintance and his great reputation for good deeds all his life long.

Felix de Hault de Lassus de St. Vrain[2] (such was his full name) in personal appearance was tall and slightly built, with black eyes and black curling hair, worn rather long. He was born in St. Louis, Missouri, March 23d, 1799. His grandfather, Pierre Charles de Hault de Lassus et de Luziére, Knight of the Grand Cross of the Royal Order of St. Michael, was born in Bouchain in Hainault (now Department of the North), where his ancestors had lived from time immemorial, holding offices of the highest importance and trust. This grandfather was compelled to leave France during the "Reign of Terror," for the Spanish possessions on the Mississippi, where the oldest son subsequently became Governor de Lassus of Upper Louisiana. Mr. Felix St. Vrain's father, Jacques, was an officer in the French navy. After the transfer of Louisiana to the United States members of the family, with the exception of the Governor, were appointed to offices of trust under our Government. St. Vrain married Mademoiselle Marie Pauline Grégoire, daughter of Charles Cyril Grégoire, also of France.

The Indians had always recognized him to be a man of unusual bravery and devotedly attached to their welfare; in fact, he was opposed to the use of the military that spring in sending Black Hawk back to the west side of the Mississippi, and early in April he went to St. Louis to dissuade the authorities from interfering, but the many and constantly increasing depredations of Black Hawk's band were perverting the well-disposed Indians to similar acts, and it was decreed that the murderers of the Menominees must be taught a substantial lesson in behavior. Accordingly St. Vrain boarded the boat with General Atkinson and returned to Fort Armstrong. Upon this boat he was detected with the soldiers by the Indian spies, who immediately reported the fact to Black Hawk. Without investigating their charge of treason, all of St. Vrain's life of devotion to the Indians was blotted out. In the manner of all his miserable judgments in the past, Black Hawk now swore revenge on the agent and selected "The Little Bear" as his deputy to execute the decree.

Gen. George W. Jones, brother-in-law of St. Vrain, identified the body and took back to camp with him the dress coat and pouch which he wore on that day. These articles are to this day in the possession of the Grégoire family.

---
[1] Galenian, June 13, 1832.
[2] Correspondence of St. Vrain's granddaughter, Julie de St. Vrain Schwankovsky, of Detroit.

CHAPTER XXIV.

ATKINSON'S MARCH TO MOUTH OF FOX RIVER—DODGE'S MARCH TO MEET HIM—CAPTAIN ILES' MARCH.

On the 29th of May General Atkinson crossed over from Dixon's Ferry to Ottawa to take up his headquarters opposite the mouth of Fox River, where Fort Johnston was established, and where he remained until June 8th, Col. Zachary Taylor returning to Dixon's to take charge of that post with the regulars who returned with him. On May 29th Atkinson issued General Order 26:

"Colonel Fry of the Illinois volunteers will assume command of the troops at this place, and give the orders necessary for its defense and the protection of the inhabitants in its vicinity until the troops shall have been organized and officers elected according to the laws of the state, which election will take place to-morrow[1] morning, and the officers elected will be obeyed and respected accordingly. Mr. Achilles Morris and William Kirkpatrick[2] are appointed to appraise the horses, the equipage and private arms of the troops."

To give additional protection to the northwest corner of the State, the companies of Captains Iles and Snyder were selected from Fry's regiment and ordered forward.

Captain Iles' company marched first, reaching Galena by way of the Apple River Fort route, June 10th. On June 11th[3] it leisurely started on its return trip, remaining over in Taylor's camp at Dixon's a short time, and then as leisurely continued to Fort Wilbourn, where it was mustered out by Lieut. Robert Anderson June 16th, after having served its period of twenty days' enlistment. No event of interest transpired to give character to the march, and had it not been for the prominence of its men during subsequent years, it would probably never have been chronicled. In 1883 Captain Iles published a book, entitled "Early Life and Times," in which, on pages 45 *et seq.* we have happily preserved to our use that march of celebrated men:

---

[1]The muster rolls invariably show the election to have been held on the 31st. Possibly the election was held the 30th, but the officers were not sworn in until the 31st.
[2]Lincoln's opponent in the election for captain.
[3]Galenian.

THE BLACK HAWK WAR. 173

"A few companies from the disbanded troops again enlisted for twenty days, to remain and protect the settlers until new troops could assemble. I was elected captain of one of these companies, although there was hardly a man in it but what was better suited to be a commander. It was made up of generals, colonels, captains, and distinguished men from the disbanded army. I was proud of it.

"My company was mustered in by young Lieut. Anderson, a graduate of West Point, acting as adjutant (of Fort Sumter fame). While the other companies were ordered to scout the country, mine was held by Gen. Atkinson in camp as a reserve. One company was ordered to go to Rock River (now Dixon), and report to Col. Taylor, afterwards president, who had been left there with a few United States soldiers, to guard the army supplies. The place was also made a point of rendezvous. Just as the company got to Dixon, a man came in and reported that he and six others were on the road to Galena, and in passing through a point of timber about twenty miles north of Dixon, they were fired on and the six killed, he being the only one to make his escape. One of the number killed was Col. St. Vrain, Indian agent. Colonel Taylor ordered the company to proceed to the place, bury the dead, go on to Galena, and get all the information they could about the Indians. But the company took fright, and came back to the Illinois River helter-skelter. (Note.—This is purely a flight of the imagination. No such company was sent, and none fled.)

"Gen. Atkinson then called on me[1] and wanted to know how I felt about taking the trip; that he was exceedingly anxious to open communication with Galena, and to find out, if possible, the whereabouts of the Indians before the new troops arrived. I answered the general, that myself and men were getting rusty, and were anxious to have something to do, and that nothing would please us better than to be ordered out on an expedition; that I would find out how many of my men had good horses and were otherwise well equipped, and what time we wanted to prepare for the trip. I called on him again at sunset, and reported that I had about fifty men well equipped and eager, and that we wanted one day to make preparations. He said, 'Go ahead,' and he would prepare our orders.

"The next day[2] was a busy day, running bullets and getting our flintlocks in order—we had no percussion locks then. Gen. Henry, one of my privates, who had been promoted to the position of major of the companies, volunteered to go with us. I considered him a host, as he had served as lieutenant in the war of 1812, under Gen. Scott; was in the battle of Lundy's Lane, and in several other battles. He was a good drill officer, and could aid me much. Mr. Lincoln, our late president, was a private in my company. After Gen. Atkinson handed me my orders, and my men were mounted and ready for the trip,[3] I felt proud of them, and was confident of our success, although numbering only forty-eight. Several good men failed to go, as they had gone down to the foot of the Illinois rapids to aid in bringing up the boats of army supplies. We wanted to be as little encumbered as possible, and took nothing that could be dispensed with, other than blankets, tin cups, coffee pots, canteens, a wallet of bread, and some fat side meat, which we ate raw or broiled.

"When we arrived at Rock River[4] we found Col. Taylor on the opposite side, in a little fort built of prairie sod. He sent an officer in a canoe to bring me over. I said to the officer that I would come over as soon as I got my men in camp. I knew of a good spring half a mile above, and I determined to camp at it. After the men were in camp I called on General Henry, and he accompanied me. On

---
[1] June 4.
[2] June 5.
[3] June 6.
[4] Evening, June 7.

meeting Colonel Taylor (he looked like a man born to command) he seemed a little piqued that I did not come over and camp with him. I told him we felt just as safe as if quartered in his one-horse fort; and, besides, I knew what his orders would be, and wanted to try the mettle of my men before starting on the perilous trip I knew he would order. He said the trip was perilous, and that since the murder of the six men all communication with Galena had been cut off, and it might be besieged; that he wanted me to proceed to Galena, and that he would have my orders for me in the morning, and asked what outfit I wanted. I answered nothing but coffee, side meat and bread.

"In the morning[1] my orders were to collect and bury the remains of the six men murdered, proceed to Galena, make a careful search for the signs of Indians, and find out whether they were aiming to escape by crossing the river below Galena, and get all information at Galena of their probable whereabouts before the new troops were ready to follow them.

"John Dixon, who kept a house of entertainment here and had sent his family to Galena for safety, joined us and hauled our wallets of corn and grub in his wagon, which was a great help. Lieutenant Harris, U. S. Army, also joined us, and I now had fifty men to go with me on the march. I detailed two to march on the right, two on the left, and two in advance, to act as lookouts to prevent a surprise. They were to keep in full view of us and to remain out until we camped for the night.

"Just at sundown the first day, while we were at lunch, our advance scouts came in under whip, and reported Indians. We bounced to our feet, and having a full view of the road for a long distance, could see a large body coming toward us. All eyes were turned to John Dixon, who, as the last one dropped out of sight, coming over a ridge, pronounced them Indians. I stationed my men in a ravine crossing the road, where any one approaching could not see us until within thirty yards; the horses I had driven back out of sight in a valley. I asked General Henry to take command; but he said 'No, stand at your post,' and walked along the line talking to the men in a low, calm voice. Lieutenant Harris, U. S. A., seemed much agitated; he ran up and down the line and exclaimed: 'Captain, we will catch hell!' He had horse pistols, belt pistols, and double-barrelled gun. He would pick the flints, reprime, and laid the horse pistols at his feet. When he got all ready he passed along the line slowly, and, seeing the nerves of the men all quiet—after General Henry's talk to them—said, 'Captain, we are safe; we can whip five hundred Indians.' Instead of Indians they proved to be the company of General Dodge, from Galena, of one hundred and fifty men, en route to find out what had become of General Atkinson's army, as, since the murder of the six men, communication had been stopped for more than ten days. My look-out at the top of the hill did not notify us, and we were not undeceived until they got within thirty steps of us. My men then raised a yell and ran to finish their lunch.

"Next morning,[2] in passing into a grove of timber, my front scouts again came under whip and reported Indians. I asked where? They pointed to my two scouts on the right, trying to catch an Indian pony; one had on a red shirt, and they mistook them for Indians. These two men had been in Stillman's defeat, and as their horses were weak and it was easier to march out of line, I had detailed them to go in the road in front. I now ordered them to the rear and to drop behind as far as they chose, and detailed two other men, on whom I could rely, to take the advance.

"When we got within fifteen miles of Galena, on Apple River, we found a stockade filled with women and children and a few men, all terribly frightened.

[1] June 8.
[2] June 9.

LIEUT. GURDON S. HUBBARD.

CAPT. ELIJAH ILES.

CHARLES BRACKEN.

KELLOGG'S GROVE MONUMENT.

THE BLACK HAWK WAR.   175

The Indians had shot at and chased two men that afternoon, who made their escape to the stockade. They insisted on our quartering in the fort, but instead we camped one hundred yards outside, and slept—what little sleep we did get—with our guns in our arms. General Henry did not sleep, but drilled my men all night, so the moment they were called they would bounce to their feet and stand in two lines, the front ready to fire and fall back to reload while the others stepped forward and took their places. They were called up a number of times, and we got but little sleep. We arrived at Galena the next day,[1] and found the citizens prepared to defend the place. They were glad to see us, as it had been so long since they had heard from the army. The few Indians prowling about Galena and murdering were simply there as a ruse.

"On our return from Galena,[2] near the forks of the Apple River and Gratiot roads, we could see General Dodge on the Gratiot road on his return from Rock River. His six scouts had discovered my two men that I had allowed to drop to the rear. Having weak horses they had fallen in the rear about two miles, and each took the other to be Indians, and such an exciting race I never saw until they got sight of my company; then they came to a sudden halt, and after looking at us for a few moments wheeled their horses and gave up the chase. My two men did not know but that they were Indians until they came up with us and shouted 'Indians!' They had thrown away their wallets and guns and used their ramrods as whips.

"The few houses on the road that usually accommodated the travel were all standing, but vacant, as we went. On our return we found them all burned by the Indians. On my return to the Illinois River I reported to General Atkinson, saying that from all we could learn, the Indians were aiming to escape by going north with the intention of crossing the Mississippi River above Galena. The new troops had just arrived and were being mustered into service. My company had only been organized for twenty days, and as the time had now expired, were mustered out. All but myself again volunteered for the third time.

"Of all the men in my company in the Black Hawk war, I know of no one now living but John T. Stuart. Major Stuart was elected to Congress over Stephen A. Douglas, and was the first and last one who ever beat Douglas in his race for office. Mr. Lincoln was assassinated in Washington, while president; Dr. Early was killed in Springfield; General Henry died in New Orleans; General Anderson, of Fort Sumter memory, who mustered my company in and out, is dead."

With the exception named, and the further one that Henry had been promoted to lieutenant-colonel and was such at the time, the history of that march is accurate, remarkably so.

General Henry in this instance had the abiding confidence of the men, and his presence alone was a battalion in strength.

Following closely after Iles' departure, Captain Snyder started out to cover the same territory and report depredations.

---

[1] June 10, Galenian.
[2] Left Galena June 11.—Galenian.

CHAPTER XXV.

CAPTAIN SNYDER'S BATTLE—MURDERS IN THE LEAD MINES COUNTRY—BATTLE OF THE PECATONICA—CAPTAIN STEPHENSON'S BATTLE.

Kellogg's Grove, by reason of the many fights with the Indians at and around the place, was the most conspicuous locality during the campaign, with the possible exception of Dixon's Ferry, which was headquarters of the army during the different campaigns. To Mr. J. B. Timms, present owner of the grove, and Mrs. E. B. Baker, daughter of O. W. Kellogg, who built there the first building in 1827, I am indebted for a description of the same as it appeared in 1832.

O. W. Kellogg (brother-in-law to John Dixon), after running "Kellogg's Trail" from Peoria to Galena in 1827, selected that large and beautiful grove of burr oak timber for his home, erected substantial buildings, and brought much live stock to it, with his family. There he lived until the spring of 1831, when, in order to be near the Dixons, he removed south to Buffalo Grove, another fine grove about one mile due west of the present site of the city of Polo, twelve miles north of Dixon. There again he built and removed his family, where he was living at the breaking out of hostilities in 1832.

In that year Kellogg's Grove was known as "Kellogg's Old Place," and generally designated as such in the public and private journals of that day. Previously to 1827, however, by reason of the character of the timber, it had been designated "The Burr Oak Grove," and thus it is we find the battle fought there by Capt. A. W. Snyder sometimes denominated "The Battle of Burr Oak Grove," naturally confusing one as to its exact location. As a matter of fact, it was fought about two and a half miles from Kellogg's buildings, but still Kellogg's Grove, as it covered a vast area, including the battlefield. The Timms family bought it and moved thence in 1835, since which time the present owner has continually resided there, conferring upon it the name of "Timms' Grove," which it still enjoys.

In 1832 the buildings comprised log cabins, a barn, large for those days, and outbuildings to the number of seven, strung along a distance of 120 feet, each approximating seven feet in height, sixteen in length, and all covered with basswood bark.

The site of the monument erected on the site of that grove is in Kent township, Stephenson county, about thirty-five miles to the southeast of Galena, thirty-seven miles north of Dixon and seven or eight miles from Lena.

After Stillman's battle its strategic advantages quickly impressed the mind of General Atkinson, and as marauding Indians from Black Hawk's band began their incursions into that territory, his first thought in disposing his new twenty-day troops was to send a company of strong men and there establish a base for operations between Dixon's Ferry and Galena. The company of Capt. Adam W. Snyder of sixty-nine men was selected for that perilous duty, and almost concurrently with Captain Iles' company marched from the mouth of Fox River for Dixon's Ferry. In Captain Snyder's company, as privates, were the late Joseph Gillespie, Pierre Menard, Richard Roman, James Semple, Gen. Samuel Whiteside and John Thomas, just elected Major, whose headquarters were properly opposite the mouth of Fox River with the other regimental officers; but preferring the dangers and privations of the field, he resumed his position of private under Captain Snyder and marched in the ranks.

At Dixon's Ferry Captain Iles' company had been detached for separate duty, but Brevet-Major Bennet Riley, with two companies of regulars, accompanied the Snyder expedition to Kellogg's Grove, and without event on the road thither, other than the death of private Loren Cleveland on June 12th, it quickly reached its destination. Remaining there for a brief rest, Captain Snyder, leaving Riley and the regulars behind, pushed on to Galena to familiarize himself with the country, arriving there June 13th about noon. The following day he returned to Kellogg's Grove.[1]

On the night of June 15th the troops were snugly ensconced in the various buildings, after sentinels had been picketed about eighty yards out, at different points of the compass around the camp. The night was cloudy and dark, though intermittently illuminated with flashes of lightning, rendering possible a sight of the surroundings during those periods. Near midnight the presence of the enemy was detected by a sentinel, who in the instantaneous period allowed him, attempted to run the Indian he discovered through with his bayonet, so close had he crawled; but the flash of light was so brief that the sentinel missed his mark and only rubbed the Indian's arm. Dropping his gun, the sentinel clinched with his adversary and by reason of superior strength was rapidly mastering him and would soon have had him a prisoner, but for another flash which discovered two other Indians within twenty feet, making for the rescue

---

[1]Correspondence Capt. Snyder, Mo. Republican of June 26, 1832.
Correspondence Judge Joseph Gillespie in Brink's Hist. Madison County.
Reynold's "My Own Times," p. 377, etc.
Ford's Illinois, 124.

as rapidly as the inpenetrable darkness would permit. Quickly releasing his antagonist, the sentinel ran to camp, shouting: "Indians, Indians," while the Indians pursued him as far as they dared. With a shot into the darkness they turned and fled, leaving the men in camp to lie upon their arms after that until morning.

From the fact that one horse was stolen during the night, color was given to the theory that plunder was the sole aim of the enemy's presence, but events of the following day exploded it.

Early in the morning Captain Snyder took a detachment of his men and pursued the enemy's trail in a southwesterly direction, hoping to overtake and punish him before escape was possible. For twenty miles it was followed in vain, but Captain Snyder would not permit it to be abandoned, and wise indeed was his decision, for after a few rods more of travel the detachment came upon four of the Indians preparing a meal in a deep ravine just ahead. Flight by them in a circuitous, back-track manner was instantly taken, which nearly baffled the troops, but after another weary but exciting chase the Indians were again discovered half a mile ahead climbing a high hill within three miles of camp at Kellogg's Grove. The troops were delayed in their pursuit by a deep and muddy creek, but on finally crossing it discovered the Indians firmly intrenched in a deep gulch, where, in a sharp hand to hand encounter, all four were killed, with loss to the whites of one man, private William B. Mecomson (or Mekemson), who received two balls in the abdomen, inflicting a mortal wound. While the engagement lasted it was as fierce and wicked a frontier fight as has ever been recorded, and in the many shots exchanged by the Indians the marvel is that the loss to the whites was no greater; but poor Mecomson received the only effective ones.

A litter was constructed of poles and blankets, upon which the wounded man was placed and, carried by his comrades, he was conveyed toward camp. In ministering to his needs his bearers were compelled to deliver their guns and horses to the keeping of others, the exchange and relief causing some delay and a little temporary confusion; men were necessarily scattered along with no regard for order; the troops were flushed with the first victory of the campaign, and while danger was to be at all times apprehended, having disposed of one enemy, the presence of other Indians was not a very strong probability. Thus the men marched along for three-quarters of a mile, when the dying man asked for a brief rest and a cup of water. As no fresh water was carried, two squads were detailed by Captain Snyder to search for some. General Whiteside, First Sergeant Nathan Johnston and Third Sergeant James Taylor went to one side, while Dr. Richard Roman, Benjamin Scott, Second Corporal Benjamin McDaniel, Dr. Francis Jarrott and Dr. I. M. McTy Cornelius searched the other side for water with which to quench the wounded man's thirst. While the last named squad was moving slowly down a ridge

CAPT. ADAM W. SNYDER.

MAJ. JOHN DEMENT.

CAPT. JAMES W. STEPHENSON.

PAYMASTER ZADOCK CASEY.

to a point having a bushy ravine on each side it was fired on by a large party of Indians, instantly killing Benjamin Scott and Benjamin McDaniel and slightly wounding Dr. Cornelius. The three survivors retreated while the Indians, estimated from fifty to ninety in number, hideously yelling, rushed upon poor Mecomson and chopped off his head with a tomahawk; then wheeling, they directed their fire upon the main body of the whites, who were somewhat scattered, as stated. Closing in as well as possible, the detachment fell back in good order, formed again and returned a brisk fire, which checked the enemy's advance. Quickly following up the advantage gained, Captain Snyder moved rapidly forward, bringing his men at close range with the enemy and making the engagement general. Trees were many times used for protection. During the thickest of the fight the apparent leader of the Indians, mounted on a white horse, rode backward and forward, urging his men on with shouts and gestures; but the intrepid volunteers were pouring lead into the ranks of the Indians with such deadly effect that they were gradually forced back. After a little the white horse was seen leaving the field without a rider; at the same time the Indians temporarily wavered and the whites pushed their lines closer. The Indians, having evidently lost their leader, sullenly retired out of range and Captain Snyder held his advanced position.

Major Thomas had in the meantime volunteered to go alone to Kellogg's Grove, less than three miles distant, for reinforcements from Major Riley, and though the trip was perilous in the extreme he made it safely, returning in an incredibly short time with the reinforcements. When they arrived Captain Snyder had driven the Indians to the timber and was anxious to press his advantage, but the lateness of the hour prevented. He then insisted on camping on the spot for the night, that he might pursue his advantage early in the morning, but Major Riley persuaded him to return to camp at Kellogg's, which he reluctantly did, after gathering up the dead for burial the following day.

Early the following morning Captain Snyder, with his full company, returned to the scene of the previous day's engagements in search of the enemy, but he was nowhere to be found, and, burying the dead, the company at once returned to camp, where it remained a few days longer, by which time the new levies having been rapidly massed at Dixon's Ferry for the final struggle, Captain Snyder marched to that point, and his company was mustered out by Colonel Taylor on June 21.[1]

That same band of Sac Indians had been lurking about that locality for some time, and was, in fact, engaged in all the fights with the whites until

---

[1] Captain Adam Wilson Snyder was born in Connellsville, Fayette Co., Pa., Oct. 6, 1799. Came to Cahokia, Ill., on foot, June, 1817. Elected Dist. Attorney by the Illinois Legislature January, 1823. Elected State Senator, 1830 and in 1832. Elected to Congress 1836. Elected State Senator and Presidential Elector 1840. Nominated for Governor by Democratic convention, Dec. 11, 1841. Died in Belleville of consumption May 14, 1842, before election. He would have been elected. Gov. Ford, the candidate selected in his place, was elected.

Black Hawk's forces withdrew to the swamps of the Rock River country, more than a month later.

On June 3d the Hall girls were brought to the fort at Blue Mounds from the camp of the Sacs where the Winnebagoes had found them. Here they were delivered to Col. Henry Gratiot, who was momentarily stopping on his return trip from his "talk" with the Winnebagoes, at the head of the Four Lakes.

Colonel Dodge had barely returned to his headquarters when he received word that an attack on Mound Fort was threatened and that reinforcements were promptly needed. Without delay Dodge summoned the companies of Capt. J. R. B. Gratiot and Captain Clark, which had been formed during his absence, and detachments of two other companies, and started for the fort. When within three miles of it an express met him with information of the return at that fort of the Hall girls. Arrived there, he found the report of the contemplated attack had been exaggerated, though some of the Winnebago party were that night suspected and taken into custody. Arrangements were promptly made for the payment of the $2,000 promised by Atkinson, which the Indians agreed to accept in money, ponies and other useful and valuable chattels.

That night[1] signs of hostilities were made to Capt. J. R. B. Gratiot, which he quickly communicated to Dodge. Awakening him, the two walked over to the brush, to which the particular Indians had retired, and took White Crow and five others into custody, marched them to a cabin and ordered them to lie down and remain there until morning. Dodge himself laid down beside them, having first placed a strong guard around the cabin and a double guard around the whole encampment. The next day the whole band, despite the complaint that their feet were sore, were taken with the Hall girls to Morrison's Grove, fifteen miles to the west, where Dodge held a talk with them June 5th. Candidly speaking his fears, he demanded that Whirling Thunder, Spotted Arm and Little Priest be held as hostages until the end of the month, to which the Indians assented, and thus doubtless was prevented the formation of a cabal which might have brought disaster to the whites.

By way of Fort Defiance the girls were, on June 8th, taken to Gratiot's Grove, where a junction was formed with the command of Capt. J. W. Stephenson, then departing to find the bodies of the St. Vrain party, and there the girls were left with Col. Henry Gratiot. There, too, the murder of Aubrey was reported.

On the 6th of June[2] one William Aubrey, first captain[3] of Mound Fort, was killed by the Sacs while after water at a spring near the dwell-

---
[1] Life of Henry Dodge, by William Salter, p. 31.
[2] Smith's Hist. Wis., Vol. 1, page 272.
[3] Bouchard's Narrative, Vol. 2. Wis. Hist. Collections.

ing of Ebenezer Brigham, a mile and a half distant to the north of the fort, to which place the Sacs had been led by Winnebago renegades.

Being then south bound, Dodge sent an express with instructions to Fort Defiance and Mineral Point to proceed with men to the scene and bury the murdered man, which was done.

By noon of the 8th the troops reached Kirker's farm, where they halted to consider the numerous murders constantly committed in their midst. Here Dodge delivered a short address to the troops, which fired them with an enthusiasm that none but Dodge could inspire. In fact, it may be said for the troops from the mining districts that they fought and dragooned their country night and day, with never a thought of flinching or flagging. In the afternoon the men marched south and found and buried the bodies of St. Vrain, Hale and Fowler, after which Stephenson returned to Galena, while Dodge moved on to Hickory Point to camp for the night. The next morning he marched to Dixon's Ferry and camped that night with General Brady. There it was learned that Atkinson had gone over to the mouth of Fox River, below which the new levies were massing. With twenty-five men Dodge escorted Brady thence,[1] and on the 11th the two had a conference with Atkinson, at which plans for the future campaign were fully mapped out. By midnight Dodge had returned to Dixon's. His faculty for quick marches has seldom been equaled. In fact, to keep track of him, Colonel Hamilton and Captain Stephenson during their rides over the frontier was impossible to any save members of their commands. Night and day they rode tirelessly. From Ottawa and Fort Wilbourn to the south to Mineral Point and the Four Lakes to the north, they were incessantly moving and charging bands of thieves and murderers, and to their work this pen cannot do justice.

With little or no rest, Dodge started back for the mining country, reaching Gratiot's Grove June 13th. There, worn and exhausted, he dispersed his command to their respective forts to recuperate the strength of the horses and await further orders.

No sooner had the men reached Fort Defiance at sundown of the 14th, than one David, as an express, arrived with news of the murder that day of Spafford, Searles, Spencer, McIlwaine and an Englishman nicknamed John Bull, at Spafford's farm on the Pecatonica, six miles southeast of Fort Hamilton. Captain Hoard at once dispatched an express to Dodge at Dodgeville, and ordered Lieut. Charles Bracken with a detachment to Fort Hamilton, which was reached late that night. The following morning, under guidance of Bennett Million, a survivor of the party which had been attacked, Bracken took a detachment over to Spaf-

---

[1] Fort Johnston, opposite Ottawa.

ford's farm and buried the dead men, who as usual had been shockingly mutilated.

Early in the morning of the 16th Dodge sighted the fort about one mile away, where he met a German named Henry Appel going to his cabin for blankets. In a few minutes shots were heard, and just as Dodge was entering the fort, Appel's horse, bedabbled with the blood of its owner, came galloping back to the fort.

A detachment of twenty-nine men immediately started in pursuit of the murderers, with another small detail to bury poor Appel, whose mutilated body was expected to be found as a matter of course. High creeks, muddy roads and other difficulties gave the Indians many advantages in their escape[1] to the Pecatonica, which they reached and crossed a considerable time before the whites reached it.

"After crossing the Pecatonica, in the open ground, I dismounted my command, linked my horses, left four men in charge of them, and sent four men in different directions to watch the movements of the Indians if they should attempt to swim the Pecatonica; the men were placed on high points that would give a view of the enemy should they attempt to retreat. I formed my men on foot at open order and at trailed arms, and we proceeded through the swamps to some timber and undergrowth, where I expected to find the enemy. When I found their trail, I knew they were close at hand. They had got close to the edge of a lake, where the bank was about six feet high, which was a complete breastwork for them. They commenced the fire, when three of my men fell, two dangerously wounded, one severely, but not dangerously. I instantly ordered a charge on them made by eighteen men, which was promptly obeyed. The Indians being under the bank, our guns were brought within ten or fifteen feet of them before we could fire on them. Their party consisted of thirteen men. Eleven were killed on the spot, and the remaining two were killed in crossing the lake, so that they were left without one to carry the news to their friends."[2]

As a matter of fact, there were seventeen in the party of Indians; eleven were found dead, two were killed in crossing the river or swampy widening of it and were scalped by the Winnebagoes, Colonel Hamilton, when he came up, found the body of another, and late the succeeding winter a French trapper found three more in the swamp close by, beneath brushwood, under which they had crawled when wounded.[3]

Thus with the loss of the three whites in the first fire, but eighteen whites remained to charge the seventeen Indians behind formidable breastworks.

Dodge marched to that battlefield to settle many a bloody murder or leave his own bones to bleach upon the banks of the Pecatonica. That battle meant death to the Indians or death to the family of every man in the mining regions, and in this connection it may be well to recall the words of Mrs. Dodge when urged to retire to Galena for safety: "My

---
[1]Dodge said thirty minutes.
[2]Dodge's Report.
[3]Bouchard's Narrative.

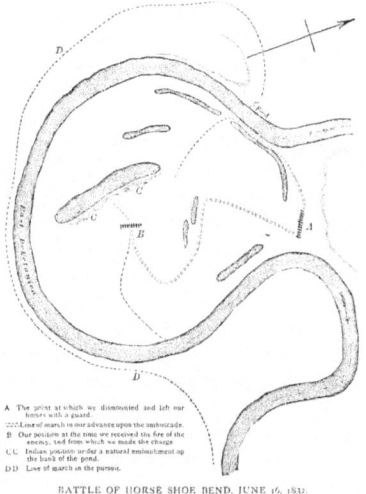

A The point at which we dismounted and left our
 horses with a guard.
:::: Line of march in our advance upon the ambuscade.
B Our position at the time we received the fire of the
 enemy, and from which we made the charge.
C C Indian position under a natural embankment on
 the bank of the pond.
D D Line of march in the pursuit.

BATTLE OF HORSE SHOE BEND, JUNE 16, 1832.

COL. WILLIAM S. HAMILTON.

SITE OF THE BATTLE OF THE PECATONICA.

husband and sons are between me and the Indians. I am safe so long as they live." Those heroic words must have echoed in the husband's heart while grappling those brawny murderers, and hand to hand, body to body, and inch by inch, in the death struggle, with gun, bayonet and knife, over the breastworks, into the enemy's intrenchment, into the jaws of death, the little band charged and fought until every last Indian was dead and the many murders were avenged.

The names of Dodge's men, so far as can be learned, were Lieut. Charles Bracken, Lieut. Bequette, Lieut. D. M. Parkinson,[1] Peter Parkinson, Jr., —— Porter, R. H. Kirkpatrick, Dr. Allen Hill, Thomas Jenkins, W. W. Woodbridge, John Messersmith, Jr., Asa Duncan, Benjamin Lawhead, Samuel Patrick, William Carnes, John Hood, Levin Leech, Alexander Higginbotham, who was of the St. Vrain party, Samuel Black, Dominick McGraw, Samuel Bunts, Van Waggoner, Wells, Morris, Rankin, Thomas H. Price, H. S. Townsend, —— Devies, M. G. Fitch and J. H. Gentry, but the horse of the last-named became mired and his gun became useless, both of which accidents prevented his participation in the fight. Samuel Black was almost instantly killed and Samuel Wells and F. M. Morris, wounded, were left at Fort Hamilton, where both died soon after. Thomas Jenkins was wounded, but not severely, and Levin Leech, while wresting a spear from a brave, got his hand badly lacerated. The troops at once dispersed for their respective forts to prepare for further developments. On the 18th a fifth company was organized with D. M. Parkinson captain.

On the 20th Lieut. George Force and Emerson Green were murdered and mutilated near the fort at Blue Mounds; one of the bodies, that of Force, was recovered by the daring of Edward D. Bouchard, and on the 24th Dodge, with a detachment of men from the companies of Captains D. M. Parkinson and J. H. Gentry, recovered and buried the body of Green. Here Dodge, piloted by Bouchard, pursued the trail of the Indians as far as the headwaters of Sugar River, and finding that they had scattered there for various points, he returned to Mound Fort.

Horsestealing became a recognized feature of Black Hawk's campaign very soon after Stillman's defeat, which he pushed with unusual vigor. He would snatch a band of horses, and if the luckless owner attempted a pursuit for their recovery he was invariably ambushed. On the night of June 8th[2] the Indians stole fourteen horses just outside the stockade of Apple River fort (now Elizabeth, Illinois), and on the afternoon and night of the 17th ten more were stolen.[3] The number was so large and the loss so great that unusual measures were adopted to

---

[1] Later captain.
[2] Hist. Jo Daviess Co., 288, and the Galenian.
[3] Charles Eames and Stephen P. Howard, who declined to "fort up," were plowing on Apple River. Indians appeared, and they escaped over the river bank, but the horses were boldly taken. The loss, among others, was reported to the fort.

attempt their recovery. As nothing but a military escort was considered equal to the search, Capt. J. W. Stephenson, with twelve of his men from Galena and nine from the Apple River fort, started on the trail early on the morning of the 18th, and overtook the thieves about twelve miles east of Kellogg's Grove, on Yellow River, southeast of Waddam's Grove, in Stephenson County. A hot pursuit followed for several miles. The Indians, seven in number, finally reaching a dense thicket, plunged into it for protection. The thicket, a short distance northeast of Waddam's Grove, was so dense that it was impossible to discover their location from the open country surrounding it, and thus secreted the Indians remained, awaiting the attack of the whites. Stephenson was impatient to dislodge them by assault. Dismounting his men, he at first attempted to sweep the thicket and draw the enemy's fire, but the wily Indians refused to shoot or otherwise indicate their position. Discarding strategy as an evidence of cowardice, Captain Stephenson detailed a guard for the horses, and with his remaining men made an impetuous charge upon the hidden reds, drawing their fire and returning it, but with the loss of one to the whites as they were retiring to the prairie to reload. Rather than accept the loss and carefully continue the assault by safer and surer methods, Captain Stephenson twice more charged the fatal thicket, losing one man with each effort, while the Indians lost but one man, who was stabbed in the neck by Thomas Sublet. Both sides had exhausted their loads in the charge and the fight became general and at close range; so close, indeed, that one could scarcely distinguish friend from foe, and rather than continue against odds entirely conjectural, the whites withdrew again to the prairie to consult—a precaution they should have exercised in the first instance.

Captain Stephenson himself was wounded so seriously that he was no longer able to continue in command. Of the whites, Stephen P. Howard, Charles Eames[1] and Michael Lovell had been killed, while the Indians had lost but the one man, and he had not been killed by the guns. Further assaults were considered useless, and, if continued, would have been wilful; therefore, leaving the dead where they fell, the men returned to Galena for assistance to return and bury the three dead soldiers and the Indian, reaching that point on the 19th.

The charges were brave and dashing, and naturally evoked the cheers of those at Galena, but, as with too many of the same character, they were not only ineffectual, but resulted in the loss of valuable lives. Governor Ford, in his history of Illinois, has justly said, "It equaled anything in modern warfare in daring and desperate courage."

On the 20th Colonel Strode, with the companies of Capt. James Craig and Captain Stephenson, marched to the scene and buried the dead.[2]

---

[1] The prints of the day have the name George Eames, but correspondence with Hiram B. Hunt and N. B. Craig, relatives, indicates that Charles is correct.
[2] Galenian.

CHAPTER XXVI.

ATTACK ON APPLE RIVER FORT.[1]

On Sunday morning, the 24th day of June, Colonel Strode sent an express of three men, Frederick Dixon, Edmund Welch and one Kirkpatrick, with dispatches for General Atkinson, then at Dixon's Ferry. By reason of the drenching rain falling at the time of their departure, the men discharged their muskets upon starting out.

Arrived at Apple River fort, twelve or fourteen miles southeast from Galena, at about noon, the express found there Capt. Clack Stone, the commandant, with only fifteen or twenty of his command with him, the others being absent on detached service. The women of the post were all out along the river, gathering berries, or else just starting for that purpose, clearly indicating that war was furthest from their thoughts. Pausing but a moment to pass the news from Galena and allow Mr. Welch to reload his musket, the express again started forward and had covered about 300 yards to the east, when Mr. Welch, who had gained about fifty yards on his companions, was suddenly fired on by a large party of Indians concealed in the high grass near a point necessary to pass on his journey. Rising instantly, they were on the point of seizing and scalping him, as he fell from his horse, shot through the thigh, when he quickly rose and fired at his assailants, some fifteen steps away. His shot was ineffectual, his horse fled, and he would surely have perished had not his companions rushed to his rescue and saved him. They had no loads to fire, but used their guns in a series of feints as though to shoot. The Indians dodged and cowered until the men were able to gain the fort, and there secure protection for two of the number. Mr. Dixon, in his frantic efforts to secure the safety of the wounded man, paid no attention to his own welfare, and, though he saw Kirkpatrick slip within, did not consider himself until the heavy timbered door slammed in his face, leaving him to face the Indians, who by this time were upon him in overwhelming numbers. Dixon was a redoubtable man and full of the resources needed in a new country, and without an instant's loss he mounted, wheeled, and

---

[1] A very spirited account of this battle, signed "Flack," appears in Wakefield's History, minutely detailing the actions of the Indians.

made for the timber, whose hidden paths he thoroughly knew. The Indians must have been more intent upon the scalps of the little garrison and plunder of the many substantial homes of the neighborhood than Dixon, for they quickly abandoned him altogether, but he, on reaching the house of Mr. John McDonald, where he expected certain relief and safety, found it filled with Indians and himself surrounded. Abandoning his horse, he fled to the rear, followed the margin of Apple River, under cover of its high bank, and, after traveling all night, reached Galena in the morning, painfully bruised and exhausted, but not so tired as to prevent his wish and determination to return to the rescue of his friends.

The shots by the Indians warned all of approaching danger and gave them time to leave the berries and the river and gain the fort, but no sooner were they all safely "forted" than the Indians, who had been massing from all points of the compass to the number of at least 200, surrounded it and hurled against the fort a terrific fire.

Providentially, a wagonload of meat and lead from Galena had been unloaded that very forenoon, which put the garrison in a tolerable state to sustain a siege.

For two hours a heavy fire was maintained by both sides. Under its first fire, the garrison showed fear of the result against such tremendous odds, but instantly Mrs. Elizabeth Armstrong, in a commanding address, inspired man and woman alike with such resolution that nothing could have driven them from their posts. She divided the women into two squads, one to mold bullets, the other to reload the muskets as they were discharged. Unfortunately, no time had been allowed to bring in a supply of water with which to quench thirst during the weary hours of that engagement. The day was hot. Confinement in close quarters of the fort, amidst the fumes of gunpowder and heat of the firing, brought on a state of suffering bordering upon exhaustion, but the almost fainting women, by their heroic disregard for danger and suffering, and by their words of cheer, propped the failing energies of the fighting men. Every advance by the enemy was met with a galling fire from within and the assailants were repulsed, only to resume the assault more fiercely than before and again retire with heavy loss.

Finding it useless to attempt a capitulation by assault, the Indians retired to the surrounding log houses, where, knocking the chinks from between the logs, they opened a deadly fire, which could not be returned with loss to themselves; but this failed to dislodge the whites, and, enraged at their failure, the Indians sought partial revenge by plundering the houses. They destroyed the furniture and crockery, emptied flour barrels and feather beds, stole the bed clothing and wardrobe and then killed the cattle and hogs, finishing their day of destruction by stealing all the horses in sight.

As night approached, Kirkpatrick, who was but a boy, resolved upon going to Galena to seek the aid which he was fearful his companion would never live to obtain. Remonstrances were of no avail, and he set out on his perilous journey in the blackness of the night. With a courage and skill known only on the frontier, he pushed bravely through, reaching Galena in time to meet Colonel Strode as he was starting out with Dixon and his relief party for the fort.

Strode moved rapidly down and left such reinforcements as were needed, but the Indians troubled Apple River fort no more. The heroic little garrison had driven them away for all time.

This band, under Black Hawk's leadership, was supposed, with good reason, to be the same that attacked Major Dement at Kellogg's Grove on the 25th. George W. Herclerode, who exposed his head too much in taking aim, and was shot through the neck and instantly killed, and James Nutting, wounded, were the only casualties to the whites.

Following the long list of the "Lead Mines" murders, the reader is brought to the murder of two men at Sinsinawa Mound, the home of George W. Jones. On June 29th three men were at work in a cornfield at Sinsinawa Mound, about ten miles from Galena, when they were attacked by a small party of Indians and two of them killed. Captain Stephenson, who had just arrived at Galena, immediately summoned thirty men of his command and started in pursuit of the Indians. Arrived at the scene, he found the bodies of James Boxley and John Thompson, mutilated as usual, and, after burial, the detachment attempted to run down the Indians. They were pursued as far as the Mississippi, which they had evidently crossed in leaving the country. As the trail could not be further followed, Captain Stephenson returned to Galena, only to be summoned to the final struggle in the pursuit from Rock River to the Mississippi.

CHAPTER XXVII.

ORGANIZATION OF FORCES AT FORT WILBOURN AND DISPOSITION OF SAME—MURDER OF PHILLIPS—MARCH TO DIXON'S FERRY.

Returning to the movements of the troops along the Illinois River, we find in the Missouri Republican that Colonel Davenport and two companies of United States Infantry arrived in St. Louis on June 11th, in the steamer Otto from the Cantonment of Leavenworth, and that they immediately took the boats Caroline and Winnebago for Fort Deposit, or Fort Wilbourn, as it subsequently was called.

On June 5th, by Order 27, Atkinson thanked the men under Colonel Fry for their services and exhorted them to re-enlist in the new campaign, which they did, almost to a man.

On the 8th Atkinson fell down the river to the foot of the rapids, fifteen miles below Ottawa, and on the 9th mustered out the company of Captain Wilbourn of Morgan, which took the steamer Caroline to Beardstown, and thence the men either re-enlisted or marched home. From the same point Quartermaster March was ordered to St. Louis to forward to Fort Wilbourn, as early as possible, the pack horses he had been directed to purchase, also fifteen to twenty two-horse wagons, and be in readiness to move to Dixon's Ferry with them on the 17th.

Back again at Ottawa on the 10th, by Order 31, Atkinson directed Capt. Cyrus Mathews' company to remain and guard supplies at Fort Wilbourn. On the 12th Capt. Morgan L. Payne, then stationed at AuxPlaines, was ordered to remove with his command to the DuPage settlement on DuPage River, remain near Captain Naper and range his company from DuPage to Hickory Creek settlements, after which, on the same day, Atkinson again moved down the Illinois River to Fort Deposit, or, as we have seen, Fort Wilbourn.

This name Deposit was given by Maj. Reddick Horn, who established it, to the point at the foot of the Illinois rapids, where the supplies were deposited when brought from St. Louis by Colonel March, Q. M., and is described in the press and documents of that day as being on the left bank of the Illinois River, one and a half miles below the mouth of the Little Vermilion River—about 300 miles from St. Louis and the head of steamboat navigation. Fort Johnston,[1] named from Albert Sidney Johnston, opposite the mouth of Fox River, and Atkinson's headquarters for some time, was about twenty miles up from Wilbourn and was placed at a distance of ninety miles from Chicago, while Wilbourn was said to be fifty miles from Dixon and Dixon 100 miles from the Four Lakes country and the neighborhood of the camp of the Sacs, which, in turn, was about sixty miles from Fort Winnebago and Chicago.

With Atkinson came his staff, Lieut. A. S. Johnston and Lieut. M. L. Clark, Aids; Lieut. Robert Anderson, Assistant Inspector-General; Lieut. G. W. Wheelwright, Ordnance Officer; Lieut. R. Holmes, Commissary of Subsistence, and Dr. Baylor, Surgeon, and Gen. Hugh Brady and his aid, Lieut. Electus Backus, who had left at Dixon's Ferry the two companies of infantry brought from Fort Winnebago. As this point was as accessible to Dixon's Ferry, the objective point of the army, as Ottawa, it was decided to remain there and notify the militia to come on from Hennepin and Beardstown, which they did.

On the 14th General Atkinson ordered Colonel Moore's regiment, with the exception of Captain Payne's company, to return to Danville to be mustered out, while Colonel Moore turned over to the quartermaster at Ottawa his surplus ammunition and supplies, Captain Payne being ordered to remain at his position till further ordered.

On the night of the 15th, Billy Caldwell, Shabbona and Wau-ban-see came into camp and offered Atkinson 100 men, to be commanded by Shabbona, who then communicated the location of Black Hawk at his last camp at the head of Rock River, with a following of warriors estimated to be from 1,000 to 2,000, and firmly intrenched against attack.

Governor Reynolds, who had rejoined the men about this time, appointed Lieut. R. Holmes on his staff, and, in turn, Atkinson appointed Thomas C. Brown, of the Gallatin County volunteers, one of his aids; accordingly, on the 19th Brown was discharged as a private, to report as aid.

On consultation with all the captains, Governor Reynolds determined that every officer above a captain should be elected by the men themselves,[2] a move which pleased everybody and which gave the army a strength unknown during the first campaign.

It was further decided that the brigade staff officers should be one brigadier-general, who should appoint one aid-de-camp, one brigade inspector, one brigade quartermaster, one paymaster and two assistant quartermasters.

On the 15th Major (Rev.) Horn, who had erected the stockade called Fort Deposit, was relieved as assistant quartermaster and Hugh McGill

---

[1] It has been said that this fort was named after Col. James Johnson, of the Fifth Regiment, but the burden of authority is in favor of A. S. Johnston.
[2] My Own Times.

was appointed by Order 34 from Atkinson. On the same day Posey's Brigade was organized and turned over to Atkinson, as follows:

Brigadier General, Alexander Posey.
Aids, Alexander P. Hall and B. A. Clark.
Brigade Inspector, John Raum.
Brigade Paymaster, William M. Wallace.
Assistant Quartermasters, John A. McClernand and Marshall Rawlings, all of Gallatin County except Raum, who was from Pope County.

The brigade was composed of three regiments and a spy battalion.

The officers of the First Regiment, so far as known, were: Colonel, Willis Hargrave; Lieutenant-Colonel, Jeff. Gatewood; Major, James Huston.

It was composed of five companies, all from Gallatin County, and commanded by Captains John Bays, David B. Russell, Harrison Wilson,[1] Joel Holliday and Achilles Coffey.

The officers of the Second Regiment, so far as known, were: Colonel, John Ewing; Lieutenant-Colonel, —— Storm; Major, Johnson Wren; Quartermaster, James F. Johnson, and Quartermaster's Sergeant, Moses Neal.

It was composed of six companies, commanded by Captains George P. Bowyer, William J. Stephenson and Obediah West from Franklin County, and Charles Dunn, Jonathan Durman and Armstcad Holman from Pope County.

The officers of the Third Regiment, so far as known, were: Colonel, Samuel Leech; Lieutenant-Colonel, —— Campbell, for a short period, when he was succeeded by William Adair; Major, Joseph Shelton, and Quartermaster's Sergeant, Levin Lane.

It was composed of five companies, commanded by Captains Ardin Biggerstaff and James Hall of Hamilton County; John Onstott of Clay County, and James N. Clark and Berryman G. Wells of Wayne County.

The officers of the Spy Battalion, so far as known, were: Major, John Dement; Adjutant, Stinson B. Anderson;[2] Paymaster, Zadock Casey;[3] Quartermaster, B. Hicks.

It was composed of the two companies commanded by Captains William N. Dobbins of Marion County, and James Bowman of Jefferson

---

[1]Captain Harrison Wilson, in the war of 1812, was an ensign in Captain James Craig's company of frontier riflemen, Fourth Regiment. His father, Alexander, was a member of the first Legislature of Illinois Territory, and drafted with his own hand the first code of English-speaking law for that territory. Gen. James H. Wilson, of Wilmington, Del., who represented the U. S. Army at King Edward's coronation, and Col. Bluford Wilson, of Springfield, Ill., late Solicitor of the U. S. Treasury, are sons of Capt. Harrison Wilson, who died in 1853. He fought by the side of Jefferson Davis against Black Hawk at the battle of the Bad Axe, while his son, Gen. James H. Wilson, captured the President of the Southern Confederacy in the Civil War. Another coincidence must be noticed: Maj.-Gen. John A. McClernand was a private in Capt. Harrison Wilson's company, and during the recent war with Spain Lt.-Col. Edward J. McClernand, son of Gen. McClernand, was adjutant to Gen. J. H. Wilson while the latter occupied Cuba.

[2]Later Lieut.-Governor.

[3]Then Lieut.-Governor.

JOHN A. McCLERNAND, ASST. BRIGADE Q. M.

MAJ. JOHN RAUM.

CAPT. JOEL HOLLIDAY.

CAPT. ACHILLES COFFEY.

CAPT. WILLIAM J. STEPHENSON.

CAPT. CHARLES DUNN.

CAPT. JOHN ONSTOTT.

CAPT. ISAAC SANDFORD.

THE BLACK HAWK WAR. 191

County, and seven detachments from the companies of Stephenson, Dunn, Russell, Durman, West, Holliday and Bowyer.

On Sunday, the 17th, an express came from the DuPage settlements, which had left there the preceding evening at 9 o'clock, bringing information of the killing of Private William Brown of Captain Payne's company by a party of Sacs on the 16th.

On the 16th the Second Brigade, consisting of three regiments, a spy battalion and a detachment, was organized, the officers of which were: Brigadier-General, Milton K. Alexander of Edgar County; Aid, William B. Archer; Brigade Inspector, Stephen B. Shelledy; Brigade Quartermaster, Henry G. Smith.[1]

The officers of the First Regiment, so far as known, were: Colonel, James M. Blackburn; Lieutenant-Colonel, William Wyatt; Major, James S. Jones; Surgeon, J. J. Parrish; Quartermaster, Leonard B. Parker.

It was composed of six companies, commanded by Captains Thomas B. Ross of Coles County, Royal A. Nott of Clark County and Samuel Brimberry, Isaac Sandford, Robert Griffin and Jonathan Mayo of Edgar County.

The officers of the Second Regiment, so far as known, were: Colonel, Samuel Adams; Lieutenant-Colonel, J. W. Barlow; Major, George Bowers; Adjutant, Samuel Dunlap; Quartermaster, Walter L. Mayo.

It was composed of the companies of Captains John Barnes (only one-half thereof, the other half being sent to Isaac Parmenter's detachment with the Third Regiment), Alexander M. Houston and part of William Highsmith's of Crawford County and John Arnold and Elias Jordan of Wabash County.

The officers of the Third Regiment, so far as known, were: Colonel, Hosea Pearce; Lieutenant-Colonel, C. Jones; Major, William Eubanks; Adjutant, Isaac Parmenter; Quartermaster, John T. Hunter; Surgeon, Aaron Thrall.

It was composed of five companies, commanded by Captains Solomon Hunter and Champion S. Madding from Edwards County, and John Haynes, William Thomas and Daniel Powell from White County.

The officers of the Spy Battalion, so far as known, were: Major, William McHenry; Adjutant, Nineveh Shaw; Surgeon, George Flanagan.

It was composed of the companies of Captains John F. Richardson from Clark County, Abner Greer from Lawrence County and John McCown from White County.

Attached to the Third Regiment were fourteen small detachments commanded by Isaac Parmenter.

On Monday, the 18th, the company of Capt. David Smith, Madison

---

[1] By Col. Smith's report, in my possession, he certified that his brigade was furnished from June 21 to July 10, by U. S. Government, with six baggage wagons; from July 10 to July 26 with four wagons, and from the 26th to Aug. 14 with three pack horses. The wagons were each drawn by two horses, and on an average drew 500 pounds. Distance traveled, 1,200 miles.

County, First Regiment, Third Brigade, was detached to occupy the post at Fort Johnston. On the same day an express arrived from the Henderson River which reported the murder on Bureau Creek of Elijah Phillips, one of a party of six who had been passing the night in the cabin of John L. Ament. As this murder created a great scare at the time, it may be well to relate the circumstances:

On the 17th Phillips, Ament, J. Hodges, Sylvester Brigham, Aaron Gunn, James G. Forristall and a lad of sixteen, named Ziba Dimmick, left Hennepin to look after cattle which had been left to run at large on Bureau Creek. On arriving at Ament's cabin, a mile and a half north of the present site of Dover, they ate their lunch and were preparing to return to Hennepin, when a heavy rain set in and the party retired to the cabin for the night, after first securely barricading the door.

To the west of the cabin lay the sugar camp of the Indians, which had for years been their headquarters. The presence of Ament in the country had greatly angered the Indians, and it required no great effort by Black Hawk's emissaries to persuade them to rid themselves of the presence of the hated settlers. The presence of the whites was at once discovered by them and during the night a cordon was formed around the house to ambush them the moment any of the number appeared. Mr. Phillips arose and left the cabin alone to look after the horses. Proceeding but a few feet, he walked square upon the Indians in the hazel bushes, who, with deafening yells, rose and shot him. Wishing the full fruition of their victory, they rushed upon his body to secure the scalp, but the other whites within, thrusting their muskets through the chinks, frightened the Indians away. Young Dimmick volunteered to return to Hennepin for reinforcements, a dangerous trip, but, calling a horse to him, he mounted, and, reaching Hennepin, was able to secure, after much persuasion, some reinforcements from two companies of the rangers who had been discharged and were returning home. The body of Phillips was secured and taken to Hennepin for burial.

On Tuesday, the 19th, Posey was ordered to draw ten days' rations and start for Dixon's Ferry that night or the following morning. Major Dement's battalion, however, was ordered first to scour the woods around the Bureau settlements to see if it could not run down the murderers of Phillips, and then go on to Dixon's to receive further orders from Colonel Taylor, who had remained at that point all the time since the discharge of the first levy on May 27th and 28th, with his force of regulars, which included Jefferson Davis, his aid, and some 200 volunteers. Just previous, Taylor had sent forward with Captain Snyder's company two companies of the regulars under Major Bennet Riley, to be stationed at Kellogg's Grove, as has been noticed before.

Governor Reynolds had on the 12th ordered a battalion to be organized to guard the frontiers between the Mississippi and Peoria on the

GEN. MILTON K. ALEXANDER.

SAMUEL DUNLAP.

S. B. SHELLEDY.

CAPT. THOMAS B. ROSS.

REV. SAMUEL WESTBROOK.

L. B. PARKER.

CAPT. JONATHAN MAYO.

CAPT. JAMES BURNS.

north of the Illinois River, and selected Samuel Bogart Major to command the same, the name of no other officer being known. The companies, so far as can be ascertained, were those of Captains Peter Butler of Warren County, John W. Kenney of Rock Island, James White, Hancock County, John Sain, Fulton County, William McMurtry, Knox County, and Asel F. Ball of Fulton County, all of which were mustered out September 4th and 5th at Macomb.

The Governor also, on the 19th, appointed his staff: Aids, Alexander F. Grant of Gallatin and Benjamin F. Hickman of Franklin; Adjutant-General, Judge Theophilus W. Smith of the Supreme Court;[1] Paymaster-General, James Turney, and Quartermaster-General, Enoch C. March.

On this same day the Governor organized a battalion to guard the frontier between Ottawa and Chicago with the companies of Captains Nathaniel Buckmaster, Aaron Armstrong, James Walker, Morgan L. Payne, Holden Sessions and — — Draper, and appointed Buckmaster Major, and it may be said that this battalion did excellent service. Without loss, it cleared its territory of the last hostile Indian, and the setttlers, in less than three weeks' time, were permitted to return to their homes, relieved of the dangers which had for so long a time compelled them to remain inside of forts at Chicago and Ottawa.

At the same time Major Bailey was given command of a battalion and was sent to Chicago to take charge of that very important post. So well did he manage the duties entrusted to him that he received the thanks of the President, Andrew Jackson.

On the 20th Posey's Brigade marched at 1 o'clock, under the command of General Hugh Brady, who took with him the two companies of regulars from the Cantonment of Leavenworth, under orders of Colonel Davenport, who was ordered to accompany the brigade and perform such staff duties as should be demanded of him. Lieutenant-Colonel Baker of the Sixth United States Infantry was assigned to command the detachment of two companies.

On the same day the Third Brigade, consisting of four regiments and a spy battalion, was organized, the officers of which, so far as known, were: Brigadier-General, James D. Henry; Aid, Alexander P. Field;[2] Brigade Inspector, Murray McConnel; Brigade Paymaster, Cornelius Hook; Brigade Wagonmaster, Nathan Hussey; Assistant Brigade Quartermasters, N. H. Johnston and Milton B. Roberts.

The officers of the First Regiment, so far as known, were: Colonel, Samuel T. Matthews; Lieutenant-Colonel, James Gillham; Major, James Evans; Adjutant, William Weatherford; Surgeon, E. K. Wood; Pay-

[1]Selected June 5, according to Wakefield.
[2]Then Secretary of State.

master, Alexander Beall; Quartermaster's Sergeant, Nathan Hart; Surgeon's Mate, Milton K. Branson.

It was composed of six companies, commanded by Captains David Smith of Madison County, detailed as stated, William Gillham,[1] William Gordon, George F. Bristow, J. T. Arnett and Walter Butler of Morgan County.

The officers of the Second Regiment, so far as known, were: Colonel, Jacob Fry; Lieutenant-Colonel, Jeremiah Smith; Major, Benjamin James; Adjutant, John O'Melvany; Paymaster, Benjamin Bond; Quartermaster, C. V. Halsted; Surgeon, William H. Terrell; Surgeon's Mate, J. B. Logan; Hospital Steward, John Hawthorne.

It was composed of five companies, commanded by Captains Hiram Rountree of Montgomery County; James Kincaid, Gershom Patterson (the first captain, Alexander Smith having resigned July 15), Aaron Bannon of Greene County and Thomas Stout of Bond County.

The officers of the Third Regiment, so far as known, were: Colonel, Gabriel Jones; Lieutenant-Colonel, Sidney Breese; Major, John D. Wood; Adjutant, David Baldridge; Paymaster, Martin W. Doris; Quartermaster's Sergeant, Joseph Orr; Sergeant-Major, John Hawthorn.

It was composed of six companies, commanded by Captains Andrew Bankson of Clinton County, William Adair of Perry County, Josiah S. Briggs, James Thompson and James Connor of Randolph (Connor's company was first commanded by Jacob Feaman, who resigned July 25th) and James Burns of Washington County.

T. W. Smith was first elected Lieutenant-Colonel, and Sidney Breese, Major, of the Third Regiment, but upon the appointment of Smith to be Adjutant-General, Major Breese was promoted.[2]

The officers of the Fourth Regiment, so far as known, were: Colonel, James Collins; Lieutenant-Colonel, Powell H. Sharp; Major, William Miller; Adjutant, Dr. E. H. Merriman; Surgeon's Mate, John Warnsing.

It was composed of six companies, commanded by Captains Bennett Nowlen of Macoupin County, Ozias Hale of Pike County, Jesse Claywell,

---

[1] Henry S. Riggs, a private in Gillham's company, who still lives at Lynnville, in Morgan County, has given the march of his company and of Capt. Gordon's as follows: "We first met at a farm near Exeter, and encamped the first night on the bank of the Mauvaisterre, northeast of Jacksonville. We then marched in a northeasterly direction and forded the Sangamon River near Petersburg. The journey across country to the vicinity of Ottawa, and later Rock Island, occupied a week, and a detachment of one company was left at Ft. Wilbourn. At this point there were, besides the whites, a good many friendly Indians who needed or desired our protection. I was one of those left on guard at the fort, so did not take part in any of the skirmishes with the Indians. Black Hawk and his braves were so far outnumbered that they knew the folly of continued resistance, but in the final struggle seventeen whites were killed and the Indian loss was heavy. Peace was finally declared, and when the volunteers returned to their homes they had been in the service just 104 days. For this campaign each man furnished his own horse and weapon and the greater part of his ammunition."

[2] Wakefield, p. 31, is authority for the statement that the regiment reached Beardstown June 3, elected officers, and that T. W. Smith was made a staff officer June 5, and that the march was taken up on the 6th for Ft. Wilbourn, where Maj. (Rev.) Horn had stored provisions.

W. L. MAYO.

ISAAC PARMENTER.

CAPT. CHAMPION S. MADDING.

CAPT. WILLIAM THOMAS.

CAPT. DANIEL POWELL.

CAPT. WILLIAM McMURTRY.

NATHAN HUSSEY.

CAPT. PETER BUTLER.

Reuben Brown[1] and Thomas Moffett of Sangamon County and Henry L. Webb of Alexander County.

The officers of the Spy Battalion, so far as known, were: Major, William L. D. Ewing; Paymaster, Frederick Remann; Quartermaster, David H. Moore; Surgeon, John Allan Wakefield; Quartermaster's Sergeant, Alanson Powell. It was composed of the companies of Captains Allan F. Lindsay of Morgan County and Samuel Huston of Fayette County.

On the 21st Brady was ordered to take command of the forces at Dixon's when he arrived there, but before starting out he was to detail ten men from each brigade for duty with the convoys of wagons, which said detail was to report daily to Col. E. C. March, Quartermaster-General.

At 2 o'clock of the same day Alexander's Brigade started for Dixon's Ferry, after receiving General Order No. 41:

"Headquarters, Army of the Frontier,
"Rapids of the Illinois, 20 June, 1832.

"The movement of the mounted volunteers on the march, whether in division or brigade, will be in columns by heads of regiments or battalions. An advance flank and rear guard will be constantly thrown out on the march; its distance from the main body will be regulated according to the nature of the ground, by the officer of the day, under the direction of the commander or senior officer present. Should the troops be attacked in front, flank and rear on the march, the line would be formed in either direction by regiments on foot previously named (as will also the reserve in either case). The form of the encampment will be a square. The troops having occupied the ground designated for the encampment will remain on horseback until the guard is posted, when the order to dismount will be given by a signal, and tents pitched; the train of wagons will then go formed in line within a square, in rear of the line of tents. The horses will be grazed until night, when, at a given signal, to be given for that purpose, they will be picketed in lines in the area within the line of wagons.

"The fires will be at least forty yards in front of the line of tents. Should the camp be attacked, the line will be formed on foot immediately in front of the line of tents.

"It is of the utmost importance that the ammunition should not be wasted. The commanders of brigades will see that the greatest care is taken of that issued to their respective commands.
"A. S. JOHNSTON, A. D. C., A. A. A. General."

"Headquarters, Army of the Frontier,
"Foot of the Rapids of the Illinois, June 21, 1832.
"Order No. 43.

"In organizing the Third Brigade of Illinois Volunteers, the Commanding General orders as follows, to-wit: That Captain Jones' company of volunteers from Randolph County be and is hereby attached to the Third Regiment of said brigade. Captain Smith's company of said Third Regiment is transferred to and is attached to the First Regiment of said brigade, to which is also attached Captain Matthews'

---

[1] The great pioneer Methodist preacher, Peter Cartwright, was a private in Brown's company.

company of volunteer infantry. Captain Matthews' company of infantry being stationary, the equipments belonging to said company will be turned over to Colonel Fry, and the necessary receipts taken for the same. The equipments drawn by Colonel Matthews at this place will be turned over to Colonel Collins. The regiment under Colonel Matthews is assigned to duty on this immediate frontier, and will garrison Forts Ottoway and Wilbourn, two companies to be stationary at the latter post. The residue to be stationed at Fort Ottoway for its garrison and for succoring the frontier and scouring the neighboring country. From two to three companies will generally be kept out for the latter purpose. The security of the public property at the forts above mentioned is confided to the commanding officer of the regiment.

"A. S. JOHNSTON, A. D. C., A. A. A. General."

The following independent companies, reporting direct to General Atkinson, joined the new levies to do scouting duty: Jacob M. Earley's, of which Abraham Lincoln was a private, Alexander M. Jenkins' and B. B. Craig's.

CAPT. A. M. JENKINS.

COL. T. W. SMITH.

LIEUT. COL. JAMES GILLHAM.

DR. J. B. LOGAN.

LIEUT. JOHN MORRISON.

LIEUT. COL. SIDNEY BREESE.

MAJ. JOHN D. WOOD.

CAPT. JAMES THOMPSON.

CHAPTER XXVIII.

March to Dixon's Ferry—Major Dement's Battle.

It has already been stated that Major Dement's battalion was ordered on detached service. Following is a copy of his order:

"Headquarters, Army of the Frontier,
"Rapids of the Illinois, 18 June, 1832.
"Order No. 37.

"Major Dement's Battalion of Volunteers will be prepared for detached service as early to-morrow morning as practicable, supplied with provisions for ten days. Major Dement will make a requisition on the ordnance officer for ammunition for his command, and report to the commanding general for instructions relative to the service to be performed.

"A. S. Johnston, A. D. C., A. A. A. General."

Pursuant to these orders, Major Dement called on General Atkinson and was directed to detach his battalion from Posey's Brigade, scour the Bureau woods to find, if possible, the murderers of Phillips, and then go on to Colonel Taylor at Dixon's and report the depredations committed by the Indians, so far as he could learn them.

Early the following morning Major Dement marched for Henderson Creek, where he thoroughly scoured the woods, only to find that the Indians had crossed the Mississippi and escaped every effort that might be made to punish them. Concluding this very tedious duty, the battalion, after a weary march through portions of the Winnebago swamps, high creeks and through pouring rains, reached Dixon's Ferry on the night of the 22d, just after Major Bennet Riley's two companies of regulars had returned from their efforts to keep open the road between Dixon's and Galena.

¹Colonel Taylor met Dement when he arrived, and informed him that his arrival was opportune, that he had just the place for him, and directed him to swim his horses across the river early to receive his orders. In Major Dement's command were men who had held nearly every office in the State, from Governor down, and Taylor's abrupt manner, if displayed before the troops, would not be calculated to promote the dispatch re-

---
¹Maj. Dement's narrative, in my possession.

quired, and which Taylor was in the habit of receiving; in fact, Major Dement felt that he could not, in justice to his relations with the men and his future comfort, repeat the orders given, at least verbatim; therefore he requested Taylor to read or deliver them personally.

The men, fatigued from their long march, expected a short respite when they reached the river, and were not in good humor.

Taylor had consented personally to deliver his orders, and promptly at daylight he was rowed to the south side of the river, where the men were formed in line, awaiting his approach. Taylor was nothing if not picturesque, and in the delivery of those orders his speech and actions were calculated to perpetuate his reputation; they amounted to a speech, in fact. He raked the Illinois militia fore and aft, virtually accusing them of cowardice, and finally concluding with these words:¹ "You are citizen soldiers and some of you may fill high offices, or even be President some day, but never unless you do your duty. Forward! March!" Prophetic words! He became President, and Jefferson Davis, his aid, was present. Abraham Lincoln, the second President to be elected from that little army, arrived the third time upon the scene, soon after, with Henry's Brigade.

Taylor's remarks, just as Major Dement had divined, evoked a storm of passion, smothered, 'tis true, but the men were almost ready to fight Taylor rather than obey him. Major Dement had foreseen the unfortunate consequences and was prepared to propitiate the angry militia by replying with spirit, to the effect that the default of the militia had been grossly exaggerated, concluding with these words: "Sir, your allusions are unjust and entirely uncalled for from a man who, with the experience of the regular army, would intrench himself behind walls (Fort Dixon) and send to the front men who had never seen service. Men! You need not obey his orders. Obey mine and follow me," and then, wheeling, he swam his horse across the river, the men following, with one exception, in good humor, with a commander who did not fear "Old Rough and Ready." Colonel Taylor saw the point in an instant, and after Major Dement rejoined him at Fort Koshkonong he said he told the story to his brother officers at Fort Dixon, who roared with laughter.

²The battalion reached Kellogg's "old place" that night, Saturday, the 23d, and enjoyed Sunday in hunting. On the night of Sunday, the 24th, a Mr. Funk of McLean County, on his way from Galena to Dixon's, stopped at Kellogg's and informed Major Dement that he had seen a large party of Indians passing near them, and that without doubt a very large band of the enemy was then close by. Major Dement's command contained not one-half the estimated number of the enemy, and, to meet the emergency,

---

¹History of Lee County, p. 249, Ed. 1893. Col. Whittlesey's Narrative, 10 Wis. Hist. Collections, p. 177.
²Reynolds' "My Own Times," p. 388.

CAPT. JACOB FEAMAN.

CAPT. THOMAS MOFFETT.

W. S. HUSSEY.

MATTHEW RICE.

he called a council of war in the night to decide on a plan of action, and this plan, when fully matured, was given to the men in detail.

At daylight of the 25th Major Dement called for twenty-five volunteers to reconnoiter, and these instantly responded and moved out. [1]Just as Major Dement and Governor Zadock Casey were mounting their horses an express came in from the advance party, informing them that three or four Indians were seen on the prairie. This information operated like an electric shock on the men, and the orders, so carefully elaborated, were cast to the winds as one and all, regardless of order, security, experience or common sense, dashed after the reported Indians helter-skelter. Though Dement tried times without number, at the risk of his life, to bring the troops off in good order, his efforts were unavailing. Refusing to learn from the experience of Stillman, the foremost men dashed headlong on to some timber where Dement had surmised the enemy was concealed. He shouted to his men to beware, but once more old Black Hawk's videttes decoyed the whites to destruction. About four hundred yards from Kellogg's, Major Dement halted and formed a line to await the charge he was positive would follow, and he had not long to wait. Stillman's fight was to be duplicated in large measure, and by Black Hawk, too, for he was personally leading his men. Just as the whites neared the edge of the timber, the enemy opened a galling fire, which killed two men and wounded a third; then, with hideous yells, a large force poured from the grove to the right and left, to flank the little band about Major Dement. The Indians, all well mounted, were stripped to the skin and painted. As they reached the bodies of the dead soldiers they clubbed, scalped and otherwise mutilated them in the usual way.

Major Dement stood his ground, firing volley after volley with deadly effect into the advancing ranks of the enemy, but the Indians continued to pour from the timber until the whites realized that delay in their perilous position meant wilful death. Then they wheeled about, and a most exciting race for life began, with the Indians on both flanks fighting at every step and gaining at every foot of the chase. Then happened a melancholy event. Three men, whose horses had strayed away during the night, had early in the morning started in search of them, and, returning, were caught in one of the flanks of the enemy, who swept over and killed them in an instant, after which every man was scalped, but, to their everlasting honor, no three men ever sold their lives at heavier cost to the enemy than they, for five dead Indians were found close to their own bodies.

During this tragic respite, Major Dement rallied a few men about him and made another stand to give the shrieking savages battle, but it was momentary only; the men caught but a sight of the returning enemy and abandoned their intrepid little commander to his fate. At the last and supreme moment he dashed to cover and only reached it by a neck.

---

[1]Reynolds, 390.

In this engagement Governor Casey's horse was badly wounded and his escape was made only after a terrific fight with the enemy. Reaching Kellogg's, the men sprang from their horses and occupied the log house and barn. On the least exposed side of the house was a workbench, over which Major Dement threw his bridle, and shot through an open window; into this same partially sheltered place the horses instinctively huddled.

As the Indians swarmed into the grove and covered themselves behind trees, portholes were made in the chinks of the log buildings and the best shots were detailed to pick off the Indians who might expose themselves, but very few of them were so rash. For many hours the garrison was stormed, it being apparently the determination of Black Hawk to exterminate the battalion to the last man, as he assailed it again and again, the Indians becoming finally careless of their security as the assault progressed. Making no impression on the besieged, the enemy finally began the merciless butchery of the horses, killing above twenty-five in their savage rage.

The reinforcements sent for were, fortunately, near at hand, for Posey's Brigade had that very morning been ordered to march, and was then actually in motion for Kellogg's Grove, on its way to Fort Hamilton to join General Dodge. The Indians finally retired, leaving nine dead on the field, and escaped with others, before the arrival of Posey, who had met Lieut. Trammel Ewing, who, though shot through the thigh, had offered to start for Dixon's for reinforcements and had met Posey[1] north of Buffalo Grove. When he delivered his dispatches to General Posey that officer hastened to the scene with incredible swiftness, while Lieutenant Ewing journeyed on to Dixon to carry the news.

The killed, whose names have been left to us, were William Allen, James Black, James B. Band and Abner Bradford, the wounded being Lieut. Trammel Ewing and Marcus Randolph, while Major Dement had holes shot through his hat and coat.

Black Hawk, in his autobiography, Second Ed., p. 104, in noticing this battle and Major Dement, used the following language:

"The chief, who seemed to be a small man, addressed his warriors in a loud voice, but they soon retreated, leaving him and a few braves on the battlefield.

"A great number of my warriors pursued the retreating party and killed a number of their horses as they ran.

"The chief and a few of his braves were unwilling to leave the field. I ordered my braves to rush upon them, and had the mortification of seeing two of my chiefs killed before the enemy retreated.

"The young chief deserves great praise for his courage and bravery, but, fortunately for us, his army was not all composed of such brave men."

When Colonel Taylor so soundly berated the militia, Major Dement knew as well as any man that every word was true, but the time for the address was inopportune, and, further, if the correction was to be expected

---
[1] Journal of A. S. Johnston.

from any source, he believed it should have emanated from an officer of the militia, but when he saw his men, contrary to orders, rushing headlong on to an ambush, and then rushing headlong back again, his heart rankled with indignation, and he almost regretted having resented Taylor's animadversions. In fact, when he finally reached Hamilton's fort, where the question arose of turning Posey's command over to Dodge, Major Dement cried:[1] "He will lead us to victory and retrieve for us the honors we have lost at Stillman's Run and at Kellogg's Grove," and, failing in the election of Dodge over Posey, he[2] resigned and fought the remainder of the campaign with another brigade.

But a man was soon to rise who, when these independent militia disturbers, with their usual tactics of insubordination, attempted again, at a crucial moment, to obstruct the orders of their superiors, crushed them into obedience with an iron hand, and that man's name was James D. Henry, the towering genius of the Black Hawk war.

[1] Salter's "Life of Henry Dodge," p. 44.
[2] Wakefield.

CHAPTER XXIX.

MURDERS NEAR OTTAWA—POSEY'S DIVISION ORDERED FORWARD—ALEXANDER'S DIVISION ORDERED TO PLUM RIVER—HENRY'S DIVISION, WITH REGULARS, MOVED.

At 12 o'clock of the 23d General Henry's Brigade marched for Dixon's Ferry with General Atkinson, camping for the night eight miles out. About 7 o'clock of the 24th they resumed the march, camping for the second night at the "Winnebago Inlet," twelve miles from Dixon's.

On the morning of the 25th, Atkinson and staff pushed forward, escorted by Capt. Stephen H. Webb's company of regulars, and reached Dixon's by 10 o'clock, General Henry's Brigade reaching the same point at 10 that evening. As before stated, Posey's Brigade was early this morning detached by General Brady from this post, with orders to report to General Dodge at Fort Hamilton, and was safely on the march when Atkinson arrived, fortunately meeting Lieutenant Ewing north of Buffalo Grove as the latter was making for Dixon's for reinforcements.

Ewing's statement on reaching Dixon's, that many fresh trails indicated the presence of large numbers of Indians in the party making westerly to escape beyond the Mississippi, caused Atkinson to at once detach Alexander's Brigade with orders to march to the mouth of Plum River to intercept such escape if possible, and, unless otherwise ordered, to return to Dixon's. Accordingly, the brigade moved at 6:30 the following morning.

Very soon after its departure an express brought news of the murder, on Fox River, of two citizens employed in conducting a wagon; also of the death of one of Captain McFadden's men in an expedition, June 24, on Indian Creek, the details of which Hon. George M. Hollenback has kindly furnished me:

"The last depredations committed by the Indians in this vicinity were done on a Sunday, about the last of June. Upon that day, a mounted detachment, numbering about 150 men, under Captain Arnett, left Ottawa for the purpose of proceeding to the Hollenback settlement and collecting and driving to a place of safety the settlers' stock.

"About the time the detachment left, something happened to one of the men which delayed him a few minutes, when he proceeded to rejoin the rest of the men.

Upon his way, he fell in with two men named Schermerhorn and Hazelton, in a wagon, following up the detachment, in order to visit their homes not far distant from the old Mission, and were, as they supposed, perfectly secure.

"The party had reached a place not far from William L. Dunnivan's, when they were fired upon, and both men in the wagon were killed; the soldier on horseback escaping. An Indian threw a spear at him as he turned to flee, cutting in its flight some of the mane from the horse, just in front of the rider. He immediately returned to Ottawa, and procuring sufficient reinforcements, returned to the scene, and found the dead bodies of the men, which were taken to Ottawa for burial. The detachment had heard the firing a mile or so in the rear, but thought nothing of it until the killing was subsequently learned. During the afternoon of the same day the other tragedy was enacted on the west side of Fox River, near Indian Creek.

"On that day, four of McFadden's company, Captain George McFadden himself and two brothers, Third Corporal Ezekiel, and Daniel Warren, and Private James Beresford left Ottawa and proceeded up the west side of Fox River, near Beresford's home, in search of strawberries. They were in fine spirits and it was Beresford's twenty-first birthday.

"They presently dismounted and, after picking strawberries until they were satisfied, proceeded to remount, which all did save Beresford, who was in the act when they were fired upon by Indians. This so frightened Beresford's horse that he could not remount, and he broke and ran, leaving him helpless to escape. The volley was effective upon McFadden, he receiving a ball through the ankle, which at the same time mortally wounded his horse, which, after running nearly four miles, dropped dead. The Warrens escaped, but poor Beresford, when last seen by his companions, was fleeing for his life, with the Indians in close pursuit. His fate was ever veiled in mystery, for no friendly eye ever rested on him afterward. His death and the manner of it were, of course, unknown."

Brady had been given his choice, whether to command the First and Second Brigades or the Third, with the regulars. He chose the latter, and at noon of the 28th marched with them up the left bank of Rock River, making twelve miles that afternoon and halting for the night. Before moving, Orders 44, 45, 46 and 47 were issued, as follows:

"Order No. 44.

"Headquarters, Army of the Frontier,
"Dixon's Ferry, 26 June, 1832.

"The combined army of regular and volunteer troops, comprising the force under the Commanding General, is organized as follows in the following manner:

"The First and Second Brigades of Volunteers constitute the first division under the senior Brigadier[1] thereof, when acting in conjunction, and the brigade of regular troops and the Third Brigade of Volunteers constitute the second division under the orders of Brigadier-General Brady, and the whole under the immediate orders of the Commanding General.

"One company of regular troops, or a detail of that strength, and one company of mounted men of the Third Brigade, with the dismounted men of the brigade of volunteers, will remain at this post and constitute its garrison. The detail of regular troops for this duty to be made by Colonel Taylor, and the volunteer company for the same service by Brigadier-General Henry. The duty hereby required is

---

[1] Posey.

of the most honorable and important nature, and will, it is hoped by the Commanding General, be embraced by those detailed with cheerfulness. After fifteen or twenty days, the volunteer company thus detailed may be relieved by another company from the same brigade, or from some other brigade, as the Commanding General may direct.

"The brigade of regular troops, and the Third Brigade of Volunteers, will hold themselves in readiness to move at a moment's notice. The regular troops are to fill their haversacks with provisions for the march, and the Third Brigade of Volunteers will complete its supply of provisions, in addition to what it has on hand, to fifteen days' ratons per man. Each will draw a full supply of ammunition."

"Order No. 45.
"Headquarters, Army of the Frontier,
"Dixon's Ferry, 26 June, 1832.

"Lieutenant Bowman,[1] of the Illinois Volunteers, will march this evening with a detachment of seventeen men to Kellogg's Grove for the purpose of protecting the provisions at that place. Lieut. Bowman is charged with the defense of the station, and will be obeyed and respected by the officers and men left by General Posey in charge. He will return to this place early in the morning."

On the 28th final preparations were made for caring for the frontier in the absence of the army and arranging for the departure of the troops at an early moment, as will be seen by the following order:

"Order No. 46.
"Headquarters, Army of the Frontier,
"Dixon's Ferry, 28 June, 1832.

"Lieutenant Holmes, Asst. Com. Sub., is charged with procuring and furnishing the army with such further supplies of provisions as may be requisite. He will station himself at this post, visiting Forts Wilbourn and Galena, if it should be necessary, or other points where the nature of his duties may call him. The staff of the Commissariat attached to the Army of the Frontier will be subject to the orders of Lieut. Holmes. Lieut. Gardenier of the First Infantry, now at Galena, will act as Asst. Com. Sub. at that place, take charge of such provisions as may be sent to that post, and make issue to such volunteer troops as have been enrolled and mustered into the service, and when there is a deficiency, make purchases to meet emergencies. He will send an express to Fort Crawford, with a request that the Commanding Officer there will send from the depot at that place, to Galena, 200 barrels of flour and 150 barrels of pork, and hire transportation for the same. Lieut. Gardenier will procure, if practicable, a steamboat at Galena to go up for it, in preference to any other mode of transportation.

"In addition to the supply of provisions expected from Fort Wilbourn, by the teams now gone for it, Lieut. Holmes will cause an equal quantity, or more, to be brought to this place without delay. Escorts to the wagons will be furnished by the Commanding Officers at Ottoway and this place when called on by Lieut. Holmes. Lieut. Crossman, Asst. Quartermaster, will remain in this district of country and attend to the disbursements of all expenses which may be necessarily incurred in the Quartermaster's Department."

At this period George E. Walker called at headquarters to report the presence at the mouth of Sycamore Creek of Shabbona, Caldwell and

---

[1] 2d Lt. Samuel Bowman of Capt. Gershom Patterson's Company, who was killed at the Battle of the Bad Axe, Aug. 2.

others, who at Fort Wilbourn had signified a willingness to command a force of Pottowatomies, and desired a detachment to meet and confer with them at that point. .Accordingly, the final order issued at Dixon's was promulgated:

"Headquarters, Army of the Frontier,
"Dixon's Ferry, 28 June, 1832.
"Order No. 47.
"General Henry will detach Colonel Fry, with his regiment, this morning, to the mouth of Sycamore Creek, where Caldwell and several of the principal men of the Pottawattomies, with 75 warriors, are encamped, waiting to join the army to co-operate with us against the Sac Indians. The object of the movement is to give countenance to the party under Caldwell till the main army comes up, which will move to-day as early as practicable. Col. Fry will, of course, use the necessary precautions for the security of his command."

On the 29th Atkinson and staff moved from Dixon's Ferry, reaching Stillman's battlefield that evening, where they camped—as stated by Albert Sidney Johnston in his journal—a distance of six miles from the "Sycamore Creek, or Kishwaukee, where Colonel Fry's Regiment is now encamped." Four miles were made June 30th, Atkinson resting on Rock River for the day.[1] On the 1st of July seven more miles were made in the forenoon, the army stopping for the night in the fork of Turtle Creek and Rock River, just above the mouth of Turtle Creek.[2]

Lack of water was felt the following day for the first time, and after a severe march, on the 2d, the army camped above and near the mouth of "the river of the Four Lakes," on the banks of a large pond, the first water to be found after a march of five hours.

About 10 o'clock of the 3d, scouts brought in news of a deserted Indian camp, broken up three nights before, which gave signs of the recent burial of five Indians. Several scalps and many feathers were also left there. The division halted at "Lake Koshkonong, or Mud Lake," a large body of water formed by the widening or enlargement of Rock River. Trails were everywhere abundant, but no enemy was in sight, nor was his position then conjectured.

At night Captains Gordon and Menard arrived from Alexander's command, which had steadily moved thence from the mouth of Plum River, with word that it was marching to form a junction with Atkinson's forces.

On the 4th the old reliable and ever-ready Colonel Fry was sent forward with his regiment and several other independent companies to reconnoiter both sides of the river, but, notwithstanding the utmost vigilance, the shadowy enemy was nowhere to be found. Early in the day Captain Briggs was dispatched with a detachment to reach Alexander, then

---

[1] It has been said he crossed the boundary line between Illinois and the present state of Wisconsin on this day, at a point where the Turtle Village was located, where Beloit now stands. Wakefield, p. 4; Thwaites, 32. Ford, 31. Moses, 372. But I quote Johnston's Journal, written on the day and on the spot.
[2] A. S. Johnston's Journal.

twenty miles distant, and urge that officer to lose no time in joining Atkinson at that point, which he did during the afternoon.

At 1 o'clock one of Briggs' men returned and reported an old blind Sac at the deserted camp, who was brought in and gave information which was not believed. Investigation was made in the vicinity of the "Lake we live on" and trails of Indians who had three or four days' advance were discovered to lead to the northwest. At this point General Dodge's approach was noticed, "with a strong force from the Four Lakes."[1]

Again on the 5th the regiments of Colonel Fry and Colonel Jones were detailed to scout the west side of the river and discover, if possible, the route and position of the enemy. For fifteen miles they advanced through mires and undergrowth, until, becoming satisfied that he had moved up the river a considerable distance, they returned, meeting Posey and Dodge's brigades encamped on the west side of the lake, ten miles from Atkinson.

Provisions were becoming scarce by reason of the usual wastefulness of the volunteers, who still continued their disobedient and independent tactics, and Atkinson, becoming alarmed, issued general order No. 48:

"Order No. 48."
"Headquarters, Army of the Frontier,
"Camp on Cooshkenong Lake, 5 July, 1832.

"The Commanding General has been disappointed in not finding, on his arrival at this place (day before yesterday), the enemy, who had occupied a strong position in the immediate neighborhood for the last six weeks, and which it was understood he would not abandon without a struggle. He has, however, retreated precipitately in various directions with a view, it is thought, of concentrating at some more favorable point not remote from us, where he will make a stand on the defense. Hence it is necessary that the greatest vigilance should be observed, and the Commanding General therefore calls upon the officers and men composing this command to observe and enforce the strictest obedience of orders and discipline, and he admonishes every soldier against the smallest waste of the provisions issued to him, as a contrary course will certainly subject him to suffering and want, detached as we all are at a distance from our depots.

"It is not at all improbable but we shall come in conflict with the enemy in a day or two. On such an occasion it is only necessary for the troops to be firm. If they stand, and more particularly if they advance upon the enemy, success is inevitable.

"The several corps and brigades will be in readiness to move to-morrow morning."

Superior officers seemed not to know how to manage the men, all of whom had votes they dared not antagonize at home, and here, surrounded with swamps, provisions scarce and no enemy in sight, with a remarkable spirit of procrastination rampant, the capture of Black Hawk seemed ex-

---

[1] Ford states that this old Indian was put to death by a later detachment, but that is a mistake.
[2] Johnston's Journal.

tremely remote. While it was the boast of the army of volunteers that it contained the leading spirits of the state, we are forced to the conclusion that it had been much better for the state and the reputation of the army if there had been in it and commanding fewer judges of the Supreme Court, members of Congress and candidates for various other offices, and more of such men as Henry and Dodge.

CHAPTER XXX.

CONSOLIDATION OF THE DIVISIONS—CAPTAIN DUNN SHOT—HENRY, ALEXANDER AND DODGE DETACHED TO MOVE TO FORT WINNEBAGO— POSEY SENT TO FORT HAMILTON—DISINTEGRATION OF THE ARMY —ALEXANDER'S RETURN.

Alexander marched to the mouth of Plum River, found no Indians to intercept, and, receiving orders to meet the right wing at Lake Koshkonong, marched thence and joined Atkinson. Posey, after reinforcing Major Dement, marched on to Fort Hamilton, as ordered, and there joined Dodge's Battalion, June 28, with orders for both, under Posey's command,[1] to join the right wing on the Koshkonong. This order provoked jealousy and a storm of protests broke out against Posey. Dodge conceived a poor opinion of him. He was admitted all round to be a fine gentleman, affable, upright and well disposed, but to lack energy and ability to maintain discipline, which rendered his men insubordinate and disorderly.[2] The miners to a man demanded that they be joined to either the brigade of Henry or Alexander, which brought about conditions likely to result in complete disorganization. Major Dement, after the disobedience of his own men, was particularly vehement in demanding the substitution of Dodge for Posey.[3] Dodge answered the request to accept the command with the reply that he would not accept it without election to it by the men. Accordingly, a vote was taken, at which, by the fidelity of his old men, Posey was re-elected to command by a small majority.

Gen. George W. Jones has described that election and his letter was published on page 54 of William Salter's "Life of Henry Dodge:"

"On our arrival at the encampment, Col. Dodge refused to assume command unless the volunteers would elect him as their commander, over their own general, although Col. Davenport of the U. S. Army, was present, under orders from Gen. Atkinson, to make the transfer or substitution in the command. All of the volunteers were entire strangers to Col. Dodge. At his request, they were drawn

---
[1] Thwaites, "The Black Hawk War," p. 33.
[2] Peter Parkinson, Vol. 2. Wis. Hist. Colls., p. 405.
[3] Dement's grievance began when, after his battle and the resumption of the march for Fort Hamilton, Posey encountered fresh trails on the first day out and, instead of following them to a possible fight, returned to Kellogg's and there camped until the next day, to "await the baggage wagons," as claimed by Wakefield on p. 39. Dement charged this as an act of cowardice.

up into a hollow square, when he addressed them, and was followed by Gen. Posey, who appealed to his old neighbors not to desert and disgrace him. His entreaties had the desired effect."

At this point, we are told by Wakefield, Major Dement resigned his command.

Dodge's command now consisted of five mounted companies, commanded by Captains D. M. Parkinson, James H. Gentry, George W. Jones, Joseph Dickson and Clark—two hundred men in all.

On July 2d the forces marched from Fort Hamilton, crossing the East Pecatonica, then much swollen, by swimming the horses and rafting the baggage and provisions, and camping at a point subsequently called Argyle. The night of the 3d the division camped at Devee's old smelting works on Sugar River, near Exeter, at which point Stephenson, with his Galena company, and Colonel Hamilton, with his company of Indians, joined them. The night of the 4th was spent in a wilderness between Exeter and Rock River, where the present township of Oregon may be said to lie, and where the Winnebago chief, White Crow,[1] with a band of some thirty Indians, joined the division. Here also Stephenson was elected Lieutenant-Colonel of Dodge's forces, and he was detached to do all the scouting duty for the division.

Passing along as rapidly as the country permitted, the division spent the night of the 5th on a sandy ridge ten or twelve miles west from Atkinson's camp, and on the 6th on Rock River opposite Atkinson, where and when Order 49 was issued:

"Headquarters, Army of the Frontier,
"On Lake Cooshkenong, 6 July, 1832.

"Order No. 49.

"General Alexander will move with his brigade this morning across Rock River and join General Dodge and co-operate with him and the troops under his command against the enemy above this lake. On Gen. Alexander joining the troops on the opposite side of the lake, Gen. Posey will march with his command across Rock River, below the lake, and join the Commanding General above this point. Gen. Alexander will call on the Commanding General for special instructions."

This order effectually settled the controversy between Dodge's men and the Illinois troops, which never should have been raised, for Posey had many soldierly qualities, as good as any Dodge possessed.

The troops now moved, Alexander with Dodge on the west bank of Rock River, Brady's on the east, which marched five miles to the Burnt Village, at the junction of the Rock River with Bark River,[2] and to which point Posey rapidly followed.

---

[1] During this march White Crow offered to conduct Posey and Dodge with a few followers to Black Hawk's camp which was singularly strong, and had the officers gone, certain death had followed. This conclusively proved that White Cloud designedly sought to have the party annihilated.

[2] Wakefield, 45. Moses, 373. Brown, 368. Journal, A. S. Johnston.

At 9 o'clock of the 7th Atkinson crossed a deep, boggy creek, one mile above the encampment, and reached a branch of the White Water at noon, but as no ford could be found it was decided to march nine miles up and cross a creek said to be there. After four miles' march Atkinson halted and camped, Posey and Alexander joining later and camping in the same place.

Captain Dunn, who was officer of the day on the 7th, was accidentally wounded by a sentinel, as was then thought, fatally.

On the 8th the one-eyed Winnebago chief, Decori,[1] came into camp and informed Atkinson that Black Hawk was camped lower down the river,[2] whereupon a council of war was called to consider further movements.

A moment's reflection should have exploded this ridiculous statement, because Fry, Jones, Early and other independent companies had explored every foot of debatable country in the vicinity named.

At this council Governor Reynolds urged Atkinson to move on up without delay, before Black Hawk could evacuate his present position and flee to the west, but to none of his appeals would the commanding general listen. He averred that his artillery had not then reached him, and without it he could do nothing, therefore did he not only decline to push forward, but he ordered the army to fall back to the Burnt Village at the mouth of the White Water for a base.[3] There Early returned from another scout and reported the main trail of the Indians, not two hours old, to be three miles beyond. Early next morning detachments marched for the trail, only to find, after fifteen miles' march, that Early had been wrong. Reynolds insisted that another day would bring them to Black Hawk's camp, and, as subsequent events demonstrated, the Governor was correct. As a matter of fact, Atkinson was upon the wrong side of the river to successfully reach Black Hawk.

Further reconnoisances made by Early's company and other detachments demonstrated conclusively, and with no delay, that the Indian Decori had deliberately fabricated the story, to allow Black Hawk a respite for retreat to the Mississippi. The 8th and most of the 9th were spent in these fruitless scouting expeditions through impassable underbrush and bogs, morasses and over "trembling lands," until the men were not only exhausted, but throughly discouraged. A party of Indians under Colonel Hamilton covered nine or ten miles of country with equal disappointment. Provisions had now run exceedingly low; intense dissatisfaction prevailed; a second campaign, planned with great pomp and expense, was coming to naught, and even the sanguine Governor Reynolds, who was energetic, though impractical and moved to many acts by consid-

---

[1] Reynolds, "My Own Times," 395.
[2] Others allege a few miles to the east on an Island in the Bark.
[3] A. S. Johnston's Journal.

THE BLACK HAWK WAR.   211

eration of policy for his future, lost heart and left camp, with his staff, Colonel Breese and others, for his home in Illinois, by way of Galena.

Late the afternoon of the 9th it was decided to send Henry, Alexander and Dodge to Fort Winnebago for provisions, with positive injunctions to hasten. It was further decided to send Posey with his command back to Fort Hamilton to guard the mineral country, as will be seen by orders 51 and 52:

"Headquarters, Army of the Frontier,
"Camp on Whitewater River, 9 July, 1832.
"Order No. 51.
"Brig.-Gen. Alexander and Brig.-Gen. Henry, brigade of Illinois mounted volunteers, will march to-morrow morning to Fort Winnebago and draw twelve days' rations of provisions (exclusive of the subsistence of their respective commands during their stay at the fort) and return to these headquarters without delay.
"A. S. JOHNSTON, A. D. C., A. A. A. General."

"Headquarters, Army of the Frontier,
"Camp on Whitewater River, 9 July, 1832.
"Order No. 52.
"Brig.-Gen. Posey will march his brigade of Illinois volunteers to Fort Hamilton in the mineral district, and remain there till further orders. Brig.-Gen. Posey will furnish from his command such escorts as may be required for the safety of supplies destined for the Army of the Frontier.
"A. S. JOHNSTON, A. D. C., A. A. A. General."

The miserable condition and character of the country, which did not permit of carrying more than twelve days' provisions at a time; the usual wastefulness of the volunteers; the ever-vanishing enemy, and the general feeling of melancholy at having so far accomplished nothing, made this disposition of the troops necessary. In addition, the regiment of Col. John Ewing was detached to escort to Dixon's Captain Dunn, whose recovery was now considered a possibility. Captain Early's entire company was mustered out at this point, and all others who were horseless, or physically incapacitated from making the weary marches required to reach Black Hawk's camp, were also ordered to report at Dixon's Ferry. These troops, a comfortable brigade of themselves, left on the 10th to return to Dixon's by the same route pursued in ascending Rock River, and consumed practically the same time in making the march. The loss of those men reduced the volunteer force nearly one-half,[1] and the departure of the other brigades, under orders, left the regulars, about 400, alone.

As the movements thereafter of the regulars were few and simple, it is considered best to briefly state them before continuing with Henry, Alexander and Dodge and the more important features of the campaign which followed.

On the 11th, while at the mouth of the Whitewater, Captain Harney was dispatched up Rock River, in command of a small reconnoitering party, to ascertain and examine the position of the enemy. Scouts return-

[1] Ford, 134.

ing that evening brought information of the Indians' further retirement up Rock River.

On the 12th Harney's party, which had ascended the river thirty miles, returned, reporting the flight of Black Hawk into the recesses of the swamps of Rock River, fifty or sixty miles above, if not further. On the same day three soldiers and two Indians went down to Lake Koshkonong in a canoe to explore. They found a small Indian camp, which they robbed, but on returning were attacked by a party of Indians, and in turn robbed of their spoils of war and also their canoe.

On the 13th Capt. Samuel McRee, with a detachment of fifty men, started in pursuit of the Indians, but returned late in the evening, after a long march, reporting no discoveries.

During the day Colonel March arrived from the Blue Mounds, reporting thirty-six wagons loaded with provisions on the way for this point.

During the 14th and 15th the camp was inactive and awaiting events. On the 16th dispatches from General Scott, who had been sent to supersede Atkinson,[1] were received, reporting the ravages in his army from Asiatic cholera. The thirty-six wagons of provisions arrived from Blue Mounds in the evening; also the pack horses sent to Fort Winnebago for provisions. On the following morning Alexander arrived with his men, thoroughly fatigued, many of them dismounted through the loss of their horses.

On the 19th the regulars and Alexander's Brigade marched up the Whitewater, with the intention of reaching Black Hawk and ending, by forced marches, the campaign, which General Jackson felt had been already dragged out to twice its needed length. The troops proceeded ten miles, when the most furious storm of that very stormy season compelled them to halt and await its passing. It raged all night long, with increasing fury, and not till morning did it abate. Here the trembling lands were reached, making further progress, as the Indian guides declared, impossible. It was then discovered that the wrong side of the river was being followed to ever reach Black Hawk, therefore it was resolved to retrace their steps, cross the river below Lake Koshkonong and ascend the west bank of Rock River. (Narrative Capt. Henry Smith, 10 Wis., 150, etc.) At this time (20th) an express from Henry and Dodge arrived early, bringing information of the movements of the Indians toward the Mississippi.[2] General Alexander at once dispatched Major McHenry, with his spy battalion, to explore the country between the forks of the Whitewater and Rock River and ascertain if all the Indians had left the country or only Black Hawk's immediate band. He found the country explored by him to be abandoned by them, and, with the other troops, fell back to Fort Koshkonong, where Capt. Gideon Lowe, with thirty or forty men, had been called from Fort Winnebago to do garrison duty.

[1] Lt. Robert Anderson. X Wis. Hist. Colls., p. 171.
[2] Wakefield, p. 72, has made the statement that Atkinson at once expressed to Henry to proceed.

CHAPTER XXXI.

FORT WINNEBAGO REACHED—STAMPEDE—HENRY'S TREATMENT OF DISOBEDIENT OFFICERS—BLACK HAWK'S TRAIL TO WESTWARD DISCOVERED—FORCED MARCH—BATTLE OF THE WISCONSIN—AT BLUE MOUNDS.

When Henry, Dodge and Alexander left, on the 10th, for Fort Winnebago, their horses were in none too good a condition for such a march, but it was begun early and continued diligently through the wilderness, until the fort was reached, at the end of the second day, a distance of sixty or seventy miles.

The horses, several hundred in number, were turned out to graze on the evening of the 12th,[1] and with no delay the men retired to their tents, pitched about three feet apart, and were very soon wrapped in sound slumber, during which occurred a calamity entailing greater disaster and more suffering than the loss of a battle. In the night (12th) it is supposed a party of thieving Indians, in attempting a wholesale theft, so thoroughly frightened the animals that a stampede followed. Running furiously in a northerly direction, directly over the camp, men and munitions were crushed under foot. A call to arms followed, but the loss of arms in the darkness and confusion, the loss of bearings, and almost of reason, prevented all possibility of order and concerted action. If it had been an attack of the enemy, as was first conjectured, the bruised and confused troops could easily have been annihilated.

The horses reached the Wisconsin River, where they were turned back by it, and, with the fury of the hurricane, rushed back and over the camp for the second time, bruising and crippling men and hopelessly wrecking tents and guns. The men had not recovered their senses when this second stampede drove them into the ground, and by the time the furious beasts had passed, the poor soldiers were in the saddest possible plight.

Two days were consumed in repairing the wreck, recovering the horses and drawing the twelve days' rations. The stampede at this crisis was painfully unfortunate. For thirty miles the horses ran, over ground

[1] Wakefield, p. 61.

almost impassable, which added to those already consumed in reaching the fort, ruined many and crippled others to such an extent that they soon gave out. The search for them added many miles of weary travel, wearing those used in it, going and coming, until it was considered doubtful if the men could get back to General Atkinson.

At this place it was ascertained through the Winnebagoes that Black Hawk occupied a strong position at the rapids on Rock River.[1] Henry at once called a council of war, composed of every officer from the rank of captain up, at which he disclosed his information and proposed the question of disobeying Atkinson's orders by pursuing the enemy. Dodge had so exhausted his men and disabled his horses in forcing a march to be in first at Fort Winnebago, that he reported he could not muster a force worth taking along.[2] Alexander reported the unwillingness of his men to disobey orders, leaving Henry alone to make the pursuit, if it were to be made at all. He quietly yet firmly resolved that it should be made. Thereupon he reorganized his brigade by disencumbering his command of the sick, injured and dismounted men, and appointed noon of the 15th for the hour to march. The disaffection of Alexander's men had a demoralizing influence on Fry's Regiment, belonging to Henry's Brigade, which resulted in the signing of a remonstrance, headed by Lieut-Col. Jeremiah Smith, and the presentation of the same to Henry as that officer was ready to march. Fry did not sign this document and had no sympathy with it. On the contrary, he was bitterly opposed to such action. This action, emanating from so conspicuous a person and officer as Smith, would, under usual conditions, have frustrated Henry's plans and demoralized his brigade, but he was the man for an emergency, with the will to meet it and the physique to enforce it against ordinary opposition. His genius rose to this occasion and his action ended the Black Hawk war, as it would have been ended long before could he have ordered the volunteer forces as he desired.

Day after day, week after week, the army had dawdled away valuable time in fruitless marches. Every command had been ignored or ridiculed. Protests had been constantly made, and at every turn the commanding influence of the militia and its votes had been consulted and obeyed.

In camp and on the march they had constantly murmured, and in action they had disobeyed and disgraced themselves and their state. Here Henry was alone and supreme in command, unhampered by a superior. He was a candidate for no office.

When this remonstrance was presented to him he quietly read it and deliberated carefully for some minutes; then, without bluster or useless fanfaronade, he ordered every man who had signed it under arrest, with orders to Colonel Collins' Regiment to escort them to Atkinson for trial,

---

[1] Wis. Colls., Vol. 2, p. 354.
[2] Ford, 139.

THE BLACK HAWK WAR.   215

at which, he had no doubt, they would be shot for disobedience. No man knew Henry better than Lieutenant-Colonel Smith, and no doubt remained in his mind of Henry's determination to enforce his order, thereupon he begged permission to retire to consult his brother officers who had signed the paper, which he was permitted to do. In less than ten minutes every one of them had returned and begged Henry's pardon, urging that they knew not the full import of the document when attaching their signatures. In the greatness of his heart that forgiveness was extended them and, with no further allusion to the incident, it was from that moment dropped. In justice to those officers, it must be said that Henry had no more devoted followers in his ranks from that time.

Alexander now moved for Atkinson's headquarters, and almost simultaneously came Capt. James Craig of Dodge's Battalion from Galena, with fresh horses and men, bringing Dodge's command up to 120 strong, when he pronounced himself ready for concerted action with Henry, whose brigade had fallen from about 1,200 to 600 men, but not more than 450 were then fit for service.

From Fort Winnebago Henry and Dodge took up their march, July 15th, accompanied by Pierre Poquette as interpreter, and twelve Winnebagoes,[1] including The White Pawnee, as guides. Heavy underbrush and swamps continually hampered their march, while each new morass cost them horses, but after three days of hard marching the rapids (now Hustisford) were reached.[2] No Indians were found. Henry thereupon ordered the little army to camp. Here three Winnebagoes reported that Black Hawk had gone further up the river to Cranberry Lake. Relying on this information, it was determined to ascend the river by a forced march the following morning. In the meantime Adjutants Dr. E. H. Merryman of Springfield and W. W. Woodbridge of Dodge's Battalion were dispatched, at 2 o'clock P. M.,[3] to Atkinson's camp, accompanied by Little Thunder as guide, to post Atkinson as to its movements.

About dark they had proceeded about eight miles to the southwest, when they suddenly came upon the broad fresh trail of the enemy in his endeavor to escape to the Mississippi River. At the sight of this trail Little Thunder manifested unusual and extreme symptoms, and, without permission, hastened back to camp, where he informed his two Winnebago friends of his discovery. Merryman and Woodbridge hastily followed. On returning, these two Winnebagoes, after communicating with their friends, attempted to escape, but in passing Major Murray McConnel of the staff, who was reconnoitering, they were arrested and returned to camp. Merryman and Woodbridge followed soon after, and in crossing

---
[1] Wakefield, p. 62.
[2] Wakefield says the 18th, p. 62.
[3] Wakefield, p. 63.

the picket lines Woodbridge was fired at by a sentinel and barely escaped with his life.

Under an examination by Henry, the Winnebagoes confessed that they had given false information in order to facilitate the escape of Black Hawk.

Early the following morning (19th) the army was ready for a fresh march along this trail. The same express was sent to Atkinson to post him as to its movements, Little Thunder safely guiding it.[1] Five baggage wagons were discarded[2] and most of the camp equipage left in a pile in the wilderness. Even blankets and parts of wardrobe were discarded to facilitate travel, so that positively nothing could hamper man or beast in the contemplated forced marches to overtake Black Hawk. Provisions were tightly packed on shoulders and then over creeks, mires, through groves, thickets and forests the chase began, men marching and almost running a-foot to keep pace with those mounted, to please the leader they knew to be the man for the hour.

A fearful storm arose the first day and continued the following morning, and though without shelter, the men cheerfully pushed forward, covering fifty miles by nightfall. The sight of Henry dismounting to give some tired footman a rest inspired others to do the same, and a valor before unknown inspired the men.

Until 2 o'clock of the morning of the 20th the storm raged. No fires could be built by which to cook supper, so meat was eaten raw and flour mixed with water into a raw dough was substituted for more substantial fare. The men, exhausted but uncomplaining, threw themselves upon the wet earth for a brief rest, without blankets or other covering, thus enduring a night of hardship which before that time would have produced the dissolution of the army.

Breakfast on the 20th was little better than supper of the preceding night. Scouts captured an Indian, who was brought to Henry, where he disclosed the information that the main body of the Indians was not far ahead. Henry at once formed an order of battle for the day, with Dodge and Ewing in front to bring on the fight, Fry to the right, Jones to the left and Collins in the center.

Poquette and the White Pawnee, still marching, had in every instance been found to be reliable in their bearings, and now that they proclaimed the presence of the enemy, a battle was momentarily promised, but their expectations were a little premature, and all day of the 20th the march was continued in the order stated, until nightfall, when the army camped on the east bank of the Third Lake, where for the first time fires could be made and a substantial supper cooked. That night was passed in the same manner, upon the ground, without event, save for the sight of a

---

[1] Wakefield, p. 63 and 72.
[2] Wakefield, p. 64.

WISCONSIN HEIGHTS BATTLEFIELD.

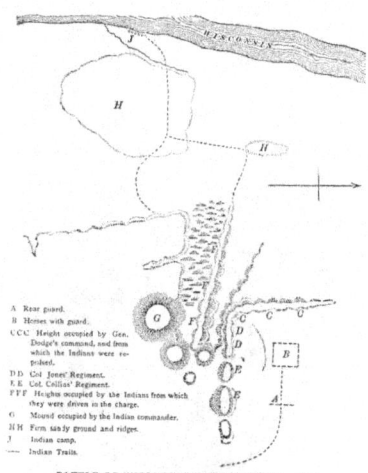

A Rear guard.
B Horses with guard.
CCC Height occupied by Gen. Dodge's command, and from which the Indians were repulsed.
DD Col. Jones' Regiment.
EE Col. Collins' Regiment.
FFF Heights occupied by the Indians from which they were driven in the charge.
G Mound occupied by the Indian commander.
HH Firm sandy ground and ridges.
J Indian camp.
— Indian Trails.

BATTLE OF WISCONSIN HEIGHTS, JULY 21, 1832.

CAPT. JOSEPH DICKSON.

GOV. JOHN WOOD.

COL. GABRIEL JONES.

MAJ. MURRAY McCONNEL.

CAPT. D. M. PARKINSON.

THE BLACK HAWK WAR. 217

rapidly disappearing Indian, who was fired at by a sentinel while fading away on the lake.

Passing around the lake early on the 21st, the army continued its march with the spy battalions of Major William L. D. Ewing and Colonel Dodge still in front, the footmen continuing the pace set by the horsemen, who had discovered unmistakable evidences that the enemy was but a short distance ahead.

The sight of discarded Indian camp equipment encouraged them with the hope that a few hours only would intervene before a battle and the possible termination of the war.

In Smith's History of Wisconsin, Vol. I, p. 279, this pursuit is described as follows:

"Pursuit commenced immediately, and the trail was followed down the river until it diverged from it westward. The detachment crossed the Crawfish River near Aztalan, and followed the trail, which bore to the west of Keyes Lake (Rock Lake). It was still followed westward until the ground between the Third and Fourth Lakes was reached, now the site of Madison; thence it was followed around the southern end of the Fourth Lake, where it appeared that an admirable position for a battleground, with natural defenses and places of ambush, had been chosen by the enemy, and here they apparently had lain the previous night. This place was near Slaughter's farm."

About noon the scouts fell upon two Indians and killed one while trying to escape.[1] Dr. Addison Philleo at that moment scalped him, and for many years afterward was in the habit of exhibiting the scalp to strangers as a trophy of his valor in that war.[2] The terrific pressure on the horses had been severely felt by this time, and before the day was half done forty or fifty of them gave out. About 3 o'clock the company of Capt. Joseph Dickson's spies reported the enemy reaching the bluffs of the Wisconsin River, which reanimated the troops with unusual vigor to increase their speed, and, if possible, overtake the enemy before he crossed the river. The men pushed on so rapidly that the rear guard of the Indians was overtaken, and, in order to occupy the whites, stopped frequently and engaged them with firing in order to allow the main body to cross the river. Twice Henry pressed them and twice the Indians gave way, but the third time Dickson's scouts or spies drove them to the main body, which had reached a body of timber sufficiently dense to offer protection, and here the whole force of Indians made a stand.

Dismounting, every tenth man was detailed to hold horses, excepting the regiment of Colonel Fry, which was made the reserve and held to prevent the enemy from turning the flanks of the whites.

The Indians opened fire as the advance guard of the whites was passing a stretch of uneven ground, through the high grass and low brush.

---

[1] Near the spot where the Lake House subsequently stood.
[2] Ford, 144.

Major Ewing's Battalion was at once formed in front, where the Indians poured their fire into it from behind trees. In a few moments Henry arrived with the main army and formed the order of battle, Colonel Jones being placed to the right, Colonel Collins to the left, Fry in reserve and Ewing in front, with Dodge on the extreme right. In this order Henry ordered the forces to move. The order to charge the enemy was splendidly executed by Ewing, Jones and Collins, routing the Indians, who retreated to the right and concentrated before Dodge's Battalion, with the obvious intention of turning his flank.[1] Henry sent Major McConnel to Dodge, ordering him to charge the enemy, but this Dodge preferred to delay until he received a reinforcement, whereupon Henry sent Colonel Fry to his aid, and together they charged into the brush and high grass, receiving the fire of the whole body of the enemy.

Advancing and returning this fire, Dodge and Fry pursued the Indians with bayonets, driving them out with loss. Retreating rapidly, the enemy fell back to the west and took up a new and a stronger position in the thick timber and tall grass at the head of a hollow leading to the Wisconsin River bottom.[2] A determined stand was made here, but Ewing, Jones and Collins dashed upon them and drove them in scattered squads down into the Wisconsin bottoms, covered with a swale so high that pursuit in the gathering darkness was impossible, and Henry, withdrawing his forces, lay all night on the field.

During the night a sonorous voice was heard from a neighboring hill, supposedly giving orders to the enemy, but as nothing came of it, no commotion or preparation to renew the fight followed. It proved to have been Ne-a-pope suing for peace in the tongue of the Winnebagoes, supposing that the guides and interpreter present from that nation would understand and secure a parley, but as all the Winnebagoes had fled in the beginning of the action, his words were wasted. Had he been understood, no doubt can exist but Henry would have closed the war then and there, for Black Hawk now realized that he was no longer fighting Stillman's command. The loss of the Indians was sixty-eight in killed and many more wounded, twenty-five of whom were found dead on the trail, subsequently resumed, while the loss to Henry was but one man killed, Private Thomas J. Short of Captain Briggs' company, Randolph County, and eight wounded, of whom the following are known: John White, Joseph Wells, Armstead Jones, Meredith S. McMillen, James Thompson and Andrew McCormick and John McNair of Capt. D. M. Parkinson's company. As all the casualties were from the Third Regiment,[3] commanded by Col. Gabriel Jones, it is to be inferred that he bore the brunt of the fight.

The following morning Henry advanced to the Wisconsin, only to find the enemy had retreated during the night across the river to the hills

---
[1] Ford, 145.
[2] Ford, 145.
[3] Except McNair.

beyond. Had supplies been plenty, he would have pressed his victory by following, but being in great need of provisions, he was compelled to fall back to the base at the Blue Mounds.

This was the first time Black Hawk in person had met signal defeat during the campaign, and he realized that more would follow, because a man who cared nothing for politics and feared not mortal man was after him.

Henry was exceedingly modest, retiring and submissive; so modest that when others were writing flaming press reports and conspiring to make way with his laurels, he attempted no intervention. Quiet, indeed, he was, yet resolute in duty to the last degree, and when an arrogant officer headed a mutinous document he was ordered in irons to the commanding General for punishment.

This inflexible regard for duty, even in the face of criticism and intrigue, moved him forward with the irresistible force of the glacier, and in this instance, with no contrivance, it pushed him forward at a bound to be the most popular man in the State of Illinois, and very soon the nominee of his party for Governor. Had he lived, nothing could have prevented his election. He died of pulmonary consumption, at New Orleans, March 4th, 1834, at his hotel lodgings.

Though a giant in stature and rugged to a degree, proof, as was thought, against the rigors of any campaign, this one undermined his health, and to find relief he sought the milder climate of New Orleans, but here he gradually sank, and in a little while passed away, so quietly that no one knew who he was until friends from Illinois proclaimed him. Then the honors due a soldier were his.

On the 22d Henry dispatched an express to Atkinson and Dodge wrote a letter to the commandant at Prairie du Chien,[1] dispatching it by the hand of Captain Estes of his command, which later found its way into the Missouri Republican and Niles Register. Following is a copy of the letter:

"Camp Wisconsin, July 22, 1832.

"We met the enemy yesterday, near the Wisconsin River, and opposite the old Sac village, after a close pursuit for nearly 100 miles. Our loss was one man killed and eight wounded; from the scalps taken by the Winnebagoes, as well as those taken by the whites, and the Indians carried from the field of battle, we must have killed forty of them. The number of wounded is not known; we can only judge from the number killed that many were wounded. From their crippled situation, I think we must overtake them unless they descend the Wisconsin by water. If you could place a field-piece immediately on the Wisconsin that would command the river, you might prevent their escape by water.

"General Atkinson will arrive at the Blue Mounds on the 24th, with the regulars and a brigade of mounted men. I will cross the Wisconsin to-morrow, and should the enemy retreat by land, he will probably attempt crossing some twenty miles above Prairie du Chien; in that event the mounted men would want some

---
[1] Capt. Loomis.

boats for the transportation of their arms, ammunition and provisions. If you could procure for us some Mackinaw boats, in that event, as well as some provision supplies, it would greatly facilitate our views. Excuse great haste. I am, with great respect, your obedient servant,

"H. DODGE, Col.-Com. Michigan Mounted Volunteers."

This letter created much criticism by subsequent historians, notably Governor Ford in his History of Illinois. Answers, replies and rejoinders were exceedingly numerous for a while, but when time had passed and mellowed the controversy, Henry, the chief in command, and Dodge, the second in command at that battle, remained with the people of Illinois and Wisconsin first among their fighters and first among their favorites, and surely both deserved the best portions of the good things said of either. The letter may have been a little presumptuous, but it never marred the good feeling which existed between the two men.[1]

Litters were constructed for the wounded, the march was taken up and in two days (24th) the Blue Mounds were reached and there the army met Posey, Atkinson and Alexander, the two latter having pushed on from Ft. Koshkonong after learning of the discovery of Black Hawk's westward trail.

---

[1] Smith's comment on the above letter, Vol. 3, page 426, History of Wisconsin: "The above letter is extracted from Niles Register of August 18th, 1832, and it does not appear to whom it is addressd; but it is highly probable that it is the letter which was sent to the commandant of Fort Crawford, at Prairie du Chien, which Captain Estes carried as express.

"The singularity of the language of the letter will be evident, when it is considered that General Henry had the chief command at the battle of Wisconsin Heights, and not Colonel Dodge."

CHAPTER XXXII.

Pursuit Resumed—Battle of the Bad Axe.

[1]On the 20th Alexander received an express from Scott giving particulars of the inefficiency of his army.

On the 21st Atkinson and Alexander marched from Ft. Koshkonong' in the direction of the Blue Mounds in the midst of a heavy rain, which continued all day and all night. The convoy of wagons met was turned back.

On the 22d the troops crossed the ford below Lake Koshkonong.

On the 23d the forces marched from the encampment of the morning, eight miles south of "the river of the Four Lakes," towards the Blue Mounds, to two miles west of Davitt's.

On the 24th they marched to the Blue Mounds, after suffering much for water, having marched twenty miles without any. The express sent from Henry, which informed Atkinson of the "Battle of the Wisconsin," was met, and on inspection the entire force of militia was now found to be reduced to the strength of one original brigade.

A certain coolness was found to be in store for the volunteers when they reached the Blue Mounds, by reason of their winning a victory which should have gone to others, according to program, and this, too, in the face of disobedience of orders. Victories then were crimes, pretty much the same as they were before Santiago in 1898, unless won by rule and by those selected for the purpose by those above, and very soon Henry was made to feel the displeasure his victory had brought.

From there Dodge's battalion scattered to the various forts for supplies and equipment, to meet later and take up the line of march at Helena on the 29th.

On the 25th the army marched for the "Ouisconsin," to overtake Black Hawk and finish the war, before he could reach and cross the Mississippi. In this Henry's men, though subordinated in their position in the line of march, cheerfully submitted. In this march the regu-

---

[1]Johnston's Journal.
[2]**Wakefield**, p. 72 and 75. Lt. Col. Sharp was left at Ft. Koshkonong in charge of the men who had lost their horses.

lars went first, Posey and Alexander following, while Henry was given the rear in charge of the baggage. Such men as Fry resented this treatment, but Henry commanded obedience to orders and trudged along behind, doing the drudgery of the army.

By evening the army reached a point within three miles of the Wisconsin, where it camped for the night.

On the 26th the Wisconsin was reached, where preparations had been made the day previous by Col. Enoch C. March for the passage of the army, and here at Helena the army, joined by Dodge, whose forces reassembled here,[1] crossed on the 27th and part of the 28th. Colonel March, whose record as a Quartermaster[2] has never been equaled in Illinois history, was given the heartiest credit from all sides for never failing in the greatest emergencies to be upon the spot when needed and with the supplies desired. In his duties he was ably assisted by John Dixon of Dixon's Ferry, who accompanied the army to the end of the campaign.

The last of the troops having passed the river on the 28th[3] and moved up the Wisconsin River three or four miles, the trail of the enemy was discovered bearing down stream and followed by turning the columns to the left; then pursuing it twelve or fifteen miles over a flat and sandy prairie, which terminated at a deep creek, where the army camped for the night.

From this point the trail was pursued with vigor all day over a rough, almost mountainous country, passing several of the enemy's encampments, which clearly indicated how hard he was pressed for provisions, horseflesh alone being left to him. The bodies of Indians who had died from the lack of proper dressing of their wounds were here seen in greater numbers than before. Reaching the summit of a very high hill, the horses, for lack of grass to eat amongst the timber, were tied up without food.

All day the 30th the march was continued over a similar country. On the 31st about fifteen miles were made over an unusually hilly country thickly timbered. At evening the first stream flowing west was reached and crossed, the army camping within six miles of the Kickapoo River.[4] August 1st the Kickapoo was crossed at ten o'clock at a shallow ford where commenced another rough prairie covered with growths of oak timber. It was a long day's march for the troops because they were forced to go further than usual for water. The trail indicated the immediate presence of the enemy and if darkness had not prevented he could have been reached very soon. The camp was made that night near a small spring. Here Atkinson gave orders to be prepared at two o'clock the following morning to move for the bank of the Mississippi.

As Captain Throckmorton, commanding the Warrior, was ascend-

---
[1] Smith's Wis., Vol. 3, p. 223.
[2] Lt. Robert Anderson, X Wis. Hist. Colls., 170.
[3] Col. W. B. Archer went to the battleground but found nothing new. Wakefield, 76.
[4] Johnston's Journal.

ing the river, he noticed a band of Indians near a camp on the bottoms at the mouth of the Bad Axe hoisting a white flag. Suspecting treachery, he ordered them to send a boat on board for a conference, which they declined. Without comment, except to allow fifteen minutes to remove their squaws and children, he shot a six-pounder into their midst, following it for an hour with a heavy fire of musketry which cost the Indians many lives. Needing fuel to continue the contest, the boat fell down the river to Prairie du Chien to wood up preparatory to returning the following day and finishing the action, but by the hour of its return the battle of the Bad Axe had been finished and Black Hawk's race was run.

Promptly at 2 the morning of the 2d the troops rose, hastily ate breakfast and by sunrise resumed their march.

Black Hawk was aware of the presence of Atkinson's forces, and to give time for a retreat across the river deployed a party of about twenty to meet him, commence the attack and by gradual retreats turn him three or four miles above the camp.

About one hour after sunrise the rising fogs indicated the presence of the river and Dickson's spies were sent forward; they soon returned with a report that the enemy was drawn up in position and near at hand. Dodge thereupon ordered Dickson forward to reconnoiter the enemy and occupy his attention while he drew up his line and reported to Atkinson. This Dickson did, killing eight of the enemy. The regulars under Taylor and Alexander and Posey were ordered forward. The regulars immediately in Dodge's rear moved forward on his right; Dodge's men, dismounting, moved forward at the left in extended order for some minutes before Posey's command came up. This officer was posted on the right of the regulars and Alexander on his right, while Henry, trudging along with the baggage, came upon the scene—just in time to be ordered to send Fry's regiment to Atkinson, which was done.[1]

When the forces moved against the Indian decoys, they of course gave way and were hotly followed by the whites.

Henry clearly saw the stratagem when Major Ewing discovered and reported to him the main trail leading to the river lower down. This trail he rapidly followed to the foot of the high bluff bordering on the bottoms, covered with timber, driftwood and underbrush, through which the trail ran. Halting here and leaving the horses, he formed his men on foot and advanced, after first sending forward a forlorn hope of eight men to draw the enemy's fire. These eight men boldly advanced until they were in sight of the river, when they were suddenly fired upon by a party of Indians and five of the eight men fell. Retreating to the cover of trees, the other three stood their ground until Henry came up.

Deploying his men to the right and left from the center, a charge

---

[1] Reynolds, "My Own Times," 415.

was made and the battle began along the whole line. At this time Henry despatched Major McConnel to Atkinson to report the presence of the entire force, which massed after the first charge and, with the loss of Fry's regiment, was now larger than Henry's force.

The Indians fought desperately from tree to tree, falling back step by step until the river was reached, when by a bayonet charge they were driven into the river. Some tried to swim; others took shelter in a small willow island near by. This charge practically ended the battle, when Atkinson, Dodge, Posey and Alexander, hearing the continued heavy firing, and receiving Major McConnel's message, came up, and while Henry's men were finishing the fight, poured a galling fire into the vanishing remnant, which killed many women and children, to the sincere regret of all, but as many of the squaws were dressed as men and mingled freely with them, it was a misfortune none could have foreseen or avoided.

To put the finishing strokes to Black Hawk's power, Dodge, Fry and Ewing, with the regulars under Taylor, Bliss, Harney and Smith, plunged breast deep into the water to the willow island, where most of the remaining Indians had taken a last stand and where in the face of a heavy fire the whites either killed, captured or drove them into the river. It was there in that little side contest that the greatest loss was supposed to have occurred to the whites, whose casualties in the engagement were twenty-four killed and wounded, while that of the enemy were upward of one hundred and fifty, forty captured, mostly women and children, and about forty or fifty horses taken. The loss to the regulars was five killed and four wounded; to Dodge six wounded;[1] Posey one wounded; Alexander one wounded,[2] and Henry seven killed and wounded.[3]

Black Hawk, with his sons and the Prophet, escaped to the Dalles of the Wisconsin.

On the 3d one hundred and fifty men under Colonels Blackburn and Archer crossed the river, searching the islands and bottoms for fugitives, but found none. Their trail indicated that they had gone along the Iowa River.

A party of Sioux called upon General Atkinson to receive permission to follow the fugitives, which was given, and in that pursuit Neapope was captured and many more Sacs perished.

At that battle again, contrary to plans, Henry won the deciding and final fight of the war, but there he received from every officer of the regular service a hearty congratulation,[4] and in his journal no stronger

---

[1] Privates Smith, Hood and Lowry died of their wounds. Capt. Joseph Dickson wounded. Sergeant George Willard and Private Skinner were wounded.
[2] The brother of Adam Payne.
[3] Lt. Samuel Bowman, killed. 1st Sergt. Wm. C. Murphy, wounded. Private Hutching, wounded and died the 3d. Privates John White, Joseph L. Young, Andrew McCormick and Robert R. Smith, wounded.
[4] Capt. Henry Smith's narrative, X Wis. Hist. Colls., 165.

MAJ. W. L. D. EWING.

FREDERICK REMANN.

BAD AXE BATTLEFIELD.

COL. JAMES M. BLACKBURN.

COL. W. B. ARCHER, FOR WHOM ARCHER AVENUE, CHICAGO, WAS NAMED.

LIEUT. ALBERT SIDNEY JOHNSTON, U. S. A.

CAPT. R. B. MASON, U. S. A.

THE BLACK HAWK WAR.

praise could be accorded a brother than that given by Albert Sidney Johnston.

Covered with glory and the hearty good wishes of every officer and man in the army, Henry returned home, only to be cut off in the zenith of his career, as before stated.

At the close of the fight Atkinson, Dodge, Posey, R. B. Mason and other officers and U. S. Infantry boarded the Warrior and dropped down the river to Prairie du Chien, arriving in the evening of the 4th.

On August 17th the regular troops which left Jefferson Barracks in April had returned to the same point.[1]

---
[1] Capt. Henry Smith's narrative.

CHAPTER XXXIII.

THROCKMORTON'S NARRATIVE—ATKINSON'S REPORT—BLACK HAWK'S FLIGHT—CAPTURE—DELIVERY TO GENERAL STREET—COUNCIL.

After darkness had finished the battle of the Wisconsin, many of the fugitives, women, children and old men, were sent by Black Hawk down the Wisconsin to escape, but on receipt of Dodge's letter, Gov. Joseph M. Street, agent of the Winnebagoes at Prairie du Chien, sent Lieutenant Ritner with a small detachment of regulars up the river to the ferry, later called Barrett's, to intercept them, which he did by firing into the party, killing fifteen men and capturing thirty-two women and children and four men. Nearly as many more were drowned, while the others who escaped to the woods, with few exceptions, perished with hunger or were massacred by a party of Menominees from Green Bay under Colonel Stambaugh.[1]

[2]In addition to this precautionary move, General Street, on July 25th, directed Mr. J. P. Burnett, sub Indian Agent for the Winnebagoes, to ascend the Mississippi and order all the Winnebagoes to descend with their canoes and other water craft to the Agency at once, thus to prevent the Sacs from securing assistance in crossing the Mississippi, and, in case any excuses were offered, to threaten the objectors with non-payment of their annuities.

Mr. Burnett carried out his instructions faithfully on the following day, but found Winneshiek and several other prominent Indians absent hunting.

On the 27th supplemental instructions were sent to Mr. Burnett to send for them, which was likewise done, and on the 28th all had gathered at the Agency that General Street desired, making escape across the Mississippi by Black Hawk practically impossible.

Among the numerous incidents related of the Battle of the Bad Axe is one of Lieut. Robert Anderson, printed in the Galenian and copied into Niles Register for November 3d, 1832, in Vol. 43, page 147.

"When our troops charged the enemy in their defiles near the bank of the Mississippi, men, women and children were seen mixed together in such a manner

---

[1]2 Wis. Hist. Colls., 258. 12 Wis. Hist. Colls., 254, Thwaites.
[2]2 Wis. Hist. Colls., 259.

as to render it difficult to kill one and save the other. A young squaw of about nineteen stood in the grass at a short distance from our line, holding her little girl in her arms, about four years old. While thus standing, apparently unconcerned, a ball struck the right arm of the child above the elbow and shattered the bone, passed into the breast of its young mother, which instantly felled her to the ground. She fell upon the child and confined it to the ground also. During the whole battle this babe was heard to groan and call for relief, but none had come to afford it. When, however, the Indians had retreated from that spot and the battle had nearly subsided, Lieutenant Anderson, of the United States Army, went to the spot and took from under the dead mother her wounded daughter, and brought it to the place we had selected for surgical aid. It was soon ascertained that its arm must come off, and the operation was performed without drawing a tear or a shriek. The child was eating a piece of hard biscuit during the operation. It was brought to Prairie du Chien, and we learn that it has nearly recovered. This was among the many scenes calculated to draw forth a sympathetic tear for human misery."

As the Warrior played an important part in Black Hawk's fall, it may be well to copy the Captain's letter:

Letter of Captain Throckmorton, 3d August, 1832 (Prairie du Chien).

"I arrived at this place on Monday last (July 30), and was dispatched, with the Warrior alone, to Wa-pe-shaw's village, one hundred and twenty miles above, to inform them of the approach of the Sacs, and in order to bring down all the friendly Indians to this place. On our way down we met one of the Sioux band, who informed us that the Indians, our enemies, were on Bad Axe River to the number of four hundred. We stopped and cut some wood and prepared for action. About four o'clock on Wednesday afternoon (August 1st) we found the gentlemen where he stated he left them. As we neared them, they raised a white flag and endeavored to decoy us; but we were a little too old for them, for instead of landing, we ordered them to send a boat on board, which they declined. After about fifteen minutes' delay, giving them time to remove a few of their women and children, we let slip a six-pounder loaded with canister, followed by a severe fire of musketry; and if ever you saw straight blankets, you would have seen them there. I fought them at anchor most of the time, and we were all very much exposed. I have a ball which came in close by where I was standing, and passed through the bulkhead of the wheelroom. We fought them for about an hour or more, until our wood began to fail, and night coming on, we left and went on to the Prairie. This little fight cost them twenty-three killed and, of course, a great many wounded. We never lost a man and had but one man wounded (shot through the leg). The next morning, before we could get back again, on account of a heavy fog, they had the whole army upon them. We found them at it, walked in, and took a hand ourselves. The first shot from the Warrior laid out three. I can hardly tell you anything about it, for I am in great haste, as I am now on my way to the field again. The army lost eight or nine killed and seventeen wounded, whom we brought down. One died on deck last night. We brought down thirty-six prisoners, women and children. I tell you what, Sam, there is no fun in fighting Indians, particularly at this season, when the grass is so very bright. Every man, and even my cabin-boy, fought well. We had sixteen regulars, five riflemen, and twenty of ourselves. Mr. How of Platt, Mr. James G. Soulard and one of the Rolettes were with us and fought well.

General Atkinson's report of the battle is also given as follows:

"Headquarters, First Artillery Corps, Northwestern Army,
"Prairie du Chien, August 25, 1832.

"Sir:—I have the honor to report to you that I crossed the Ouisconsin on the 27th and 28th ultimo, with a select body of troops, consisting of the regulars under Col. Taylor, four hundred in number, part of Henry's, Posey's and Alexander's brigades, amounting in all to 1,300 men, and immediately fell upon the trail of the enemy and pursued it by a forced march, through a mountainous and difficult country, till the morning of the 2d inst., when we came up with his main body on the left bank of the Mississippi, nearly opposite the mouth of the Ioway, which we attacked, defeated and dispersed, with a loss on his part of about a hundred and fifty men killed, thirty-nine women and children taken prisoners—the precise number could not be ascertained, as the greater portion was slain after being forced into the river. Our loss in killed and wounded, which is stated below, is very small in comparison with the enemy, which may be attributed to the enemy's being forced from his positions by a rapid charge at the commencement, and throughout the engagement. The remnant of the enemy, cut up and disheartened, crossed to the opposite side of the river and has fled into the interior, with a view, it is supposed, of joining Keokuk and Wapello's bands of Sacs and Foxes.

"The horses of the volunteer troops being exhausted by long marches, and the regular troops without shoes, it was not thought advisable to continue the pursuit; indeed, a stop to the further effusion of blood seemed to be called for, till it might be ascertained if the enemy would surrender. It is ascertained from our prisoners that the enemy lost in the battle of the Ouisconsin sixty-eight killed and a very large number wounded. His whole loss does not fall short of three hundred. After the battle of the Ouisconsin, those of the enemy's women and children, and some who were dismounted, attempted to make their escape by descending that river, but judicious measures being taken by Capt. Loomis and Lieut. Street, Indian agent, thirty-two women and children and four men have been captured, and some fifteen men killed by the detachment under Lieut. Ritner.

"The day after the battle of this river, I fell down with the regular troops to this place by water, and the mounted men will join us to-day. It is now my purpose to direct Keokuk to demand a surrender of the remaining principal men of the hostile party, which, from the large number of women and children we hold prisoners, I have every reason to believe will be complied with. Should it not, they should be pursued and subdued, a step Maj-Gen. Scott will take upon his arrival.

"I cannot speak too highly of the brave conduct of the regular and volunteer forces engaged in the last battle and the fatiguing march that preceded it. As soon as the reports of officers of the brigades and corps are handed in, they shall be submitted with further remarks.

5 killed, 2 wounded, 6th Inft.
2 wounded, 5th Inft.
1 captain, 5 privates Dodge's Bat. mounted.
1 lieutenant, 6 privates, Henry's.
1 private wounded, Alexander's.
1 private, Posey's.

"I have the honor to be, with great respect,
"Your obedient servant,
"H. ATKINSON, Brevet Brig-Gen., U. S. A.
"MAJOR-GEN. MACOMB, Com.-in-Chief, Washington."

Whipped so thoroughly that no more fight remained in him, Black Hawk, at the close of August 2d, fled to the woods of the North with his sons and principal officers, hoping that he would be protected by his whilom friends, the Winnebagoes, when once in the fastnesses of the Dalles of the Wisconsin, far from the scenes of conflict; but General Street, in calling the Winnebagoes to the Agency on August 4th, had anticipated and frustrated every plan and move of the defeated and fugitive Indians. From the Agency he sent in pursuit of them the one-eyed Decori and Chaeter, who caught first Black Hawk and the Prophet, and later the Sioux caught Ne-a-pope. The most authentic account of that capture seems to be the one made by David McBride, and is to be found in Vol. 5 of the Wisconsin Historical Collections, page 293, verbose, but in the main correct:

"He became satisfied the battle was lost, and hastily retreated to a surrounding height, overlooking the sanguinary battleground, accompanied by his faithful adjunct, the Prophet, and for an instant turned to view the scene of his disastrous defeat, his haughty bosom filled with mingled feelings of disappointment and despair, * * * then hastily fled, to seek a temporary refuge among his pseudo friends, the Winnebagoes of the Lemonweir valley.

"The fugitive chief fled northward with his follower, until he entered the valley of the Lemonweir, where he hoped to secrete himself among its numerous bluffs and rocky cliffs. * * * When he reached what is now known as the Seven Mile Bluff, from its lofty and precipitous heights he could see an enemy or friend in their approaches for many miles. Here he felt secure for the present, and cast himself down under the shade of its evergreens to rest his wearied body, that had for many days known no respite or repose, dispatching his companion in search of food, and to ascertain whether any of his Winnebago friends were in the vicinity. Late in the evening, the messenger returned without food, but with information that they were pursued; that either friends or foes were on their trail. Not a moment was to be lost; they must separate and each secrete himself as best he could. The Prophet sought refuge in a cliff of the romantic chimney rocks, at the east end of the bluff,[1] and Black Hawk selected a unique hiding place, where he had often, years before, secreted himself, when on hunting excursions, to watch for game. On a bold promontory of the bluff that stretches far out into the valley, on its northern face, and high on the summit of a towering crag, stands an isolated gray pine, with its dwarfed and straggling limbs. About twenty feet from its base, a remarkable thicket of small branches starts suddenly out from its trunk like a cradle from the ship's mast, covered with a dense mass of deep green foliage closely matted together, forming a complete protection from outward view to a much larger animal than man, and from which an extended view was readily obtained of the leading trail, which passed to the foot of the cliff, up and down the valley for many miles, and which has since the above event, been familiarly known as Black Hawk's Nest, by the early settlers of the valley.

For two whole days and nights he kept still in his eyrie. Twice during the first, runners passed on the trail, but doubtful of their character as friends or foes, the accustomed signal was not given. Towards evening of the third, two tall chiefs approached in view; the quick, discerning eye of the fugitive recognized the well-

---

[1]Prophet captured on Black River and Black Hawk at the Dalle on the Wisconsin, forty miles above the Portage. Galenian, Sept. 5, 1832, which corresponds with account quoted.

known costume and gait of his former Winnebago friends, Cha-e-tar and One-Eyed De-cor-ra. They had been friends in the early period of the contest, had given him important intelligence of the movements of the white men, and had even piloted him to the settlement at Spafford's Farms and Fort Mound, while another of their chiefs, White Crow, was acting as guide to Col. Dodge. Soon these runner chiefs came close to the hiding place of Black Hawk and encamped for the night at the base of the cliff upon which he was perched. Before they slept, in soft whispers, the purport of their journey was disclosed to the deeply interested ear of their intended victim. Their errand was to make him captive. Overwhelmed with disappointment at their duplicity and treachery, but fearful of the result of an attempt at this moment to seek revenge, with characteristic stealthiness, at midnight, he quickly descended and again sought safety in flight. After communicating with his friend, the Prophet, on his future plans of escape from the grasp of his pursuers, they both started for Prairie La Crosse, one hundred miles up the Mississippi, where he could cross to the west side and again be secure.

"But in this he was alike deceived and unfortunate. As day broke, Cha-e-tar and De-cor-ra, believing he had sought refuge in the great cave in one of the twin bluffs about fifteen miles west, started on their hurried journey, and had proceeded but a few miles ere they came upon the well-known trail of the fugitives. Though prepared for the emergency, their instructions were to take them alive, if possible, and their policy was to keep close on their footsteps, well knowing they could make the capture before crossing the river. For two days these wary chiefs kept close in Black Hawk's rear, until, on the evening of the second day, they saw their victims enter the wigwams of their band at the river, and in a few moments after they were in the presence of the fugitive chief and his companion. Black Hawk saw at once his fate was sealed; he was in the hands of his captors, his long-cherished visions of triumph over his white enemies instantly vanished, but he was still a brave, a warrior that could meet his worst fate with dignified composure. * * * He silently held out his hands for the accustomed cord."

On the 27th of August the two were delivered to General Street at Prairie du Chien, which important event was fully chronicled in a letter written by General Street to the St. Louis Globe, dated Prairie du Chien, 3d September, 1832:

"F. P. Blair, Esq.:

"Dear Sir:—The Indian war is over. The celebrated leaders of the hostile Indians, Black Hawk and the Prophet, were delivered to me at this place on the 27th ultimo, by the Winnebagoes of my agency. The day after Generals Scott and Atkinson left this place, I sent out two parties of Winnebagoes to bring Black Hawk, the Prophet and Ne-a-pope to me. They returned the 27th ult., about 10 or 11 o'clock, and delivered the two first. The same day I turned them over to Col. Taylor, commanding Fort Crawford, and expect to accompany them with a military escort to the headquarters of Gen. Scott at Rock Island in a day or two.

"I am now waiting the return of an express sent up the Wisconsin, by which I expect to receive about fifty or sixty more prisoners taken by the Indians. There are now forty-eight in the fort, delivered me by the Winnebagoes of my agency, and I have previously delivered to Gen. Atkinson forty-three taken by the Winnebagoes and Menominees.

"The moment the hostile Indians entered the limits of my agency by crossing the Wisconsin, with the aid of the commanding officer at the fort, I assembled the

Indians of my agency and encamped them before my door, where they remained until the battle of the Mississippi and the rout of the hostile Indians.

"I herewith convey to you an account of the delivery of Black Hawk and the Prophet to me.

"Your most obedient servant,

"JOSEPH M. STREET."

"Prairie du Chien, 27th August, 1832.

"At 11 o'clock to-day, Black Hawk and the Prophet were delivered to Gen. Joseph M. Street by the One-Eyed Decori and Chaeter, Winnebagoes, belonging to his agency. Many of the officers from the post were present. It was a moment of much interest.

"The prisoners appeared in a full dress of white tanned deerskins. Soon after they were seated the One-Eyed Decori rose up and said:

"'My Father:—I now stand before you. When we parted, I told you I would return soon, but I could not come any sooner. We have had to go a great distance (the Dalle on the Wisconsin, above the portage). You see we have done what you sent us to do. These are the two that you told us to get (pointing to Black Hawk and the Prophet).

"'My Father:—We have done what you told us to do. We always do what you tell us, because we know it is for our good.

"'My Father:—You told us to get these men, and it would be the cause of much good to the Winnebagoes. We have brought them, but it has been very hard for us to do so. That one—Mucatamish-ka-kaik (Black Hawk)—was a great way off. You told us to bring them to you alive. We have done so. If you had told us to bring their heads alone, we would have done so, and it would have been less difficult than what we have done.

"'My Father:—We deliver these men into your hands. We would not deliver them even to our brother, the chief of the warriors, but to you, because we know you, and believe you are our friend. We want you to keep them safe. If they are to be hurt, we do not wish to see it. Wait until we are gone before it is done.

"'My Father:—Many little birds have been flying about our ears of late, and we thought they whispered to us that there was evil intended for us, but now we hope these evil birds will let our ears alone.

"'My Father:—We know you are our friend, because you take our part, and that is the reason we do what you tell us to do.

"'My Father:—You say you love your red children. We think we love you as much, if not more, than you love us. We have confidence in you, and you may rely on us.

"'My Father:—We have been promised a great deal if we would take these men; that it would do much good to our people. We now hope to see what will be done for us.

"'My Father:—We have come in haste; we are tired and hungry. We now put these men into your hands. We have done all that you told us to do.'

"General Street said: 'My children:—You have done well. I told you to bring these men to me, and you have done so. I am pleased at what you have done. It is for your good, and for this reason I am pleased. I assured the great chief of the warriors that, if these men were in your country you would find them and bring them to me; that I believed you would do whatever I directed you, and now that you have brought them, I can do much for your good. I will go down to Rock

Island with the prisoners, and I wish you who have brought these men especially to go with me, with such other chiefs and warriors as you may select.

"'My Children:—The great chief of the warriors when he left this place directed me to deliver them and all other prisoners to the chief of the warriors at this place, Col. Taylor, who is here by me.

"'My Children:—Some of the Winnebagoes south of the Wisconsin river have befriended the Saukies, and some of the Indians of my agency have also given them aid. This displeases the great chief of the warriors and your great father, the President, and was calculated to do much harm.

"'My Children:—Your great father, the President, at Washington, has sent a great war chief from the far east, Gen. Scott, with a fresh army of soldiers. He is now at Rock Island. Your great father, the President, has sent him and the Governor and chief of Illinois to hold a council with the Indians. He has sent a speech to you, and wishes the chiefs and warriors of the Winnebagoes to go to Rock Island to the council on the 10th of next month. I wish you to be ready in three days, when I will go with you.

"'My Children:—I am well pleased that you have taken the Black Hawk, the Prophet and other prisoners. This will enable me to say much for you to the great chief of the warriors and to the President, your great father.

"'My Children:—I shall now deliver the two men, Black Hawk and the Prophet, to the chief of the warriors here; he will take care of them till we start to Rock Island.'

"Col. Taylor said:—'The great chief of the warriors told me to take the prisoners when you should bring them, and send them to Rock Island to him. I will take them and keep them safe, but I will use them well and send them with you and General Street when you go down to the council, which will be in a few days. Your friend, General Street, advises you to get ready and go down soon, and so do I.

"'I tell you again I will take the prisoners. I will keep them safe, but I will do them no harm. I will deliver them to the great chief of the warriors, and he will do with them and use them in such a manner as shall be ordered by your great father, the President.'

"Chaeter, a Winnebago warrior, then said to General Street:

"'My Father:—I am young and do not know how to make speeches. This is the second time I ever spoke to you before people.

"'My Father:—I am no chief; I am no orator; but I have been allowed to speak to you.

"'My Father:—If I should not speak as well as others, still you must listen to me.

"'My Father:—When you made the speech to the chiefs, Wau-kon Decorri, Carramana, the One-Eyed Decorri and others 'tother day, I was there. I heard you. I thought of what you said to them. You also said to me, you said, "If these two (pointing to Black Hawk and the Prophet) were taken by us and brought to you, there would nevermore a black cloud hang over your Winnebagoes."

"'My Father:—Your words entered into my ears, into my brains, and into my heart.

"'My Father:—I left here that same night, and you know you have not seen me since until now.

"'My Father:—I have been a great way. I have had much trouble; but when I remembered what you said, I knew what you said was right. This made me continue and do what you told me to do.

"'My Father:—Near the Dalle, on the Wisconsin, I took Black Hawk. No one did it but me. I say this in the ears of all present, and they know it, and I now appeal to the Great Spirit, our grandfather, and the earth, our grandmother, for the truth of what I say.

"'My Father:—I am no chief; but what I have done is for the benefit of my nation, and I hope to see the good that has been promised to us.

"'My Father:—That one, Wa-bo-kie-shiek (the Prophet), is my relation. If he is to be hurt, I do not wish to see it.

"'My Father:—Soldiers sometimes stick the ends of their guns (bayonets) into the backs of Indian prisoners when they are going about in the hands of the guard. I hope this will not be done to these men.'"—Copied in Niles Weekly Register, Vol. 43, page 78, issue of Sept. 29, 1832.

CHAPTER XXXIV.

Stambaugh's Expedition.

On the 23d of June Col. George Boyd, Agent for the Menominees at Green Bay, wrote Atkinson offering or suggesting the services of the Indians of this agency, to which Atkinson replied on the 12th of July, requesting him to raise a company of 200 Menominees to arrest the progress of Black Hawk toward the Milwaukee River. This letter was entrusted to Colonel Hamilton and safely delivered.

On the 12th July Colonel Boyd replied as follows:[1]

"Indian Agency Office.
"Green Bay, July 20, 1832.

"Sir:—I have the honor to acknowledge the receipt of your letter of the 12th instant, in answer to one of mine of the 23d ult., by the hands of Col. Hamilton, three days since, and to inform you that arrangements are making, with all possible expedition, to forward to your aid the services of two hundred Menominees, with a view to arrest the progress of the enemy towards the Milwaukee country. They will be placed under the immediate command of Col. Stambaugh, the former agent of these people, who, on my first arrival in this country, demanded as a favor that, in the event of the Menominees being called into the field, that Col. Stambaugh should be placed at their head. This request was formally granted them by me in council, and it is to redeem this pledge, as well as to enable me consistently to relinquish a command for which my present state of health wholly unfits me, that this arrangement has been made. It has been my earnest wish to employ the talents and experience of Col. Hamilton, by associating him with the expedition, with that rank which would bring him second in command. This offer, I regret to say, Col. Hamilton has at once declined. I trust, however, that the Menominees will effect what you calculated from their presence in the field under the present management, and that they will be ready to take the line of march in order to aid you in your intended operations against the enemy in about seven days from the present time. * * * "With great respect, etc.,

"G. Boyd, U. S. Ind. Agent.
"Brig.- Gen. H. Atkinson, U. S. Army, Commanding Camp Whitewater, Rock River."

There were no arms for them when the communication arrived. They were scattered about in a manner to require unusual trouble in

---

[1] 12 Wis. Hist. Colls., p. 270. Lack of knowledge of the country and its geography caused Atkinson to call it the Milwaukee country. He intended to cut off a possible retreat to Canada *via* Green Bay. 4 Wis. Hist. Colls., p. 185.

LIEUT. JAMES M. BOYD.

LIEUT. ALEXANDER J. IRWIN.

CAPT. AUGUSTIN GRIGNON.

COL. HART L. STEWART.

THE BLACK HAWK WAR. 235

collecting them and upon putting the plan into practical operation Colonel Boyd almost despaired enlisting the desired 200. He attempted to engage recruits from the ranks of the New York Indians, the Oneidas and Stockbridges under Alexander J. Irwin of Green Bay, but they to a man refused and Irwin enlisted under Stambaugh.

There was no overt hostility to the command of Hamilton, but the Menominees held Colonel Stambaugh in such veneration that they were unwilling to trust another to command them.

After much discouraging work, the quota was finally secured and, divided into two commands or companies, the battalion was ready to march.

¹S. C. Stambaugh, Commander; Augustin Grignon, Sr., Captain; Chas. Grignon, Jr., First Lieutenant and Interpreter; Robert Grignon, Second Lieutenant; George Johnston, Captain; James M. Boyd, First Lieutenant; William Powell, Second Lieutenant and Interpreter, and Alex J. Irwin, charged with the commissariat, with the rank of First Lieutenant Infantry.

After which Colonel Stambaugh received the following instructions:

"Indian Agency, July 25, 1832.

²"Sir:—As you have been selected by the Menominees to lead them in the coming conflict, and having yielded to their choice, I consider it my duty to enclose to you a copy of the Commanding General's instructions to Col. Hamilton, as to their movements in the field, and the position to be occupied by them in regard to the main army, and to request your strict adherence to them, as far as practicable.

"As much time, however, has elapsed since the above instructions were given, and the general line of operations of our army perhaps materially changed, it is determined, under all circumstances, to direct you to proceed with all possible expedition to Fort Winnebago, and, immediately on your arrival there, to report yourself forthwith, by express, to the Commanding General in the field, and to await his orders as to your further movements.

"Wishing you all the success which the Government has a right to anticipate from the movements of the Menominees, and that the honor and the interest of the nation may be your leading star, to guide you in all your operations, I have the honor to be, Yours, etc.,

"GEORGE BOYD, Indian Agent."
"Col. S. C. Stambaugh, Com. the Menominee Expedition, Green Bay, M. T."

On the 26th³ the battalion moved, and for the only authentic account extant of their movements from that hour I am indebted to Augustin Grignon, one of the captains in the expedition, which is to be found in Vol. 3 of the Wis. Hist. Soc. Colls., p. 293 et seq.

"Col. Stambaugh had previously been the Menominee Indian Agent, but had been superseded by Col. Boyd, who had been directed to raise a party of the Menominees to serve against the hostile Indians.

---
¹12 Wis. Hist. Colls., p. 279.
²12 Wis. Hist. Colls., p. 282.
³12 Wis. Hist. Colls., p. 284.

"Col. Boyd gave the command of the expedition to Col. Stambaugh. The Menominees rendezvoused at Green Bay early in July, 1832. There were over 300, all Indians except the officers, about nine in number.

"Osh-kosh, Souligny, I-om-e-tah, Grizzly Bear, Old Po-e-go-nah, Wau-nau-ko, Pe-wau-te-not, Osh-ka-he-nah-niew, or the Young Man, La Mott, Carron, and, indeed, all the principal men of the Menominees, were of the party. Alexander Irwin was Commissary and Quartermaster. The Indians were arranged into two companies. I commanded one, having my son, Charles A. Grignon, and my nephew, Robert Grignon, for lieutenants. George Johnson of Green Bay was chosen to the command of the other company, with William Powell and James Boyd, a son of Col. Boyd, for lieutenants. George Grignon served as a volunteer.

"With a few pack horses and each man a supply of provisions, we started from the Bay and proceeded to the Great Butte des Morts, and there crossed over to the present place of Robert Grignon. Went to Portage, and the next day renewed our march, and the first night camped on Sugar Creek, some half a dozen miles short of the Blue Mounds, and the second night at Fort Dodge, then to English Prairie, thence with one other camping we reached Prairie du Chien;[1] before reaching which, Grizzly Bear, his son and two or three others, descending the Wisconsin in a canoe, discovered a Sauk girl on an island alone. The Grizzly Bear's son went and took her and found her half starved. She was about 10 years old, and on the return of the party, Colonel Stambaugh took her to Green Bay and placed her in the Indian mission school, and the next year, when Black Hawk reached Green Bay on his way home, he took her with him.

"From Col. William S. Hamilton we learned at Prairie du Chien that a trail of Sauks had been discovered down the river. Fully one-half of our party, with George Grignon and William Powell, remained at Prairie du Chien while Oshkosh, I-om-e-tah, Souligny, Carron, Pe-wan-te-not, with their warriors, proceeded by land, accompanied by Colonel Hamilton.

"We stopped at Barrett's Ferry on the Wisconsin and started early the next morning, and about noon struck the Sauk trail and pursued it till the sun was about an hour and a half high, when we discovered the smoke of Indians encamped in a low spot beside a small stream in the prairie. There were only two men and a youth about twelve years old; three or four women and as many children. We at once surrounded them and rushed upon them, with orders to take them prisoners; but the Menominees were fierce for a fight and killed the two men and took the others prisoners. They fired a volley at the two Sauks, and when they fell they were riddled with bullets by those coming up, who wished to share in the honor of having participated in the fight. In the melee one of the children was wounded and died the next day.

"Lieutenant Robert Grignon was badly wounded in the side with a buckshot, and, coursing round his back, lodged. He thought he was shot by the Indian lad, but I think it was quite as likely to have been done by some of our own party, firing as they were in every direction.

"This little affair occurred not far back from the Mississippi and some ten or fifteen miles north of Cassville. Colonel Hamilton participated in it.

"We camped on the battleground that night, and next day went to Cassville, carrying Robert Grignon on a litter, and thence to Prairie du Chien; he was conveyed in a canoe, while we returned by land. We delivered the prisoners at

---

[1] On August 8, as stated by Wakefield, p. 83.

Prairie du Chien; we had to leave Robert Grignon there; the shot could not be extracted, and he was not able to return till in the autumn.

"We commenced our return home in three days, and nothing happened on our march worthy of particular notice."

While Stambaugh's expedition accomplished little, it was an integral part of the general scheme and has been given the consideration it demanded.

CHAPTER XXXV.

Examination of the Indians—Black Hawk a Prisoner.

With the exception of Black Hawk's immediate party, the prisoners were sent to Fort Armstrong, and in a report from General Scott to Hon. Lewis Cass, Secretary of War, dated at Fort Armstrong, August 19th, he states that he had examined many of the 118 prisoners taken, from whom he had learned that at one time ten lodges of Winnebagoes had been with Black Hawk's party, and that Winnebagoes brought in scalps eight different times. They also stated that the Agent St. Vrain was killed by Winnebagoes; in consequence whereof, the general had sent a talk to the Winnebagoes, demanding of them that their chiefs, warriors and principal men meet him on the 10th of September and bring such Sacs, Foxes and Kickapoos of Black Hawk's party as may have taken refuge amongst them, and such Winnebagoes as may have been engaged in the war, or may have given assistance to the enemy.

Ne-a-pope, the principal war brave of Black Hawk's band, in his examination[1] said:

"I always belonged to Black Hawk's band. Last summer I went to Malden; when I came back, I found that, by the treaty with General Gaines, the Sacs had moved across the Mississippi. I remained during the winter with the Prophet, on Rock River, 35 miles above the mouth. During the winter the Prophet sent me across the Mississippi to Black Hawk with a message, telling him and his band to cross back to his village and make corn. That if the Americans came and told them to move again, they would shake hands with them—if Americans had come and told us to move, we should have shaken hands and immediately have moved peacefully.[2] We encamped on Sycamore Creek—we met some Pottowattamies and I made a feast for them. At that time I heard there were some Americans near us (Stillman's). I prepared a white flag to go and see them, and sent two or three young men on a hill to see what they were doing. Before the feast was finished I heard my young men were killed; this was at sunset. Some of my young men ran out; two were killed, and the Americans were seen rushing on to our camp. My young men fired a few guns and the Americans ran off, and my young men chased them about six miles."[3]

---
[1]Made on the 19th.
[2]He entirely forgot the many requests of Atkinson to move peacefully.
[3]Also copied in 43 Niles Reg. for Sept. 29, 1832, p. 69.

Ne-a-pope continued by stating that the Pottowatomies of the village immediately left them, and that no Kickapoos joined them but those who were originally with Black Hawk; but the Winnebagoes did, and brought in scalps frequently; that at last, when they found the Sacs would be beaten, they turned against them.

Na-ni-sa, a Sac woman, aged 25, sister of a head warrior, stated that in the hottest of the fight of August 2d she kept her infant close in her blanket by the force of her teeth, seized a horse's tail, and got across the Mississippi, where they were afterwards attacked by the Sioux. She ran off, but during the firing she heard some of those who fired, hallo—"I am a Winnebago."

When, on August 27th, Black Hawk was brought a prisoner before General Street, he is reported to have addressed the latter as follows:[1]

"My warriors fell around me. It began to look dismal. I saw my evil day at hand. The sun rose clear on us in the morning; at night it sunk in a dark cloud, and looked like a ball of fire. This was the last sun that shone on Black Hawk. He is now a prisoner to the white man, but he can stand the torture. He is not afraid of death. He is no coward. Black Hawk is an Indian. He has done nothing of which an Indian need be ashamed. He has fought the battles of his country against the white man, who came year after year to cheat his people and take away their lands. You know the cause of our making war. It is known to all white men. They ought to be ashamed of it. The white men despise the Indians and drive them from their homes. But the Indians are not deceitful. Indians do not steal. Black Hawk is satisfied. He will go to the world of spirits contented. He has done his duty. His father will meet and reward him. The white men do not scalp the heads, but they do worse—they poison the heart. It is not pure with them. His countrymen will not be scalped, but they will in a few years become like the white man, so that you cannot hurt them; and there must be, as in the white settlements, as many officers as men to take care of them and keep them in order. Farewell to my nation! Farewell to Black Hawk!"

Black Hawk and his fellow prisoners were placed aboard the steamboat to be delivered to General Scott at Fort Armstrong, where treaties were to have been negotiated at once with the Sacs and Foxes and Winnebagoes. Soured at his restraint he sought, in a speech at Galena, to shift his guilt to the shoulders of Keokuk, as has been reported in the Galenian of September 5th, 1832:

"Black Hawk this morning desired to speak to General Street. The amount of what he said was: That he was not the originator of the war. He was now going where he would meet Keokuk and then he would tell the truth. He would tell all about this war which had caused so much trouble. There were chiefs and braves of his nation who were the cause of the continuance of the war. He did not wish to hold any council with him. He only wanted to tell him that when he got where Keokuk was, he would tell the whole of the origin of the differences and those who continued them. He wanted to surrender long ago; but others refused. He wanted to surrender to the steamboat Warrior, and tried to do so till the second

---

[1] Fulton's "Red Men of Iowa," p. 210.

fire. He then ran and went up the river and never returned to the battleground. His determination then was to escape if he could. He did not intend to surrender after that; but when the Winnebagoes came upon him, he gave up—and he would tell all about the disturbances when he got to Rock Island."

It is a noteworthy fact that when he did meet Keokuk he made no startling disclosures. On the contrary, he leaned upon Keokuk and cultivated the latter's assistance, with the expectation that Keokuk would be able to aid him to escape further captivity.

Upon the arrival at Fort Armstrong of the boat, the cholera was raging with such virulence that General Scott directed the prisoners to be taken on down to Jefferson Barracks until the fury of the disease had abated.[1] This angered Black Hawk, for he was determined to make a speech to Scott and doubtless endeavor to unload all his offenses upon Keokuk.

This memorable trip from Prairie du Chien to Jefferson Barracks was made in charge of Lieut. Jefferson Davis, and of his kindness and consideration for the feelings of the distinguished prisoners, Black Hawk has this to say:[2]

"We remained here (Prairie du Chien) a short time, and then started for Jefferson Barracks in a steamboat under the charge of a young war chief (Lieut. Jefferson Davis) who treated all with much kindness. He is a good and brave young chief, with whose conduct I was much pleased. On our way down we called at Galena and remained a short time. The people crowded to the boat to see us, but the war chief would not permit them to enter the apartment where we were—knowing, from what his feelings would have been if he had been placed in a similar situation, that we did not wish to have a gaping crowd around us."

Arriving safely at Jefferson Barracks,[3] the prisoners were delivered to General Atkinson, who put them in irons and thus laid the finishing stroke to Black Hawk's pride. On this feature of his captivity he had Colonel Patterson write: "We were now confined to the barracks and forced to wear the ball and chain. This was extremely mortifying and altogether useless. Was the White Beaver (Atkinson) afraid I would break out of his barracks and run away? or was he ordered to inflict this punishment upon me? If I had taken him prisoner on the field of battle I would not have wounded his feelings so much by such treatment, knowing that a brave war chief would prefer death to dishonor. But I do

---

[1] The Captain, prior to leaving, had pledged his passengers not to stop at Ft. Armstrong, Mo. Rep., Sept. 11, 1832.
[2] Autobiography 2d Ed., p. 111.
[3] Mo. Republican of Sept. 11, 1832, contains statement that steamboat Winnebago arrived in St. Louis en route for Jefferson Barracks "ten miles below," on Sept. 10. That the "boat left Galena with Black Hawk, The Prophet, two sons of Black Hawk and nine braves, together with about 50 warriors." The latter were landed south of the lower rapids on their pledge of neutrality. Black Hawk, The Prophet, two sons and nine braves were taken to Jefferson Barracks to remain as hostages. On the preceding Thursday Ne-a-pope and six or seven warriors were taken there by Lt. Cross and five men under his command.

not blame the White Beaver for the course he pursued, as it is the custom among the white soldiers, and I suppose was a part of his duty."

The White Beaver probably had in mind the many previous breaches of faith exhibited by the prisoner, after having made promises and treaties to behave himself, when he applied the shackles, and Black Hawk realized for the first time that the whites would suffer him to disturb them no longer. In his lofty speech to General Street, stating that "he can stand the torture," one would expect to find Black Hawk glorifying the pleasure of manacled martyrdom; but in the contrast between the speech and the complaint, we find the true Black Hawk, from young manhood to his capture. The inconvenience of prison life made of him the poorest example of martyrdom that ever posed.

CHAPTER XXXVI.

Scott's Expedition—Treaty.

Allusion to the presence of General Scott in this campaign has been made, but for the purpose of receiving substantial treatment later on was temporarily dropped.

He may not have participated in any of its pitched battles, but in his conflict with an enemy more dreadful than bullets, he displayed a genius and heroism seldom found in military annals.

For the first time in the history of this continent, Asiatic cholera had appeared in Quebec and Montreal during the early days of warm weather. Few knew its character and none its treatment.

Jackson, who had grown impatient at what he considered a policy of procrastination and conduct which he is said to have characterized as pusillanimous on the part of the volunteers, ordered Scott to take nine companies from the Atlantic coast, proceed to the seat of war and put an end to it.

On June 28th General Scott started from Fortress Monroe with them, and with four of his nine companies made the trip to Chicago in the incredibly short space of eighteen days. His departure was noticed in Niles Register for June 30, 1832. The trip was prosperous enough to Buffalo, where four steamboats, the Sheldon Thompson, Henry Clay, Superior and William Penn, were chartered to carry the expedition around the lakes to Chicago. Down Lake Erie all went well, but when Detroit[1] was reached, two cases developed on board the Thompson while moored to the wharf, which excited alarm. The victims died and the boats all passed on up the St. Clair River to Fort Gratiot, some forty miles distant, by which time the contagion had assumed such proportions that it became necessary to land five companies of 280 men. Many had died; others died immediately after landing; others fled, and later, when seized with the pest, were shunned and denied assistance. Thus abandoned and exhausted, the miserable wretches perished in woods and fields, only to be discovered when birds of prey surrounded their bodies or the odor

---

[1]Davidson & Stuve, Ills., p. 406. Brown Hist. Ills., p. 373.

from decomposition became apparent. Of the entire body of 280 men, we are told that but nine survived.

Scott, in his autobiography, Vol. 1, p. 218, has stated that the disease broke out on his boat and that the only surgeon aboard, after drinking half a bottle of wine, was frightened into a sickness which kept him to his bed. He further adds with some asperity that the surgeon "ought to have died."

Preparatory to departure, Scott, who was always forehanded, had consulted Surgeon Mower of New York about the disease, and, adopting all his suggestions, had laid in a supply of medicines to use if the plague overtook him. These he supplied with his own hand to one and all, from the moment of its appearance to the final eradication of the scourge from the ranks of his army. In Niles Register for August 4th, Vol. 42, p. 402, we are told that Lieut. Gust. Brown and Second Lieut. Franklin McDuffie had died July 15th,[1] and Col. W. J. Worth, Capt. John Munroe and Lieut. William C. DeHart were ordered east July 14th from Chicago, being too ill to travel. In the issue of August 11th Captain Gath (probably meant for Galt), the other member of "the staff," is mentioned as being sent in the same party.

Decimation of the ranks of the men is noticed in Vol. 42, Niles, p. 423, for August 11th: "Of the 208 soldiers attached to the command of Colonel Twiggs, 30 died and 155 deserted. Of three companies of artillery under him, consisting of 152 men, 26 died and 20 deserted. Of Colonel Cummings' detachment of 80 men, 21 died and 4 deserted. Of Colonel Crane's artillery, 220 men, 55 died. Of the 850 men who left Buffalo, not more than 200 were left fit for the field."

While a slight discrepancy may be found to exist between items and their totals, they are but natural to all statements, and do not overestimate the awful mortality and the conditions, which can readily be realized. The following letter, published in the same issue of Niles and dated Fort Dearborn, July 12th, will probably convey a better idea of those conditions than any deductions I may make:

"We have got at last to our place of rendezvous, but in what a condition! We have traveled 600 miles in a steamboat crowded almost to suffocation and the Asiatic cholera raging amongst us. The scenes on board the boat are not to be described. Men died in six hours after being in perfect health. The steerage was crowded with the dying and new cases were appearing on the deck, when the demon entered the cabin. The first case occurred at Fort Gratiot; the man attacked belonged to the company I commanded. I found that the soldiers hesitated about attending him at first, so that I went to the sick man, felt his pulse and stood by his bed, and in a short time the soldiers became reconciled. This was only at first, for when the disease came upon us with fury and the boat became a moving pestilence, every soldier who was well became a nurse for the sick. The disease

---
[1]Wentworth's, Ft. Dearborn, p. 31.

was met with resolution, and never did a body of men stand more firmly by each other than the soldiers in our boat.

"To give you an idea of the disease: You remember Sergeant Heyl? He was well at nine o'clock in the morning—he was at the bottom of Lake Michigan at seven o'clock in the afternoon! I was officer of the day when we arrived and had to move all the sick men to the shore; I had scarcely got through my task when I was thrown down on the deck almost as suddenly as if shot.

"As I was walking on the lower deck, I felt my legs growing stiff from my knees down. I went on the upper deck and walked violently to keep up a circulation of the blood. I felt suddenly a rush of blood from my feet upwards, and as it rose my veins grew cold and my blood curdled. I was seized with a nausea at the stomach and a desire to vomit. My legs and hands were cramped with violent pain. The doctor gave me eight grains of opium and made me rub my legs as fast as I could; he also made me drink a tumbler and a half of raw brandy, and told me if I did not throw up the opium I would certainly be relieved; but not until I had had a violent spasm. The pain is excruciating."

Another letter, written by Capt. A. Walker to Capt. R. C. Bristol, which first appeared in the Chicago Democrat, March 23d, 1861, was afterward copied in "Fort Dearborn," page 72, in an address delivered by John Wentworth, May 21st, 1881, and published the same year by the Chicago Historical Society, and is as follows:

"* * * It will also be remembered, as stated in my former communication, that four steamers, the Henry Clay, Superior, Sheldon Thompson and William Penn, were chartered by the United States Government for the purpose of transporting troops, equipments and provisions to Chicago during the Black Hawk war, but owing to the fearful ravages made by the breaking out of the Asiatic cholera among the troops and crews on board, two of those boats were compelled to abandon their voyage, proceeding no further than Fort Gratiot. The disease became so violent and alarming on board the Henry Clay that nothing like discipline could be observed; everything in the way of subordination ceased. As soon as the steamer came to the dock each man sprang on shore, hoping to escape from a scene so terrifying and appalling. Some fled to the fields, some to the woods, while others lay down in the streets, and under the cover of the river bank, where most of them died unwept and alone.

"There were no cases of cholera causing death on board my boat until we passed the Manitou Islands (Lake Michigan). The first person attacked died about four o'clock in the afternoon, some thirty hours before reaching Chicago. As soon as it was ascertained by the surgeon that life was extinct, the deceased was wrapped closely in his blanket, placing within some weights, secured by lashing some small cordage around the ankles, knees, waist and neck, and then committed, with but little ceremony, to the deep.

"This unpleasant, though imperative duty, was performed by the orderly sergeant, with a few privates detailed for that purpose. In like manner twelve others, including this same noble sergeant, who sickened and died in a few hours, were also thrown overboard before the balance of the troops were landed at Chicago.

"The sudden and untimely death of this veteran sergeant and his committal to a watery grave caused a deep sensation on board among the soldiers and crews, which I will not here attempt to describe. The effect produced upon General Scott and the other officers in witnessing the scene was too visible to be misunderstood, for the dead soldier had been a very valuable man, and evidently a favorite among the officers and soldiers of the regiment.

"Some very interesting and appropriate memoranda were made by the steward of the boat at the time on one of the leaves of his account book (which is still in my possession) by quotations from one of the poets, such as 'Sleep, soldier, sleep; thy warfare's o'er,' etc.

"On another leaf is a graphic representation of a coffin, made by pen and ink, placed opposite the account on the credit side of one of the volunteer officers, who died after reaching Chicago, with this singular and concise device or inscription written upon the lid of the coffin: 'Account settled by death.'

" 'H. BRADLEY, Clerk and Steward,

" 'Steamer Sheldon Thompson.

" 'Chicago, Ill., July 11, 1832.' "

"There was one singular fact—not one of the officers of the army was attacked by the disease while on board my boat with such violence as to result in death, or any of the officers belonging to the boat, though nearly one-fourth of the crew fell a prey to the disease on a subsequent trip while on the passage from Detroit to Buffalo.

"We arrived in Chicago[1] on the evening of the 10th of July, 1832. I sent the yawl boat on shore soon after with General Scott and a number of the volunteer officers, who accompanied him on his expedition against the hostile tribes, who, with Black Hawk, had committed many depredations. Before landing the troops next morning, we were under the painful necessity of committing three more to the deep, who died during the night, making in all sixteen who were thus consigned to a watery grave. These three were anchored to the bottom in two and a half fathoms, the water being so clear that their forms could be plainly seen from our decks. This unwelcome sight created such excitement, working upon the superstitious fears of some of the crew, that prudence dictated that we weigh anchor and move a distance sufficient to shut from sight a scene which seemed to haunt the imagination and influence the mind with thoughts of some portentous evil.

"In the course of the day and night following eighteen others died, and we interred their bodies not far from the spot where the American Temperance House (northwest corner Lake Street and Wabash Avenue) has since been erected. The earth that was removed to cover one made a grave to receive the next that died. All were buried without coffins or shrouds, except their blankets, which served for a winding sheet, and there left, as it were, without remembrance or a stone to mark their resting place. During the four days we remained at Chicago fifty-four more died, making an aggregate of eighty-eight who paid the debt of nature."

The disease was dreadful enough, but its reputation had spread such consternation abroad that Scott was compelled to write to Governor Reynolds a letter, asking for it general circulation, to allay the fright of the people:

"Headquarters, Northwest Army, Chicago,
"July 15, 1832.

"Sir:—To prevent or to correct the exaggerations of rumor in respect to the existence of cholera at this place, I address myself to your Excellency. Four

---

[1]Lt. Humphrey Marshall, later General and a Member of Congress from Kentucky, came to Chicago with Scott.—Early Chicago, Ft. Dearborn, p. 31.

steamers were engaged at Buffalo to transport United States troops and supplies to Chicago. In the headmost of these boats, the Sheldon Thompson, I, with my staff and four companies, a part of Colonel Eustis' command, arrived here on the night of the 10th inst. On the 8th, all on board were in high health and spirits, but the next morning six cases of undoubted cholera presented themselves. The disease rapidly spread itself for the next three days. About 120 persons have been affected. Under a late act of Congress six companies of rangers are to be raised and marched to this place. General Dodge of Michigan is appointed major of the battalion, and I have seen the names of the captains, but I do not know where to address them. I am afraid that the report from this place in respect to cholera may seriously retard the raising of this force. I wish, therefore, that your Excellency would give publicity to the measures I have adopted to prevent the spread of this disease and of my determination not to allow any junction or communication between uninfected and infected troops. The war is not at an end and may not be brought to a close for some time. The rangers may reach the theater of operations in time to give the final blow. As they approach this place I shall take care of their health and general wants.

"I write in great haste, and may not have time to cause my letter to be copied. It will be put in some postoffice to be forthwith forwarded. I have the honor to be your Excellency's most obedient servant,

"WINFIELD SCOTT.

"His Excellency, GOVERNOR REYNOLDS."

From Fort Gratiot the remnant of the troops proceeded around the lakes, hopeful that no further signs of the cholera would appear. In this Scott was gratified until the shores of Mackinac were reached, when, notwithstanding the utmost care of his troops, another case suddenly developed, and from that hour until the expedition reached Chicago, July 10th, and from thence into the fort, which became a hospital, it continued its relentless ravages, until the last of the month, at which time, by Scott's tireless exertions, it was thought to have been thoroughly eradicated.[1]

[2]At this time Major William Whistler was commandant of Fort Dearborn, which contained one company of infantry under the immediate command of Capt. Seth Johnson, with Samuel G. I. DeCamp, Surgeon; Julius J. B. Kingsbury, First Lieutenant, and Hannibal Day, James W. Penrose and Edwin R. Long, Second Lieutenants. In many narratives of this expedition, it has been stated that Scott arrived before Fort Dearborn July 8th, but the letters heretofore copied herein, and which should be accurate, make the date July 10th, and that is the date which should be considered in all future references to the subject. Here, for want of harbor facilities, Scott was compelled to unload his men in boats one-half mile out and row them to shore.[3] In all this long journey, with its

---

[1] An entry in the records of the War Dept. reads: "Fort Dearborn having become a general hospital on July 11th, no returns were received until its reoccupation: Companies G and I, 2d Infantry, returned to the fort on October 1st from the campaign." Wentworth's address on Ft. Dearborn.

[2] Ft. Dearborn by Wentworth, p. 12.

[3] Ft. Dearborn by Wentworth, p. 34.

GEN. SCOTT'S HEADQUARTERS AT
FORT ARMSTRONG.

MAJ. GEN. WINFIELD SCOTT.

LIEUT. JOSEPH E. JOHNSTON,
U. S. A.

MAJ. WILLIAM WHISTLER, U. S. A.

horrors, and in his long stay at Fort Dearborn, Scott never wearied in his ministrations to the suffering men, whose brows he smoothed as they died in agony, trying with a last gasp to bless him for his patient and loving care.

In many a campaign did this fine old hero distinguish himself, but in none did he win more fame than in this, against an enemy with whom he could not treat; in which, as he subsequently stated to John Wentworth: "Sentinals were of no use in warning of the enemy's approach. He could not storm his works, fortify against him, nor cut his way out, nor make terms of capitulation. There was no respect for a flag of truce and his men were falling upon all sides from an enemy in his very midst."[1]

Among those who sought fortune in this war were most of a class of forty-five cadets of the class of 1832. Twenty-nine of them left Buffalo for the Black Hawk campaign, but nearly all were sent back from Fort Gratiot.[2]

On board the ship, amidst stifling air, the dying and dead; on land, in hospital—a very pest house—everywhere, was Scott; and not until the last case had disappeared did he think of relinquishing his fatherly care of the suffering soldiers. Then, on July 29th,[3] finding the spread of the contagion once more checked, he set out with three staff officers for Prairie du Chien, following the route subsequently adopted in 1834 as the mail route from Galena to Chicago, via Fort Payne,[4] Naperville, Aurora, along through what subsequently became DeKalb County, across Lee, up to Dixon's Ferry, arriving there August 2d with the report that the troops under Eustis were en route for Dixon's, and leaving on the same day for Galena, which he reached August 3d with his staff officers, Captains Patrick H. Galt, Hartman Bache and William Maynadier. Leaving Galena on the 5th, on the steamboat Warrior, for Fort Crawford, at Prairie du Chien, that point in turn was reached August 7th, when and where he assumed command of the entire army.

His first act was to order the discharge of the volunteer forces, which immediately·marched to Dixon's Ferry for that purpose, Dodge's battalion excepted, and then on the 10th, at 6 o'clock, he started down the Mississippi for Fort Armstrong, on the boat Warrior, with two companies of U. S. Infantry, eight members of the Sixth Infantry and General Atkinson and staff, transferring the scene to Fort Armstrong.[5] On the 11th Fort Armstrong was reached.

On leaving Chicago, Scott left orders for Lieut.-Col. Abraham Eustis to follow his general route to Fort Crawford with all the well troops

---
[1] Ft. Dearborn by Wentworth, p. 34.
[2] Ft. Dearborn by Wentworth, p. 37, where the names are given.
[3] Scott's letter, Mo. Republican for Aug. 7, 1832.
[4] Scott's letter to Capt. J. R. Brant, A. Q. M., St. Louis, pub. in Mo. Rep. Aug. 7, 1832.
[5] Johnston's Journal.

which had arrived, or might arrive before the 3d August,[1] which Colonel Eustis did, but upon reaching Dixon's Ferry an express from Scott informed the Colonel of the termination of the war and ordered him to follow Rock River down its left bank, along the route used by Atkinson, to its mouth, and establish his camp at Fort Armstrong on Rock Island. On this march Colonel Eustis reached Dixon's Ferry on the 17th,[2] resting there until the 22d of August,[3] when he moved down to Fort Armstrong and camped a short distance from the mouth of Rock River, about four miles from Atkinson's men.

On the 12th Scott sent Lieutenant Buchanan on the steamboat Warrior to bring down all prisoners[4] surrendered to that period, after which he began the examination of witnesses to ascertain the names of those who actively assisted Black Hawk and those who were his passive allies, in order to act intelligently in adjusting the treaties expected to be made September 10th, with reference to the settlement of damages sustained by the United States. On the evening of the 13th Keokuk, with fifty or sixty Sacs and Foxes, arrived in camp and reported that he had visited all the Sac and Fox villages, and that none of Black Hawk's band had yet arrived. He further reported that he had ordered forty-two braves in the direction of the "Ioway," to intercept and bring in any stragglers as they might appear. On the 14th Keokuk delivered to Scott a brave who had murdered a white man, just before, in the vicinity of the Yellow Banks.

On the 15th Atkinson, with his staff, viz., Lieutenants Johnston, Wheelwright and Dorrance, and Captains Smith, Rogers and Hatton, Sixth Infantry, and Lieutenant Richardson, left on the steamboat Warrior for St. Louis.

On or about the 26th of August the cholera again broke out with unusual virulence,[5] and again Scott actively participated in conquering it. So many Indians became affected that it became necessary to dismiss them all until they could be re-assembled by special summons. The following order became imperative:

"Order No. 16.

"Assistant Adjutant-General's Office,
"Fort Armstrong, August 28th, 1832.

"1. The cholera has made its appearance on Rock Island. The two first cases were brought by mistake from Captain Ford's company of U. S. Rangers; one of those died yesterday, the other is convalescent. A second death occurred this morning in the hospital in Fort Armstrong. The man was of the 4th Infantry and had been there some time under treatment for debility. The ranger now convalescent was in the same hospital with him for sixteen hours before a cholera hospital could be established outside the camp and fort.

[1]Scott's letter to Hon. Lewis Cass, dated Aug. 10, 1832.
[2]Davidson and Stuve, p. 407. Galenian of Aug. 22d.
[3]Niles, Vol. 43, p. 51.
[4]118 as reported by Scott. Niles, Sept. 29, p. 69.
[5]Capt. Henry Smith, X Wis. Hist. Colls., p. 165.

"2. It is believed that all these men were of intemperate habits. The Ranger who is dead, it is known, generated this disease within him by a fit of intoxication.

"3. This disease having appeared among the Rangers[1] and on this island, all in commission are called upon to exert themselves to the utmost to stop the spread of the calamity.

"4. Sobriety, cleanliness of person, cleanliness of camp and quarters, together with care in the preparation of the men's messes, are the grand preventives. No neglect under these important heads will be overlooked or tolerated.

"5. In addition to the foregoing, the Senior Surgeon present recommends the use of flannel shirts, flannel drawers and woolen stockings; but the Commanding General, who has seen much of this disease, knows that it is intemperance which, in the present state of the atmosphere, generates and spreads the calamity, and that, when once spread, good and temperate men are likely to take the infection.

"6. He therefore peremptorily commands that every soldier or Ranger who shall be found drunk or sensibly intoxicated after the publication of this order, be compelled, as soon as his strength will permit, to dig a grave at a suitable burying place large enough for his own reception, as such grave cannot fail soon to be wanted for the drunken man himself or some drunken companion.

"7. This order is given as well to serve for the punishment of drunkenness as to spare good and temperate men the labor of digging graves for their worthless companions.

"8. The sanitary regulations now in force respecting communications between the camp near the mouth of Rock River and other camps and posts in the neighborhood are revoked. (They had provided for sending all the sick to the hospital on Rock Island.) Colonel Eustis, however, whose troops are perfectly free from cholera, will report to the Commanding General whether he believes it for the safety of his command that these regulations should be renewed.

"By order of Major-General Scott,

"P. H. GALT, Ass't Adjutant-General."

Cold rains fell; many soldiers were afforded protection from them only by the most miserable of tents, and soon out of 300 cases there were fifty deaths. Finally, as a last resort, the men were removed across the river, where the last case disappeared. It has been said that in this last visitation the Rangers suffered most.[2]

At the time of the appearance of the cholera the three Sacs were confined in the military prison at Fort Armstrong on a charge of complicity in the murder of the Menominees near Prairie du Chien on the 31st of July, 1831. By reason of the cholera, General Scott set them at liberty, taking their promise to return upon the exhibition of a certain signal to be hung from the limb of a dead tree at an elevated point of the island when the epidemic should be over. The signal was subsequently hung up, and, true to their parole, the Indians reported themselves. They were again paroled and subsequently released.[3]

Having again checked the disease, Scott sent out the summons to

---

[1]Cholera appeared in the ranks of Capt. Jesse B. Brown's company just below Dixon's Ferry. Nurses were left behind to care for the sick. At Fort Armstrong thirteen of the company died and were buried in the woods. X Wis., 231.
[2]Capt. Henry Smith, X Wis., 165.
[3]Scott's Autobiography.

the Winnebagoes, who assembled on the 15th[1] to sign a new treaty. Before proceeding with its details it was considered best to prepare them for the forfeitures they must necessarily sustain by reason of their assistance to Black Hawk at nearly all stages of the campaign, as ascertained by the examinations of witnesses:

> "Such is justice between nation and nation, against which none can rightfully complain; but as God, in his dealings with human creatures, tempers justice with mercy—or else the whole race of man would soon have perished—so shall we, commissioners, in humble imitation of divine example, now treat you, my red brethren, who have offended both against God and your great human father at Washington."[2]

Thereupon the following treaty was made and signed, on the 21st day of September, 1832, and promulgated by the President's proclamation, February 13th, 1833, after having been ratified by the Senate:

ARTICLES OF A TREATY OF PEACE, FRIENDSHIP AND CESSION, concluded at Fort Armstrong, Rock Island, Illinois, between the United States of America, by their Commissioners, Major-General Winfield Scott, of the United States Army, and His Excellency John Reynolds, Governor of the State of Illinois, and the confederated tribes of Sac and Fox Indians, represented in general council by the undersigned Chiefs, Headmen and Warriors.

WHEREAS, Under certain lawless and desperate leaders a formidable band, constituting a large portion of the Sac and Fox nation, left their country in April last, and, in violation of treaties, commenced an unprovoked war upon unsuspecting and defenseless citizens of the United States, sparing neither age nor sex; and whereas, the United States, at a great expense of treasure, have subdued the said hostile band, killing or capturing all its principal chiefs and warriors, the said States, partly as indemnity for the expense incurred, and partly to secure the future safety and tranquility of the invaded frontier, demand of the said tribes, to the use of the United States, a cession of a tract of the Sac and Fox country, bordering on said frontier, more than proportional to the numbers of the hostile band who have been so conquered and subdued.

Article I. Accordingly, the confederated tribes of Sacs and Foxes hereby cede to the United States forever all the lands to which the said tribes have title or claim (with the exception of the reservation hereinafter made) included within the following bounds, to-wit: Beginning on the Mississippi River, at the point where the Sac and Fox northern boundary line, as established by the second article of the treaty of Prairie du Chien of the fifteenth of July, one thousand eight hundred and thirty, strikes said river; thence, up said boundary line to a point fifty miles from the Mississippi, measured on said line; thence, in a right line, to the nearest point on the Red Cedar of the Ioway, forty miles from the Mississippi River; thence in a right line to a point in the northern boundary line of the State of Missouri, fifty miles, measured on said boundary, from the Mississippi River; thence by the last-mentioned boundary to the Mississippi River, and by the western shore of said river to the place of beginning. And the said confederated tribes of Sacs and Foxes hereby stipulate and agree to remove from the lands herein ceded to the United States, on or before the first day of June next;

---
[1] Postponed from the 10th.
[2] Scott's Autobiog., Vol. 1, p. 227.

and in order to prevent any future misunderstanding it is expressly understood that no band or party of the Sac or Fox tribes shall reside, plant, fish or hunt on any portion of the ceded country after the period just mentioned.

Article II. Out of the cession made in the preceding article the United States agree to a reservation for the use of the said confederated tribes of a tract of land containing four hundred square miles, to be laid off under the directions of the President of the United States, from the boundary line crossing the Ioway River, in such manner that nearly an equal portion of the reservation may be on both sides of said river, and extending downwards, so as to include Ke-o-kuk's principal village on its right bank, which village is about twelve miles from the Mississippi River.

Article III. In consideration of the great extent of the foregoing cession, the United States stipulate and agree to pay to the said confederated tribes annually, for thirty successive years, the first payment to be made in September of the next year, the sum of twenty thousand dollars in specie.

Article IV. It is further agreed that the United States shall establish and maintain within the limits, and for the use and benefit of the Sacs and Foxes, for the period of thirty years, one additional black and gunsmith shop, with the necessary tools, iron and steel; and finally make a yearly allowance for the same period, to the said tribes, of forty kegs of tobacco and forty barrels of salt, to be delivered at the mouth of the Ioway River.

Article V. The United States, at the earnest request of the said confederated tribes, further agree to pay to Farnham and Davenport, Indian traders at Rock Island, the sum of forty thousand dollars without interest, which sum will be in full satisfaction of the claims of the said traders against the said tribes, and by the latter was, on the tenth day of July, one thousand eight hundred and thirty-one, acknowledged to be justly due for articles of necessity, furnished in the course of the seven preceding years, in an instrument of writing of said date, duly signed by the Chiefs and Headmen of said tribes, and certified by the late Felix St. Vrain, United States agent, and Antoine LeClaire, United States interpreter, both for the said tribes.

Article VI. At the special request of the said confederated tribes, the United States agree to grant, by patent in fee simple, to Antoine LeClaire, Interpreter, a part Indian, one section of land opposite Rock Island, and one section at the head of the first rapids above said island, within the country herein ceded by the Sacs and Foxes.

Article VII. Trusting to the good faith of the neutral bands of Sacs and Foxes, the United States have already delivered up to those bands the great mass of prisoners made in the course of the war by the United States, and promise to use their influence to procure the delivery of other Sacs and Foxes, who may still be prisoners in the hands of a band of Sioux Indians, the friends of the United States; but the following named prisoners of war, now in confinement, who were Chiefs and Headmen, shall be held as hostages for the future good conduct of the late hostile bands, during the pleasure of the President of the United States, viz.: Muk-ka-ta-mish-a-ka-kaik (or Black Hawk) and his two sons; Wau-ba-kee-shik (the Prophet), his brother and two sons; Na-pope, We-sheet Ioway, Pa-ma-ho, and Cha-kee-pa-shi-pa-ho (the Little Stabbing Chief).

Article VIII. And it is further stipulated and agreed between the parties to this treaty that there shall never be allowed in the confederate Sac and Fox nation any separate band, or village, under any chief or warrior of the late hostile bands; but that the remnant of the said hostile bands shall be divided among the neutral bands of the said tribes according to blood—the Sacs among the Sacs and the Foxes among the Foxes.

Article IX. In consideration of the premises, peace and friendship are declared, and shall be perpetually maintained between the United States and the whole confederated Sac and Fox nation, excepting from the latter the hostages before mentioned.

Article X. The United States, besides the presents delivered at the signing of this treaty, wishing to give a striking evidence of their mercy and liberality, will immediately cause to be issued to the said confederated tribes, principally for the use of the Sac and Fox women and children whose husbands, fathers and brothers have been killed in the late war, and generally for the use of the whole confederated tribes, articles of subsistence as follows: Thirty-five beef cattle, twelve bushels of salt, thirty barrels of pork and fifty barrels of flour, and cause to be delivered for the same purposes, in the month of April next, at the mouth of the lower Ioway, six thousand bushels of maize or Indian corn.

Article XI. At the request of the said confederated tribes, it is agreed that a suitable present shall be made to them on their pointing out to any United States agent, authorized for the purpose, the position or positions of one or more mines, supposed by the said tribes to be of a metal more valuable than lead or iron.

Article XII. This treaty shall take effect and be obligatory on the contracting parties as soon as the same shall be ratified by the President of the United States, by and with the advice and consent of the Senate thereof.

Done at Fort Armstrong, Rock Island, Illinois, this twenty-first day of September, in the year of our Lord one thousand eight hundred and thirty-two, and of the Independence of the United States the fifty-seventh.

WINFIELD SCOTT,
JOHN REYNOLDS.

SACS.

Kee-o-kuck, or He Who Has Been Everywhere.
Pa-she-pa-ho, or The Stabber.
Pia-tshe-noay, or The Noise Maker.
Wawk-kum-mee, or Clear Water.
O-sow-wish-kan-no, or Yellow Bird.
Pa-ca-to-kee, or Wounded Lip.
Winne-wun-quai-saat, or The Terror of Men.
Mau-noa-tuck, or He Who Controls Many.
Wau-we-au-tun, or The Curling Wave.

FOXES.

Wau-pel-la, or He Who is Painted White.
Tay-wee-mau, or Medicine Man (Strawberry).
Pow-sheek, or the Roused Bear.
An-nau-mee, or the Running Fox.
Ma-tow-e-qua, or the Jealous Woman.
Mee-shee-wau-quaw, or the Dried Tree.
May-kee-sa-mau-ker, or the Wampum Fish.
Chaw-co-saut, or the Prowler.
Kaw-kaw-kee, or the Crow.
Mau-que-tee, or the Bald Eagle.
Ma-she-na, or Cross Man.

Kaw-kaw-ke-moute, or the Pouch (Running Bear).
Wee-shee-kaw-kia-skuck, or He Who Steps Firmly.
Wee-ca-ma, or Good Fish.
Paw-qua-nuey, or the Runner.
Ma-hua-wai-be, or Wolf Skin.
Mis-see-quaw-kaw, or Hairy Neck.
Waw-pee-shaw-kaw, or White Skin.
Mash-shen-waw-pee-tch, or Broken Tooth.
Nau-nah-que-kee-shee-ko, or Between Two Days.
Paw-puck-ka-kaw, or Stealing Fox.
Tay-e-sheek, or the Falling Bear.
Wau-pee-maw-ker, or the White Loon.
Wau-co-see-nee-me, or Fox Man.

In presence of R. Bache, Cap. Ord. Sec. to the Commission; Abrm. Eustis, Alex. Cummins, Lieut.-Col. 2d Infantry; Alex. R. Thompson, Major U. S. Army; B. Riley, Major U. S. Army; H. Dodge, Major W. Campbell; Hy. Wilson, Major 4th U. S. Inf.; Donald Ward, Thos. Black Wolf, Sexton G. Frazer, P. H. Galt, Ass't Adj.-Gen.; Benj. F. Pike, Wm. Henry, James Craig, John Aukeny, J. B. F. Russell, Isaac Chambers, John Clitz, Adj. Inf.; John Pickell, Lieut. 4th Art'y; A. G. Miller, Lieut. 1st Inf.; Geo. Davenport, Ass't Quar. Mas.-Gen. Ill. Mil.; A. Drane, Aeneas Mackay, Capt. U. S. Army; I. R. Smith, 1st Lieut. 2d Inf.; Wm. Maynadier, Lieut. and A. D. C.; I. L. Gallagher, 1st Lieut. A. C. S.; N. B. Bennet, Lieut. 3d Art'y; Horatio A. Wilson, Lieut. 4th Art'y; H. Day, Lieut. 2d Inf.; James W. Penrose, Lieut. 2d Inf.; J. E. Johnston, Lieut. 4th Art'y; S. Burbank, Lieut. 1st Inf.; I. H. Prentiss, Lieut. 1st Art'y; L. I. Beale, Lieut. 1st Inf.; Addison Philleo, Thomas L. Alexander, Lieut. 6th Inf.; Horace Beall, Act'g Surgeon U. S. Army; Oliver W. Kellogg, Jona. Leighton, Act'g Surg. U. S. Army; Robert C. Buchanan, Lieut. 4th Inf.; Jas. S. Williams, Lieut. 6th Inf.; John W. Spencer, Antoine LeClaire, Interpreter.

To the Indian names are subjoined marks.[1]

On November 11, 180 men, the remains of the six companies sent out with Scott, arrived at Norfolk on the steamboat Potomac, Captain Hubbell commanding: Capt. John Monroe, Fourth Artillery; Capt. Elijah Lyon, Third Artillery; Capt. Upton S. Fraser, Third Artillery; Capt. Patrick H. Galt, Fourth Artillery, with Lieutenants John Pickell, H. A. Wilson, W. A. Thornton, Joseph E. Johnston, Charles O. Collins, Edwin Rose and James H. Prentiss.[2]

[1] Vol. 7, U. S. Statutes at Large by Peters, p. 374.
[2] Niles Reg., Vol. 43, p. 180, Nov. 17, 1832.

CHAPTER XXXVII.

MOVEMENTS OF THE MICHIGAN MILITIA.

In the year 1832, Michigan, as a Territory, embraced that territory later erected into the State of Wisconsin, and while the latter was storm-swept with the troops, the peninsula was in no danger whatever. A great danger was anticipated, and during the tremendous scare which spread over it from one end to the other, enough correspondence passed between Acting Governor Stevens T. Mason, Gen. J. R. Williams and his subalterns to have sufficed for a war of two years' duration. From the first, a fear that Black Hawk intended to go to Malden with his people and there end his days prevailed among the people of the Territory, in which event bloodshed and all the horrors of a border warfare were feared. From statements made by Black Hawk at subsequent periods, notably to Col. John Shaw, some foundation might appear for this position, but prior to his surrender the officers did not entertain such a thought, and it was contrary to his repeated declarations before Stillman's battle. At any rate, a supernatural fear ran through the entire peninsula, to check which and provide every means of defense for the settlers the following order was issued:

"Executive Office, Detroit, May 22, 1832.
"MAJOR-GEN. JOHN R. WILLIAMS.

"Sir:—By dispatch received at this office from Chicago and St. Joseph, it seems that the Indians have assumed an attitude of hostility towards the frontier settlements in that quarter.

"I am satisfied that the public safety requires immediate movements on the part of the militia of the Territory.

"You are authorized to raise such a number of volunteers as in your opinion may be necessary for co-operating with Brig.-Gen. Brown, who has rendezvoused at Jonesville.

"When you arrive there, you will take such steps as may then in your opinion be necessary.
"STEVENS T. MASON,
"Acting Governor of the Territory.

"The Quartermaster-General will issue to Major-Gen. John R. Williams such stores, ammunition and arms as he may require. "STEVENS T. MASON,
"Acting Governor of the Territory.
"Detroit, May 22, 1832."

GOV. STEVENS T. MASON.

GEN. J. R. WILLIAMS.

CAPT. JOSEPH F. MARSAC.

LIEUT. COL. ABRAHAM EDWARDS.

THE BLACK HAWK WAR. 255

An order for the Division Quartermaster to call on the military storekeeper for 200 pounds of rifle powder, 100 pounds of bar lead, 1,000 musket flints, 1,000 rifle flints and cartridge boxes was thereupon made by General Williams, as well as a call for the volunteers authorized by the acting Governor, who, in a letter attached, limited the number to 300.

Henry Dodge was at this time acting as Colonel of Michigan militia, under a commission dated October 15th, 1829. Major-General Williams, just mentioned, was the Major-General in command, under appointment the same year, and notice of the appointment was sent him by Lewis Cass in the following letter:

"Washington, March 10, 1829.

"Dear Sir:—I have the pleasure to inform you that your nomination as a major-general has been confirmed by the Senate. I shall now confidently rely upon your exertions to place our militia on a respectable footing, and I am well satisfied that this confidence will not be misplaced. Larned and Stockton are the brigadiers.

"Sincerely your friend,

"Lewis Cass."

Following General Williams' call for volunteers, an order on the Division Quartermaster for 3,000 rations of bread and salt pork, to last 300 men ten days, was issued, and the work of recruiting proceeded, but slowly. To the call for volunteers, not a volunteer responded. On the 23d, pursuant to peremptory orders to call out such companies or parts of companies of the state militia as would insure a force of 300 men, General Williams at once issued his second order for the First Regiment and Major Davis' battalion of riflemen and the city guards to assemble at Ten Eyck's, on the 24th, at 10 o'clock. Meantime he had engaged to forward to General Brown 200 stands of arms and bring to Ten Eyck's 200 additional stands for distribution at 2 o'clock P. M. The militia arrived and General Williams requested a voluntary enrollment. Capt. Joseph F. Marsac and his men of the First Regiment, and the city guards, under Capt. Isaac Rowland, and Captain Jackson's troop of cavalry and parts of some companies of cavalry volunteered, to the number of 100, leaving 200 to be drafted from the others present, some 400 in number. From these he drafted the required number and organized them. One ration was at once issued, but no blankets could then be issued, as they had not arrived. During the night and on the morning of the 25th parts of Davis' battalion arrived, which Williams was induced to accept (discharging a like number from the drafted men), and to make a second organization.

At 12 noon Williams left Ten Eyck's, reaching Willow Springs, a place within three miles of Ypsilanti, making a march of seventeen miles for the afternoon before camping.

On the morning of the 26th the troops were again put in motion, notwithstanding a heavy rain, which finally compelled them to halt at

Ypsilanti until afternoon, when the storm subsided and the march was resumed. At evening a halt was made at Saline for the night, where Colonel Schwarz presented orders from Mason, directing the detachment under Colonel Brooks to return to Detroit and ordering Williams to "overtake General Brown and to continue part of his regiment in the field for the purpose of quieting the fears of the timid, and further directing Williams to see the arms sent General Brown secured before he returned." After issuing the order to Colonel Brooks, Williams parted with them and reached Blackmaar's, sixty-seven miles from Detroit, that night, at which time and place he received word by express of the murders on Indian Creek.

On the 31st, at a point three miles from Niles, he met the Eighth Regiment, which had been discharged by General Brown, and on his arrival at Niles he was informed that several detachments of volunteers which had been called out and others, in all 350,—80 of which were mounted—had moved forward to the Door Prairie. After conferring with General Brown, it was agreed that he should proceed to the Door Prairie, about thirty-five miles to the west, and then take such measures as he might deem necessary and proper to secure that settlement from aggression, Williams to remain at Niles until the detachment under Colonel Brooks should return, when the combined forces of Williams and Brooks were to move forward to the Door Prairie. On the evening of the 1st June Brown received a peremptory order from Mason to march to Chicago, which so mixed the plans made by the two officers that it became impossible to act intelligently. Such orders as the one to Brooks recalling him, and then ordering him to return to Williams, marching and countermarching to no purpose, as well as exhausting the men, had a most disastrous effect. Not only did men thereafter refuse to enlist, but, in the face of a campaign, many then in the ranks refused to leave their families in danger from such incompetence as had up to that moment been displayed. General Williams' righteous indignation rose many times in this perplexing campaign.

On the 2d it was ascertained that the entire force under Brooks, then returning, numbered thirty of Jackson's men, the others having been disabled by their frivolous march through trackless forests. Subalterns in the commissary's department quibbled about the construction of orders and haggled over imaginary slights in the giving of orders to such an extent that the troops, with abundance in sight, actually suffered for want of food.

On the 2d Colonel Brooks arrived at Niles with twenty-six men of Jackson's troops, and, contrary to orders and all sense of decency, General Brown returned to Niles on the same day, with all his men, and without the least show of authority discharged them. This high-handed act threw Williams into a passion, which was clearly shown in a letter written at the time, in which he declared he would prefer charges against Brown on his return to Detroit. That astounding action demanded an order to counteract the effect on the troops, which was issued and instantly forwarded to the Door Prairie as follows:

"The volunteers and other companies or corps of militia which have been called out by a recent order from Gen. Brown and were directed to march to and concentrate at the Door Prairie are not discharged. The major-general, after having arrived at the Door, will judge of the expediency of discharging a part of the troops or not, according to circumstances, and the public service and safety to the frontier.

"The quartermaster of the Third Brigade will immediately provide transportation for the provisions, arms, ammunition and other public property which it is necessary to forward for the use and subsistence of the troops. The volunteer companies of mounted men are hereby placed under the immediate command of Colonel Edward Brooks. He is charged with their instruction and discipline in all matters connected with their improvement and efficiency.

"Order will be observed on the march, and no arms shall be discharged without the special permission of the senior officer in command.

"The troops now about to march from this place will be furnished with six rounds to each man.

"The brigade quartermaster, Capt. Ullman, will remain at this place to take charge of all provisions, arms and accouterments, ammunition and other public property that may remain in store or arrive for the use of the troops, and to be in readiness to forward such articles as may be required by the major general.

"By order of Major-General J. R. WILLIAMS,
"CHARLES W. WHIPPLE, Aid-de-Camp."

Brown having applied for a leave of absence, by reason of the appearance of measles in his family, was allowed it and departed.

While every effort had been made by Williams to retain the men under Brown, his efforts must have been ineffectual, for on the 3d, after ordering his men to remove to Door Prairie, and directing A. Huston to wheel from Terra Coupa Prairie and return to the same destination, he also asked the services of 300 mounted militia. To this call Col. Hart L. Stewart was the only man able to respond, and he with only fifteen or twenty men of Captain Martin's company. Provisions had also given out, and, with all the Quartermaster's exertions, he could get none.

On the 5th Williams reached Door Prairie, at which point he learned, on the 6th, of Stillman's defeat and the consequent panic into which the country had been thrown. On the 8th orders were given to march on the 9th for Chicago, which was taken up promptly and continued till the 12th, at which time Williams reached Chicago and placed Col. Edward Brooks in charge of Fort Dearborn until the arrival of Major Whistler of the United States Army. On the 13th General Williams, finding to what fears the people had been driven, put all his energy into making the fort safe against attack. Reports coming in from the Naper settlements of threatened attack, Williams dispatched Brooks, with thirty-five horsemen, to assist in the defense of Fort Payne. Here they remained until the threatened danger passed, and Major Whistler arrived on the 17th to take charge of the post. On the 13th General Williams also requested Colonel Huston to bring 100 men to Chicago, but the action of Brown had such a depressing influence on the men that he replied on the 17th, "It will not be in my power to obey your call. I should have been extremely happy to come through and join you again, but it would be a hard matter to march a hundred men from this regiment at this time. * * *" Thus, for all the assistance rendered by the militia in those parts, the people in the western portion of their territory might have been murdered to the last man.

A detachment of 300 men from Indiana having arrived at Fort Dearborn on the 22d, General Williams issued the following order, which terminated the duties of the troops from the peninsula, all having returned agreeably with its contents:

"General Order. "Headquarters, Chicago, June 22d, 1832.

"A detachment of 300 mounted militia having arrived at this place from the State of Indiana, under the command of Colonel Russell, with special instructions from the Executive of that State.

"The Major General directs that the detachment of militia, under the immediate command of Lieut-Col. Abraham Edwards, embark immediately on board the Napoleon, and be conveyed to the mouth of the river St. Joseph and there landed, and under the direction of the officers present be marched in good order to Niles, and when arrived there, will be honorably discharged. The mounted men, including Captain Jackson's troop and the staff officers of the detachment, will be in readiness to march at 2 o'clock p. m. this day. They will return to Detroit under the orders of Col. Brooks. The quartermaster will take charge of all public property, including arms, ammunition, etc., and see that it is carefully shipped and conveyed to the mouth of the St. Joseph, and there safely stored to await further orders. The stores belonging either to the territory of Michigan or to the United States that may now be on the way to this place, shall be carefully shipped to Niles. The Major General takes this opportunity to express his entire approbation of the good conduct and behavior of every officer, non-commissioned officer, musician and private of this command, and therefore tenders his thanks to all in behalf of our common country, with his best wishes for the welfare and happiness of every individual member of the command.

"By order of the Major General, J. R. WILLIAMS,

"J. M. WILSON, Aid-de-Camp."

On the 5th of August General Williams had returned to Detroit, but not before he had paid his respects to the miscarriages of his command.

CHAPTER XXXVIII.

PRISON LIFE—EASTERN TRIP—RETURN—COUNCIL AT FORT ARMSTRONG—BLACK HAWK'S APOLOGY—BLACK HAWK RELEASED.

In every way possible for those early days, Keokuk endeavored to make the confinement of Black Hawk tolerable. Early in the spring he took with him the wife and daughter of Black Hawk, together with Colonel Davenport, Antoine LeClaire and many prominent Sacs and Foxes, to pay the old prisoner a visit and cheer him up. Further than that, he endeavored to secure his release, pledging himself to General Atkinson to be responsible for the good behavior of Black Hawk and his fellow prisoners. Black Hawk was delighted to see his wife and daughter and hoped to be released under Keokuk's promise, but the orders from the War Department were to take the prisoners to Washington under the escort of an officer of the army. Accordingly they were sent there, arriving the latter part of April, 1833. Black Hawk was first presented to the President, then the Prophet, who remarked:

"We expected to return immediately to our people. The war in which we have been involved was occasioned by our attempting to raise provisions on our own lands, or where we thought we had a right so to do. We have lost many of our people, as well as the whites Our tribes and families are now exposed to the attacks of our enemies, the Sioux, and the Menominees. We hope, therefore, to be permitted to return home to take care of them."

Black Hawk, taking up the conversation, continued:

"I am a man and you are another. * * * We did not expect to conquer the whites. They had too many houses and too many men. I took up the hatchet, for my part, to revenge injuries which my people could no longer endure. Had I borne them longer without striking, my people would have said, 'Black Hawk is a woman; he is too old to be a chief; he is no Sac.' These reflections caused me to raise the war whoop. I say no more of it; it is known to you. Keokuk once was here; you took him by the hand, and when he wished to return to his home, you were willing. Black Hawk expects that, like Keokuk, we shall be permitted to return too."

He says he took up the hatchet. He attempted to create the impression, in his formal announcement, when he crossed the Mississippi, that he was simply taking up the hoe, to go among the Winnebagoes to make corn.

But it was not the policy of President Jackson to again let him off without feeling, to a slight degree, the hand of the Government. Therefore, on April 26th, the prisoners were all taken to Fortress Monroe and placed in charge of Colonel Eustis, where they remained until the 4th of June, the date of the order made by the President for their liberation. During his confinement, Black Hawk was treated with the utmost courtesy by Colonel Eustis, which was thoroughly appreciated by all the prisoners; so much, indeed, that upon their departure, Black Hawk made him a speech:

"Brother:—I have come, on my part, and in behalf of my companions, to bid you farewell. Our great father has at length been pleased to permit us to return to our hunting grounds. We have buried the tomahawk, and the sound of the rifle will hereafter only bring death to the deer and the buffalo. Brother, you have treated the red men very kindly. Your squaws have made them presents, and you have given them plenty to eat and drink. The memory of your friendship will remain till the Great Spirit says it is time for Black Hawk to sing his death song. Brother, your houses are as numerous as the leaves upon the trees, and your warriors like the sands upon the shore of the big lake that rolls before us. The red man has but few houses, and few warriors, but the red man has a heart that throbs as warmly as the heart of his white brother. The Great Spirit has given us our hunting grounds, and the skin of the deer which we kill there is his favorite, for its color is white, and this is the emblem of peace. This hunting dress and these feathers of the eagle are white. Accept them, my brother. I have given one like this to the White Otter. Accept it as a memorial of Black Hawk. When he is far away this will serve to remind you of him. May the Great Spirit bless you and your children. Farewell."

These sentiments are truly poetical and worthy a place in any literature, but they did not represent the life of Black Hawk. He had all his life long been a warrior, fonder of warfare than of life, but no doubt a change was coming over his heart with the scenes of peace and progress around him. The futility of further war upon the Americans had doubtless finally impressed him, and he realized that they were a people no longer to be trifled with. Therefore, he had resolved to submit for all time to the inexorable fate of civilization's western march.

Under the escort of Major John Garland, on the 5th of June, Black Hawk and his companions took their departure from Fortress Monroe. Visiting the Norfolk navy yard, the Prophet, from the balcony of his hotel, addressed a large concourse of people:

"The Great Spirit sent us here, and now, happily, we are about to return to our own Mississippi, and our own people. It affords us much happiness to rejoin our friends and kindred. We would shake hands with all our white friends assembled here. Should any of them go to our country on the Mississippi we would take great pleasure in returning their kindness to us. We will go home with peaceable dispositions towards our white brethren, and make our conduct hereafter more satisfactory to them. We bid you all farewell, as it is the last time we shall see each other."

The party went on to Baltimore on the 6th, where it was greeted by thousands of curious spectators, and where again Black Hawk met President Jackson. At night both were present at the same theater, and Black Hawk is said to have attracted as much attention as the President. In an interview the following day the President advised the Indians to return to their homes and listen to the counsels of Keokuk, their principal chief:

"When I saw you in Washington, I told you that you had behaved very badly in raising the tomahawk against the white people and killing men, women and children upon the frontier. Your conduct last year compelled me to send my warriors against you, and your people were defeated with great loss and your men surrendered, to be kept till I should be satisfied that you would not try to do any more injury. I told you I would inquire whether your people wished you to return and whether, if you did return, there would be any danger to the frontier. Gen. Clark and Gen. Atkinson, whom you know, have informed me that Keokuk, your principal chief, and the rest of your people are anxious you should return, and Keokuk has asked me to send you back. Your chiefs have pledged themselves for your good conduct, and I have given instructions that you should be taken to your own country.

"Major Garland, who is with you, will conduct you through some of our towns. You will see the strength of the white people. You will see that our young men are as numerous as the leaves in the woods. What can you do against us? You may kill a few women and children, but such a force would soon be sent against you as would destroy your whole tribe. Let the red men hunt, and take care of their families; but I hope they will not again raise their hands against their white brethren. We do not wish to injure you. We desire your prosperity and improvement; but if you again plunge your knives into the breasts of our people, I shall send a force which will severely punish you for all your cruelties. When you go back, listen to the counsels of Keokuk and the other friendly chiefs. Bury the tomahawk and live in peace with the frontiers. And I pray the Great Spirit to give you a smooth path and a fair sky to return."

The reply of Black Hawk to this address was brief:

"My Father:—My ears are open to your words. I am glad to hear them. I am glad to go back to my people. I want to see my family. I did not behave well last summer. I ought not to have taken up the tomahawk; but my people have suffered a great deal. When I get back I will remember your words. I won't go to war again. I will live in peace. I shall hold you by the hand."

On the 10th Philadelphia was reached, where all remained until the 14th, with their headquarters at Congress Hall. While there they witnessed a military display of such impressive interest as to evoke a speech from Black Hawk:

"My heart grew bitter against the whites, and my hands strong. I dug up the tomahawk, and led on my warriors to fight. I fought hard. I was no coward.

Much blood was shed. But the white men were mighty. They were as many as the leaves of the forest. I and my people failed. I am sorry the tomahawk was raised. I have been a prisoner. I see the strength of the white men. They are many; very many. The Indians are but few. They are not cowards. They are brave, but they are few. While the Great Spirit above keeps my heart as it now is, I will be the white man's friend. I will remain in peace. I will go to my people and speak good of the white man. I will tell them that they are as the leaves of the forest, very many and very strong, and that I will fight no more against them."

Among other interesting sights seen was Fairmount waterworks, after which the party started for New York City, where it arrived the evening of the 14th. Among the novel sights seen there was a balloon ascension from Castle Garden, which greatly astonished the Indians, one of whom asked the Prophet if the aeronaut was "going to see the Great Spirit." Crowds of people gathered about the Exchange Hotel to see them, and exchange a word with "General Black Hawk," as they called him. He was obliged to make his appearance upon all sorts of occasions to gratify the curious crowds. His rooms were daily and hourly visited by ladies and gentlemen, and each evening the Indians were escorted to the theater or other places of amusement. They received many handsome presents, and one of the ceremonies was the presentation to Black Hawk of a pair of topaz earrings for his wife or daughter, by John A. Graham, who said:

"Brothers, open your ears. You are brave men. You have fought like tigers, but in a bad cause. We have conquered you. We were sorry last year that you raised the tomahawk against us; but we believe you did not know us then as you do now.

"We think that in time to come you will be wise and that we shall be friends forever. You see that we are a great people—numerous as the flowers of the field, as the shells on the seashore, or the fish in the sea. We put one hand on the eastern, and at the same time the other on the western ocean. We all act together. If some time our great men talk long and loud at our council fires, but shed one drop of white men's blood, our young warriors, as thick as the stars of the night, will leap on board of our great boats, which fly on the waves, and over the lakes, swift as the eagle in the air; then penetrate the woods, make the big guns thunder, and the whole heavens red with the flames of the dwellings of their enemies. Brothers, the President has made you a great talk. He was but one mouth. That one has sounded the sentiments of all the people. Listen to what he has said to you. Write it on your memories. It is good, very good.

"Black Hawk, take these jewels, a pair of topaz earrings, beautifully set in gold, for your wife or daughter, as a token of friendship, keeping always in mind that women and children are the favorites of the Great Spirit. These jewels are from an old man, whose head is whitened with the snows of seventy winters; an old man who has thrown down his bow, put off his sword, and now stands leaning on his staff, waiting the commands of the Great Spirit. Look around you, see all this mighty people; then go to your homes, open your arms to receive your families. Tell them to bury the hatchet, to make the bright chain of friendship, to love the white men, and to live in peace with them as long as the rivers run into the sea, and the sun rises and sets. If you do so, you will be happy. You will then insure the prosperity of unborn generations of your tribes, who will go hand in hand with the sons of the white men, and all shall be blessed by the Great Spirit. Peace and happiness by the blessing of the Great Spirit attend you. Farewell."

To which Black Hawk replied:

"Brother:—We like your talk. We will be friends. We like the white people. They are very kind to us. We shall not forget it. Your counsel is good. We shall attend to it. Your valuable present shall go to my squaw. We shall always be friends."

Patrick Shirriff in his "tour," page 29, alludes to this hippodrome in the following manner:

"An Indian chief named Black Hawk, who had been taken prisoner the preceding year, in a war to the west of Lake Michigan, and who was carried through some of the great towns with a view of impressing him with the power of the states preparatory to his liberation, arrived in New York the day after the President and divided public attention. The ladies declared in favor of Black Hawk, some of them actually kissing him, which it is said affected the old President's health. The chief of the white men and the chief of the red were alike objects of curiosity, the President holding a levee by day, the Hawk by night, in Niblo's Gardens. Had a mammoth or elephant appeared, the mighty ones of the earth would have been eclipsed in public favor."

It had been the intention to visit Boston, but, greatly to the disappointment of its citizens, the route was changed, and on the 22d the party left New York in a steamboat up the Hudson for Albany, where it arrived the following day. There the party remained until the 25th, when it resumed its western journey, reaching Buffalo on the 28th. In that city the members remained three days, where, among other people who came to call on Black Hawk, was Kar-lun-da-wa-na, a chief of the Senecas, who made an address, counseling Black Hawk and his companions to return home and remain in peace. To this Black Hawk replied:

"Our aged brother of the Senecas has spoken the words of a good and wise man. We are strangers to each other, though we have the same color, and the same Great Spirit made us all and gave us this country together. Brothers, we have seen how great a people the whites are. They are very rich and very strong. It is folly for us to fight against them. We shall go home with much knowledge. For myself, I shall advise my people to be quiet and live like good men. The advice which you gave us, brother, is very good, and we tell you how we mean to walk the straight path in future, to content ourselves with what we have, and with cultivating our lands."

From Buffalo the party embarked by water for Detroit, after which it proceeded to Green Bay, thence up the Fox and down the Wisconsin River to the Mississippi, on to Fort Armstrong, which was reached about the 1st of August, and which had been chosen as the spot for the final liberation of Black Hawk. Upon landing, messengers were sent to notify the Sacs and Foxes to assemble and meet the returned captives. In response came Keokuk, Pash-e-pa-ho, Wapello and others, Keokuk leading a convoy of canoes floating the American flag and landing opposite Black Hawk's quarters. After several hours spent in arranging their dress and other preliminaries, they all returned to their canoes, and, with shouts and songs and drums, crossed over to the island. There, with Keokuk at the head, each Indian cordially greeted Black Hawk and his companions. After smoking the pipe of peace, they then returned to the west bank of the river to await the grand council set for the following day, when Black Hawk was to be taken home.

About 10 o'clock of the following morning Keokuk, with about 100 of his followers, crossed over to Fort Armstrong, where a room had been especially prepared to receive him, and here Black Hawk was escorted to a seat opposite Keokuk. The occasion was one of deep humiliation to Black Hawk, and his appearance indicated as much. Major Garland opened the council with a speech, referring to the good feeling manifested by all toward Black Hawk. This was followed by reading the speech made by the President to Black Hawk in Baltimore, to which Keokuk, as the future custodian of Black Hawk's conduct, rose and replied:

"I have listened to the talk of our great father. It is true we pledged our honor for the liberties of our friends. We thought much of it; our councils were long. Their wives and children were in our thoughts. When we talked of them our hearts were full. Their wives and children came to see us, which made us feel like women; but we were men. The words which we sent to the great father were good. He spoke like the father of children. The Great Spirit made his heart big in council. We receive our brothers in friendship. Our hearts are good towards them. They once listened to bad counsel; now their ears are closed. I give my hand to them. When they shake it, they shake the hands of all. I will shake hands with them, and then I am done."

Major Garland then stated that he wished it distinctly understood that their great father would hereafter acknowledge Keokuk as the principal chief of the Sac and Fox nation, and that he wished Black Hawk to listen and conform to his counsels. This remark was construed by Black Hawk to mean that he *must* conform to the counsels of Keokuk, and at once his bad blood arose; all his old animosities mastered him, and in his impulsive way he cried:

"I am a man, an old man. I will not conform to the counsels of anyone. I will act for myself; no one shall govern me. I am old; my hair is gray. I once gave counsel to my young men. Am I to conform to others? I shall soon go to the Great Spirit, where I shall be at rest. What I said to our great father at Washington, I say again. I will always listen to him. I am done."

His resentful, passionate nature stubbornly refused, as it always had refused before, to acknowledge any standard of conduct except such as emanated from his own limited capacities. He flew into a rage, no doubt expecting to combat this inexorable decree as he had opposed every former American institution, by quibbling or fighting, but at that supreme moment of helplessness, more than at any previous time in his life, his incapacity to comprehend and act was manifested, and had it not been for the soothing gentleness of Keokuk, who realized his old enemy's helplessness and his weaknesses, the question of liberty might have been deferred for an indefinite period. After the excitement of Black Hawk's speech had subsided, Keokuk stepped to the side of his gloomy old foe, and in a low voice said to him: "Why do you speak so before the white men? I will speak for you. You trembled; you did not mean what you said."

Without changing his sullen looks, though recognizing his deplorable mistake, he nodded assent, and Keokuk again addressed the council, as follows:

"Our brother who has again come to us has spoken, but he spoke in wrath. His tongue was forked; he spoke not like a man or a Sac. He knew his words were bad. He trembled like the oak whose roots have been wasted away by many rains. He is old. What he said let us forget. He says he did not mean it. He wishes it forgotten. I have spoken for him. What I have said are his own words, not mine. Let us say he spoke in council to-day—that his words were good. I have spoken."

Keokuk's kind apology, followed by speeches from Col. William Davenport, then in command of Fort Armstrong, Wapello and Pash-e-pa-ho, lulled him back into a full realization of his helplessness, and again rising, he deliberately said:

"I feel that I am an old man. Once I could speak; now I have but little to say. To-day we met many of our brothers. We were glad to see them. I have listened to what my brothers have said; their hearts are good; they have been like Sacs since I left them; they have taken care of my wife and children, who had no wigwam. I thank them for it; the Great Spirit knows that I thank them.

"Before the sun gets behind the hills to-morrow I shall see them. When I left them, I expected soon to return. I told our great father in Washington that I would listen to the counsel of Keokuk. I shall soon be far away; I shall have no village, no band. I shall live alone. What I said in council to-day I wish forgotten. If it has been put upon paper, I wish a mark to be drawn over it. I did not mean it. Now, we are alone, let us say we will forget it. Say to our great father and Governor Cass that I will listen to them. Many years ago I met Governor Cass in council, far across the prairies, to the rising sun. His counsels were good, but my ears were closed. I listened to the great father across the waters. My father listened to him, whose band was very large. My band, too, was once large. Now I have no band. I and my son, and all the party, thank our great father for what he has done. He is old and I am old. We shall soon go to the Great Spirit, where we shall rest. He sent us through his great villages. We saw many of the white men, who treated us with kindness, and we thank them. We thank you and Mr. Sprague for coming with us. Your road was long and crooked. We never saw so many white men before. When you were with us we felt as though we had some friends among them. We felt safe, for you knew them all. When you come upon the Mississippi again you shall come to my wigwam. I have none now. On your road home you will pass where my village was. No one lives there now. All are gone. I give you my hand. We may never meet again, but I shall long remember you. The Great Spirit will be with you, and your wives and children. Before the sun rises I shall go to my family. My son will be here to see you before we go. I will shake hands with my brothers here, and then I am done.."

After Keokuk's apology and Black Hawk's same, Wapello arose (chief of the Foxes) and said:

"I am not in the habit of talking. I think—I have been thinking all day. Keokuk has spoken. Am glad to see my brothers. I will shake hands with them. I am done."[1]

The chiefs all arose, a general shaking of hands, followed by an interchange of civilities, ensued, and the council adjourned. In the evening Major Garland invited the principal chiefs, together with Black Hawk, to his quarters, as it would afford a good opportunity to ascertain explicitly the feeling which existed among them toward their fallen foe. About 7 o'clock they arrived. They took their seats in silence, passed the pipe of peace and then drank a round of champagne. Pashepaho first shook hands with all present and said:

"We met this morning. I am glad to meet again. That wine is very good. I never drank any before. I have thought much of our meeting to-day. It was one that told us we were brothers—that we were Sacs. We had just returned from a buffalo hunt. We thought it was time for our brothers to be here, as our father at St. Louis told us this was the moon. We started before the rising sun to meet you. We have met and taken our brothers by the hand in friendship. They always mistrusted our counsels, and went from the trail of the red men, where there were no hunting grounds nor friends. They returned and found the dogs howling around their wigwams, and wives looking for their husbands and children. They said we counseled like women; but they have found our counsels were good. They have been through the country of our great father. They have been to the wigwams of the white men. They received them in kindness and made glad their hearts. We thank them. Say to them that Keokuk and Pashepaho thank them. Our brother has promised to listen to the counsels of Keokuk. What he said in council to-day was like the Mississippi fog. The sun has shone and the day is clear. Let us forget it. He did not mean it. His heart is good, but his ears have been open to bad counsels. He has taken our great father by the hand, whose words are good. He listened to them, and has closed his ears to the voice that comes across the great waters. He now knows that he ought to listen to Keokuk. He counseled with us and our young braves, who listened to his talk. We told our great father that all would be peace. He opened his dark prison, and let him see the sun once more and gave him to his wife and children, who were without a lodge. Our great father made straight his path to his home. I once took the great chief of the Osages prisoner. I heard the cries of his women and children. I took him out by the rising sun and put him upon the trail to his village. 'There,' said I, 'is the trail to your village. Go and tell your people that I, Pashepaho, the chief

[1]Drake, 223.

of the Sacs, sent you.' We thank our great father. Our hearts are good towards him. I will see him before I lay down in peace. May the Great Spirit be in his councils. What our brother said to-day let us forget. I am done."

Keokuk, after going through the usual ceremonies, followed, saying:

"We feel proud that you have invited us here this evening to drink a glass with you. The wine which we have drank, we never tasted before. It is the wine which the white men make, who know how to make anything. I will take another glass, as I have much to say. We feel proud that we can drink such wine. To-day we shook hands with our brothers, who you brought to us. We were glad to see them. We have often thought of our brothers. Many of our nation said they would never return. Their wives and children often came to our wigwams, which made us feel sad. What Pashepaho has said is true. I talked to our young men, who had the hearts of men. I told them that the Great Spirit was in our councils. They promised to live in peace. Those who listened to bad counsels, and followed our brothers, have said their ears are closed. They will live in peace. I sent their words to our great father, whose ears were open, whose heart was made sad by the conduct of our brothers. He has sent them to their wigwams. We thank him. Say to him, Keokuk thanks him. Our brothers have seen the great villages of the white men. They traveled a long road and found the Americans like grass. I will tell our young men to listen to what they shall tell them. Many years ago I went through the villages of our great father. He had many. They were like the great prairies; but he has gone. Another is our father. He is a great war chief. I want to see him. I shall be proud to take him by the hand. I have heard much of him. His head is gray. I must see him. Tell him as soon as the snow is off the prairie, I shall come. What I have said I wish spoken to him, before it is put upon paper, so that he shall hear it as I have said it. Tell him that Keokuk spoke it. What our brother said in council to-day, let us forget. He told me to speak. I spoke his words. I have spoken."

Early next morning Black Hawk went to his family and the Sacs hailed his return with great joy. Though shorn of power, no allusions were made to his new conditions; everywhere his old friends, who never before sympathized with him, now exercised every effort to make his declining years pleasant. He settled quietly down and for some time made his home near Keokuk's village, on Iowa River.[1]

---

[1]Fulton's "Red Men of Iowa," 212 *et seq.*

CHAPTER XXXIX.

SECOND TRIP EAST—A QUIET LIFE—JULY FOURTH TOAST AT FORT MADISON—INTERVIEW WITH IOWAS—DEATH—BURIAL—HIS GRAVE ROBBED—BONES RECOVERED—CONSUMED BY FIRE—DEATH OF MADAM BLACK HAWK.

In 1837 it became necessary for a delegation of Sacs and Foxes to go to Washington. Keokuk, who was at its head, prudently took Black Hawk along, fearing perhaps that during his absence he might create some new disturbance.[1] Knowing that he was neither a delegate nor chief, he remained indifferent to the attention given him while traveling through the various cities of the East, and little can be said of his trip.

After his return, in the autumn of 1837, Black Hawk and his family spent the winter in Lee County, Iowa, residing on a small stream known as Devil's Creek. His family then consisted of his wife, As-shaw-e-qua (Singing Bird[2]), two sons, Nes-se-as-kuk and Na-som-see, and his daughter, Nam-equa. It is related that a young man from Baltimore, who met Namequa, became charmed with her comely appearance, and, with continued acquaintance, became desperately in love with her. The young lady received his advances with favor and a wedding was among the immediate possibilities at Fort Madison. All arguments by friends failed to dissuade the young gentleman from marrying the maid. He was coaxed, bantered and threatened, but nothing would affect him in the least until one more resourceful than his other friends asked how he would enjoy such comments from his Baltimore friends as, "There goes ——— and his squaw." That possibility settled the affair against the young lady, who became thereby another victim of the white man's fickleness, but contrary to the usual trend in matters of that character, Nam-e-qua indifferently dropped the subject and later married a young Indian of her tribe, living happily thereafter, probably more happily than she ever could have lived with the impulsive young white.

In the spring of 1838 Black Hawk and his family removed to the vicinity of the chiefs of the Sacs and Foxes, on the Des Moines River,

---

[1] Fulton's "Red Men of Iowa," 222.
[2] Annals of Iowa, May, 1902.

near Iowaville, the site of the famous battle where the Sacs annihilated the tribe of Iowas many years before. Here he had a comfortable cabin, furnished in humble imitation of the white settler's on the frontier. As the whites moved into the country he formed their acquaintance and mingled very largely in their pleasures and pastimes with hearty goodwill. He occasionally imbibed too freely of liquor and made himself as merry or ridiculous as the white man under the same condition, but it must be said in his favor that when found indulging in spirits it was at the invitation of his white brother.[1] His usually morose disposition gradually underwent a radical change, for he was frequently found receiving the chaff of the whites in a spirit of the utmost jollity and to the very best of his ability giving it back again, which, considering the few English words he could master, was said to have been remarkable.

This feature of "mixing," which he cultivated, had much to do with bringing to him during the last years of his life the general verdict that he was a martyr and a person of ability far above his actual worth. His travels and the universal interest taken in him during them led others to seek his acquaintance and to place him in all sorts of conspicuous attitudes, comical and otherwise. The following, kindly furnished me by Prof. B. F. Shambaugh of the University of Iowa, is a fine illustration of that phase of Black Hawk's amusement.

"TO GENERAL 'BLACK HAWK.'"[2]

"Sir:—As there is at present a vacant seat in the council chamber, which certainly ought to be filled by some talented and influential person, and as you seem to be the theme of men, women and children in this place, and your political character well known and established, I would, in common with many others of my fellow-citizens, beg, with great deference, to bring you upon the carpet, by nominating you as a suitable person, worthy of our elective franchise, to fill the vacancy in question, conscious as I am that, once elected and seated beyond the threshold of the Council chamber, there to be installed as one of the councilors, in all the privileges and honors connected with that station, that your voice and vote shall not be found wanting when any question or cause is in agitation involving the rights of the people. Your inherent spirit of independence is well known to this community; also that your political views and principles are honorable, and that you have no earthly connection with that obnoxious and diabolical phalanx who would fain exclude (as they have recently attempted to do) the people from a voice in the management of the territorial affairs. Methinks your system would be more liberal. I doubt not but the grand and noble feature of your legislative acts will be recognized in the unerring vigilance to protect the liberties and rights of the citizens of this young and mighty republic, and that you will guard against speculative innovation, which, unfortunately, in this our day, sways men's best judgments.

---

[1] Page 164, Vol. 3, Smith's Wis. Foot note by W. R. Smith, the author: "I can vouch myself that I came up the Mississippi in a steamboat, on board of which was Black Hawk, his wife and son and a number of his warriors, in July, 1837, and that Black Hawk was apparently particularly fond of brandy, as he often indulged himself with it at the bar on board of the boat; but to this act, it must be confessed, he was always invited by the white passengers."

[2] Copied from "The Iowa News," Vol. 1, No. 29, June 6, 1838.

"As you are fully alive to the present depressed and truly deplorable state of our commercial affairs, which, if some relief more than the stay of action upon executions for twelve months is not immediately devised, will most assuredly prostrate and render our young and enterprising merchants of this territory bankrupts, and thus, alas! pave the way to ruin, and bring into active operation the machinery of the debtor laws, with their ruinous and demolishing consequences.

"It need hardly be observed that, upon installation in office, your actions will be public, so that they need not blush at daylight; besides, as you know, privacy is generally hateful, and is indeed more worthy and characteristic of nocturnal clubs than that of legislative assemblies, and thereby give every facility of watching and judging the whole course of your official career for your own exoneration and the satisfaction of your constituents. You will, in all cases, particularly in the passage of bills, laying off county lines and seats of justice, faithfully obey the people's instructions and correspond with them timorously; in short, be entirely, as far as consistent, guided by petitions from the people, and by so doing you will, in a great measure, get rid of responsibility which otherwise you might not, and if your acts do not turn out so favorable as have been anticipated, they (your constituents) cannot, and will not, justly charge you with dereliction of duty. Let it not be heard said of you, as of some others, that you legislate for your own and that of your friends' private interests, but for the general good of the country.

"In conclusion, I beg you to be very guarded how and in what manner you vote, not voting for the cause one day, and the next day jump about from 'post to pillar,' like jumping 'Jim Crow,' and vote differently. These hints may be of some service to you. Indeed, were it not that I have special interest in your welfare, I should be the last individual in this community to advise you in any shape or form. I have the honor to be, with due respect,

"ONE OF THE PEOPLE.

"Burlington, Dec. 9, 1837."

Black Hawk's constant mingling with the whites taught him another familiar characteristic; one more likely than any other to get him into difficulty—that of borrowing money. From Louisiana, Mo., I was furnished with the copy of one of his financial engagements, presented herewith, and for which I am under obligations to Mrs. Fannie Anderson of Louisiana, Mo.

Thus in a tranquil, careless way Black Hawk was passing the remainder of his days, without responsibilities and with the hearty good will and esteem of every person who knew him. An old "plug" hat was his passion; he so dearly loved it that some contend it was placed upon his head when he was buried. In this and similar eccentric adornments he one day rode into Fort Madison, by special invitation, to attend a Fourth of July banquet, and it must be said that it was a sorry day in his declining years in which he allowed the whites to inveigle him into a speech. While his animosity toward Keokuk was as bitter as ever, he had latterly learned to curb it with discretion. Among the toasts for that occasion was one to which he was asked to respond: "Our Illustrious Guest, Black Hawk—May his declining years be as calm and serene as his previous life has been boisterous and full of war-like incidents. His attachment and present friendship to his white brethren fully entitle him to a seat at our festive board." After the sentiment was explained to him by an interpreter, he responded as follows, his words being taken down by two interpreters:

"It has pleased the Great Spirit that I am here to-day. I have eaten with my white friends. The earth is our mother; we are now on it, with the Great Spirit above us. It is good. I hope we are all friends here. A few summers ago I was fighting against you. I did wrong, perhaps, but that is past. It is buried; let it be forgotten. Rock River was a beautiful country. I loved my towns, my cornfields and the home of my people. I fought for it. It is now yours. Keep it as we did. It will produce you good crops. I thank the Great Spirit that I am now friendly with my white brethren. We are here together. We are friends. It is his wish and mine. I thank you for your friendship. I was once a great warrior. I am now poor. Keokuk has been the cause of my present situation, but do not attach blame to him. I am now old. I have looked upon the Mississippi since I was a child. I love the great river. I have dwelt upon its banks from the time I was an infant. I look upon it now. I shake hands with you, and as it is my wish, I hope you are my friends."

It is to be hoped that on this occasion Black Hawk was intoxicated, not with liquor, but with pride at his flattering reception, and that he forgot himself (as he once before did), when he thus uncivilly spoke of Keokuk, the man who implored him to desist from entering his disastrous campaign of 1832; the man who urged that Black Hawk was deceived by liars; the man who, when Black Hawk was imprisoned, took to him his wife and child and friends to cheer his fallen spirits; the man who, with all the strength of his mighty eloquence, urged the old man's liberation; the man who pledged his every resource as a guaranty of Black Hawk's future good behavior for that liberation; the man who stood at Black Hawk's side when in an evil hour he flew into a passion and defied those who were giving him that liberation on Keokuk's pledge, and who whispered in the angry old man's ear words of moderation, and then who rose and in the greatness of his heart apologized for Black Hawk's haste and begged that it be overlooked; the man who at all times had but the kindest of words for the old man's failings and who, to please a whim of passing envy, actually resigned his chieftainship into the hands of his tribe to avoid friction, that his exalted position might no longer wound the false pride of Black Hawk. No sacrifice was ever demanded that he did not make for Black Hawk.

It was a shame to compromise the old man as he was drifting so rapidly to the grave, and expose his foibles, then long forgotten. In the fullness of his eloquence he made himself to speak of "my towns, my cornfields, and my people," as though he had been autocrat of all the Indian tribes, when, in fact, he never had been a chief and had naught whatever to say more than another about their disposition or their government; but no blame shall go to Black Hawk for that speech. Let the reader peruse and remember its concluding words, which are as sweet and gentle and pathetic as one will find in all literature, and forget the old man's follies, for he was mistaken, as many another has been before and since.

Black Hawk's cabin stood about one hundred feet from the north bank of the Des Moines River, a few rods from that of Mr. James H. Jordan, the agent. Near it, on the sloping bank, stood two large trees, an elm and an ash, so intertwined as to appear like one tree. Close by flowed the clear waters of what was known as Black Hawk's Spring. Here, during the sultry days of summer, he would sit and dreamily ponder over the scenes of his long and turbulent career. Before him was spread that old battlefield on which his nation snatched from the Iowas their country and their homes—the same country then passing to others. Then came a gloomy period of melancholy, which enveloped him so completely that he said but little, and that to his few intimates. In the summer of 1838 a party of Iowas returned on a friendly visit to their old home and Black Hawk held a friendly council with them at a place about half a mile from his cabin. On that spot he directed that his body should be buried. At this time he regarded the usual indifferences of the Indians as personal slights, and while it may be true that many of his whilom companions neglected to show him many of the little civilities which white men might observe, the whites supplied them with unusual attentions, and he should not have fretted as he did fret. General Street, observing the same, thoughtfully made the family a present of a cow, a property very unusual with an Indian. This pleased him and the family immensely. Madam Black Hawk and her daughter learned to milk, and during the warm days of 1838 the two were often seen sitting beside their beloved cow, patiently brushing away the troublesome flies and other insects. This daughter, though married, remained with her parents to the time of Black Hawk's death and, it may be said, was the mainstay in their domestic affairs; a model of neatness. It has been said that she and Madam Black Hawk were so neat that the little yard was swept during the warmer months once a day. One October day was designated as "ration day," which was attended by nearly every Indian, leaving Black Hawk almost alone. Though he had been sick of a fever[1] for many days, nothing serious was feared. Mr. Jordan was with him to the last moment his official duties would permit, leaving him, as he supposed, on the high road to recovery; but the old man took a sudden turn for the worse and within three hours after Mr. Jordan left his bedside Black Hawk was dead, after a sickness of fourteen days.

During Black Hawk's sickness his wife, As-shaw-e-qua (Singing Bird), was devoted in her attentions to him and deeply mourned his death.

---

[1] Bilious fever.

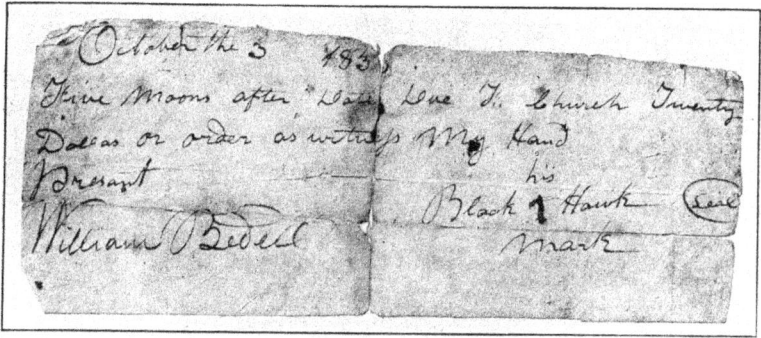

BLACK HAWK'S PROMISSORY NOTE.

BLACK HAWK'S TOWER.

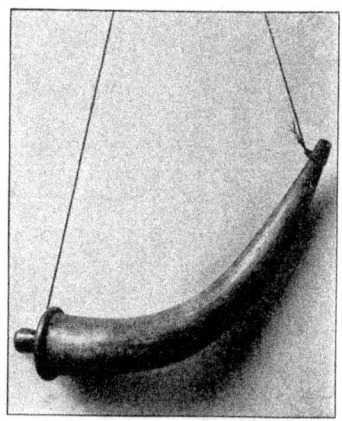

BLACK HAWK'S POWDER HORN.

Some days before it occurred she said: "He is getting old; he must die. Monoto calls him home."

His remains were followed to the grave by the family and about fifty of the tribe, the chiefs and all others being absent at Fort Armstrong to receive their rations. He was buried on the spot selected by him prior to his death, which is best described by James H. Jordan[1] in a letter to Dr. J. F. Snyder of Virginia, Ill., who has written the best account of Black Hawk's burial to be found,[2] and to whom I am much indebted for points in this work:

"Eldon, Iowa, July 15, 1881.

"Black Hawk was buried on the Northeast Quarter of Section Two, Township 70, Range 12, Davis County, Iowa, near the northeastern corner of the county, on the Des Moines River bottom, about ninety rods from where he lived at the time he died, and on the north side of the river. I have the ground where he lived for a dooryard, it being between my house and the river. The only mound over the grave was some puncheons split out and set over his grave and then sodded over with blue grass, making a ridge about four feet high. A flagstaff, some twenty feet high, was planted at his head, on which was a silk flag, which hung there until the wind wore it out. My house and his were only four rods apart when he died. He was sick only about fourteen days. He was buried right where he sat the year before when in council with the Iowa Indians, and was buried in a suit of military clothes, made to order, and given to him when in Washington City by Gen. Jackson, with hat, sword, gold epaulets, etc., etc."

His body was placed on the surface of the ground in a sitting posture, with his head toward the southeast, the body supported in position by a wooden slab or puncheon. On his left side was placed a cane given him by Henry Clay, with his right hand resting on it. Three silver medals, the gifts of prominent persons in the east, hung upon his breast.[3] There were also placed in the grave two swords, a quantity of wampum, an extra pair of moccasins and other articles of Indian costume, with a supply of provisions sufficient to last him three days on his journey to the spirit land. Around the body and the articles buried with him two large blankets were closely wrapped. On his head was placed a military cap elaborately ornamented with feathers. Forked sticks were firmly driven at the head and foot of the grave and across these a pole was placed, extending over the body. Against this pole split puncheons were laid to a peak, the gables of the primitive vault being closed with boards and the whole then sodded over. Near by was a hewn post inscribed with Indian characters. Enclosing all was a strong circular picket fence ten or twelve feet high.

One morning about the 1st of July, 1839, Madam Black Hawk, bitterly weeping, called upon Mr. Jordan and informed him that the grave

---

[1] The Indian trader, beloved of Black Hawk and his family. Fulton, p. 117.
[2] Magazine of American History, Vol. XV, No. 5, p. 494 *et seq.*
[3] It has been said these were given him respectively by Pt. Jackson, John Quincy Adams, Ex-Pt., and the City of Boston. If the latter made such a present it must have been during his last visit east, because he did not go to Boston during his first trip.

of her husband had been opened and rifled of everything within.[1] Mr. Jordan immediately instituted a search and traced the act to a Dr. Turner of Lexington, in the County of Van Buren, who had sent the body to St. Louis, where the bones were cleaned and then removed to Quincy, where they were articulated. Much contention as to the details of the body's pilgrimage has existed, but the letter to be found on page 10 hereof, written at the time, should conclusively settle the matter.

At once Governor Lucas, then governor of the Territory of Iowa, learned of the location of the bones; he sent for and received them very soon thereafter, but when the sons of Black Hawk called upon the Governor and found them "in a good dry place," they concluded it was best to allow them to remain in storage. Governor Lucas allowed them to remain in his office for a little while and then deposited them in the collections of the Burlington Geological and Historical Society, where they remained until the year 1855, at which time they were consumed by the fire which destroyed the building and all the society's collections. Thus all that remained mortal of Black Hawk passed away in fire and smoke after the manner of his stormy life.

It was a spectacular finish and one Black Hawk might possibly have courted in his strenuous days had it been less ignoble; but ignoble it was and unworthy the man. To Madam Black Hawk and her children it was an act of inhumanity which can never be forgiven by civilization. If Black Hawk had faults, they were buried with his body, which by all rules of decency should have remained sacred.

When the Sac nation was again removed to its new reservation in Kansas, Madame Black Hawk with her family followed and there remained until the 29th of August, 1846, when she died at the fine old age of 85 years.

---

[1] Fulton, on page 228, insists that the head was first stolen, but being frightened, Turner threw it into his saddle-bags and ran away to return later and procure the body; but as a discrepancy exists as to his dates, it is possible he was mistaken in other details.

APPENDIX

CAPT. ABRAHAM LINCOLN.

APPENDIX NO. 1.

Abraham Lincoln in the Black Hawk War.

Little consideration should be given to the great majority of stories told of Mr. Lincoln's service in the Black Hawk War. If one were to believe them all, one would find every man in the army to have wrestled and vanquished him or otherwise participated in some undignified frolic wherein he was made to appear ludicrously delightful. While the age was one of jest and joust, and Mr. Lincoln was apt at both, yet his career as captain in that war was temperate and dignified.

In 1832 all of his young companions were strenuous, as were all the young men of Illinois—itself young and vigorous. They bubbled over with buoyant animal spirits and paid little heed to formalities. It was especially an era of independence; discipline being regarded an evidence of femininity, and formality a certain indication of snobbishness. In the towns of (then) importance—more mature, perhaps—that spirit might have been modified; but the times were essentially of the open air order.

An atmosphere of politics likewise pervaded and the majority of candidates affected that spirit of contempt for the little amenities of life and comfort. When, therefore, those young spirits did not like a command, the first impulse was not to obey it, and in point of fact very few commands were obeyed, at least to the letter.[1] To attempt enforcement generally meant disaster, whether the officer was General or Second Lieutenant. Some scheme was usually found to counteract the order, if at all distasteful to the volunteers.

While Mr. Lincoln was as stalwart as his generation, he was self-possessed and handled his headstrong company with consummate skill and was thoroughly beloved by his men. His known honesty, fearlessness and prowess and willingness to back the same made it possible to control his men, and from the most unmanageable in the army they became at his request tractable. These characteristics then made him a leader where others failed by swagger and vulgarity.

On the march and in camp stories were told; but Mr. Lincoln's

---

[1] A story has been told that Capt. Lincoln's first command was answered by being told to "go to the devil."

stories were not ribald recitals, told only to express a vicious conclusion. They were droll, quaint, homely perhaps, but full of humor; new and invariably to the point.

When men congregate it is natural to seek entertainment; the best adapted to surroundings, story-telling always finding the most favor, consequently the best story-tellers were soon discovered and courted. Thus in the camps in Beardstown and Rushville and on the march to Yellow Banks, the genius of Mr. Lincoln was discovered and quickly popularized.

At each resting-place diversion was sought in wrestling matches, horse racing, foot racing and other kindred sports, and quickly enough came Mr. Lincoln's reputation as a champion in the manly sports of the day, notably wrestling, which then, as now in new and small villages, was made to measure a man's standing. No one was above a "match." If he was, his presence in that locality soon became a reminiscence. Add, then, the two accomplishments of Captain Lincoln, and no imagination is required to account for his tremendous popularity in the army.

At New Salem Mr. Lincoln adapted himself to his surroundings by accepting the first challenge for a match that Mr. Offutt unwittingly caused to be sent him by John Armstrong, and notwithstanding the threatened interference by the "Clary's Grove Boys," he asserted his strength and bravery to such advantage that he became from that hour a respected leader, and the following year that same Armstrong became his First Sergeant, while William and Royal Clary became privates in his company. During the annual muster in the fall of 1831 those same influences elected him captain of the militia.

Being "out of a job" in the spring of 1832, the Black Hawk war offered him employment which was at once accepted. On April 21st sixty-eight men volunteered[1] to serve the state from "Richland, Sangamon County," and at the election which followed for captain Mr. Lincoln was chosen by more than three-fourths of the men. Another, one William Kirkpatrick, aspired to the same position. He was pretentious, assumed a prominence in the neighborhood, questioned at times, but never severely challenged, and when he announced a desire for the office, he expected to get it. The two candidates were placed a short distance away and the men were requested to fall in behind the man they preferred for their captain. The proceeding was simple, brief and overwhelmingly in favor of Mr. Lincoln, and he was hilariously declared elected. Enrolling his company for sixty days' service, he marched at its head to Beardstown to be mustered in.

Captain Lincoln owned no horse and to make that march he was forced to borrow, a not very difficult matter in those days; but on that

[1] Another volunteered at Beardstown, April 29th, and another at Dixon's Ferry, May 19, making the total strength of the company seventy men.

MUSTER ROLL OF CAPT. ABRAHAM LINCOLN.

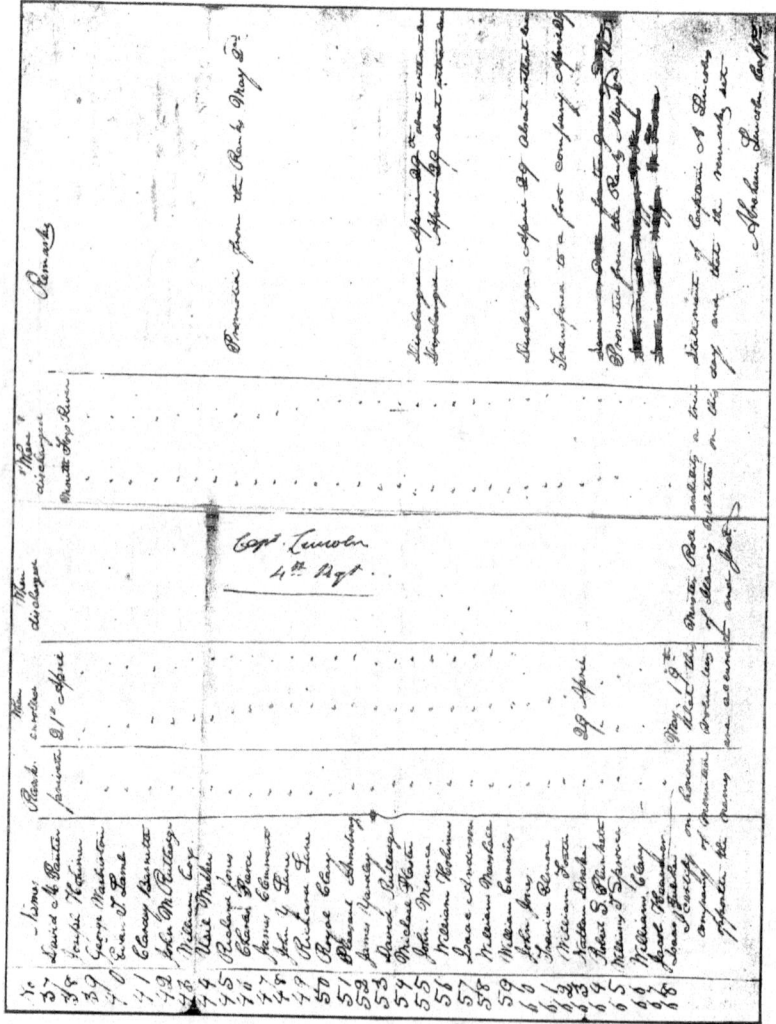

MUSTER ROLL OF CAPT. ABRAHAM LINCOLN.

borrowed horse, at the head of his men, he marched into Beardstown, "forty miles from the place of enrollment," the proudest man in the state. On April 28th the company was mustered into the service of the state of Illinois by Col. John J. Hardin, Inspector-General of the state and Mustering Officer. Two muster rolls were made out, one by Colonel Hardin and one by Captain Lincoln, both of which are in existence and one reproduced herein.

At Beardstown Captain Lincoln's company was assigned to the Fourth Regiment, of which his First Lieutenant, Samuel M. Thompson, was elected Colonel April 30th, and William Kirkpatrick, late candidate for captain, was made Quartermaster's Sergeant, both quoted as coming from "Richland Creek."

On the 30th the last of the army, including Captain Lincoln's company, left Beardstown and encamped four miles north of Rushville. On Tuesday, May 1st, the march for Yellow Banks, seventy or seventy-five miles distant, was resumed and about twenty-five miles covered, the army camping at a point on Crooked Creek in McDonough County. On Wednesday, the 2d, another distance was made and the army encamped in a large prairie, two miles from timber or water. The night was cold and tempestuous.

At about 12 o'clock of Thursday, the 3d, the Henderson River was reached and crossed, and before night the Yellow Banks in Warren County was reached, where the army again encamped.[1] There, by reason of delay in the arrival of the boat with provisions, the army was compelled to remain the 4th, 5th and 6th, on which last-named day the provisions arrived. On the morning of the 7th the army moved for the mouth of Rock River, reaching that point about nightfall.

About Beardstown Captain Lincoln absorbed all the information to be found concerning tactics and imparted the same to his company to the best of his ability by frequent drills, stories of which have caused many a hearty laugh. The best version of one of those celebrated drills has been told by Ben. Perley Poore and is to be found on page 218 of "Reminiscences of Abraham Lincoln": "I remember his narrating his first experience in drilling his company. He was marching with a front of over twenty men across a field when he desired to pass through a gateway into the next enclosure.

" 'I could not for the life of me,' said he, 'remember the proper word of command for getting my company endwise so that it could get through the gate, so as we came near the gate I shouted: "This company is dismissed for two minutes, when it will fall in again on the other side of the gate!" ' " The story was told to picture the position of someone in debate who could find no tactful way out of a dilemma he had worked himself into. But Captain Lincoln was proud of his company and ex-

---

[1] Journal O. H. Browning.

pressed his pride on many occasions. Leonard Swett obtained the story of that company direct from the lips of the captain and it is to be found in the book last quoted, on page 465: "Together with the talk of organizing a company in New Salem began the talk of making Lincoln captain of it. His characteristics as an athlete had made something of a hero of him. Turning to me with a smile at the time, he said: 'I cannot tell you how much the idea of being the captain of that company pleased me.'

"But when the day of organization arrived a man who had been captain of a real company arrived in uniform and assumed the organization of the company. The mode of it was as follows: A line of two was formed by the company, with the parties who intended to be candidates for officers standing in front. The candidate then made a speech to the men, telling them what a gallant man he was, in what wars he had fought, bled and died, and how he was ready again, for the glory of his country, to lead them; then another candidate, and when the speech-making was ended they commanded those who would vote for this man, or that, to form in line behind their favorite. Thus there were one, two or three lines behind the different candidates, and then they counted back, and the fellow who had the longest tail to his kite was the real captain. It was a good way. There was no chance for ballot-box stuffing or a false count.

"When the real captain with his regimentals came and assumed the control, Lincoln's heart failed him. He formed in the line with the boys, and after the speech was made they began to form behind the old captain; but the boys seized Lincoln and pushed him out of the line and began to form behind him, and cried, 'Form behind Abe,' and in a moment of irresolution he marched ahead, and when they counted back he had two more[1] than the other captain."

The lawlessness of the troops in camp and on the march caused Governor Reynolds much annoyance and chagrin. When Major Long's battalion was ordered down the river the troops were especially charged not to fire their guns aboard the boat, a charge unnecessary with most men. So prevalent had that amusement become that the celebrated order of April 30th was issued just as the little army was taking up its march for the Yellow Banks. At the Henderson River a crossing was effected only after great labor and more inconvenience in the way of wet clothing, and probably to celebrate so successful an event the firing was resumed, this time by Captain Lincoln himself, which promptly brought upon his head his first disgrace by being reprimanded and, as is generally conceded, by being compelled to wear a wooden sword. That punishment was accepted in good spirit, but no more firing was charged to his account during the campaign; in fact, it made him more punctilious and

---
[1] His strength was full three-fourths of the company.

JOHN CALHOUN.

WILLIAM POINTER.

ORDER OF APRIL 30, FORBIDDING THE FIRING OF ARMS.

REV. PETER CARTWRIGHT.   WILLIAM H. LEE.

I CERTIFY, That Lewis W. Farmer volunteered and served as a Private in the Company of Mounted Volunteers under my command, in the Regiment commanded by Col. SAMUEL M. THOMPSON, in the Brigade under the command of Generals S. WHITESIDE and H. ATKINSON, called into the service of the United States by the Commander-in-Chief of the Militia of the State, for the protection of the North Western Frontier against an Invasion of the British Band of Sac and other tribes of Indians,—that he was enrolled on the 21st day of April 1832, and was HONORABLY DISCHARGED on the 7th day of June thereafter, having served 48 days

Given under my hand, this 21st day of September 1832.

A. Lincoln Capt.

watchful and more insistent with his men. When off duty, however, he allowed himself and his men the harmless diversions of camp life without restraint.

Captain Lincoln was magnetic and his men were drawn toward him from admiration, and not alone because they knew he was a man of courage and strength. That magnetism drew not only his immediate acquaintances at New Salem, but his superior officers, and as he advanced in life, it drew about him the men of influence and power who later made a new and powerful political party. It attracted John T. Stuart to invite him to his office to read law; it attracted the voters of his district to beat Peter Cartwright, then the best-known man in Illinois probably, for the legislature. That discipline kept Captain Lincoln vigilant until the mouth of Rock River was reached, and even the affair there was not one of commission.

During the night of May 9th one Royal P. Green, of the company of Capt. Thomas McDow of Greene county, entered the officers' quarters and, with the assistance of a tomahawk, four buckets and some of Lincoln's command, secured enough liquor to enjoy a comfortable lark and place a large number of Captain Lincoln's men *hors de combat*. On the morning of the 10th, the date fixed to begin the march up Rock River, few were able to answer the roll call and few indeed were able to take up the march for the Prophet's town. For this offense, which had been committed without the knowledge of the Captain, and to his great surprise and mortification, that officer was again reprimanded and ignobly compelled to wear for two days the wooden sword. This he did "for the boys" with grim humor. As the men sobered up and gradually straggled into camp that night, they realized what their disgraceful behavior had brought to their captain. Remorse, or some equally powerful agency, made Captain Lincoln's company a model one from that hour.

To claim that sports were not a feature of camp life and that Captain Lincoln did not participate in them, were ridiculous. Nine-tenths of that army were Kentuckians or Tennesseeans, every man of which loved a horse. There were close upon two thousand horses in camp; some better, some worse, and when off duty no time was allowed to lapse without a horse race, a foot race or a wrestling match. Into those contests Captain Lincoln did not obtrude himself, but he was always counted on as "being ready" and on the spot. His men knew his prowess and were proud of it, as was Offutt when he got the Captain into the Armstrong affair. They were alert to advertise that prowess at all times and willing to stake their last earthly possession on his success. Such is human nature to-day. The best foot runner, quoit pitcher, boxer or wrestler in a body of men has followers constantly boasting the prowess of their favorite and getting him into business, and many times into troubles. So Captain Lincoln, to oblige his men, and likely his own inclination, took on wrestling matches and vanquished his antagonists one after another to the end of his service as a soldier.

The story of the match with Thompson, the wrestler, is no doubt true, though difficult to locate. Some authorities have asserted that Thompson came from Union County,[1] but as Union County supplied but one company, that of Captain B. B. Craig, in which no person named Thompson can be found, the Union County portion of it must be eliminated. This is unfortunate when attempting to locate the situs. Had Thompson been from Union County his company never could have met either of the three companies with which Lincoln was connected, because it did not reach the main army until Lincoln had been discharged and was on his way home.

The story contains, with all its variations, the reference to his position as captain, and no loss of prestige with his men; therefore the event must have occurred at Beardstown, Rushville, Yellow Banks, Dixon's Ferry, Ottawa or some one of the camps along that route, and prior to May 27th, the date of his muster out. At any rate the story is as follows:

Thompson, a man of burly form, champion of his section, was tendered to Captain Lincoln for a match in a way that to decline it would have disgraced his men and his friends. Captain Lincoln was not given to separating himself from a responsibility at any time, and without formality accepted the challenge. Up to that date there had been no pay-day and it is safe to assume that the entire company could not inventory five dollars in money; but the men had knives, souvenirs, watches and knickknacks, the last one of which was staked on the issue of the match. The combatants grappled and it soon became evident that Thompson was qualified to bear championship laurels. The tussle was long and uncertain and keyed all the men up to a high tension, as each contestant was being cheered to a victory; but Thompson, after a hard battle, secured the first fall. Lincoln could recognize a worthy antagonist and before taking on the second bout said to his friends: "This is the most powerful man I ever had hold of. He will throw me and you will lose your all unless I act on the defensive." Accordingly, when the men came together again, Captain Lincoln played for a "crotch holt," which Thompson was able to avoid. Then, as the struggle progressed, the trick of "sliding away," was tried. In this Captain Lincoln was more successful, for in the scramble for advantage both men went to the ground in a heap, which, according to the ethics of frontier wrestling, is denominated a "dog fall," hence a draw. Armstrong claimed a victory, at which a storm of protest went up from Captain Lincoln's backers, and a free fight was imminent. Believing that trouble was imminent, Captain Lincoln came forward, and in a voice which compelled attention, exclaimed,

---
[1] Nicolay and Hay.

"Boys, the man actually threw me once fair, broadly so, and the second time, this very fall, he threw me fairly, though not apparently so,"[1] and that settled the question for all time, though "dog fall" was frequently repeated during the remainder of the campaign by the Captain's partisans. That defeat and the acknowledgment of it in no sense diminished the influence or standing of Captain Lincoln with his men or those who were beginning to know and like him.

In later years men took advantage of his prominence to claim many untrue familiarities in the Black Hawk war. For instance: William L. Wilson, who was a private in Capt. M. G. Wilson's company, wrote, under date of February 3d, 1882: "I have during that time had much fun with the afterwards President of the United States, Abraham Lincoln. I remember one time of wrestling with him, two best in three, and ditched him. He was not satisfied and tried it in a foot race, for a five-dollar bill. I won the money and 'tis spent long ago. And many more reminiscences could I give, but I am of the Quaker persuasion and not much given to writing." There are some other qualities belonging to the Quaker persuasion which might have been regarded with advantage in the manufacture of that story.

A story for which there is no warrant of authority, except constant repetition, is the one of the drinking contest. At first the scene was located at Beardstown, but afterward Colonel Strode, having heard it, appropriated the glory of the contest to himself, at least one-half of it, and located the same at Dixon's Ferry. The question of strength having arisen, Captain Lincoln was quoted as being the strongest man in the army. Strode challenged the statement by offering to bet that he and nobody else could raise a barrel of whisky and drink from its bunghole. The partisans of Captain Lincoln accepted the challenge, produced the whisky and their favorite, and Colonel Strode made his boast good by raising the barrel and taking his drink from the bunghole. The feat seemed impossible, but having been witnessed by a reputable crowd of men, could not be gainsaid.

Captain Lincoln is said to have then stepped forward, and with much greater ease swung the barrel to his lips and taken his drink, thereby besting Strode in his boast.

An addition was made to the story in later years by having Strode exclaim, "Well, I thought you said you never drank any whisky, Captain Lincoln!"

"I don't drink whisky, Colonel Strode," replied Captain Lincoln, and forthwith he spat the whisky upon the ground.

At the mouth of the Rock River the company was sworn into the United States service by Gen. Henry Atkinson. It is but recently that the author has been able to determine that much disputed point, and it

---
[1] Lamon 110.

must be admitted that the discovery was made with pain. From the days of his earliest boyhood, he had believed that Jefferson Davis was the mustering officer and that there the two men who later became so conspicuous, yet divergent, in the eyes of the world, met for the first time, the one asking the other if he would support the constitution of the United States and fight for the flag.

For generations that tradition has obtained. It has been repeated by the highest authorities, even by President Lincoln himself, if we may believe Ben. Perley Poore and others who have claimed the distinction of hearing him so state. The point was generally fixed at Dixon's Ferry, the birthplace of the author, and for that reason, steeped with the tradition from his earliest boyhood, it must be admitted that the discovery of the truth was made with profound grief. There can be no mistake about the truthfulness of that discovery. Major Nathaniel Buckmaster was second in command of the army. He was a careful and conscientious officer. He wrote the fact in a letter to his wife on the following day, and that letter is herewith reproduced as evidence. It may be said that General Atkinson might have sworn in the general officers, while a minor officer like Lieutenant Davis might have administered the oath to the captains and men, but it is not conceivable why more than one officer should be employed for so small a body of men, and it cannot be imagined why the captains would be separated from the few officers of the general staff. In fact, if General Atkinson were to have made a specialty of or distinction, it seems fair to presume that he would have included the captains with the officers sworn in.

On the 9th General Atkinson issued orders to the troops to march on the morning of the 10th, which they did, reaching the Prophet's town in the afternoon, where camp was established for the night.

The following day, instead of remaining at that point, Reynolds pushed up the river twelve miles and again camped.

On the morning of the 12th the baggage was abandoned and a forced march made to Dixon's Ferry. There Captain Lincoln remained the 12th, 13th and 14th, at which last-named date Stillman was defeated and his men returned to Dixon's pell-mell during all hours of the night.

On the 15th he went up the river, reaching the battlefield just before dark. After the burial of the dead he camped and next day returned to Dixon's, where he remained until the 19th, when he pushed up the river in pursuit of the Indians. Twelve miles out he camped until the 20th, when he again marched to Stillman's battlefield, at which point Captain Goodan was placed under arrest for some breach of duty, demonstrating that Captain Lincoln was not the only officer of that rank to suffer punishment.

On the 21st the army moved over to a point on Rock River, where it camped until the 22d, moving then over to the Kishwaukee and up the

Mouth of Rock River Camp No 30
May 9th 1832 —

Dear Wife
 yesterday we was mustered in to service of the United States by General Atkinson, and we go to Monoco Morning Start to the Prophets village — perhaps from thence to Dixons Ferry on Rock River, where it is believed the hostile Indians are, and should they be gone before our arrival, it is the calculation to follow them until we come up with the body back and capture all the young women, and as to your inquiry respecting my manner of living, we have in abundance and that of the best. Would meet a supply ... I have been much exposed since I left home, it is my fate, I suppose, since I have to perform all the duty of what ever department I may be thrown into. The duties assigned me in this expedition is ordinary in their extream but it is my fate to what I meanis
I expect to come home by way of

LETTER OF MAJ. NATHANIEL BUCKMASTER.

feel better but at what season of the year is uncertain so do not look for me untill you see me, but I intend to return accedants exceptd And afford me greate pleasure when I reflect that you and Grand Mauggh has the meens of supplying you [with?] untill I Returned should the clerk [illegible] Shrouder Muchin be all of whome will Supply you with articles they &c. I know of no opsetty for you to write for it were uncertain abdugns our movements but I shall write the first opptty that presents it self Say to Denyer Bush and all my friend to watch over my intress untill I return should I not get home before the Election I shall I hope after ward Give my love to grand Maclef and permit me to say to you have the Warmest place in my affections

N Buckmaster

Mrs. H. A. Buckmaster
[illegible] I will not look over his [illegible] I will love it up

LETTER OF MAJ. NATHANIEL BUCKMASTER.

same about ten miles from its mouth, where camp was established and the army rested until the following morning.

On the 23d the army moved about twelve miles in a southeasterly direction to the Pottawatomie village on Sycamore Creek, at which point, after a consultation with all the captains, it was decided to march to the mouth of Fox River and there discharge the volunteers. At the village were found the scalps of Stillman's men and evidences of Indians, but no sentiment could move the men to continue the pursuit of them. Some few articles of Indian property were found at the village, all of which were confiscated by the men. Much confusion has in the past been caused by the terms Kishwaukee and Sycamore Creek, when no such name as the latter can now be found on the maps, but an explanation can be found in the fact that in those days many called the stream by both names, interchangeably, while others especially called the south branch of the Kishwaukee River by the name of Sycamore Creek. Afterward the latter branch continued by the name Sycamore Creek until settlements increased, when finally, to avoid confusion, the present name of Kishwaukee River was given to both branches. Sycamore Creek meant then the south branch of the Kishwaukee.

On the morning of the 24th the march was resumed, the army camping near the "Paw Paw village," which was also robbed by the men. On the 25th Fox River was reached, most of the day being spent there in searching men for articles of plunder taken from the two Indian villages. On the 26th, being very near the end of the journey, the march was very leisurely pursued for twelve miles, where the last camp before reaching Ottawa was established, and where the men remained until the following morning, the 27th, when Ottawa was reached. On that and the following days the Illinois volunteers were mustered out by Major Buckmaster.

During that march along Sycamore Creek the story is told of an old Pottawatomie Indian who came into camp, tired and hungry. His age should have commanded respect, and probably would under circumstances at all different, but in that instance the first chance to kill a supposed enemy was presented and his death was demanded. The poor old Indian produced from his garments a safe conduct signed by Gen. Lewis Cass, pleading protection under it. "Make an example of him," cried one. "The letter is a forgery," cried others, and still others called him a spy, and the poor old fellow was in danger of death, when Captain Lincoln, "his face swarthy with resolution and rage," stepped forward, even between the cowering Indian and the guns pointed at him, and shouted, "This must not be; he must not be shot and killed by us," and the men recoiled. "This is cowardly on your part, Lincoln," one man said; to which Captain Lincoln instantly replied, "If any man thinks I am a coward let him test it." Still defiant, another cried, "Lincoln, you are larger and heavier than we are," but that miserable objection was quickly disposed of by the rejoinder from the Captain, "This you can guard against; choose your weapons." It is needless to add that no one chose a weapon and that the Indian departed in safety.

On the 27th, the day Captain Lincoln was mustered out, he re-enlisted as a private in the company of Elijah Iles, which was one of the six companies to enter the twenty-day service,[1] pending the organization of the new levies at Fort Wilbourn. He remained with the company at Ottawa and in camp on the opposite bank of the river until the morning of the 6th, when the company marched for Dixon's Ferry. The first night out the company camped at a point a little south and east of what is now Sublette in Lee County, and reached Dixon's Ferry the evening of the 7th. On the morning of the 8th the company started for Galena, camping that night about twenty miles out; the night of the 9th near Apple River Fort, now Elizabeth, in Jo Daviess County, and in the forenoon of the 10th the company reached Galena.

On the 11th it started on its return march over the same trail pursued in going, camping at the same places, reaching Dixon's Ferry the night of June 13th, from which point it started on the 14th, and reached Fort Wilbourn, where, on the evening of the 15th, the company was mustered out by Lieut. Robert Anderson, and where, on the following day, Mr. Lincoln was mustered into the company of Dr. (Captain) Jacob M. Early, along with John T. Stuart and other ex-captains, majors and minor officers.

On the 20th his company, which was an independent one, reporting direct to General Atkinson, started for Dixon's Ferry, arriving there the evening of the 21st, and remaining at that point until noon of the 27th, when he, with the second division of the army, began his final march in pursuit of Black Hawk. Twelve miles out he camped, and in the afternoon of the 29th once more reached and camped on Stillman's battlefield, six miles from Sycamore or Kishwaukee Creek, as stated by Albert Sidney Johnston at the time.

On the morning of the 30th, he traveled four miles above Sycamore Creek, to a point on Rock River "which is very narrow at this place, and continues so."

July 1st, the journal tells us: "Marched this morning seven miles from the last encampment. Came to Rock River, which is scarcely one hundred yards wide at this point. There is in the bluff a remarkably fine spring, thickly shaded with cedar trees, the first I ever saw. The bluff is pebbly. About half a mile above, a narrow, rapid creek empties into Rock River, one mile below Pecatonica, known by

---

[1] Lt. Robert Anderson mustered Private Lincoln into that company.

the name of Brown's Creek. Encamped this evening in the fork of Turtle Creek and Rock River, above the mouth of Turtle Creek."

On the 2d he proceeded, after considerable suffering for want of water, to the mouth of "the river of the Four Lakes," on the banks of a large pond.

On the 3d Lake Koshkonong, or "Mud Lake," was reached, and there the troops remained the 4th, 5th and 6th, Captain Early's company doing constant duty as a spy company or scouting party.

On the 7th the army moved up to Whitewater River and about four miles up that stream, to which point the divisions of Posey and Alexander came and camped.

On the 8th a council of war was held, at which it was resolved to return to the mouth of the Whitewater and operate from that point. On reaching the point where the troops were encamped on the 7th, the army halted for the night. From that point Captain Early's company was constantly engaged in scouring the country in search of the fleeing Indians, without any success at all. Many trails were reported, but on following them up each proved abortive.

Provisions had become scarce. The enemy was as far away as ever. The necessity of a different campaign became apparent. Captain Dunn, who had been shot by accident, was recovering and was about to be returned to Dixon's Ferry under escort of Col. John Ewing's Regiment. Henry and Alexander had been detached to go to Fort Winnebago for provisions, thus virtually disrupting the army. At that stage General Atkinson considered it best to dismiss the independent commands. Accordingly, on July 10th, 1832, the company of Captain Early was mustered out of the service, and its members, including Private Abraham Lincoln, started for Dixon's Ferry with the detachment of Colonel Ewing, who took with him all the sick and decrepit men of the army.

The men fell down the river to Dixon's Ferry, along the same route pursued by them up that stream, but did not move so rapidly for the reason that many of the men had lost their horses by death, theft and one or another cause.

Among those to have lost their horses were Mr. Lincoln and his chum, George Harrison, but during the march those who had horses cheerfuly gave up the use of them to the unfortunate, and on the whole a jolly time of it was had all the way down the river.

On that march up the river Mr. Lincoln's mess was composed of five men—himself, his stepbrother, John D. Johnston, G. B. Fanchier, George Harrison, all privates, and First Corporal R. M. Wyatt, all of Captain Early's company. During all of Mr. Lincoln's service he was ever ready to march or move upon the phantom enemy. While scouting up in the swamps around Lake Koshkonong, he was the first to say,

"Let's go." He was tireless on the march and overflowing with anecdote at all times.

The story has been told of him that while returning to Dixon's Ferry after his discharge, his shoes were so worn that he preferred going without them. One morning was particularly chilly, which brought out the complaint that he was very cold. "No wonder," replied his neighbor, "there is so much of you on the ground." That story may be truthful, but nevertheless the skeptical listener is forced to wonder how anyone could suffer to any great extent during the last few days of July, the hottest of the year. It is also a noteworthy fact that the story has never been authenticated by the names of eye-witnesses.

From Dixon's Ferry Mr. Lincoln, with his companion, George Harrison, crossed the country to the point on the Illinois River later called Peru; thence to Peoria, where they bought a canoe in which to paddle themselves down the Illinois River as far as Havana. While Harrison supplied the commissary, Mr. Lincoln made an oar or paddle to be used as motive power—one large enough to endure hard service. Just below Pekin they overtook two men on a log raft, upon which the two soldiers were invited. It was meal time, and, western fashion, the hungry men were invited to join the raftsmen. Cornbread, fish, eggs, butter, coffee and similar luxuries were lavishly supplied, and from Mr. Lincoln's own statements he did justice to the meal.

Arrived at Havana, the canoe was sold without trouble and the two companions set out overland for New Salem, Lincoln's long strides blazing the way and leading poor Harrison a pace he never forgot.

While no military achievement brought glory to Mr. Lincoln, he was ever after fond of recording his experiences in the Black Hawk War and relating stories of the ridiculous things which were done in his campaigns. Repetition by others caused their enlargement, until the number and variety became very great. Those stories attracted attention to him in Congress and brought him a considerable following, and finally a reputation, when he made his celebrated speech on "Military Coat-tails," into which he injected portions of his Black Hawk War experiences in a way to ridicule the life out of the military pretensions of Lewis Cass.

Again quoting from Ben. Perley Poore, we find:[1]

"Soon after the presidential campaign of 1848 was opened, Alfred Iverson, a Democratic Representative from Georgia, made a political speech, in which he accused the Whigs of having deserted their financial and tariff principles and of having 'taken shelter under the military coat-tails of General Taylor,' then their presidential candidate. This gave Mr. Lincoln as a text for his reply, 'Military Coat-tails.' He had written the heads of what he had intended to say on a few pages of foolscap paper,

---
[1]Reminiscences of Abraham Lincoln, p. 219.

which he placed on a friend's desk, bordering on an alleyway, which he had obtained permission to speak from. At first he followed his notes, but as he warmed up, he left his desk and his notes to stride down the alley toward the Speaker's chair, holding his left hand behind him so that he could now and then shake the tails of his own rusty black broadcloth dress coat, while he earnestly gesticulated with his long right arm, shaking the bony index finger at the Democrats on the other side of the chamber. Occasionally, as he would complete a sentence amid shouts of laughter, he would return up the alley to his desk, consult his notes, take a sip of water and start off again.

"Toward the close of his speech Mr. Lincoln poured a torrent of ridicule upon the military reputation of General Cass, and then alluded to his own exploits as a soldier in the Black Hawk War, 'where,' he continued, 'I fought, bled and came away. If General Cass saw any live, fighting Indians at the battle of the Thames, where he served as aide-de-camp to General Harrison, it was more than I did, but I had a good many bloody struggles with the mosquitoes, and although I never fainted from the loss of blood, I can truly say I was often very hungry. Mr. Speaker,' added Mr. Lincoln, 'if I should ever conclude to doff whatever our Democratic friends may suppose there is of black-cockade Federalism about me, and thereupon they shall take me up as their candidate for the Presidency, I protest they shall not make fun of me as they have of General Cass, by attempting to write me into a military hero.'"

"Mr. Lincoln received hearty congratulations at the close, many Democrats joining the Whigs in their complimentary comments. The speech was pronounced by the older members of the House almost equal to the celebrated defense of General Harrison by Tom Corwin, in reply to an attack made on him by a Mr. Crary of Ohio."

---

[1]Mr. Poore was not exact in his quotations from that speech, but near enough the truth to escape the charge of error.

APPENDIX NO. 2.

JEFFERSON DAVIS IN THE BLACK HAWK WAR.

In the year 1832, when the State of Illinois was but fourteen years of age, there was to be found on the south bank of Rock River, sixty-five miles above its mouth, a frontier post called Dixon's Ferry. It was an unpretentious affair, consisting of a solitary tenement laid east and west, in three sections, and built of logs—a cozy but rambling affair ninety feet in length.

At this point the great "Kellogg's trail," run by O. W. Kellogg in the year 1827, crossed the river, and John Dixon, from whom the ferry derived its name and its existence, had lived here with his family since early in the year 1830, entertaining travelers, operating the ferry and trading with the "suckers" who journeyed to and from the mining district and Indians. This famous old trail was then the route pursued by the argonauts of all the southern country in search of sudden wealth in the mines. It was the great thoroughfare from Peoria, then more commonly referred to as Fort Clark, to Galena, sought by those from the St. Louis country on the southwest and the old Vincennes country to the southeast, and followed on northwesterly past Dixon's Ferry to Galena, where the crowds dispersed and scattered for the "diggings" over northwestern Illinois and southwestern Wisconsin, then a part of Michigan Territory. Later the Government mail route changed the old trail to a straighter course between Galena and Dixon's Ferry, thence leaving it for an easterly direction through DeKalb, Kane, DuPage and Cook counties the route continued to Chicago.

Famous old days were those in the West and famous men traveled that trail in those old days! From the miner and prospector to the merchant; from the mail carrier to the soldier; from the circuit preacher to the circuit law rider following a peripatetic court. From Peter Cartwright, the energetic Methodist preacher, who swam swollen streams and rivers to keep his word, and who, if rumor be true, brought in more than one obstreperous recruit with a flogging, to Col. James M. Strode, the then noted but erratic criminal lawyer of Galena; from Lieut.-Col. Zachary Taylor, who afterward became President of the United States,

LIEUT. JEFFERSON DAVIS.

THE BLACK HAWK WAR. 291

and Gen. Winfield Scott, who wanted to be, to Lieut. Jefferson Davis, who was President of the Southern Confederacy, and Capt. Abraham Lincoln, who dissolved it, we find them all associated with the old trail and eating and lodging with mine host Dixon, singly and together; those who were later to become Cabinet Ministers, United States Senators, Representatives, Governors, and soldiers and statesmen without number.

White men and Indians alike made their pilgrimages along that trail, stopping over with Mr. Dixon to strengthen the inner man and replenish their stock of supplies. With the Indians he was particularly popular, insomuch that he became their counselor and arbitrator, and likewise their banker. In turn, as a recognition of his many and kindly offices, the Winnebagoes adopted him into their tribe, naming him Na-chu-sa (long hair white). This affection for the old patriarch was equally manifested by the whites, and when the time came to bespeak it there was left no uncertainty respecting the judgment. His silent influence became so potent that in the year 1840, with Galena the political and commercial power of the Northwest, he took from her to his own town the United States Land Office.

When the subject of removal was first broached it appeared so ridiculously impossible that nothing in Galena but laughter protested, but John Dixon's tavern was stronger than the politics and commercial prestige of the giant philistine, and her haughty pride was humbled. Singly he journeyed on to Washington, and for the simple asking, the office, the most potential factor in the politics of that day, was ordered removed to Dixon—the miracle of the century in Illinois politics.

'The man's venerable personality, his charming sweetness of disposition, his rugged honesty, and possibly his little account book, were altogether too powerful for the antagonists of those rugged days, and before passing that same little account book it may be well to run hastily over its pages.

Colonel Strode was exceedingly familiar with them; one might say that he took liberties with them. First we find Colonel Strode Dr.—To Cash—$10.00, and again Strode was Dr.—To Cash—$5.00; invariably cash, running clear through from cover to cover.

Col. William S. Hamilton, son of General Alexander Hamilton, whose business ventures were as varied as they were numerous, was favored with merchandise to the extent of many pages and many hundreds of dollars, and so, by the by, was Col. Zachary Taylor, only to more modest amounts. One entry characteristic of the times is laughable enough. Here it is: "Col. Z. Taylor—To Md'se. (including a shirt pattern), $6:50, and then follows its liquidation in a still more laughable manner: "Settled by note."

There is humor for you! The hero of more than one war and President of the United States settling an account of $6.50 by note of hand! But the note was paid in due time, we are assured by Miss F. Louise Dixon, the owner of the little book with such historic credits and debits.

Even the dignity of Gen. Winfield Scott was not above the acceptance of the hospitality of those friendly pages, for we find entries which tell of the manner they had obliged him, but the punctilio observed by him in the discharge of those little accounts was manifested by the same precision one would expect from the dignified old soldier, who was nothing if not precise.

Men came and traded, traveled afar off and returned to settle, sometimes a year from date and sometimes at a still longer date, but they returned, and the score at Mr. Dixon's was never forgotten. Today the debtor was a miner; tomorrow he might be a contractor, and later he might be a lawyer, but in meeting his obligations he was always a man.

On one occasion we find this same Colonel Hamilton, who had contracted two hundred steers to be delivered to the Government agency at Green Bay, Wisconsin, driving them from Springfield, Illinois, through Chicago, and thence northward to his destination. In the same month he was operating "Hamilton's diggings," and subsequently he was defending a noted Mormon at Nauvoo, Illinois, charged with the commission of a crime, and yet again he was commanding a band of Menominee Indians in the Black Hawk War; always strenuous and always unqualifiedly successful.

Backward and forward the people came, forgetting never to stop over with genial Mr. Dixon. Travel was constant, and in a general sense men were prosperous, particularly in the mines.

Though freely encroaching on the land of the Winnebagoes, no troubles had ensued since the "Winnebago scare" of 1827, when Red Bird was captured for an unwarranted attack upon the whites.

A little riffle was caused in 1831 by Black Hawk, but nothing serious arose to disturb the tranquillity of the settlements until the year 1832. Possibly if the affair of 1831 had been more serious the one of 1832 would have been less disastrous.

In the spring of the year 1832, Black Hawk and his "British band," as it was denominated, of the Sac tribe of Indians, disregarding all former treaties, one of them so late as the preceding summer, crossed the Mississippi in search of trouble. He had traveled up Rock River, stopping one day with Mr. Dixon, and then continued to a point some thirty miles above, where Stillman and his militia in attempting later to dislodge them, were signally defeated, and in consequence consternation spread over the entire West.

Then it was the log cabin of John Dixon took on a national reputation, which its memory has ever since maintained, and which must stand by it so long as our country endures, and then, indeed, the account books

LIEUT. J. J. ABERCROMBIE. U. S. A.

LIEUT. GEORGE WILSON. U. S. A.

COL. NATHAN BOONE.

LIEUT. ROBERT ANDERSON, U. S. A.
(Copyrighted, as stated in index.)

THE BLACK HAWK WAR. 293

took on an importance seldom acquired in the affairs of bookdom. Then the tide turned, too, from lawyers and "suckers" to soldiers, and the flower and chivalry of the State and Nation went forth to concentrate at Dixon's Ferry to contest the advance of Black Hawk and his mercenaries, who had fought the Americans at every opportunity from the beginning of the century.

In addition to those named there were Gen. Hugh Brady, Gen. Henry Atkinson, Col. Nathan Boone, son of Daniel Boone, Capt. W. S. Harney, Robert Anderson, Jefferson Davis, N. J. Eaton, Albert Sidney Johnston, Joseph E. Johnston, Bennet Riley, W. M. Graham, George Wilson, Kearney, Abercrombie, Gardenier, William Whistler, M. L. Clark, of the regular army, and of the militia, Capt. Abraham Lincoln, Gen. Henry Dodge, Gen. George W. Jones, Gov. John Reynolds, Gen. E. D. Baker, O. H. Browning, John A. McClernand, John Dement, Harrison Wilson, James D. Henry, Sidney Breese, Jacob Fry, Samuel Whiteside, Adam W. Snyder and others without number, who became famous in the history of the country at subsequent periods.

The regulars stationed at Jefferson Barracks (St. Louis) started under Atkinson up the Mississippi for Fort Armstrong (Rock Island), from which point the General, with a small detachment, proceeded further up to Fort Crawford (Prairie du Chien), to secure the assistance of the troops stationed there under Lieut.-Col. Zachary Taylor, and those at Fort Winnebago (Portage, Wisconsin) under Lieut.-Col. Enos Cutler. Those under Taylor returned with Atkinson to Fort Armstrong to meet the militia of the State of Illinois, then gathering at Beardstown, preparatory to moving up to the mouth of Rock River, where a junction was to be formed with the regulars. Other troops under General Scott were subsequently ordered from Fortress Monroe. Others under Brady were ordered to Dixon's Ferry from Detroit, taking in the Fort Winnebago men, the whole finally making an army formidable enough to annihilate all the Indians in the West if Indians could have been drawn into a general engagement.

On the 12th of May, 1832, the militia under Governor Reynolds and Gen. Samuel Whiteside arrived, almost simultaneously with a company of troops from the mining district under the intrepid Gen. Henry Dodge. On the 17th the regulars under General Atkinson arrived, and on this day Jefferson Davis assisted in mustering into the United States service the newly-formed Fifth Regiment, of which James Johnson of Macon County had been made Colonel just before.

In this first campaign of 1832 Lincoln was captain of a company of militia composed of sixty-nine as intractable and headstrong men as could be found at that very independent period, extravagantly opposed to discipline, acknowledging no superior, yet managed with skill and credit to all by the captain, who, under ordinary circumstances, chafed under restraint much less severe than that which military authority imposed and which few western men respected.

The age was one of independence, and that, more than anything else, was the cause of Stillman's defeat. Private differences were settled without the assistance of courts, which were few and far between. One man was as good as his neighbor, and if anyone disputed the proposition it generally cost him a sore head. Those men who had fought in the war of 1812, without the assistance of the general Government, looked with profound contempt on the gold trappings of the regular officer and his tedious routine, and Governor Reynolds, diplomat that he was in handling western character, was put to the limit of his ability and endurance in smoothing over the difficulties which were needlessly created by this miserable spirit of independence. But by appointing officers of the regular establishment on his personal staff, requesting General Atkinson to accept some of the militia on his staff,[1] which he cheerfuly did, and finally instructing others in the gentle art of "mixing," he was finally able to overcome almost every obstacle which arose. Officers of the militia were invited to mess with the regulars, and vice versa, and through the friendly offices of the Governor, Abraham Lincoln and Jefferson Davis were brought together for the first time and "messed" at Mr. Dixon's table.

Albert Sidney Johnston, then a second lieutenant, accompanied the expedition from Jefferson Barracks and was appointed on the Governor's staff with Robert Anderson. Lieutenant Johnston's journal, kept regularly during the entire campaign, and which is fortunately preserved to us at this day, is a valuable and entertaining document.

When Atkinson was ordered to the front, Lieut. Robert Anderson was at Jefferson Barracks making an inspection. Asking and obtaining leave to accompany the expedition, he was appointed Assistant Inspector-General of the militia, and, as before stated, made a member of the Governor's staff, with the rank of Colonel.

Gen. W. S. Harney, then a captain, and Jefferson Davis, then a lieutenant, were both absent on furlough when Black Hawk crossed the Mississippi, but on hearing of his purpose, each at once returned, rejoined his regiment at the mouth of Rock River and continued throughout the campaign to its close.[2]

The season was unusually rainy, and by the time the troops had reached Dixon's Ferry they were nearly exhausted with fording creeks and towing the unmanageable keel boats up the river, many times wading waist deep in mire and water to propel them.

Stillman had been defeated on the 14th, and by the time General At-

---
[1] Col. E. C. March and others.
[2] Flagler's Rock Island Arsenal, p. 21.

kinson's forces reached the ferry the militia and its officers were a panicky lot.

The War Department at Washington shows that Lieut. Jefferson Davis applied for a leave of absence and left Fort Crawford to go upon the same on the 26th day of March, 1832, and that he formally rejoined his command from leave August 18th, 1832, sixteen days after the battle of the Bad Axe, the last engagement of the campaign, which would inferentially indicate that he was absent from duty all the time between those dates and inferentially not in the campaign.

In a letter written by Mr. Davis on the 8th day of August, 1882, from Beauvoir, Mississippi, to Gen. George W. Jones of Dubuque, Iowa, he stated: "In the spring of 1832 I was relieved by Lieut. I. R. B. Gardenier, as private matters required me to go to Mississippi, my home. * * * "

So far there is no conflict. But while his official letter acknowledging his return to his regiment is not dated till August 18th, he was present in flesh and blood from start to finish, delaying that perfunctory duty until he was once more back to quarters and relieved of the fatigues and manifold annoyances of a campaign through swamps and bogs and innumerable privations. And while touching upon the general subject of war records, I beg to state that I attended the funeral of an officer killed at the battle of Shiloh—literally shot to pieces—yet there stands to this day against his name in the Adjutant-General's reports this "record:" "Absent on furlough." The officer had no opportunity to take the furlough, and it took the affidavits of half the town to make the department believe he was not actually alive. The facts in the case are exactly stated by Col. William Preston Johnston, late President of Tulane University, in his very interesting "Life of General A. S. Johnston," at page 36: "Jefferson Davis, who was with General Gaines in his operations in 1831, was absent on furlough in Mississippi when the Black Hawk war broke out, but gave up his furlough, and, joining his company, served in the campaign." This was told him by Mr. Davis himself when Colonel Johnston was writing the book, as well as many other little incidents, including one of Stillman's defeat, and should be regarded as conclusive for all time. But as various writers, with more regard for revenue than right, have sought to discredit the truth because a negative inference from the record gave them the opportunity of avoiding a little labor, I have collected from various sources a complete detail of Mr. Davis' movements during the campaign.

On the 17th day of May, when General Atkinson arrived at Dixon's Ferry, the militia were discontented, disconcerted and on the verge of insubordination. Governor Reynolds had on the morning of the 15th issued a call for two thousand more troops to rendezvous at Hennepin, and only by the most frantic appeals had he been able to hold the others together until Atkinson arrived.

It is true the provisions had been exhausted and the volunteers were living on less than half rations, but it is equally true that this was due entirely to their own improvidence and wastefulness.

The troops under Stillman, after their defeat on the 14th, had consented to remain in the service to protect the frontier until a new levy could be raised. Accordingly, so soon as they returned from the burial of their dead, on the 16th, the Fifth Regiment was organized, and on the following day, when the troops under the commanding general arrived, the regiment was sworn into the United States service.

On the 15th Strode, who was colonel and commander of the militia of Jo Daviess County, had been instructed to hasten back to the mines and organize his forces to protect that very important frontier, which all recognized as the one to suffer from the attacks of the Indians at almost any hour. He quickly returned, but, being utterly unable to manage the intractable spirits of that locality, he had declared martial law. This act inflamed the people to a high degree of passion and rumors of its effects had reached the ears of Governor Reynolds.

General Atkinson was consulted at once on his arrival, and Lieut. Jefferson Davis and two or three other officers were detailed to go post haste to Galena and, if possible, bring order out of the chaos which Strode had precipitated.

The departure of Lieutenant Davis on the 17th and his mission to Galena have been related to me by Mr. Dixon on more than one occasion. Fortunately, others remembered the circumstance and reduced it to writing, making a mistake impossible on that point. Among the many documents which have come to my attention in connection with this search is an old yellow letter in the possession of Gen. John C. Smith of Chicago, written to him years ago by H. Hezekiah Gear, who was a captain and served throughout the Black Hawk campaign. Captain Gear was a man of character and influence in the community and his memory or veracity has never yet been called into question. This letter details this very visit in a concise yet luminous fashion:

"I had a partial acquaintance with Lieut. Jefferson Davis. I had a partial acquaintance with him when this whole domain was under savage rule, except ten miles square about Galena and western garrisons. He was, I *think,* at the Winnebago disturbance in 1827. He was at Fort Winnebago on the Wisconsin River, and in 1832 stationed at Prairie du Chien, in the then Colonel Taylor's regiment.

"He came at the commencement of the Sauk and Fox war to Galena to counsel with us in relation to defense, with a number of officers, his superiors, for a day or so.

"At the same time the Governor of Illinois, by proclamation, called every able-bodied man into the field. Came to Galena on Saturday; all in commotion. Colonel Strode commanding.

"We held a council of war, yet had no arms. I urged them to have spontoons forged. He gave me the order to have 250 manufactured, I remember, and on Monday morning I brought them into quarters, when I then mounted my horse to go to the diggings, when I was accosted by the Colonel: 'Where are you going, Gear?' 'To plant my potatoes.' 'What, leave us here to take care of your family?' 'No, I act as a picket guard,' having my rifle on my shoulder.

"'Gear, we cannot spare you.' 'Why?' said I. He said, 'The Governor had called every able-bodied man into the field.' I looked along the crowd and he had a company of about sixty." 'Are these all?' was my reply. 'Yes,' was his answer. 'Why,' said I, 'I can raise more men at the sound of a whistle. Now there is but one to command and the balance to obey, Colonel, if we are in such danger. Now would you dare declare martial law, as General Jackson did at New Orleans?' He then said as Nathan said to David, 'Thou art the man; make out your order now and I will see it obeyed.' I dismounted at once, armed and equipped, shortly reporting at his headquarters, where his order was handed me, countersigned by the adjutant. I, reading, replied, 'It was a good order, but do you suppose a soul will obey me? No, not one, unless I have a force sufficient to carry it out. Will you give me a sergeant's guard?' 'I will.' 'Will you give me that fife and drum?' 'I will.' 'I will see it carried to the extent of my life.'

"I that day raised 240 recruits, was appointed officer of the day, had sixty-four to mount for guard; got quarters for my men and rations and part of their blankets, and refused other blankets that would not pass muster by me as a soldier's blanket; put the commissary in mud in the streets of Galena, for endeavoring to pass them on my men, and the next day received a pair of blankets for all. Well, the last round: I told the boys we would have some sport.

"Mrs. Barnes kept a bakery house on Brush street, which was the quarters of several officers of the United States Army.

"B. Miller, Esq., called the Chesterfield of the bar of Illinois, was there cracking jokes, and I halted at their quarters, requesting orders to report. He said to fall into line. 'What are you going to do with us?' 'The army wants just such men as you. Now we will find a place for you.' I then made my bow to Captain Kearney, or Major Harney, I do not know which. 'Will you and your brother officers fall into line? We belong to the United States Army.' 'Well, then, read them the Governor's proclamation and the order from Colonel Strode of the Twenty-seventh Regiment declaring martial law. Now, gentlemen, you know my duty,

[1]Stephenson's.

and if you hail General Jackson you will march. Now I cannot discharge my duty by leaving you behind, but the Colonel can dispose of you after you arrive in headquarters.' So we all fell into line, and under double-quick marched to quarters.

"Now their names were as follows, to wit: Captain Harney, Captain Kearney, Lieutenant Anderson, Lieutenant Gardenier, Lieutenant Jeff Davis."

Those companies were formed at Galena on the 19th day of May, and the presence of Lieut. J. R. B. Gardenier on that day, as mentioned by Captain Gear, is substantiated by reference to page 138 of a "Record of the Services of Illinois soldiers in the Black Hawk War," published by the Adjutant-General of Illinois in 1882, where it will be found that Lieut. J. R. B. Gardinier acted as commandant of Nicholas Dowling's company from May 19th to July 14th, "by request."

Captain Gear takes considerable credit unto himself for the accomplishment of this muster, but that is a latitude allowed every person who narrates a statement of fact so prominent, and especially when so successful. He has the detail of Strode's order a trifle confused, but that is of no consequence when the story is considered as a whole. He has given the days of the week with such accuracy that there remains no reason to doubt the statement of John Dixon, which it confirms.

Mr. John K. Robison was at the time a resident of Galena. Subsequently he removed to Dixon, and later removed to Melugin's Grove, in the same county, where he passed most of his long and honored life. He was fourth sergeant in Captain Gear's company.

In his lifetime I had many conversations with him about the campaign and his famous comrades, in the course of which he has more than once alluded to this meeting of Lieutenant Davis and Lieutenant Gardenier at Galena while they were encountering such trouble with Colonel Strode and his pig-headed tactics. He also told me of meeting Lieutenant Davis on several occasions thereafter, particularly at the time Lieutenant-Colonel Taylor's troops, with others, crossed the Wisconsin River on the march to the Bad Axe, where Black Hawk was overtaken and his band annihilated.

From Galena Lieutenant Davis and his companions, with the exception of Lieutenant Gardenier, returned to Dixon's Ferry, where, with the exception of scouting duty from time to time, and the march up Rock River, the troops under Taylor remained until the 27th day of June at 12 o'clock, when the militia under General Henry and the regulars under Atkinson and Brady started up the east bank of Rock River for the headquarters of Black Hawk among the morasses of the river above Lake Koshkonong.

It was during that period of over one month at Dixon's Ferry that Mr. Dixon became so well acquainted with Lieutenant Davis and his

CAPT. H. HEZEKIAH GEAR.

SERGT. JOHN K. ROBISON.

GEN. GEORGE W. JONES.

GEN. A. C. DODGE.

companions that error was impossible. He with others were guests at Mr. Dixon's house. They traded with him, buying his merchandise and paying for it or "having it charged." They hunted the wild duck, the grouse, the squirrel, the deer and the wild bee trees, and they fished and trapped and enjoyed life with a zest allowed no man of the present day of dirty pavements, crowded streets and dusty roads.

For weeks they were present, conversing, dining, playing, romping the prairies like so many schoolboys just dismissed from the termination of a long and arduous term of school. And thus were the images of those army officers impressed upon the memory of John Dixon, who, by the by, continued with them clear through the campaign, as army guide and contractor, till the battle of the Bad Axe ended the campaign.

After wearisome efforts around the Koshkonong country to dislodge the enemy, Henry and Dodge found his trail leading to the west, in a final effort to escape destruction, which was so surely coming upon him.

Taylor's division, including Lieutenant Davis, who was Taylor's adjutant, marched immediately for the Wisconsin River and the Blue Mounds, and thence on to the Bax Axe. After this engagement, the troops marched to Fort Crawford, their headquarters, and there, freed from the dangers and fatigue of the campaign, Lieutenant Davis formally wrote out a letter notifying the department of his return to duty. From that point the Illinois troops were marched back to Dixon's Ferry and mustered out by Capt. Zalmon C. Palmer.

During this period of five weeks, while Taylor remained at Dixon's Ferry, he was constantly on the alert, intercepting marauding bands of Indians, assisting the volunteers who had temporarily offered their services while the new levy was forming at Hennepin and Fort Wilbourn, and generally protecting the frontiers, and in this connection it may be said that the bloodiest and most destructive skirmishes were made between the Ferry and Galena during this period.

It may also be recorded that while the little account book was at all times open to the service of the officers there stationed, Mr. Dixon always laughingly spoke of the fact that, while he often sold them bills of goods, yet Lieutenant Davis and Lieutenant Anderson were always cash customers. In the fullness of time, Mr. Dixon, who had never taken thought for the morrow, particularly when his fellow man was in need or distress, came to an age when he felt constrained to marshal all of his resources and call in his few overlooked accounts. Among them was a large one against the United States Government, which of right should have been paid years before, but being in no immediate need, it had slipped along without attention. He finally applied for a land warrant for a quarter section of land to recompense him in a measure for the many and valuable services he had rendered his country during the Black Hawk War. A bill was introduced in Congress, passed by the Lower House, and in the

Senate was referred to the usual committee for consideration. This committee reported adversely on the bill, and when it was reported to the Senate for final action, Senator Trumbull, who well knew the merit of the case and greatly desired the passage of the measure, dispatched a message at once to Dixon to inquire if Mr. Dixon did not know of some friend in the Senate, as he did in the House, who would assist in its passage. On a moment's thought he replied to a friend, "Why, yes, there is Lieutenant Davis," whereupon the attention of Senator Jefferson Davis was called to the bill, and here is the record of what transpired:

From the Congressional Globe, First Session, 36th Congress.—June 8th, 1860, page 2751:

"JOHN DIXON.

"The Senate, as in Committee of the Whole, next proceeded to consider the bill (H. R. No. 236) for the relief of John Dixon, which had been reported adversely from the Committee on Public Lands. It directs the Secretary of the Interior to issue a bounty land warrant for one hundred and sixty acres to John Dixon, of Dixon's Ferry, in the State of Illinois, for services rendered in the Black Hawk war.

"Mr. Trumbull: 'I ask that the bill may be put upon its passage. I will remark that the Chairman of the Committee on Public Lands, with whom I had a conversation on the subject, stated that he reported adversely on this bill to grant a land warrant to Mr. Dixon, for the reason that the testimony before the Committee did not seem to be sufficient of his having rendered any service. He was not enlisted in the service, but he performed valuable service in the Black Hawk war—furnished supplies and acted as a guide and interpreter. He is an old man, over eighty years of age, and is now in very reduced circumstances. Some of his friends have made this application to get the old man a land warrant, and comes, I think, within the spirit of the law. The Senator from Mississippi (Mr. Davis), who served in the war, knows him personally, and perhaps he would make a statement to the Senate of his knowledge of the services for which it is proposed to grant a land warrant to this poor old man.'

"Mr. Davis: 'As stated by the Senator from Illinois, I do know this individual personally and believe him to be a very honest man, and I should have great confidence in his statement. He was one of the first pioneers in the country near what is now the town of Dixon, formerly known as Dixon's Ferry. He lived there in an isolated position when I first knew him. His house was reached by crossing a wide prairie country inhabited only by Indians. He was of great service in the first settlement of the country. He was of service to the troops when they ascended the Rock River in the Black Hawk campaign. For some time a post was established at or near his house. He was of service at that time in furnishing supplies and giving information in regard to the country, and afterwards in taking care of the sick. In a liberal spirit toward camp followers, we have since that time provided for packmen, for teamsters and for clerks, giving them bounty land warrants equally with the soldiers who were serving in the same campaign. I think the only objection in this case is the want of testimony, but I have such confidence in the individual, together with my recollection of the circumstances, that I would say that he was within the spirit of the law, and I should be glad, because of his many services in the first settlement of that country, to see him thus rewarded.'"

After a few exchanges of explanations, the bill passed the Senate, and the recollections of Senator Jefferson Davis of the days he spent at and about Mr. Dixon's log cabin saved the day for the bill.

It is not to be considered by any intelligent person that Mr. Davis would state on the floor of the United States Senate those facts, "from my recollection of the circumstances," if he had not been present in that campaign and witnessed them with the pleasantest of memories. The little old log tavern-store-house of the 1832 campaign came back to him with all its memories and Senator Davis saved the bill, as the records of the proceedings show.

The days when a man of years was young and his associations are never forgotten, and if any association under Heaven will evoke assistance from one to another it is an appeal to those early associations. And so it was with Senator Davis and Mr. Dixon.

Among others of subsequent prominence in the history of the State of Illinois, who formed the acquaintance of Mr. Davis during that campaign, and particularly while Taylor was stationed at Dixon's Ferry, was Col. John Dement, later a resident of the city of Dixon, where he died. For fifty years Colonel Dement was one of the foremost men of Illinois, and whenever he made a statement it carried conviction. He it was who fought the battle of Kellogg's Grove in that campaign, one of the fiercest of the many which occurred between Dixon's Ferry and Galena, retiring only after his clothing had been pierced with bullets and the Indians thoroughly checked from further molestation of the northwestern frontier.

Colonel Dement many times told me of his acquaintance with Lieutenant Davis and how it ripened into a strong friendship as the campaign progressed, and which continued for all time thereafter. He many times in his lifetime spoke of Lieutenant Davis during that campaign, in public; and in the form of historical narrative he reduced the same statements to writing, one of which I have.

At the breaking out of hostilities, Colonel Dement was State Treasurer, which station naturally carried with it considerable prestige in more ways than one, as proved to be the case a little later when he won for his bride the daughter of Gen. Henry Dodge, later Governor of Wisconsin and United States Senator, and, by the by, one of the most famous Indian fighters that ever lived.

Lieutenant Davis knew them both, bride and groom, from the early day, all through life, and at the death of the Colonel wrote to Mrs. Dement the following touching letter, in which the friendship of that famous old campaign is alluded to:

"Beauvoir, Miss., Feb. 4th, 1883.

"My Dear Friend: Of the many who will offer you condolence in your recent bereavement, there is not one who sympathizes more deeply with you than he who long years ago claimed the privilege of the sacred name of friend.

"Widely and long we have been separated, but your image has not been dimmed by time and distance.

"The gallantry and noble bearing of your deceased husband was known to all who, like myself, were on the frontier of Illinois during the campaign against Black Hawk, and from your brother, Augustus, and your friend, General Jones, I heard of him in after years.

"As your husband, he was to me the object of special interest, and it was a great gratification to me to learn that he was so worthy to be your life companion.

"If you have preserved enough of the pleasant memories of one springtime to care for one who flitted with you over the flowers of youth's happy garden, it will give me sincere gratification to hear from you and to learn of the welfare of yourself and children.

"With cordial regard for you and yours, and renewed assurance of my deep sympathy, I am ever,

"Faithfully your friend,

"JEFFERSON DAVIS."

The term "garden" is appropriately applied to the spring of the year 1832 and its successor, 1833. The summer of 1831 had been dry, and crops and vegetation had failed; the prairies had been left parched and brown, and but for the open-handed manner of the pioneer in helping his distressed brother, there had indeed been great suffering. But in 1832, barring the scare of the Indian campaign then carried on, the people were permitted to revel in a luxury of vegetation. Rains descended and the foliage of the trees was beautiful beyond description. The wild grape and cherry and plum, and the bee tree, laden with honey, were all free to him who cared to gather. Wild deer, turkeys, ducks, geese, grouse and squirrels were everywhere present in abundance for the huntsman, while the streams were plentifully stocked with fish. The wild rose spread out its blossoms over the prairies, and if man, though never so weary, could not revel in his surroundings he was sordid enough. The pathway of the pioneer was hard and coarse, but a thoughtful God seasoned his toil with many a blessing denied to us of the crowded city.

General Harney, in the latter years of his life, was very fond of speaking of those same beautiful days of springtime and the famous men he soldiered with at Dixon's Ferry and on through the campaign, and in all those reminiscences failed never to allude to Lieut. Jefferson Davis, beginning with him at the mouth of Rock River, when they began their march up to Dixon's Ferry. Reavis, in his biography, makes frequent quotations from those days and events in which both Harney and Davis took such active and conspicuous parts. In a recent correspondence with Mrs. John M. Harney of St. Louis I am told that full reliance can be placed upon the statements made by Mr. Reavis in that biography, and, furthermore, all statements contained in the same as emanating from General Harney were made in the presence of herself and Mr. Harney, and, independently of the book, Mrs. Harney confirms the presence of Lieutenant Davis in that campaign from General Harney himself, who in his lifetime so asserted many times.

Gen. John A. McClernand, the last living member of that famous band which gathered at Dixon's Ferry, wrote me, a very short time before his death, which but recently occurred, that he well knew it to be true that Lieutenant Davis was present and participated in the campaign to its close.

Later on, when Lieutenant Davis became Secretary of War, Colonel Strode, who had then removed to Woodstock, Illinois, and traveled the circuit from that point, was exceedingly fond of alluding to Jefferson Davis as his companion in arms during the Black Hawk War, and upon that point I have the correspondence, confirming the making of those claims at all times and upon all occasions, from so eminent an authority as Hon. H. W. Blodgett, for so many years United States Judge of this District.

Gen. George W. Jones, the first Senator in Congress from the State of Iowa, was a classmate of Jefferson Davis in their days of young manhood at Transylvania, and at his death was one of Mr. Davis' pallbearers. The college days, so dear to every man who has a soul, brought them together as only college days can bring men together, and if subsequent events should ever bring them together again, after separating to start out in life, it can scarcely be said that either could be mistaken in any material point concerning the history of the occasion. Certainly General Jones could not, and here is what he has written above his signature about the presence of Lieut. Jefferson Davis, his classmate, in the Black Hawk campaign:

Mr. F. R. Dixon. Dubuque, Jan. 16th, 1896.

My Dear Sir: Your letter of the 14th was received yesterday and I answer with pleasure.

My acquaintance with Mr. Jefferson Davis was formed at Transylvania University, Lexington, Kentucky, from 1821 to 1824; renewed in

1828 after he was graduated at West Point and commissioned Second Lieutenant of Infantry, U. S. A., when he served under Col. Zachary Taylor, at Fort Crawford, Wisconsin.

I, as Gen. Henry Dodge's aid-de-camp, served with Lieutenant Davis throughout the Black Hawk war, from its *inception* to its *close*. Later, we were brother United States Senators, and an intimate friendship existed between us throughout his life.

I knew your grandfather intimately, as also Colonel Dement, and esteemed them both highly. * * * Trusting that the foregoing is a satisfactory reply to your inquiry, I am,   Yours very sincerely,

GEO. W. JONES.

And here is what Gen. A. C. Dodge of Iowa, Senator in Congress with Jefferson Davis, has written on the subject:

"In 1832 we became associated in the famous Black Hawk war, he (Lieutenant Davis) as lieutenant of infantry, and I as aid-de-camp to Gen. Henry Dodge, commanding the militia of Michigan Territory. I often accepted his invitation to partake of his hospitality, as well as that of Gen. (then Captain) William S. Harney and Col. Zachary Taylor, who often divided their rations with me, as we volunteers were frequently in want of suitable food.

"The regulars were much better provided for than we volunteers were at the time. They were not only furnished with better rations and more of them, but they had tents, while we had none; and I shall never forget the generous hospitality of Lieutenant Davis, Col. Zachary Taylor, Capt. W. S. Harney and others of my brave and generous comrades of those days."[1]

There was no point in the material or political growth of that part of the then Michigan Territory (now Wisconsin), where Lieutenant Davis was stationed, that Generals Jones and Dodge were not identified with and thoroughly familiar. They were on the staff of General Dodge during the campaign, by reason of which and the exalted position of General Dodge they were upon terms of intimacy with the army officers of the war, beginning with Gen. Winfield Scott, who was chief in command after his arrival at Prairie du Chien.

In 1866, after the conclusion of the Civil War, and when the prominent men on both sides were in the minds of everyone, Rev. W. W. Harsha, then of Dixon, but later President of the Presbyterian Theological College at Omaha, Nebraska, was about to take a journey to New York City, at which point Gen. Robert Anderson was to be found, recovering from a very severe illness.

Commenting on the proposed trip to Mr. Dixon, the latter expressed a desire to have Mr. Harsha call upon the General, and, if remembered

---
[1] Jefferson Davis, a memoir by his wife. Vol. 1, p. 133.

by him, to convey to him the very best wishes of Mr. Dixon for his speedy recovery, and, in view of the prominence of Lieutenant Anderson, Lieutenant Davis and others who served in the Black Hawk campaign, recall the incidents of that early day and inquire if General Anderson remembered them. Mr. Harsha, upon his arrival, true to his promise, made the call, and the following letter, written at the time, gives the substance of the interview:

Chicago, April 29th, 1866.

My Dear Friend: Being recently in New York City on business, and finding myself one day in the neighborhood of General Anderson's residence, it occurred to me to call, and, partly on your account and partly on my own, make his acquaintance. I did so, and as soon as I told the General that I had lived eight years in Dixon, and I mentioned your name, he expressed himself greatly pleased to see me. He entered immediatly upon a minute and interesting detail of his experiences in Illinois and confirmed the statement which I had heard from you of his meeting Davis and Lincoln at your house at "Dixon's Ferry." He was very glad to hear that you were living and inquired affectionately after your health and the condition of your family. He seemed distressed to learn of your bereavements, and showed himself a man of true feeling.

He is, as you know, very much broken down in health. * * *

On parting from him the General says: "Tell my old friend, Mr. Dixon, that I shall probably not see him in this life again, but I hope to meet him in Heaven." * * *   Yours truly,

W. W. HARSHA.

To John Dixon, Dixon, Illinois.

Isaac N. Arnold, Lincoln's friend and biographer, specifically recalls a conversation with Lincoln, wherein the latter remembers and mentions the presence of Mr. Davis in that campaign.

Ben Perley Poore frequently heard Lincoln tell of Davis' presence in that campaign, and he has particularly told us so on page 218 of "Reminiscences of Abraham Lincoln."

After leaving Dixon's Ferry to march up the left bank of Rock River, the route became one of privation and hardship, particularly after reaching the bogs and swamps about Lake Koshkonong, where men fell ill by the score, and where others became so exhausted that they were sent back to the Ferry, to be later discharged. In many cases, detachments sent out among the swamps to chase the phantom Indian or guard some particular settlement against apprehended attack had nothing but pickled pork and a course dough for subsistence. The rains made the streams impassable, and many times, as at the Wisconsin, just before the battle of that name, the entire army, after making wearisome forced marches without sleep, were compelled to remain standing all night long before the battle, in a drenching rain, awaiting the hour in the morning when the attack might be made. Thus, day after day, the troops marched in clothing soaked with water, many falling by the wayside, to be carried to the rude hospitals improvised for the occasion, and even so rugged and powerful a man as General Henry, who won both the battle of the Wisconsin and the Bad Axe, sickened and died from the exposures of that campaign.[1]

Through all these vicissitudes Davis and Anderson and Johnston and Eaton were cheerful and buoyed up the men with encouraging words until back once more at Fort Crawford, where a more fearful enemy than exposure was met—the Asiatic cholera. Anderson and Johnston were stricken and suffered a long time the frightful agonies of that dread disease. There at his old and familiar quarters, Lieutenant Davis performed the duty demanded of him, of formally reporting himself back with his regiment for duty, August 16th, 1832.

Later, Black Hawk, Neapope, the Prophet and the other Indian leaders were captured and handed over to Lieut.-Col. Zachary Taylor as prisoners of war. Robert Anderson, in a letter to Hon. E. B. Washburne, has stated that he was designated as their custodian to take them to Jefferson Barracks, but that the fateful cholera prevented. In that he was mistaken; he took the second installment of prisoners.

We know from every man who served in that campaign and from every record that those prisoners were handed by Colonel Taylor to Lieut. Jefferson Davis to be taken to Jefferson Barracks. Following is from The Galenian of September 5th, 1832: "September 4th General Street, the Indian agent at Prairie du Chien, arrived to-day on board the steamboat Winnebago with about one hundred Sac prisoners, guarded by an escort of troops under command of Lieut. Jefferson Davis. Among the prisoners are the celebrated Black Hawk, the Prophet and La-ce-o-souck (The Thunder), son of Black Hawk; the latter was delivered on the night of the 3d. The prisoners were brought in by the Winnebagoes and the Sioux.

"The Winnebagoes came in, as we learn, so late on the night of the 3d with the prisoners, and the steamboat being there in waiting for them, General Street, instead of delivering them to Colonel Taylor, as heretofore, delivered them over to the charge of Colonel Anderson, who went on that commission, and who is now on his way to Rock Island with them."[2]

From the Galenian, a paper published in Galena, we find "locals" noting the presence of the noted prisoners and their guard, Jefferson Davis, at every point containing a newspaper, at which they stopped.

No reasonable person can believe that so honorable and responsible

---

[1] He died of consumption incited and accelerated by that exposure.
[2] Robert Anderson did take the second installment as far as Ft. Armstrong, where he was compelled to enter the hospital, from cholera.

THE BLACK HAWK WAR. 307

a post would have been given Lieutenant Davis had he not participated in the campaign with distinction.

With the most frightful epidemic of cholera at Fort Armstrong which they passed; with cholera about him in the boat, he reached Jefferson Barracks thoroughly exhausted, and feeling that he was entitled to the leave of absence which he had given up to enter this campaign, he applied for another and, receiving it, as he did in due time, he returned to Mississippi to enjoy it.

The experience gained in that campaign suggested his name for the command of a regiment of Mississippi troops in the war with Mexico, where he gained such fame as to bring forth the hearty thanks of Gen. Zachary Taylor on the field.

In conclusion, I wish to add a conversation which Mr. Aldrich, Curator of the Historical Department of Iowa, had with Mr. Davis about two years before the death of the latter.

Mr. Davis, in the course of this conversation, said much about Black Hawk and that campaign and his participation in it, and here is his narrative verbatim, of the Battle of the Wisconsin, in which he was engaged, taken down by Mr. Aldrich at the time: "We were one day pursuing the Indians, when we came close to the Wisconsin River. Reaching the river bank, the Indians made so determined a stand, and fought with such desperation, that they held us in check. During this time the squaws tore bark from the trees, with which they made little shallops, in which they floated their papooses and other impedimenta across to an island, also swimming over the ponies. As soon as this was accomplished, half of the warriors plunged in and swam across, each holding his gun in one hand over his head, and swimming with the other. As soon as they reached the opposite bank, they also opened fire upon us, under cover of which the other half slipped down the bank and swam over in like manner. This," said Mr. Davis, "was the most brilliant exhibition of military tactics that I ever witnessed—a feat of most consummate management and bravery, in the face of an enemy of greatly superior numbers. I never read of anything that could be compared with it. Had it been performed by white men, it would have been immortalized as one of the most splendid achievements in military history."

Black Hawk in his book, page 107, states the facts of that retreat pretty much as Mr. Davis did to Mr. Aldrich, excepting only to take no especial credit to himself or his braves for strategy.

As Black Hawk was taken down the Mississippi by Lieutenant Davis, the two were in frequent conversation, and naturally each studied the other more or less, and while Mr. Davis, in after years, always spoke of his prisoner in the very highest terms, it may be interesting to know what Black Hawk had to say about his captor when he came to write his autobiography the following year: "We remained here a short time, and then started for Jefferson Barracks in a steamboat, under charge of a young war chief (Jefferson Davis), who treated us with much kindness. He is a good and brave young chief, with whose conduct I was much pleased. On our way down we called at Galena and remained a short time. The people crowded to the boat to see us, but the war chief would not permit them to enter the apartment where we were, knowing from what his feelings would have been if he had been placed in a similar position, that we did not wish to have a gaping crowd around us."

Little can be said for the negative of this question and less can be proven, and with such a unanimity of testimony in favor of his presence, from those who saw him and there formed his acquaintance and friendship, it cannot be perceived how an assumption, an "interpretation" can be allowed to rob him of that honor.

MAJ. GEN. ALEXANDER MACOMB, COMMANDER-IN-CHIEF, U. S. A.

WA-PEL-LO, CHIEF OF THE FOXES.

FORT WINNEBAGO; ERECTED LARGELY BY LIEUT. JEFFERSON DAVIS.

INDEX

	PAGE
Abercrombie, J. J.	120
Account of Manner of Enlistment	119
Adair, William (Capt.)	194
Adair, William (L't.-Col.)	190
Adams County	117, 125
Adams, John G. (Capt.)	125, 130, 133, 134, 135, 138, 141, 145, 148
Adams, John G., Mrs.	135
Adams, Parker	140
Adams, Samuel (Col.)	191
Adopted Son Story	43
Aird, James	54
Albany, N.Y.	263
Aldenrath, Benj. J.	142
Aldrich, Charles	Introduction and 2d Appendix
Alexander County	195
Alexander, David C.	126
Alexander, Milton K. (Gen.)	93, 98, 191, 195, 202, 205, 208, 209, 210, 211, 212, 213, 214, 215, 220, 221, 222, 223, 228, 287
Alexander, of Russia	48
Alexander, T. L.	111, 120
Allen, William	200
Al-lo-tah	98
Ament, John L.	192
American Phrenological Journal	19
American Temperance House	245
Ames, Orestes	118
Amhurstburgh	68
An-a-wash-queth	64
Anderson, Fannie (Mrs.)	270
Anderson, George (L't.)	120
Anderson, Robert (L't.)	126, 172, 173, 175, 189, 226, 227, 286, 293, 294, 299, 304
Anderson, Stinson B.	190
Anderson, T. G. (Capt.)	67
Annoyances	81
Annuities of Sacs and Foxes	84
An-o-wart	64
Appel, Henry	182
Apple River	131, 174, 183, 186
Apple River Fort	172, 183, 184, 185, (battle) and 186, 187, 286
A-qua-o-sa	64
Arabian Nights	96
Archambeau, Mr.	56

	PAGE
Archer, Col. William B.	191, 224
Arenz, Francis	93
Argyle	209
Armstrong, Aaron (Capt.)	193
Armstrong, Elizabeth (Mrs.)	186
Armstrong, Gen. John	66
Armstrong, John	278, 281, 282
Armstrong, Perry A	59
Arnett, J. T. (Capt.)	194, 202
Arnold, John (Capt.)	191
A-sam-e-saw	98
Ashton, Capt. Eliakem	169
Asiatic Cholera	242
As-shaw-e-qua	268, 272, 273, 274
Atkins, A.	93
Atkinson, Henry (Gen.)	106, 110, 111, 112, 113, 114, 116, 120, 121, 127, 141, 142, 145, etc., 157, 161, 163, 169, 171, 172, 173, 175, 177, 180, 181, 185, 188, 189, 197, 202, 205, 206, 209, 210, 212, 214, 215, 216, 219, 220, 221, 222, 223, 225, 228, 230, 234, 238, 240, 247, 259, 261, 283, 284, 293, 294
Atkinson's Report Bad Axe	228
Atlas, Ill.	119
Attack on the "Oliver H. Perry" and Consort, in 1827	73, 74, 75
Aubrey, William	180
Ausbery, Griffith	82
Autobiography of Black Hawk	19, 31
Aztalan	217
Bache, Hartman (Capt.)	247
Backus, Electus (L't.)	189
Bad Axe River	20, 73, 223, 226, 227, 295
Bad Axe Battle	167, 168, 223, 295
Bailey, Maj. David	113, 125, 126, 130, 141, 145, 193, 204
Bailey, Capt. Alexander	169
Bailly, Joseph	55
Bain, John L.	82
Baird, Scipio	124
Baker, Daniel (L't. Col.)	120, 193
Baker, Edward D. (L't.)	2d Appendix
Baker, Mrs. E. B.	176
Baker, James	123
Baldridge, David	194
Ball, Azel F. (Capt.)	125, 145, 193

309

THE BLACK HAWK WAR.

	PAGE
Ball, Japhet A. (Capt.)	125
Baltimore	261, 264
Band, James B.	200
Bankson, Andrew (Capt.)	194
Bannon, Aaron (Capt.)	194
Banquet at Ft. Madison	270
Barker, Thomas (Capt.)	120
Bark River	209
Barlow, L't. Col. J. W.	191
Barnes, David W. (Capt.)	125, 135, 145
Barnes, John (Capt.)	191
Barnes, Robert (Capt.)	159
Barney, Benj. (Capt.)	120, 125
Barnhart, Peter	159
Barnsback, Julius L. (Capt.)	124
Barrel, John	82
Barrett's Ferry	226, 236
Barron, Joseph	30
Barrott	55
Bartlett, Michael	82
Batman, M. W. (L't.)	120
Battle of 1800	23
Battle of the Wisconsin Heights	218, 221
Baylor, Dr.	189
Bays, Capt. John	190
Beach, Maj. John	40
Beall, Alexander (Maj.)	123, 194
Beall, Thomas J.	126, 145
Beardstown	85, 93, 117, 154, 157, 160, 188, 278, 279, 282, 283
Beauchamp	73, 74, 75
Beauty of Rock Island	95
Beckwith, L't. Col. Daniel W.	169
Beggs, Rev. S. R.	167
Belleville	159
Bells, Mr.	154, 156
Beloit	205
Beltrami, J. C.	17, 67
Benett, Louis	55
Bennett, Hiram C.	118, 123
Bennett, Redding	142
Bequette, Paschal	131, 183
Beresford, James	203
Berry, E. C.	94, 116
Berry, Thomas G. (Col.)	160
Best, ——	55
Biggerstaff, Ardin (Capt.)	190
Big Indian Creek	147
Big Sioux River	100
Birch, Benjamin	124
Birth of Black Hawk	17
Bivens, John	143
Black Hawk, Bones	274
Black Hawk, Burial	273
Black Hawk, Capacities	20
Black Hawk, Death	272
Black Hawk, Grave Robbed	273
Black Hawk, Not a Chief	21, 80
Black Hawk, Village, See V.	
Black, James	200
Black, Samuel	183
Blackburn, James M. (Col.)	191, 224
Blackmaars, Mich.	256
Blackwell, J. A.	123
Blackwell, John H.	94

	PAGE
Blackwell, Robert	124, 139
Black Snake Hills	103
Black Thunder	87
Blair, F. P.	230
Bliss, John (Maj.)	94, 98, 106, 107, 120, 121, 145, 161, 224
Blondeaux, Maurice	61
Blodgett, H. W.	303
Bloomington, Ill.	159
Blue Earth River	101 and affair there, 102, 103
Blue Mounds	143, 153, 154, 180, 183, 212, 219, 220, 221, 236
Bogart, Maj. Samuel	193
Bolen, Hypolite	30
Bond, Benjamin	194
Bond County	117, 125, 164, 194
Bones of Black Hawk	18
Boone, Levi D. (Capt.)	125
Boone, Nathan (Col.)	2d Appendix
Boston	263
Bouchard, Edward D.	183
Bounty Land Warrants	77
Boutillier, Francois	54
Bowers, Maj. George	191
Bowman, Capt. ——	130
Bowman, James (Capt.)	190
Bowman, Samuel (L't.)	204, 224
Bowyer, George P. (Capt.)	190, 191
Boxley, James	187
Boyce, W. M. (L't.)	120
Boyd, Col. George	234, 235
Boyd, James M. (L't.)	235
Boyd's Grove	130
Bracken, Charles	131, 181, 183
Bradley, H.	245
Brady, Gen. Hugh	120, 181, 189, 193, 195, 202, 203, 209
Bradford, Abner	200
Branson, Dr. Milton K.	194
Brazhere, William	82
Breese, Sidney (L't. Col.)	194, 211
Briggs, Josiah S. (Capt.)	194, 205, 206, 218
Briggs, Benjamin (L't.)	145
Brigham, Ebenezer	143, 181
Brigham, Sylvester	192
Brimberry, Samuel (Capt.)	191
Brishois, ——	54
Bristol, John E.	136
Bristol, R. C. (Capt.)	244
Bristow, George	93
Bristow, George F. (Capt.)	194
British	40, 42, 51, 53, 55, 57, 58, 66, 67
British Agents	25, 26, 32, 38, 41, 44, 46
British Band	39, 48, 55, 63, (including Rock River Sacs) 64, 88, 97, 103, 114
British Flags	31, 58
British Indians	26, 41
Broken Shoulder	114
Brooke, L't. F. J.	120
Brooks, Col. Edward	256, 257, 258
Brown, A. C.	136
Brown, Brig. Gen.	254, 256, 257, 258
Brown, Gust. (L't.)	243

THE BLACK HAWK WAR. 311

Brown, Jacob (Capt.)............ 120
Brown, Reuben (Capt.).......... 195
Brown, William................. 191
Brown, William G............93, 123
Browne, Thomas C.............. 189
Browning, O. H............117, 118
Browning, O. H., Diary of....... 117
Brown's Creek.................. 287
Bruff, J........................ 30
Brush Creek.................... 170
Buchanan, L't.................. 248
Buckmaster, Nathaniel (Maj.).....
.....94, 116, 118, 119, 122, 125,
132, 162, 163, 167, 169, 193, 284, 285
Buffalo Grove..................
........131, 142, 169, 176, 200, 202
Buffalo, N. Y............242, 243, 263
Buisson, Louis.................. 55
Bunts, Samuel.................. 183
Burbank, Sid. (L't.)............ 126
Bureau Creek.......130, 148, 192, 197
Bureau County............154, 157
Burlington Hawk Eye............ 19
Burlington, Iowa.............78, 270
Burner, Edward................. 82
Burnett, J. P................... 226
Burning of Black Hawk's Bones.. 274
Burns, James (Capt.)............ 194
Burnt Village...............209, 210
Burr Oak Grove............156, 176
Burton, Thomas................. 124
Butler, Nathaniel 94
Butler, Peter (Capt.)............ 193
Butler, Walter (Capt.).......... 194

Cady, Albert (L't.).............. 120
Caldwell, Billy (Chief)..........
.................166, 189, 204, 205
Call of May 15.................. 139
Calumet River................... 100
Campaign of 1831,.......92, Closed 95
Campbell, John (L't.).......49, 50, 51
Campbell, John, His Battle....49, 50
Campbell, L't. Col. ———......... 190
Camp Whitewater................ 234
Camp Wisconsin................. 219
Canada 26
Cap au Gris.................49, 55
Carlin, Thomas (Capt.)........93, 125
Carnes, William................. 183
"Caroline," Steamboat.......160, 188
Caron, J. B., 64, and Caron........ 236
Carondelet 55
Carpenter, William.............. 123
Car-ra-ma-na 231
Cartwright, Rev. Peter....195, 281, 290
Case, Jonah H................... 82
Casey, Zadock............190, 199, 200
Cas-kup-wa 64
Cass County................154, 157
Cass, Lewis (Gen.)..............
.......100, 106, 238, 255, 265, 285
Cassell, Henry K................ 159
Cassville 143, 236
Castle Garden................... 262
Catch-e-nack-e-seo 61

Catlin, George.................. 84
Chadwick, Joseph M..........122, 130
Cha-e-ter 229, 231, 232
Cha-go-sort 61
Cha-kee-pax-he-pa-ho 98
Chapman, Ammyson...........83, 84
Chapman, Thomas................ 124
Charless, Joseph................. 64
Che-ka-qua 61
Cherokees 22, 23
Chicago 38, 42, 167, 169, 193,
242, 243, 254, 256, 257, 258, 290, 292
Chicago Historical Society........ 244
Chic-hon-sic 72, 76
Chick-a-ka-la-ko 98
Childs, Tyrus M................. 135
Chippewa, Battle................. 42
Chippewas 24, 72, 100, 105
Cholera, See Scott's Expedition.
Chouteau, Auguste....30, 60, 61, 63, 64
Chouteau, Pierre...............30, 61
Christy, Samuel C...........93, 94, 116
Cintajah 101
Clament 103
Clark, B. A..................... 190
Clark, Capt. ———, of Wis.......... 209
Clark County.................... 191
Clark, I., Jr. (Capt.)..........120, 180
Clark, James N. (Capt.).......... 190
Clark, Meriwether Lewis.......120, 189
Clark, William (Gov and Gen.)..38,
47, 48, 50, 55, 58, 60, 61, 63,
64, 80, 85, 86, 87, 88, 89, 90, 91, 100,
102, 103, 105, 106, 107, 154, 156, 261
Clark, Gov. William, Boat......48, 50
Clary, Royal.................... 278
Clary, William.................. 278
Clary's Grove Boys.............. 278
Clay County................103, 190
Clay, Henry.................... 273
Clay, Henry, The—A Boat........ 242
Claywell, Jesse (Capt.).......... 194
Cleveland, Loren 177
Clinton County.................. 194
Coffey, Achilles (Capt.).......... 190
Coles County.................... 191
Collins, Charles O. (L't.)......... 253
Collins, James (Col.)...........
.............194, 196, 214, 216, 218
Collins, Thomas................. 93
Columbia, Mo................... 160
Co-mee 148, 149, 157
Conditions of Early Settlers........ 78
Congress Hall Hotel............. 19
Connor, James (Capt.).......... 194
Conrod, John (L't.)............. 120
Constant, William............... 123
Converse, Daniel................ 61
Cook, Horace.................... 82
Cook, William.................. 124
Cooke, P. St. George (L't.)...... 120
Cornelius, J. M. McT.....123, 178, 179
Cornstalk 20
Correspondence of 1831....83 to 89 inc.
Council of 1831................. 92
Council of Sept. 25, 1831.......... 107

	PAGE
Covell, M. L. (Capt.)	..125, 137, 145, 159
Cowen, William (L't.-Col.)	159
Cox, Alexander D. (Capt.)	164
Cox, John	39
Craig, B. B. (Capt.)	196, 282
Craig, Capt. ——, of War 1812	56
Craig, Capt. James, War 1812	190
Craig, Capt. James, Jo Daviess Co.	142, 184, 215
Craig, Capt. Jonathan	142
Craig, N. B.	184
Crain, James W.	126
Cranberry Lake	215
Crane, Col.	243
Crawfish River	217
Crawford County	76, 191
Crocker, Thomas	117
Crooked Creek	117, 279
Cross, L't. ——	240
Crossman, G. H. (L't.)	120, 204
Crow, David	118, 125
Cuivre River	55
Cummings, Col. ——	243
Cummings, Mr. ——	167
Curran, Catherine Buckmaster—Introduction.	
Cutler, Enos (L't. Col.)	121
Cutright, Temperance	150
Dad Joe's Grove	130
Dakotas	72, 73
Dale, George W.	119
Dalles of Wisconsin	229, 231
Danforth, Joseph	82, 98
Danville	189
Davenport, George	110, 259
Davenport, William (Maj. and Col.)	120, 121, 188, 193, 208, 265
Davis, Alexander	150
Davis, Jefferson (L't.)	120, 122, 141, 142, 192, 198, 240, 284, Appendix, 290
Davis, Jimmie	157
Davis, Maj. ——	255
Davis, Robert	123
Davis, Thomas	82
Davis, William	147
Davitts, ——	221
Dawson, John	125
Day, Hannibal (Lt.)	246
Deace, Capt.	47
De Camp, Samuel G. I. (Surgeon)	246
Decatur, Ill.	159
Decori, which includes "One-eyed Decori"	210, 228, 231, 232
Dee Sulhorst, Justus	143
De Kalb County	130
De Hart, William C. (L't.)	243
De Lassus, Gov.	171
De Lassus, Pierre C.	171
Delauney, D.	30
Dement, John (Maj.)	93, 125, 130, 140, 164, 187, 190, 192, 197, 198, 208, 209, 301
Dement, Mrs. John	302
Dement's Battle	200, 201
Dennis, John H.	84

	PAGE
Desertion from British Army	42
Des Moines Rapids	37, 111
Des Moines River	37, 38, 54, 57, 100, 268, 272, 273
Des Plaines River	167, 188
Detroit	42, 254, 256, 257, 258, 263
Devees' or Devies'	183, 209
Devil's Creek	268
Dewey, Stephen	84
De Witt, A. B. (Col.)	123, 146
Diamond Grove	143
Dickson, Joseph (Capt.)	209, 217, 223, 224
Dickson, Robert	41, 42, 47, 48, 54
Dimmick, Ziba	192
Disobedience of Officers	214
Disorders	162
Dixon, Frederick	185
Dixon, F. Louise (Miss)	292
Dixon, John	129, 140, 174, 176, 222, 290, 300
Dixon, John (Mrs.)	130
Dixon Land Office	140
Dixon's Ferry	35, 113, 114, 116, 118, 119, 120, 125, 126, 127, 128, 129, 131, 139, 140, 141, 142, 146, 161, 163, 169, 172, 173, 176, 177, 179, 181, 185, 188, 189, 192, 195, 197, 198, 200, 202, 203, 204, 205, 211, 247, 248, 282, 283, 284, 286, 287, 290, et seq.
Dobbins, William N. (Capt.)	190
Dodge, A. C. (Gen.)	78, 304
Dodge, Henry (Col.)	131, 140, 142, 143, 156, 169, 173, 174, 175, 180, 181, 182, 183, 201, 202, 206, 207, 208, 209, 211, 213, 214, 215, 216, 217, 218, 219, 220, 221, 222, 223, 225, 230, 246, 255, 301, 302
Dodge, Henry L.	78, 131
Dodge, Mrs. Henry	182, 200
Dodgeville	143, 236
Donaldson, Dr.	134
Door Prairie	256, 257
Doris, Martin W.	104
Dorr, Gustavus (L't.)	120
Dorrance, L't.	248
Dorsey, Charles S. (Capt.)	159
Doty, Capt.	160
Doty, James	134, 135
Doty, James D. (Judge)	76
Dougherty, John	103
Douglas, Stephen A.	175
Dover	192
Dowling, Nicholas (Capt.)	120
Doyle, Edward	123, 142, 298
Drakeford, L't.	55
Draper, Joseph	135, 136
Draper, L. C.	108
Draper, —— (Capt.)	193
Drayton, Thomas F. (L't.)	120
Drum, R. C. (Gen.)	162
Drummond's Island	67
Dubuque	102
Dubuque Mines	47, 102, 120
Dulaney, William H., Dr.	118, 123, 164

THE BLACK HAWK WAR. 313

Duncan, Asa... 183
Duncan, Enoch... 143
Duncan, Joseph (Gen.)... 93-96
Duncan, Matthew... 124
Dunlap, Adams... 123
Dunlap, Samuel... 191
Dunn, Charles (Capt.)
  ...190, 191, 208, 210, 211, 287
Dunnivan, William L... 203
Du Page River... 145, 161, 167, 188
Du Page Settlements... 191
Durley, James... 123
Durley, William... 142, 169
Durman, Jonathan (Capt.)... 190, 191

Eads, Abner... 125, 133, 137, 145
Eames, Charles... 183, 184
Early, Jacob M. (Capt.)...
  ...175, 196, 210, 211, 286, 287
Eaton, John H... 91
Eaton, Nathaniel J... 111, 120
Ebey, Jacob... 125
Eckles, Hon. James H... 149
Edgar County... 191
Eddy, Henry (Col.)... 116
Eddy, John M... 123
Edgerton, Mr., the Phrenologist... 18
Edwards, Abraham (L't.-Col.)... 258
Edwards County... 191
Edwards, Cyrus... 122
Edwards, Ninian (Gov.)...
  ...55, 60, 61, 63, 64
Eldon, Iowa... 273
Election, Dodge vs. Posey... 201
Elizabeth, Illinois... 183, 286
Elk Grove... 143
Elkin, William F... 93
Ellis, Bird W... 135, 136
English Prairie... 236
England... 25, 38
Engle, James (L't.)... 121
English, Levin N... 123
English, The... 26, 57
Epperson, Elijah... 165
Estes, Capt. ———... 219, 220
Eubanks, William (Maj.)... 191
Eustis (Col.)... 246, 247, 248, 249, 260
Evans, James (Maj.)... 193
Ewing, John (Col.)...
  ...127, 139, 190, 211, 287
Ewing, W. L. D. (Maj.)...
  ...195, 216, 217, 218, 223, 224
Ewing, Trammel (L't.)... 200, 202
Exeter... 194, 209

Fairmount... 262
Fanchier, G. B... 287
Fal-sa-voine... 47, 55, 57
Farnham & Davenport... 251
Farris, Joseph B... 135
Fayette County... 125, 195
Feaman, Jacob (Capt.)... 194
Fevre River... 154
Field, Alex. P... 193
Fitch, M. G... 183
Fitzpatrick, William... 123

Flack... 185
Flannagan, Dr. George... 191
Flood, Wm. G... 117, 125
Floyd, Aquilla... 169
Fonda, John H... 108
Force, George (L't.)... 183
Ford, Capt. ———... 248
Ford, Thomas (Gov.)...
  ...95, 158, 184, 220
Forristal, James G... 192
Forsythe, Thomas... 67, 80, 169
Fortieth Regiment... 159
Fortress Monroe... 242-260
Foster, Amos (L't.)... 121
Foster, John F... 123
Four Lakes... 205, 206, 221
Four Lakes Conference... 143
Fourth Lake... 217
Fowler, John... 169, 170, 171, 181
Fowlers, Phrenologists... 19
Fox River, Ill... 145,
  148, 161, 177, 181, 189, 202, 203, 285
Fox River, Wis... 27, 35
Foxes Attacked by Menominees... 102
France... 24, 25, 58
Franklin County... 190, 193
Franks, Jacob... 54
Fraser, Upton S. (Capt.)... 253
Freeman, Elam S... 117, 118, 123
Freeman, Jonathan (L't.)... 120
French and English War... 26
French, Charles... 82
Frenchtown... 42
Fry, Jacob (Col.)... 93, 117,123,
  146, 164, 172, 188, 194, 196, 205,
  206, 210, 214, 216, 217, 218, 222, 223
Ft. Armstrong...
  ...66, 67, 92, 94, 95, 96, 97, 107,
  115, 121, 126, 141, 145, 166, 171,
  238, 239, 248, 249, 263, 264, 265, 273
Ft. Beggs... 167
Ft. Clark... 62, 290
Ft. Crawford... 104, 107,
  112, 114, 121, 126, 168, 204, 230, 295
Ft. Dearborn... 119, 243, 257, 258
Ft. Dearborn Massacre... 41
Ft. Defiance... 143, 180, 181
Ft. Deposit... 140, 188, 189
Ft. Dixon... 161, 198
Ft. Gratiot... 242, 243, 247
Ft. Hamilton... 143, 170,
  181, 183, 200, 201, 202, 208, 209, 211
Ft. Harmar... 32
Ft. Howard... 55, 56
Ft. Independence... 52
Ft. Jackson... 143
Ft. Johnston... 172, 189, 192
Ft. Koshkonong... 212, 220, 221
Ft. Madison... 35,
  37, 38, 39, 41, 43, 45, 46, 268, 270
Ft. Meigs... 42
Ft. Ottawa... 196
Ft. Payne... 247, 258
Ft. Selby, Including Capture and
  Loss... 47, 48, 51
Ft. Snelling... 72, 73

THE BLACK HAWK WAR.

Ft. Stephenson 42
Ft. Union 143
Ft. Wayne 38
Ft. Wilbourn.............140, 159, 172, 188, 189, 194, 196, 204, 205, 286
Ft. Winnebago....112, 114, 121,189, 208, 211, 212, 213, 214, 215, 235, 287
Fulton County........125, 132, 169, 193
Fulton, Judge A. R................. 108
Funk, Mr. ———, of McLean Co.. 198

Gagnier, Louisa.................... 76
Gagnier, Madame................72, 73
Gagnier, Registre.........72, 73, 75, 76
Gaines, Gen. Edmund P......84, 86, 88, 89, 90, 91, 92, 93, 94, 95, 96, 238
Gale, Levin (Lt.).................. 120
Galena..............120, 129, 141, 142, 154, 156, 169, 170, 172, 176, 177, 182, 184, 185, 186, 187, 197, 198, 204, 209, 211, 215, 239, 247, 286
Gallatin County.........189, 190, 193
Galt, P. H. (L't.)....243, 247, 249, 253
Gardiner, Thomas.................. 82
Gardenier, J. R. B. (L't.)—This officer's name has been written throughout the work "I." R. B., because the early prints so had it; but by reference to the old army register, "J." is now found to be correct.............120, 142, 204, 295
Garland, John (Maj.)..260, 261, 264, 266
Gatewood, Jeff. (L't.-Col.)......... 190
Gear, H. H. (Capt.).......142, 296, 297
Gentry, James H.....131, 143, 183, 209
Gentry, Maj.-Gen................... 160
General Order of Gen. Wood...... 160
George, Henry...................... 148
Gillespie, Joseph............94, 164, 177
Gillham, Isom M................... 93
Gillham, James (L't.-Col.)......... 193
Gillham, John F................... 94
Gillham, William.............93, 194
Gillispie, Capt. I. M............... 169
Givens, William T. (Capt.)......... 125
Goble, Benjamin.................... 82
Gooden, Levi W. (Capt.)......125, 184
Gordon, George.................... 124
Gordon, William (Capt.).......194, 205
Governor's Call of May 15......... 139
Graham, Duncan........54, 57, 58, 60
Graham, John A.................... 262
Graham, Mr. ———.................. 39
Graham, W. M. (L't.).............. 120
Grand Mascatin.................... 80
Grant, Alex. F..................... 193
Gratiot, Charles................... 30
Gratiot, Henry (Col.)...90, 91, 114, (His Rescue), 115, 131, 143, 153, 180
Gratiot, J. R. B. (Capt.)......143, 180
Gratiot's Grove...........114, 129, 143, 153, 180, 181
Grave Robbed...................... 273
Graves, (Ward..................... 159
Gray Tail, The.................... 101
Great Britain..................... 25

Great Butte des Morts............ 236
Great Eagle....................... 18
Greathouse, John S............... 98
Green Bay.........................
 ....41, 42, 47, 226, 234, 235, 263, 292
Green, Emerson.................... 183
Green, Royal P.................... 281
Green, Sion R..................... 124
Greene County........117, 125, 164, 194
Greenough, J. K. (L't.).........94, 120
Greer, Abner (Capt.).............. 191
Gregoire, Marie P................. 171
Gregory, Charles (L't.-Col.)...118, 123
Gregory, James (Capt.)............ 169
Gridley, Asahel (L't.)............. 137
Griffin, John...................... 30
Griffin, Robert (Capt.)............ 191
Grigneau Bros. (Grignon meant).. 54
Grignon, Sr., Augustin............ 235
Grignon, Jr., Charles (Capt.)...... 235
Grignon, Robert (L't.)............ 235
Grizzly Bear...................... 236
Guirano, Guyolde.................. 65
Gulf of Mexico.................... 109
Gunn, Aaron....................... 192

Hackleton, Mr. ———............... 132
Hail, David B..................... 82
Haines, Alfred.................... 130
Haines, James..................... 130
Haines, John...................... 93
Haines, Jonathan.................. 130
Hale, Ozias (Capt.)............... 194
Hale, William............169, 170, 171
Hall, Alex. P..................... 190
Hall, Edward H..........150, 153, 154
Hall, Elizabeth................... 150
Hall, Greenbury................... 150
Hall, James (Capt.)............... 190
Hall, John W..........149, 150, 153, 154
Hall, Mary J. R................... 150
Hall, Oliver W..............134, 136
Hall, Rachel and Sylvia..149 et seq., 180
Hall, Reason 153
Hall, William.............147, 150, 181
Halsted, C. V..................... 194
Hamilton and Bigelow............. 158
Hamilton, Alexander..........132, 205
Hamilton County.................. 190
Hamilton, Thomas (L't.)....39, 40, 58
Hamilton, William S..............
 ....131, 132, 143, 146, 181, 182, 209, 210, 234, 235, 291, 292
Hamilton's Diggings............... 292
Hancock County.............125, 193
Hardin, John J. (Col.).....93, 164, 279
Hargrave, Willis (Col.)........... 190
Harney, Mrs. John M.............. 303
Harney, W. S. (Capt.)...120, 122, 126, 141, 161, 211, 212, 224, 294, 302
Harris, John...................... 125
Harrison, George...........287, 288
Harrison, Jesse M................. 124
Harrison, Thomas.................. 125
Harrison, William Henry (Gov.)...
 ....26, 27, 29, 33, 38

THE BLACK HAWK WAR. 315

Harsha, Rev. W. W. 304
Hart, Nathan. 194
Hash-e-quar-hi-qua 27, 30, 31
Haskins, Moses. 124
Hatton, Capt. 248
Havana, Ill. 288
Hawley, Aaron. 169, 170
Haws, William (Capt.) 159
Hawthorn, John (Sg't.-Maj.) 194
Hawthorn, John (Surgeon) 194
Haynes, John (Capt.) 191
Hayse, Dr. B. M. 159
Hazleton, ——— 203
Headen, William. 124
Heans, William. 82
Helena, Wis. 221, 222
Hempstead, Charles S. 76
Hempstead, L't. 53
Henderson, John and J. H..147 et seq.
Henderson, L't. ——— 50
Henderson River. ....
 .... 84, 118, 192, 197, 279, 280
Henderson, Vawter. 124
Henry, James D. (Gen.).79, 93, 123,
 125, 127, 141, 164, 173, 174, 175,
 193, 198, 201, 202, 203, 205, 207,
 211 212, 213, 214, 215, 216, 218,
 219, 220, 221, 222, 223, 225, 228, 287
Henry, William. 82
Herclerode, George W. 187
Hewitt, ——— 118
Heyl, Serg't. ——— 244
Hickman, Benj. F. 193
Hickory Creek. 167, 188
Hickory Point. 181
Hicks, B. (Q. M.) 190
Higbee, Charles. 94
Higginbotham, Alex. 169, 183
Highsmith, William (Capt.) 191
Hill, Dr. Allen. 183
Hinman, William. 119
Hitchcock, E. A. (Capt.) 120
Hoard, Capt. ——— 143, 181
Hodges, J. 192
Hoffman, William (L't.) 120
Hogan, John S. C. (L't.) 119
Holderman Settlement. 148
Hollenback, George B. 166
Hollenback, George M. ... 166, 167, 202
Hollenback's Grove. 167
Holliday, Joel (Capt.) 190
Hollingsworth, Samuel. 125
Holman, Armstead (Capt.) 190
Holmes R. (L't.) 120, 189, 204
Hood, John. .... 183, and see p. 224
Hook, Cornelius. 193
Hook, James H. (Capt.) 120
Horine, Michael. 124
Horn, Reddick (Rev. and Maj.)...
 .... 122, 140, 154, 188, 189, 194
Horn, W. S. 150, 154
Horney, Samuel. 123
Houston, Alex. (Capt.) 191
How, Mr. ——— of Platt. 227
Howard, Allen. 147, 150
Howard, Benj. 124

Howard, Gen. 48
Howard, Stephen P. 183, 184
Hubbard, Gurdon S. (L't.) 169
Hull, ———, Surrender of. 41
Hulls, M. S. 82
Hunt, Richard. 159
Hunter, Charles W. 65
Hunter, John T. (Q. M.) 191
Hunter, Solomon (Capt.) 191
Huron, Lake. 38
Hussey, Nathan. 193
Hustisford 215
Huston, A. (Col.) 257, 258
Huston, James (Maj.) 190
Huston, Samuel (Capt.) 195
Hutching, Private ——— 224
Hutt, Corbin R. (Capt.) 169
Hutter, George C. 111, 120

Iles, Elijah (Capt.) ....
 .... 145, 164, 172, 177, 286
Illinois Rapids. 188, 195, 197
Illinois River. 26, 27, 35, 62,
 77, 111, 116, 139, 140, 146, 148, 188
Indian Creek. 146, 148, 202, 203
Indian Creek Massacre. ....
 .... 119, 146, 149 et seq., 160, 167
Indian Creek, Mich. 256
Indian Maiden at Fort Madison.... 40
Indiana 25, 258
Ingalls, Boone. 65
Interim Regiment. 164
Iometah 236
Iowa River. 80, 106, 109, 224
Iowa Village. 103, 269
Iowa Village, Battle at. 69, 70
Iowas 57, 69, 70, 100, 272, 273
Irwin, Alex. J. 235

Jackson, Andrew. ....
 57, 58, 60, 193, 212, 242, 260, 261, 273
Jackson, Capt. ——— 255, 256, 258
Jacksonville 194
James, Benj. 125, 164, 194
James, John. 124
James, Thomas (Maj.) ....
 .... 124, 125, 146, 161
Jarrot, Vital. 122
Jarrott, Francis. 164, 178
Jefferson Barracks. ....
 .... 89, 110, 121, 225, 240, 294
Jefferson County. 190
Jefferson, Thomas. 27
Jeffreon River 32
Jenkins, A. M. (Capt.) 196
Jenkins, Thomas. 183
Jo Daviess County. 19, 140, 142
Jo Daviess Militia. 131
Johnson, George (Capt.) 235
Johnson, James (Capt. and Col.)
 .... 125, 126, 145, 157, 189
Johnson, James F. (Q. M.) 190
Johnson, John 38
Johnson, John W. (Capt.) 61
Johnson, Seth (Capt.) 246

Johnston, Albert Sidney (L't.).... 111, 120, 140, 147, 161, 162, 189, 195, 196, 197, 205, 211, 225, 248, 286, 293, 294
Johnston, John D.................. 287
Johnston, Joseph E................ 253
Johnston, L. (L't.)............... 67
Johnston, Nathan.................. 178
Johnston, N. C.................... 124
Johnston, N. H.................... 193
Johnston, William P. (Col.)....... 295
Johnston, William P. (Mrs.)....... Introduction
Jones, Armstead................... 218
Jones, C. (L't.-Col.)............. 191
Jones, Edward..................... 93
Jones, Gabriel (Col.)............. 194, 206, 210, 216, 218
Jones, George W................... 170, 171, 187, 208, 209, 295, 302, 303
Jones, James S. (Maj.)............ 191
Jones, Richard.................... 123
Jones, Capt. ———, of Randolph Co. 195
Jonesville........................ 254
Jordan, Elias (Capt.)............. 191
Jordan, James H...........272, 273, 274
Jordan, Mr. ———................... 69
Jordan, W......................... 94
Jouett, William R. (Capt.)........ 120
Julien, Mr. ———................... 39

Ka-non-e-kah...................... 76
Ka-ra-zhon-sept-kah............... 76
Ka-ta-ka.......................... 61
Ka-ka-kew......................... 98
Ka-ke-ka-mah...................... 98
Ka-ke-me-ka-pes................... 98
Kar-lun-da-wa-na.................. 263
Kas-kas-kias.................24, 26
Kellogg's Grove...................156, 171, 176, 177, 178, 179, 184, 187, 192, 198, 199, 200, 201, 204, 208, 300
Kellogg, O. W..............129, 176, 290
Kellogg's Trail................... 113, 129, 168, 176, 290
Ke-me-a-lo-sha.................... 64
Kendle, Samuel F.................. 94
Kennedy, George F................. 94
Kennedy, Aid-de-Camp.............. 47
Kenney, John W.................... 193
Kenney, Thomas.................... 169
Kent, Erastus..................... 82
Kentucky...........25, 48, 58, 77, 78
Kent Township..................... 177
Ke-o-kuk..........................20, 23, 44, 45, 79, 80, 81, 88, 107, 108, 112, 113, 228, 239, 240, 248, 251, 259, 261, 264, 265, 266, 267, 268, 270, 271
Ke-o-kuk's Village, and Scenes There.....................109, 110
Ke-o-sa-tah....................... 98
Ke-o-ta-she-ka.................... 64
Kee-tee-see....................... 98
Kercheval, Gholson................ 119
Kesh-e-yi-va...................... 32
Kettle......................102, 108

Kee-was-see....................... 158
Keyes Lake........................ 217
Kick-a-poos.....55, 57, 90, 97, 238, 239
Kickapoo River.................... 222
Kincaid, James (Capt.)............ 194
Kincaid, Hiram.................... 94
Kingsley, Alpha (L't.)..........37, 38
Kingsbury, J. W. (L't.)........... 120
Kingsbury, Julius J. B. (L't.).... 246
Kinney, Mr. ———................... 127
Kinzie, John...................... 114
Kirker's Farm..................... 181
Kirkpatrick, Wm......164, 172, 278, 279
Kirkpatrick, R. H................. 183
Kirkpatrick, ———, at Apple River Fort.......................185, 187
Kish-wau-kee..............131, 205, 284
Knox County....................... 193
Koe-ko-skee....................... 98
Kosh-ko-nong, Lake................ 205, 206, 208, 209, 212, 287
Kot-te-ken-ne-kak................. 107
Kreeps, David..................... 135
Krupp, John....................... 94

La Croix, Cerre M................. 65
La Croix, Joseph.................. 55
La Croix, Mitchell................ 55
Lafayette County.................. 114
La Gouthrie, Edward........41, 54, 58
Lagoterie..................41, 54, 58
Lake We Live On................... 206
Lake House........................ 217
Lamotte, Lieut. ———............... 104
Lamotte, ———...................... 236
Land Warrants..................... 77
Lane, Levin....................... 190
Lane, Will Carr................... 111
Larned, Brig. Gen. ———............ 255
La Saillier....................... 55
La Salle.......................... 140
La Salle County................... 159
Lasley's.......................... 117
Lawrence, W. (L't.-Col.).......... 66
Lawrence County................... 191
Lawhead, Benj..................... 183
Lay-ow-vois....................27, 30
Lead Mines...................100, 187
Leavenworth, Cantonment........... 103, 121, 188, 193
Le Claire, Antoine...19, 92, 98, 251, 259
Leech, Levin...................... 183
Leech, Samuel (Col.).............. 190
Lee County........................ 130
Leighton, Jonathan............124, 164
Lemonweir Valley.................. 229
Lena.............................. 177
Levers, Thomas (L't.-Col.)........ 61
Lexington, Iowa................... 275
Lieb, Daniel...................... 94
Lillard........................... 117
Lincoln, Abraham..............125, 140, 164, 173, 175, 196, 198, App., 277
Linden, H. S. J. (L't.)........... 120
Lindsay, Allen F. (Capt.).......73, 195
Lipcap, Solomon...........72, 73, 76

THE BLACK HAWK WAR. 317

"Little Bear"............169, 170, 171
Little, Josiah...................... 124
Little Medicine Man............... 114
Little Priest................114, 180
Little Thunder................215, 216
Little Turtle...................... 20
Little Vermilion River............ 188
Lockwood, James H......103, 105, 108
Logan 20
Logan, Dr. J. B................... 194
Loomis, G. (Capt.)................ 228
Long, Edward R. (L't.)............ 246
Long, Thomas (Maj.)..........
......116, 124, 125, 141, 161, 163, 280
Loraine, John...................... 94
Lorton, John....................... 93
Louisiana 24, 29
Lovell, Michael................... 184
Lovitt, Thomas..................... 82
Lowe, Gideon (Capt.)......106, 121, 212
Lower Cuivre Ferry................. 56
Lower Iowa R...................... 111
Lowry, Private ———............ 224
Lucas, Gov. ———............18, 274
Lundy, John....................... 136
Luziére 171
Lynnville 194
Lyon, Elijah (Capt.).............. 253
Little Mascoutille................. 58

Mackinac or Mackinaw.............. 47
Mackinac, Fall of................. 41
Mackinaw Company.................. 47
Mackinaw Fencibles................ 47
Mackitee, Andrew.................. 123
Macomb, Maj.-Gen. Alex........... 228
Macomb, Ill....................... 193
Macon County................125, 159
Macoupin County.............125, 194
Madding, Champion S. (Capt.).... 191
Madison County..........125, 191, 194
Madison, Wis...................... 217
Madam Black Hawk..268, 272, 273, 274
Mah-na-at-ap-e-kah 76
Ma-ka-tai-she-kia-kiak.......17, 64, 98
Malden....................88, 238, 258
Mandeville, Jack.................. 75
Manner of Enlistments............. 119
March, Enoch C. (Col.)..........
 93, 94, 116, 140, 188, 193, 195, 212, 222
March to Rock River Mouth, in
 1831 92
March to the Wisconsin............ 216
March to Yellow Banks in 1832.118, etc.
Marie de Ogee..................... 128
Marion County..................... 100
Marsh, John....................... 102
Marshall, Humphrey (L't.)......... 245
Marshall, Thomas I. or J.......... 124
Marsac, Joseph F. (Capt.)......... 255
Martin, Capt. ———.............. 257
Martin, Philip W..........117, 118, 123
Ma-sha-she 64
Mash-co 64
Mason, R. B. (Capt.)........120, 225
Mason, Stevens T. (Gov.).....254, 256

Masonic Temple.................... 35
Massey, L't. ——— 55
Match-e-qua-wa 64
Mathews, H........................ 93
Mathews, Cyrus (Capt.)..........
 ....159, 188, 195, 196
Matthews, Samuel T. (Col.)...193, 196
Maughs, Milton M. (Capt.).....19, 142
Mauvisterre River................. 194
Maynadier, William (Capt.)....... 247
Mayo, Jonathan (Capt.)............ 191
Mayo, Walter M. (Q. M.).......... 191
Me-al-es-e-ta 64
Meau-eus, or Mee-au-mese 147, 157
Me-caitch 61
Mecomsen, William B..........177, 178
Medals 32, 67
Men-a-con 98
Menard, Peter (Capt.).159, 164, 177, 205
Mendinall, Zadock................. 135
Menominees 67,
 100, 102, 103, 110, 230, 235, 249, 259
Menominees, Murder of..........
..103, 104, 107, 110, 113, 234 et seq.
Merameg River..................... 22
Merryman, Dr. E. H...........194, 215
Messersmith, John, Jr............. 183
Methode 72, 76
Mexico, Gulf of................... 109
Michigan Militia in the War....... 254
Military Tract 77
Miller, Albert S.................. 120
Miller, Col....................... 58
Miller, Gov. of Mo................ 160
Miller, G. V...................... 82
Miller, Solomon...............94, 159
Miller, William................... 94
Miller, William (Maj.)............ 194
Million, Bennett.................. 181
Mills, Benj....................... 113
Milton, James..................... 135
Milwaukee River................... 234
Mineral Point, Wis.........131, 143, 181
Miners' Journal................... 76
Missouri, 58; Excitement in....... 160
Missouri River.......44, 60, 61, 100, 103
Mitchell, E. G. (L't.)............ 120
Moffett, Thomas (Capt.)........... 195
Mograine, Noel.................... 61
Molansat 98
Monroe County..................... 125
Montgomery County.......117, 125, 194
Montreal 17, 26
Moore Benj........................ 130
Moore, David H. (Q. M.).......... 195
Moore, Isaac R. (Col.)........169, 189
Moore, James...................... 124
Moore, James B. (Capt.)........... 61
Moore, J. Milton.................. 124
Moore, Jonathan................... 124
Moore, Risdon..................... 124
Moore, Risdon Marshall............ 124
Moore, William.................94, 124
Morgan County....................
 ....125, 140, 159, 188, 194, 195
Morgan, Joshua C.................. 126

Morgan, Willoughby (Col.)....... 98, 101, 104, 106, 107
Morgan, A. Brave................ 106
Morris, Achilles (L't.-Col.)..93, 123, 172
Morris, F. M..................... 183
Morrison, James.................. 123
Morrison, Wm. L. E.............. 123
Morrison's Grove................. 180
Morse, Jedediah.................. 67
Mosley, Roland................... 159
Mower, Surgeon Thomas G........ 243
Mud Lake........................ 205
Munroe, John (Capt.)..........243, 253
Munson, Gideon..............134, 135
Munson, William.............150, 154
Murder of Rev. Adam Payne..166, 167
Murder of Rev. James Sample..... 166
Murphy, Wm. C. (Sgt.).......... 224
Musick, David (Capt.).........55, 56
Myers, William................... 159
McAdams, William................ 164
McBride, David................... 229
McCall, Daniel................... 126
McCall, Gentry................... 82
M'Call, George A................. 98
McClure, Robert..............125, 145
McCormick, Andrew..........218, 224
McClernand, John A..........190, 303
McClernand, E. J. (Col.)......... 190
McConnel, Murray................ 123, 193, 215, 218, 224
McCown, John (Capt.)............ 191
McCoy, Charles.................. 142
McDonald, John.................. 186
McDonough County............... 118
McDow, Thomas..............125, 281
McDaniel, Benj.................. 178
McDuffie, Franklin (L't.)......... 243
McFadden, Geo. (Capt.).......... 157, 159, 202, 203
McGill, Hugh.................... 189
McGraw, Dominick............... 183
McHatton, A..................... 123
McHenry, William (Maj.)....191, 212
McIlvaine, Caroline M.....Introduction
McIlwaine, Murder of............ 181
McKay, Wm. (Col.)..........48, 67, 68
McKenney, Thomas L............. 73
McLean County.......125, 136, 150, 159
McLean Hist. Society............ 136
McMillen, Meredith S............ 218
McMurtry, William (Capt.)....... 193
McNair, John.................... 218
M'Nair, L't. ——................. 55
McNeil, H....................... 82
McRee, Capt. ——............... 212

Nabb, Mr. ——................... 39
Na-chu-sa 291
Na-i-o-gui-man ....
Na-kis-ka-wa 98
Na-ma-che-wa-na 61
Na-match-e-sa 64
Na-ma-we-nan-e 64
Name of Black Hawk............. 17
Na-mee 98
Nam-e-qua 268
Na-na-ma-kee 17
Na-ni-sa 239
Na-noch-aa-ta-sa 61
Naper, Joseph (Capt.).....157, 167, 188
Naperville 247, 257
Na-pe-ta-ka 64
Napoleon 24, 48
Napoleon Boat................. 258
Na-sa-war-ku 64
Na-she-as-kuk 18
Nashville 58
Na-som-see 268
Neal, Moses.................... 190
Neale, Thomas M............... 93
Neapope 109, 130, 218, 224, 229, 238, 239, 240
Neepeek 98
Nes-se-as-kuk 268
Ne-sho-ta 61
Neutral Strip.................. 101
Newcomb, F. D. (L't.).......... 120
Newhall, Dr. Horatio........... 142
New Salem...........278, 280, 281, 288
New York City.............262, 263
Niblo's Garden................. 263
Nichols, John (L't.)............ 120
Niles, Mich...................256, 258
Noel, Thomas...............111, 120
Norfolk 260
Norris, Robert................. 148
Norvell, Joshua................ 64
Nott, Royal A. (Capt.)......... 191
Nowlin, Bennett (Capt.)........ 194
Nute, Levi M. (L't.)............ 120
Nutting, James................. 187

Offutt, Mr....................278, 281
Ogee, Joseph................... 129
Ohio 25
Old Man's Creek........132, 137, 138
Old Mission.................... 203
Old Shullsburg................. 143
Oliphant, E. P................. 164
Omahas 103, 108
O'Melvany, John................ 194
O'Neal, John F. (Capt.)........ 143
Oneidas 235
Onstott, John (Capt.).......... 190
Order No. 12 126
Order No. 13 126
Order No. 14 126
Order No. 15 128
Order No. 16 128
Order No. 21 146
Order No. 22 161
Order Special No. 11........... 161
Order of May 24................ 163
Order No. 26 172
Order No. 41 195
Order No. 43 195
Order No. 44, Defining Divisions and Duties................... 203
Order No. 45, to L't. Lowman... 204
Order No. 46, for Subsistence... 204
Order No. 48, Urging Obedience.. 206

THE BLACK HAWK WAR. 319

Order No. 49 209
Order to Maj. Long............. 116
Order to Maj. Stillman........... 131
Orear, George.................... 123
Oregon, Wis..................... 209
Organization of Army, 1831....... 93
Orr, Joseph..................... 194
Osages..........21, 22, 23, 24, 29, 103
Oshkahenahniew 236
Oshkosh 236
Oquawka 116
Otoes 103
Ottawa 136, 146, 148,
  153, 156, 159, 167, 169, 172, 188,
  189, 193, 194, 202, 203, 204, 282, 285
Ottawas 100
"Otto," Steamboat................ 188
Ouilmette, Louis..........130, 131, 149
Out-che-qua-ha 27, 30, 31

Palmer, James (Capt.)............ 169
Palmer, Zalmon C. (Capt.).111, 120, 299
Pa-ma-ke-tah 98
Pan-se-na-nee 98
Parish, Thomas J................. 143
Parish's Fort.................... 143
Parker, Leonard B. (Q. M.)....... 191
Parkinson, Daniel M..143, 183, 209, 218
Parkinson, Peter, Jr.............. 183
Parrish, Dr. J. J................ 191
Parmenter, Isaac................. 191
Pa-she-ko-mack 64
Pa-she-pa-ho......27, 30, 31, 33, 40,
  68, 69, 70, 79, 98, 264, 265, 266, 267
Pash-qua-mee 107
Patterson, Gershom (Capt.)....194, 204
Patterson, J. B..............19, 66, 240
Patrick, Samuel.................. 183
Paul, R. 64
Paul, T. 61
Pa-we-sheek 98
Paw Paw Grove and Village...130, 285
Payne, Rev. Adam..166, 167, 168, etc.
Payne, Aaron................168, 224
Payne, Morgan L. (Capt.).........
  ....169, 188, 189, 191, 193
Pearce, Hosea (Col.)............. 191
Pearson, Ed. L................... 117
Pecatonica 286
Pecatonica, The..........170, 181, 209
Pecatonica, The Battle of........ 182
Pekin 130
Pem-e-see 98
Peoria ...55, 113, 116, 129, 176, 192, 288
Peoria County...............125, 159
Pekin 159, 288
Perkins, Isaac................... 135
Perkins, L't. —— 47
Perkins, Joseph.................. 64
Penrose, James W. (L't.)......... 246
"Perry, Oliver H., The".......... 73
Perry County.................... 194
Peru.....................77, 140, 288
Peru Road....................... 140
"Petit Boeuff".................. 76
Petition to Gov. Reynolds......82, 83

Petty, Elisha.................... 125
Petersburg 194
Pettigrew, William............... 147
Penn, William, The.............. 242
Pe-wau-te-not 236
Philip of Pokonoket.............. 20
Philleo, Addison 143, 217
Phillipps Ferry.................. 119
Phillips, Elijah............192, 197
Phrenological Comments........18, 19
Pickett, John (L't.)............. 253
Pierce, Earl (Capt.)............. 160
Pierce, Samuel C................. 93
Pike, Benjamin F........82, 83, 84, 98
Pike County.............119, 125, 194
Pike, Zebulon M. (L't.).....31, 32, 37
Pillsbury, Samuel 126
Pinckney, Ninian (Capt.).......37, 38
Plainfield 167, 169
Platoff 48
Platteville 143
Plum River............170, 202, 205, 208
Po-ca-ma 61
Poe-go-nah 236
Poin-a-ke-ta 64
Polo 142, 176
Pontiac 20, 80
Poore, Ben Perley............279, 284
Pope County..................... 190
Poquette, Pierre...........215, 216
Portage des Sioux.55, 58, 59, 60, 61, 63
Portage des Sioux, Treaty of..... 60
Portage, The, Wis..........229, 236
Posey, Alexander (Gen.)..........
  ......190, 192, 193, 197, 200, 201,
  202, 203, 204, 205, 206, 208, 209,
  210, 211, 220, 222, 223, 225, 228, 287
Posey, John F................... 124
Pottawatomies ....
  ....32, 35, 68, 82, 90, 97, 130,
  132, 133, 143, 146, 147, 205, 238, 239
Pottawatomie Council at Rock
  Creek, 166; Village............. 285
Powell, Alanson................. 195
Powell, Daniel (Capt.).......... 191
Powell, William (L't.)......235, 236
Prairie la Crosse............... 230
Prairie du Chien.41, 47, 48, 49, 50, 51,
  52, 58, 71, 72, 74, 75, 76, 89, 100,
  101, 103, 104, 105, 112, 219, 223,
  225, 226, 227, 228, 231, 237, 240, 249
Pratt Seth (Capt.)..........125, 145
Prentiss, James (L't.), James H... 253
Preuitt, Solomon...............94, 122
Price, Daniel................... 125
Price, Thomas................... 183
Prickett, David................. 122
Prince, William 30
Proclamation Opening Lands Ceded
  by 1804 Treaty................. 79
Prophet's Village...............
  ......35, 114, 126, 127, 128, 163, 284
Prosper, Samuel M............... 123
Pryor, Nathaniel (L't.)......... 38
Pugh, Isaac C. (Capt.)......125, 145
Putnam County................... 159

	PAGE
Py-e-sa	17, 22, 23
Pype-gee	148, 166
Quash-qua-me	27, 30, 31, 32, 40, 41, 44, 61, 80, 87
Quesh-qua-ing	107, 108
Quincy	18, 117, 140, 274
Ralls, William C. (Capt.)	125, 164
Ramsay, Robert	57
Ramsay, Robert (Mrs.)	57
Randall, Peter	124
Randolph County	194, 218
Randolph, Marcus	200
Rankin, ——	183
Rattan, M. E.	124
Raum, John (Maj.)	190
Rawlings, Marshall	190
Rector, L't. and Capt. ——	49, 50, 53, 54
Red Bird	72, 75, 76, 77
Red Cedar River	100
Reed, Thomas B.	133
Reed, Michael	159
Remann, Frederick	195
Return to Ft. Armstrong	267
Revell, Wallace	
Reynolds, John	81, 82, 85, 86, 88, 89, 90, 93, 96, 113, 116, 118, 119, 122, 127, 130, 132, 139, 140, 141, 157, 161, 162, 169, 189, 192, 210, 245, 280, 284, 293, 294
Reynolds, Gov., Appeal for Troops.	113, 117
Reynolds' Proclamation, May 15	139
Rhodes, Mr.	156
Richardson, Asa	111, 120, 248
Richardson, John F. (Capt.)	191
Riggs, Henry S.	194
Riggs, L't. ——	49, 50
Riley, Bennet	110, 120, 126, 177, 179, 192, 197
Rious, Senor	24
Ritner, L't. ——	226, 228
Robison, John K.	298
Robinson, Chief Alex	166
Roberts, Milton B.	193
Roberts, Calvert	118
Roberts, Calvin	123
Rochelle's Village	148
Rock Creek	166
Rock Island	48, 66, 82, 85, 86, 87, 89, 90, 95, 194, 230, 232, 240
Rock Island County	193
Rockport	94
Rock Lake	217
Rock River	17, 18, 31, 41, 47, 50, 51, 52, 53, 54, 55, 57, 58, 61, 80, 82, 83, 84, 86, 87, 89, 90, 91, 112, 115, 119, 120, 126, 129, 146, 156, 161, 166, 180, 187, 189, 203, 205, 209, 211, 214, 238, 248, 271, 281, 283, 290, et seq.
Rock River Sacs	103 and see "British Band."
Rogers, Jason	111, 120, 248

	PAGE
Roman, Richard	94, 123, 164, 177, 178
Rose, Edwin (L't.)	253
Ross, Thomas B. (Capt.)	191
Ross, William	119, 122, 125
Rountree, Hiram (Capt.)	194
Rountree, John H.	143
Rousseau, Gus S. (Lieut.)	120
Rowland, Isaac (Capt.)	255
Royster, Thomas J.	111, 120
Rushville	117, 278, 279, 282
Russia	48
Russell, William (Col.)	55, 56
Russell, David B. (Capt.)	190, 191
Russell, Col. of Mich.	258
Rutledge, Dr. John B.	164
Sain, John (Capt.)	193
Sakaegan Lake	27
Sa-kee-too	64
Saline, Mich.	256
Salter, William	208
Salt River	31
Sample, Rev. James	165
Sanders, Hiram	83, 84
Sandford, Isaac (Capt.)	191
Sangamon County	93, 125, 164, 169, 195
Sangamon River	194
Santeaux	71
Sash-au-quash	158
Sauk-e-nuk—Black Hawk's Village	17, 41, 52, 57, 67, 77, 81, 84, 94, 95, 101, 130, 165
Sauk Trail	165
Sawyer, James	65
Scales, S. H. (Capt.)	142
Schermerhorn, ——	203
Schuyler County	117-125, 159-164
Schwankovsky, Julie	171
Scott, Benj.	178, 179
Scott, John	76
Scott, John W.	164
Scott, Moses	65
Scott, Winfield (Gen.)	168, 173, 212, 221, 228, 232, 238, 239, 291, 292, 304
Scott's Expedition	242 et seq.
Schwarz, Col.	256
Searight, Joseph D. (L't.)	111, 120
Searles, Murder of	181
Semple, James	94, 122, 164, 177
Senecas, The	263
Sessions, Capt. Holden	193
Seven Mile Bluff	229
Sevier, Robert (L't.)	120
Sha-a-toc	157
Sha-bo-na or Shab-bo-na	20, 133, 147, 148, etc., 157, 166, 189, 204
Sha-bo-na's Village	128, 130
Sha-ma-ga	61
Shambaugh, Prof. B. F.—Introduction and	269
Sharp, Powell H. (L't.-Col.)	194
Shaw, John (Col.)	254
Shaw, Nineveh	191
Shelby County	125
Shelledy, Stephen B.	191
Shelton, Joseph (Maj.)	190

THE BLACK HAWK WAR. 321

Shem-e-non 157
Sherman, John (Capt.) 143
She-she-qua-nas 98
Shields, Alexander 123
Short, Thomas J 218
Simpson, Gideon 124
Singing Bird 268, 272, 273, 274
Sink Hole Battle 46, 55, 56
Sinsinawa Mound.................. 187
Sioux, The 47, 72,
  100, 101, 102, 103, 224, 227, 229, 259
Skinner, Private ——— 224
Slaughter's Farm 217
Smart, Josiah 110
Smith, Adam 93
Smith, Alex. (Capt.) 194
Smith, Brig.-Gen. ——— 58
Smith, Chester 167
Smith, David (Capt.) 191, 194, 195
Smith, George F. (Mrs.) 135
Smith, Henry (Capt.) ....
  ....111, 120, 212, 224, 225, 248
Smith, Henry B. (Q. M.) 191
Smith, James 142
Smith, Jeremiah 125, 194, 214, 215
Smith, John C. (Gen.) 296
Smith, Robert R 224
Smith, Samuel. ̣..........93, 124, 164
Smith, Theophilus W. (Col.) 193
Smith, Thomas A. (Gen.) 66
Smith, Vincent 142
Smith, William B 125
Snelling, Fort 72, 73
Snelling, Josiah (Col.) 72, 75
Snelling, William J 75
Snock-wine 157
Snyder, Adam W. (Capt.) 122,
  164, 172, 175, 176, 177, 178, 179, 192
Snyder, Dr. J. F., Introduction and 273
Solomon, Samuel 61, 64
Soulard, James G 227
Souligny 236
Spafford's Farms 230
Spafford, Murder of 181
Spain 24, 25, 29
Spanish Father 23, 24, 26
Spears, Edward (L't.) 56
Speech on Military Coat-tails 288
Spencer, J. W 82
Spencer, Murder of 181
Spotted Arm 180
Springfield 215
Sprouce, William 123
Stahl, Fred. (Serg't.) 142, 169
Stambaugh, Col. ——— .226, 235 et seq.
Stambaugh's Expedition 234
Stampede at Ft. Winnebago 213
Stapp, James T. B.............122, 130
Stapp, Wyat B.................... 130
Starkey, John 122
Starr, William E 122
Stennett John (Capt.) 159
Stephenson County 177, 184
Stephenson, James W 127, 131,
  141, 142, 143, 180, 181, 184, 187, 209
Stephenson, James W., Battle of.. 184
Stephenson, W. J. (Capt.) 190, 191
Stewart, ——— 74
Stewart, Dr. ——— 49
Stewart, Hart L. (Col.) 257
Stewart, William M. (Capt.) 159
Stillman, Isaiah ..113, 125, 126, 128,
  130, 139, 141, 145, 161, 199, 284, 292
Stillman's Defeat 119,
  ....125, 132 et seq., 143, 163,
  183, 201, 205, 218, 238, 254, 257, 294
Stillman's Defense 137
Stockbridges, The 235
Stockton, Brig.-Gen 255
Stoddard, Amos (Capt.) 30, 34
Stone, Clack (Capt.) 142, 185
Storm, L't.-Col. ——— 190
Stout, Thomas (Capt.) 194
Strawn, Jeremiah 159
Strawn, John (Col.) 159
Street, Joseph M. (Gen.) ....
  ...98, 105, 226, 228, 230, 239, 241, 272
Strode, James M. (Col.) ....
  ....113, 127, 131,
  140, 142, 184, 185, 187, 283, 290, 296
Stuart, John T 93, 164, 175, 281, 286
Ste. Genevieve 76
St. Ange 24
St. Charles 55
St. Clair County 93, 159, 164
St. Joseph 254, 258
St. Joseph Island 38
St. Louis.22, 23, 24, 27, 28, 29, 31, 32,
  34, 38, 41, 42, 44, 56, 140, 154, 188, 266
St. Peter's Indian Agency 101, 102
St. Peter's River 101, 102
St. Pierre, Ensign 50
St. Vrain, Felix ....
  ..86, 87, 88, 98, 106, 107, 169, 170;
  Death of, 171, 173 180, 181, 238, 251
Sublet, Thomas 184
Sublets, Mr 156
Sugar River 183, 209, 236
Sullivan, John (Capt.) 47, 48
Summers, John 124
"Sun, The" 76
Superior, The—Boat.........242 et seq.
Swett, Leonard 280
Sybald, Samuel 123
Sycamore Bluff 137
Sycamore Creek 137, 139,
  156, 161, 162, 204, 205, 238, 285, 286

Tah-sau-gah-now 102
Ta-ko-na 98
Taliaferro, Law 102, 106
Tate, John 124
Tavar, P. G 65
Taylor, E. D 93
Taylor, James 178
Taylor, Zachary ....
  ....47, 51, 52, 53, 54, 112, 120,
  121, 126, 128, 145, 161, 162, 172,
  173, 179, 192, 197, 198, 200, 201,
  203, 223, 224, 228, 230, 232, 290, 291
Taylor's Battle 53, 54
Tazewell Co................113, 125, 159

Te-cum-seh 20, 41, 42, 80, 109	Van Waggoner................ 183
Tennessee 58, 77	Vasquez, Burony (L't.)............ 39
Ten Eycks.................... 255	Vaughan, James W............ 124
Te-pa-kee 32	Vermillion County Regiment...159, 169
Terra Coupa Prairie............ 257	Village of Black Hawk..........
Terrell, Dr. William H.......... 194	........17, 41, 52, 57, 67,
Thames, Battle................ 42	77, 81, 84, 90, 94, 95, 101, 130, 165
Third Lake..................216, 217	Vincennes 38
Thomas, Henry................ 165	
Thomas, John (Col.)............	Wabash County................ 191
...........122, 146, 164, 177, 179	Wabash Tribes................26, 27
Thomas, John B. (Capt.)........ 169	Wabasha Village..............73, 227
Thomas, William (Capt.)........ 191	Wa-bo-ki-e-shiek—the Prophet.....
Thomas, William (Col.)........93, 122	.....87, 89, 91, 109, 112, 114, 130,
Thompson, Elias (Maj.)......... 159	229, 231, 232, 233, 238, 240, 259, 262
Thompson, James (Capt.)....... 194	Waddam's Grove................ 184
Thompson, James (Private)...... 218	Wah-pa-koo-tas 101, 102
Thompson, Joel................ 82	Wakefield, John A.127, 139, 195, 208, 209
Thompson, John................ 187	Waldron, Thomas R............ 164
Thompson, J. L................ 124	Walker, A. (Capt.)............ 243
Thompson, Samuel M. (Col.)...123, 279	Walker, George E........158, 166, 204
Thompson, The—Boat............ 242	Walker, James (Capt.)....160, 167, 193
Thompson, the Wrestler........ 282	Walker, Wilbur................ 157
Thornton, W. A. (L't.)......... 253	Wallace, William M............ 190
Thrall, Dr. Aaron.............. 191	"Wallace, William," Steamboat.... 118
Throckmorton, Capt..........222, 227	Walters, John................ 135
Throckmorton's Report.......... 227	Waniga 176
Thwaites, R. G...........Introduction	Wa-pa-la-mo 64
Timms, J. B................... 176	Wa-pa-mak-qua 64
Timms' Grove.................. 176	Wa-pa-qunt 98
Ti-or-nay 107	Wa-pel-lo, or Wa-pel-la, or Wau-
To-mah 104	pel-la ....
To-po-kia 98	79, 88, 98, 112, 113, 228, 264, 265, 266
To-qua-mee 148, 149, 157, 158	War of 1812..................38, 41
Townsend, H. S................ 183	Warnick, William (Capt.)........ 159
Tradition of Rock Island......... 66	Warnsing, Dr. John............ 194
Treaty of 1783 ....25, 47	War-pa-lo-ka 64
Treaty of 1789 32	Warrell, Vigo S................ 30
Treaty of 1804 21,	Warren County............118, 193
27, 31, 34, 60, 61, 62, 63, 71, 80, 100	Warren, Daniel and Ezekiel....... 203
Treaty of 1815 ....60, 61, 62	Warren, Peter................ 125
Treaty of 1816 ....63, 80	Warrick, Montgomery............ 124
Treaty of Ghent....55, 60, 63, 64	Warrior, The—Steamboat........
Treaty of 1824 71	..............222, 225, 227, 239, 248
Treaty of 1825 ....71, 100, 106, 107	Wash, R.....................61, 64
Treaty of 1830 101	Washburne, E. B.............. 114
Treaty of 1831 ....92, 96	Wash-e-own 46
Treaty of 1832 250	Washington 259, 261, 265, 268
Tunnell, Luther................ 118	Washington County.............. 194
Turcot, Commissioner............ 58	Wash-ut 98
Turner, Dr. —— 274	Was-sek-e-ne-qua 64
Turney, James..............122, 193	Waters, G. W................ 120
Turtle Creek...............205, 287	Watson, John B................ 123
Turtle Village................ 205	Wau-ban-se, or Wau-ban-see, or
Twiggs, David E. (Maj.)......120, 243	Wa-ban-se........133, 147, etc., 189
	Waukon Decori................ 232
Ullman, Capt. —— 257	Wau-koo-kah 76
Union Co..................... 282	Wau-nau-ko 236
Upper Iowa River...........100, 228	Wa-wap-o-la-sa 98
	Wayne County................ 190
Van Derveer, J. S...........111, 120	Weatherford, William......94, 123, 193
Vandruff, J.................... 82	Webb, Henry L. (Capt.)......... 195
Vandruff, S................... 82	Webb, Stephen H. (Capt.)........ 202
Vandruff's Island................ 94	Wee-sa-ka 61
Vansburgh, L. P............... 142	We-kau 72
Van Swearengen, J.........111, 120	Welch, Edmund................ 185

	PAGE
Wells, Albert	82
Wells, Alexander	94
Wells, Asaph	82
Wells, Berryman G. (Capt.)	190
Wells, Eli	82
Wells, Huntington	82
Wells, Joel	82
Wells, John	82
Wells, Joseph	218
Wells, Levi	82
Wells, Samuel	82
Wells, Samuel, of Wisconsin, at Pecatonica	183
Wentworth, John	244
West, A. S.	98
West, Obediah (Capt.)	190, 191
West Bureau Timber	165
Westerfield Scare	169
Wethers, Enoch B.	93
Wharton, Clifton (Capt.)	120
Wheeler, Erastus (Capt.)	94, 125
Wheelock, E. L. R.	118, 123
Wheelwright, W.	111, 189, 248
Whipple, Charles W.	257
Whirling Thunder	114, 153, 180
Whistler, William (Maj.)	246, 257, 258
White, Alexander (Capt.)	164
White Beaver	240, 241
White Cloud	209
White County	191
White Crow	114, 152, 180, 209, 230
White Elk	68
White, James	125, 145
White, James (Capt.), of Hancock County	193
White, John	218, 224
White Oak Springs	143, 153, 156
White Otter	260
White Pawnee	215, 216
Whiteside County	35
Whiteside, Samuel	53, 54, 61, 94, 98, 116, 118, 122, 125, 126, 127, 132, 145, 146, 161, 163, 164, 177, 178
Whiteside, William B.	53, 54, 94
Whitewater River	209, 210, 211, 212, 287
Whitlock, James	124
Whittlesey, Col.	198
Wick-a-up	81
Wickliffe, W. N.	120
Wilbourn, John S.	140, 159, 160, 188
Willard, George (Sergt.)	224
Will County	160, 167
Williams, J. R. (Gen.)	254, 255, 256, 257, 258
Williams, J. S.	111, 120
Williams, William (L't.)	161

	PAGE
Willis, George B. (Capt.)	159
Wilson, Alexander	190
Wilson, Bluford (Col.)	190
Wilson, Harrison (Capt.)	190
Wilson, H. A. (L't.)	253
Wilson, James H. (Gen.)	190
Wilson, J. M.	258
Wilson, Moses G.	123, 125, 283
Wilson, William L.	283
Winchester, P. H.	94
Wingville	143
Winnebagoes	35, 38, 39, 46, 47, 55, 57, 73, 76, 82, 91, 97, 100, 114, 132, 143, 146, 180, 214, 215, 216, 218, 219, 226, 229, 231, 232, 238, 239, 250, 260
Winnebago Outbreak	71, 72
Winnebago Squaws Debauched, Denied	76
"Winnebago, The"—Steamboat	188
Winnebago Swamps	197
Winneshiek	226
Winnette, James (Maj.)	67
Winona	73
Winstanley, John	124
Winters, John D.	142
Winters, Nathan	125
Wiota	143
Wisconsin	26, 100, 221
Wisconsin Bottoms	218
Wisconsin Heights, Battle of	218, 220, 221
Wisconsin River	27, 29, 35, 50, 87, 213, 217, 218, 222, 226, 228, 232
Witter, Dan S.	98
Wood, E. K. (Surgeon)	193
Wood, John D. (Maj.)	194
Woodbridge, W. W.	143, 183, 215, 216
Woodrow, Hugh	126
Woodson, Joseph C.	124
Worth, Joseph S. (L't.)	120
Worth, W. J. (Col.)	243
Wren, Johnson (Maj.)	190
Wright, David	94
Wright, Thomas	111
Wyatt, R. M.	287
Wyatt, William (L't.-Col.)	191
Yeizer, Capt.	47, 48, 50
Yellow Banks	116, 118, 119, 120, 248, 278, 279, 280, 282
Yellow River	184
Young, Joseph L.	224
Young, Richard M.	113, 158
Ypsilanti	255, 256

www.ingramcontent.com/pod-product-compliance
Lightning Source LLC
Chambersburg PA
CBHW050326230426
43663CB00010B/1758